Pre-publication REVIEWS, COMMENTARIES, EVALUATIONS . . .

"This notebook is chock-full of activities that can be used in individual or group counseling, or with training programs for gay, lesbian, and bisexual clients or students. Although the impact may be greatest for sexual minorities, many of these activities will be useful in classes devoted to helping nongay persons develop sensitivity to and awareness of the experiences of sexual minorities. Practical, clearly presented, and targeted, each activity will be helpful, whether it be for individual identity development, couple relationship enhancement, or coming out in the workplace or to family and friends. I have no doubt that clients who participate in these exercises will emerge with a clearer idea of their own sexual identity and feel freer to live in the larger world. I look forward to using this book with clients and with my students."

Bob Barret, PhD
Professor of Counseling, University of North Carolina at Charlotte;
Co-Author, *Counseling Gay Men and Lesbians: A Practice Primer*

"This is a wonderful and well-edited notebook placing a variety of helpful activities, assignments, and handouts in a collection that is both practical and usable. This edition supports the insightful use of methods and techniques that can help clinicians engage with their gay, lesbian, bisexual, and transgendered (GLBT) clients in a meaningful, supportive, and action-oriented manner. Practical exercises are offered that will make the counseling process more collaborative and experiential, leading to effective outcomes.

Drs. Whitman and Boyd have provided clinicians working with GLBT clients with an excellent resource. They have gathered individual authors whose expertise and creativity is demonstrated in the topics covered. Their helpful resources are applicable to enriching the therapeutic process with GLBT clients. This book should be included in the collections of both practitioners and educators."

Edward A. Wierzalis, PhD
Assistant Professor of Counselor Education,
University of North Carolina at Charlotte

"Finally, a resource book that doesn't require a therapist to change pronouns or try to expound on things to include issues facing gay, lesbian, bisexual, and transgendered clients. This guidebook provides numerous valuable activities and handouts for a community that has had difficulty finding resources in the past. This book can and will be valued by the therapists who work predominantly with a sexual minority clientele as well as those who have limited experience and exposure to this population.

Whitman and Boyd have organized a wonderful assortment of activities and worksheets that address the numerous difficult issues that face so many in the GLBT community. I for one cannot wait to have this manual on my shelf so that I can begin to use these activities with my clients."

Nicholas DiCarlo, MS
Nationally Certified Counselor;
Certified Alcohol and Drug Addiction Counselor;
Licensed Mental Health Counselor;
Evaluator—Tippecanoe County Court Services, Drug and Alcohol Program;
Private Practitioner at New Perspectives Counseling;
Board of Trustee Member,
Association for Gay, Lesbian, Bisexual Issues in Counseling

"This exciting collection of activities contains something for every sexual minority client, whether she or he is a neophyte counselee struggling with the coming-out process, or a 'long-time' lesbian or gay individual negotiating a relationship. Drs. Whitman and Boyd have compiled a collection of assignments that are clinically sound, grounded in theory, practical, and useful. The book provides activities for the many dilemmas that arise in psychotherapy, including those quandaries that are rarely addressed in other sources.

This notebook addresses client concerns with gender identity, passages from heterosexuality to homosexuality, surviving the trauma of heterosexism, integrating sexual orientation and ethnicity, understanding the politics of sexual orientation and identity, mixed-identity relationships, sexual dysfunction, reconciling religion and spirituality, coping with unwanted sexual behavior, and concerns of disabled sexual minorities.

The contributors provide excellent ideas for therapists, even if they choose to vary from the formats suggested by Drs. Whitman and Boyd. The instructions are specific and helpful, and the contraindications section of each activity is particularly significant, given the ethical caveat of not rendering further harm to an already-vulnerable client population."

Kathleen Y. Ritter, PhD
Professor,
Coordinator of Counseling Psychology,
California State University, Bakersfield;
Co-Author, *Handbook of Affirmative
Psychotherapy with Lesbians and Gay Men*

The Therapist's Notebook
for Lesbian, Gay, and Bisexual Clients
Homework, Handouts, and Activities
for Use in Psychotherapy

HAWORTH Practical Practice in Mental Health
Lorna L. Hecker, PhD
Senior Editor

The Therapist's Notebook
for Lesbian, Gay, and Bisexual Clients
Homework, Handouts, and Activities
for Use in Psychotherapy

Joy S. Whitman, PhD
Cyndy J. Boyd, PhD

Editors

The Haworth Clinical Practice Press
An Imprint of The Haworth Press, Inc.
New York • London • Oxford

Published by

The Haworth Clinical Practice Press, an imprint of The Haworth Press, Inc., 10 Alice Street, Binghamton, NY 13904-1580.

PUBLISHER'S NOTE
Quotes for Common Issues in Being Addicted and in Being Gay, Chapter 43, from A.A. Grapevine 1989, *AA and the Gay/Lesbian Alcoholic*. Copyright © by the A.A. Grapevine, Inc. Reprinted with permission.

Identities and circumstances of individuals discussed in this book have been changed to protect confidentiality. Any resemblance to actual persons, living or dead, is entirely coincidental.

Cover design by Marylouise E. Doyle.

Library of Congress Cataloging-in-Publication Data

The therapist's notebook for lesbian, gay, and bisexual clients : homework, handouts, and activities for use in psychotherapy / Joy S. Whitman, Cynthia J. Boyd.
    p. cm.
   Includes bibliographical references and index.
   ISBN 0-7890-1252-9 (soft : alk. paper)
   1. Gays—Mental health—Handbooks, manuals, etc. 2. Lesbians—Mental health—Handbooks, manuals, etc. 3. Bisexuals—Mental health—Handbooks, manuals, etc. 4. Psychotherapy—Handbooks, manuals, etc. 5. Psychoanalysis and homosexuality—Handbooks, manuals, etc. 6. Homosexuality—Psychological aspects—Handbooks, manuals, etc. I. Whitman, Joy S. II. Boyd, Cynthia J.

RC451.4.G39 T478 2003
616.89'14'08664—dc21
2002027283

CONTENTS

ABOUT THE EDITORS

Joy S. Whitman, PhD, is Associate Professor of Education in the Counseling and Development Program at Purdue University Calumet in Hammond, Indiana. She is on staff as a clinical supervisor at the university's Counseling Center, and also serves as Co-Chair of the university's School of Education Diversity Committee. She is a member of the American Psychological Association (Division 44 and 17), the American Counseling Association, and the Indiana Counseling Association. She is board trustee of the Association for Gay, Lesbian, and Bisexual Issues in Counseling, and serves as Chair of its student mentoring program. Her work has been presented in publications including *Innovative Higher Education, Counselor Education and Supervision,* the *Journal of College Counseling,* the *International Journal of Sexuality and Gender Studies,* and the *Journal for Specialists in Group Work.* She has given more than twenty presentations at professional conferences, focusing on issues gay, lesbian, and bisexual clients face in therapy. Dr. Whitman also maintains a private practice in Chicago. She is experienced in long- and short-term therapy with individuals and groups.

Cyndy J. Boyd, PhD, is Staff Psychologist and Director of Training at the University of Illinois Counseling Center in Chicago. She has taught an undergraduate course on counseling methods at the university that prepares students for volunteer work on the Counseling Center's In-Touch Crisis Hotline and a master's level course in career theory and lifestyle development at the Illinois School of Professional Psychology. In the past, she coordinated the Crisis Hotline and taught courses in career counseling, crisis counseling, psychopathology, and human development. She has presented nationally on topics that include counseling GLBT individuals, multicultural and feminist therapy, training and supervision, and career counseling. Her work has been published in the *Journal of Career Development,* the *International Journal of Sexuality and Gender Studies,* and the *Journal of College Counseling.* She maintains a part-time private practice in Chicago and is on the advisory committee to the Office of Gay, Lesbian, Bisexual, and Transgender Concerns at UIC.

She is a member of the American Psychological Association (Divisions 17, 35, and 44) and the American Counseling Association, and sits on the Board of Directors of the Association for Counseling Center Training Agencies (ACCTA).

CONTRIBUTORS

Eve M. Adams, PhD, is Assistant Professor in the Department of Counseling and Educational Psychology at New Mexico State University. She received her PhD from The Ohio State University in 1988. Prior to working at NMSU, she was a psychologist at the University of Akron's Counseling and Testing Center. She has worked with GLB clients and has served as an advisor to GLB student groups. Her research interests include identity development and the psychology of oppression, which she has examined in the GLB population among many others.

Sheila M. Addison, MA, is a PhD student in marriage and family therapy at Syracuse University and a student member of AAMFT. She has taught about working with GLBT clients in a variety of settings, and most recently coinstructed a PhD course at SU called "Sexual Identity and Family Therapy," which she and a colleague designed. She is the co-author of "Don't Ask, Don't Tell: Supervision and Sexual Identity," which was recently published in the *AAMFT Supervision Bulletin.* She was cocreator of a poster presented at the 1999 AAMFT Conference titled "The Sexual Orientation of Marriage and Family Therapy," and was the copresenter of "But Is It Therapy? Redefining In-Home Interventions" at the 2000 AAMFT conference.

Randall L. Astramovich, PhD, is currently Assistant Professor in the Department of Counseling at Idaho State University. He has counseled GLB clients in mental health agencies and in private practice and has presented at local, regional, and national counseling conferences on a variety of topics including spiritual and transpersonal perspectives in counseling.

Michael Barbee, MA, ATR-BC, is an art therapist and clinical psychology doctoral candidate at the California Institute of Integral Studies in San Francisco. He received his MA from the University of Louisville. He has worked with sexual minorities in several public mental health settings, including that city's intake clinic for GLBT clients and its Center for Special Problems, one of the country's only public clinics specializing in transgendered care. He has worked most often with homeless and severely mentally ill clients who do not experience a sense of gay community. Currently, he is doing dissertation research on transsexual identity, using photography and narrative, and is a developing studio artist.

Monica Bigler is a doctoral student in the Counseling Psychology Department at the University of Florida. She received her BS in psychology from the University of Florida. Prior to her academic studies in the United States, she studied and worked in Switzerland and Israel. She has been a teacher for children with mental disabilities, and has worked in various social settings, including an international human service organization and a home for the elderly. She conducts psychotherapy research, focusing upon metaphor usage across cultures and multicultural treatment methods.

Randolph Bowers, PhD, is a Counseling, Teaching, and Research Scholar at the School of Health, University of New England, New South Wales, Australia. He is a native of Canada, where he trained in Rogerian psychotherapy, neurolinguistic programming, and clinical hypnosis. His current interests include counselor education, particularly on sexual and gender minority issues; indigenous issues; and exploring transpersonal methods in counseling.

Sara K. Bridges, PhD, is Assistant Professor of Psychology and Director of the Davis House Psychology Clinic at Humboldt State University in Arcata, California. She teaches graduate and undergraduate courses in counseling techniques, couple therapy, and human sexuality; has published on topics related to constructivism and sex therapy with couples; and is currently co-editing a book titled *Cutting Edge Issues in Personal Construct Psychology: Practical Applications* *and Postmodern Directions* (Pace University Press). Her current research interests concern systems of personal and relational meanings that affect sexual satisfaction in lesbian, bisexual, and heterosexual women.

Melody M. Brown, MA, is a PhD student in marriage and family therapy at Syracuse University and an associate member of AAMFT. She specializes in working with African-American individuals, couples, and families in a clinical setting. She also has a special interest in confronting oppression in all forms. She presented a roundtable discussion at the 2000 AAMFT Conference titled, "Dismantling Stereotypes Within African-American Couples." For the past two years, she has run a therapy group for African-American teenage girls at the Brighton Family Center in Syracuse, New York.

Stuart F. Chen-Hayes, PhD, NCC, is Assistant Professor and Coordinator of Counselor Education at Lehman College, City University of New York. He has worked as a counselor in middle school, university, mental health, couple, family, and sex therapy settings. He has published on GLBT counseling and advocacy in *The Family Journal, The Journal of Lesbian and Gay Social Services, The Journal of Humanistic Education and Development,* and *The Journal of American College Health.* He has had GLBT book chapters in Lewis and Bradley's *Advocacy in Counseling,* Kumashiro's *Troubling Intersections of Race and Sexuality: Queer Students of Color and Anti-Oppressive Education,* and a forthcoming chapter in Pope, Niles, and Goodman's *Career Counseling Casebook.* He recently co-authored a culturally diverse GLBT youth/family school-counseling video series with Microtraining Associates. His research, writing, and public speaking interests include academic, career, and interpersonal equity and justice for all children, youth, and families.

Elizabeth P. Cramer, PhD, LCSW, is Associate Professor at the School of Social Work, Virginia Commonwealth University. Her primary practice and scholarship areas are lesbian and gay issues, domestic violence, and group work. For the past two years, she has been conducting a sexuality and gender group for lesbian, bisexual, transgendered, and questioning women in a residential substance abuse treatment program.

Michelle M. Crooks-Yared is a doctoral student in marriage and family therapy at Michigan State University, currently working on her dissertation, a qualitative study of parents who are seeking and affirming regarding their gay or lesbian child's sexual orientation. She has worked in the Family and Child Clinic at MSU, and for the past three years as a staff therapist at the Employee Assistance Program. She has worked with a wide variety of individuals, couples, and families with varying presenting problems. She has had the opportunity to work with many gay and lesbian clients during her time at MSU, and hopes to continue this as a specialty area in private practice in the future.

Mary J. Didelot, PhD, is Assistant Professor of Educational Psychology in the School of Education, Purdue University Calumet. She teaches courses within the teacher-education program, including diversity for professional educators. She has presented at national and international conferences, has numerous publications in the areas of diversity, learning, and counseling, and co-owns an independent psychotherapy practice.

Farzana Doctor, MSW, is currently the manager of the LesBiGay Service, an addictions program at the Centre for Addiction and Mental Health in Toronto, Ontario. She is a South-Asian lesbian who has worked with GLBT communities since 1993.

Ned Farley, PhD, is a core faculty member and the chair of the Mental Health Counseling Program in the Graduate Programs in Psychology at Antioch University, Seattle. He has been in private practice since 1984, serving adolescents and adults. Previously he was at Seattle Counseling Services for Sexual Minorities, serving in a variety of clinical roles from 1982 to 1991, including clinical director from 1988 to 1991. He helped design and administer a domestic violence program serving perpetrators and victims of same-sex domestic violence during his tenure. He has worked for almost twenty years with both perpetrators and survivors.

Karen Fontaine, RN, MSN, is a certified sex therapist, author, and professor of nursing at Purdue University Calumet. She has over twenty-five years of experience in private practice providing individual, relationship, and sex therapy. Karen has worked with diverse groups of people across the country in facilitating change for individuals and couples and providing consultation for professionals.

Nicole Noffsinger Frazier, MA, is a doctoral student in the Counseling Psychology Program at the University of Memphis. Her research interests are in the area of sexuality, identity, religion, and spirituality.

Molly L. Grimes is currently enrolled in the doctoral program at the Illinois School of Professional Psychology, Chicago. At present, she is participating in a diagnostic practicum at a Chicago private practice, where she works primarily with gay males. She is particularly interested in the areas of diversity and difference, and hopes to continue to successfully merge these interests with her love for clinical psychology.

Perry N. Halkitis, PhD, is a noted health psychologist and applied statistician, a professor in the Department of Applied Psychology at New York University, and a co-director at the Center for HIV/AIDS Educational Studies and Training, an NYU-CUNY HIV behavioral research center. He is Principal Investigator of the Protease Inhibitor Longitudinal Life Study (Project PILLS) funded between 1999 and 2003 by the National Institute on Drug Abuse, and Principal Investigator of the Club Drug Men's Health Study (Project BUMPS) funded by NIDA between 2000 and 2004. Dr. Halkitis is undertaking an assessment of bareback behavior, body image, steroid use, and conceptions of masculinity among seropositive gay and bisexual men using both qualitative methodologies and the Internet to collect these data. He is the recipient of the 1999 American Psychological Foundation Placek Award for his work on methamphetamine use among gay men and the NYU 1999 Daniel E. Griffith's research award for his study of masculinity among seropositive gay men.

Lisa A. Hollingsworth, PsyD, is Assistant Professor of Education at the School of Education, Purdue University Calumet. She trains and supervises master's level counselors within the graduate studies program, counsels students in the University Counseling Center, and is a co-owner of an independent psychotherapy practice. She has presented her research at national and international conferences, and has published in the areas of diversity, disability, learning styles, and spirituality.

Sharon Horne, PhD, is Assistant Professor in Counseling Psychology at the University of Memphis. She teaches a course on counseling gay, lesbian, and bisexual clients, and has published articles and presented at national conferences on issues of sexual identity, GLBT youth, and gender identity of lesbian women.

Heidi M. Levitt, PhD, is Assistant Professor in Clinical Psychology at the University of Memphis. Her psychotherapy research has concentrated on the roles of narrative and silence in psychotherapy. Her sexuality research has focused on butch and femme lesbian genders. She is an experiential psychotherapist and her approach to both therapy and research is rooted within humanistic and constructivist traditions.

Jackie Mascher, MEd, is a doctoral student in the Counseling Psychology program at Boston College. She received a master of counseling psychology degree, and a master of social restoration degree, both from Lehigh University. Her clinical area of interest is in the intersections of marginalized and privileged identities, including race, gender, and sexuality. She earned a bachelor's degree in psychobiology from Yale University.

Ron McLean, PhD, is Assistant Professor of Counselor Education at Hofstra University. His research and practice interests are in healthy family development, sexual minorities, multicultural counseling, and the use of spirituality in the helping professions. As a licensed professional counselor, he maintains a private practice where he works with family groups and individuals. He earned his doctorate in counselor education from Saint Louis University, Missouri.

Marie Mohler, MA, graduated with a master's degree in psychology, specializing in professional counseling, from the Georgia School of Professional Psychology in Atlanta. Since that time, she has worked for a large nonprofit organization in the Pittsburgh, Pennsylvaina, area. She provides individual and marriage counseling to predominantly low-income families, and also coordinates a pregnancy and parenting program. She is currently a member of the American Counseling Association and the Association for Gay, Lesbian, and Bisexual Issues in Counseling.

Robert A. Neimeyer, PhD, is Professor of Psychology and Director of the Psychotherapy and Psychopathology Specialty at the University of Memphis. He edits the *Journal of Constructivist Psychology,* and has published extensively on topics related to meaning-making frameworks for clinical practice. His books include *Constructivism in Psychotherapy, Constructions of Disorder,* and *Meaning Reconstruction and the Experience of Loss,* all with the American Psychological Association.

Scott D. Pytluk, PhD, is Assistant Professor at the Illinois School of Professional Psychology—Chicago, a division of Argosy University; Director of the Eating Disorders Center at the Community Hospital, Munster, Indiana; and in independent practice with Bridge Psychological Associates in Chicago, Illinois. His teaching and scholarly interests are in GLBT studies, general issues of diversity and difference, and contemporary psychodynamic theory and practice. He works with GLB clients, individuals with eating disorders, and others.

Karina Raina is a clinical doctoral student in the Psychology Department at the University of Memphis. She received her BS in psychology from Bradley University. Prior to her academic studies in the United States, she lived and studied in Germany. She conducts psychotherapy process research from a humanistic approach and concentrates on the role of silence in psychotherapy.

Katherine Schneider, PhD, is a licensed clinical psychologist who has taught, counseled, and administered counseling services at universities for the past twenty-five years. She is blind and has fibromyalgia. She has learned a lot about being an ally for others facing oppression from her experience of living with disabilities.

Julie Shulman, MS, is a doctoral candidate in counseling psychology at the University of Memphis. Her interests include women's sexualities, issues among GLBT clients, gender issues, and multicultural issues.

Todd M. Sigler, PsyD, graduated from the University of St. Thomas with a doctorate in counseling psychology. His doctoral project was titled, "The Impacts of Internalized Homonegativity on Gay Therapists Working with Gay Couples." He has worked with children, adolescents, and families in a crisis setting and in in-home family therapy. He has worked with geriatric patients in skilled nursing facilities and has worked with facilities providing residential and vocational services to people with developmental disabilities.

Diane Sobel, PhD, is a licensed counseling psychologist in Kentucky. She has worked as Staff Psychologist and Coordinator of the Group Therapy Program at the University of Kentucky Counseling and Testing Center for eight years. In addition to clinical work with college students, she has developed and facilitated prevention programs as part of her staff psychologist position in the counseling center, as a paid consultant to other professional and community organizations, and as a volunteer in the community. She conducts programs on a wide range of topics including relationship issues, gender issues, date rape, multiculturalism, and HIV/AIDS issues. She was selected as a HOPE trainer by the American Psychological Association's HIV/AIDS Office for Psychology Education in 1996, in order to better facilitate workshops for mental health professionals and paraprofessionals who work with people with HIV.

Andrew B. Suth, PhD, received his doctorate in psychology and human development from the University of Chicago. He has clinical training with clients in university, community, and in-patient settings. He has worked with the GLBT community providing psychotherapy through which he has addressed issues of identity, self, and sexuality. He currently practices in the Chicago area.

Reginald Tucker is a master's student in the Counseling and Family Therapy Department at Saint Louis University. He is also pursuing a minor in research methodology. He has a bachelor of science in business administration with a major in accounting from the University of Tulsa. He is currently a volunteer with Blacks Assisting Blacks Against AIDS, a St. Louis-based HIV/AIDS service organization, where he works on social-support issues with African-American men who have sex with men. In addition, he volunteers for St. Louis Effort for AIDS, a St. Louis-based HIV/AIDS service organization, where he works with the agency's volunteers on diversity issues. He also works as a diversity facilitator for the A World of Difference Institute.

Andrew Walters, PhD, MPH, is Professor at Hobart and William Smith College in Geneva, New York. He is a member of the Department of Psychology and the interdisciplinary program in men's studies. Certified by the American Association of Sex Educators, Counselors, and Therapists, he has presented numerous sexuality-based activities at professional conferences and has published activities and group-based demonstrations in the areas of coming out and homophobia. His research interests include HIV prevention among street youth, developmental approaches to sexuality education, and sexuality in medically compromised populations.

Leo Wilton, PhD, is a psychologist and a faculty member in the Department of Counseling and Clinical Psychology at Teachers College, Columbia University. He is also Visiting Assistant Professor in the Department of Africana Studies at Binghamton University. He completed his doctoral studies at New York University and a predoctoral fellowship in the Department of Psychiatry at the Yale University School of Medicine. His research and teaching interests are primary and secondary HIV prevention in urban communities of color, black psychological development and mental health, multicultural psychology, and GLBT psychology.

Foreword

Finally, here it is . . . a practical guidebook for therapists traversing both unique and common issues of gay, lesbian, bisexual, and transgendered (GLBT) clients. Never before has there been such a purposefully targeted and useful array of clinical activities, handouts, and homework to fit the specific needs of GLBT clients. Never before have the topics herein been focused on in such a practical yet infinitely sensitive manner. Never before have we seen a book of activities for use in psychotherapy so eloquently written specifically for the GLBT community. Therapists working with GLBT populations will be thrilled with this compendium of extremely useful tools that, for once, do not need to be modified or adapted from a heterosexist world.

Historically, social denial and ignorance of the effects of oppression served only to reinforce the problems faced by the GLBT community. It is only in the past fifteen to twenty years that the prevalence and detrimental effects of oppression have been acknowledged and support for healing been more readily accessible. This book reflects an innate understanding of what it takes to give up denial and other defenses used to keep pain away, and the authors reflect in their writing the nurturing it takes to accept, feel, and resolve issues stemming from oppression, both in its internal and external forms.

Although there are several clinical activities, worksheets, questions, interventions, and homework assignments designed to deal with facing oppression and the personal meaning of these events, all of the contributors write with great respect for the resiliency of the human spirit. The pages hereafter emanate healing, love, and understanding for the human spirit in a way that few books are able to convey.

Issues that are unique to GLBT clients are highlighted and dealt with creatively and knowingly. Coming-out issues are confronted, relationship issues are covered, and gender, ethnic, and sexual identity issues are painstakingly addressed. There are forty-nine detailed assignments, handouts, and activities in this book. The topics are diverse and include body image, disability, partner selection, multiculturalism, medication adherence for HIV-positive men, parenting, finances in lesbian relationships, and sexual pleasuring, to name a few. There are also chapters that all therapists should utilize for themselves (e.g., the daily heterosexism stressors are a must "read and reflect" for every therapist). One unique aspect of this book is that two authors, Sheila M. Addison and Melody M. Brown, give us a nomenclature for genograms for GLBT clients. This has been sadly lacking in the family therapy-related literature and should be widely referred to and appreciated.

Joy S. Whitman and Cyndy J. Boyd have pulled together a marvelous compendium of resources from authors who clearly know the territory of issues facing GLBT clients. I congratulate the many contributors on the insight, sensitivity, and intellect with which they created the chapters for this book. It is theoretically diverse, although most activities can be altered to fit a particular theoretical orientation. There is also an innate understanding of how spirit can become crushed in the face of oppression and wonderful activities and interventions that are both spiritually and emotionally enriching. Even substance abuse is thoughtfully and richly linked to experiences of homophobia.

If all this were not enough, if you read this book for no other reason, it should be for the rich listing of resources. Each chapter details readings and resources for both the clinician and the client. Since so many clients benefit from bibliotherapy and other connecting resources, it is hard to ignore this important feature.

There is something for every client and for every therapist in this book. I personally found it to be extremely exciting because of its practicality and the glaring need for a resource such as this. There will be little dust gathered on this marvelous assortment of therapeutic tools.

Lorna L. Hecker, PhD
Professor of Marriage and Family Therapy;
Editor, Practical Practice in Mental Health:
Guidebooks for Inpatient, Outpatient, and Independent Practice
Book Program, The Haworth Press

Preface

When Lorna Hecker invited us to contribute to the Practical Practice in Mental Health book program, we felt honored to have the opportunity to join a series that has so richly augmented the mental health literature. We were also excited by the prospect of giving back to the gay, lesbian, bisexual, and transgendered (GLBT) community in a way that is both respectful and meaningful. The goal of this project is to provide clinical interventions for professionals working with GLBT clients that have been developed and applied within a context of understanding the impact of the daily heterosexism, homophobia, and sexism with which GLBT individuals are faced. As a result, this book acknowledges a myriad of unique concerns to GLBT communities, addresses them in ways that normalize their experiences, and highlights the resilience and strength that GLBT individuals demonstrate in managing those concerns.

The chapters that follow vary with regard to the theoretical orientation and perspective that informs the clinical work. For this reason, most clinicians will be able to find an exercise that is consistent with his or her clinical view. All of the chapters are grounded in theory and research relevant to GLBT individuals, thereby enriching the clinician's base of knowledge in each area and clearly outlining the rationale for the implementation of each activity with GLBT clients. The authors have employed language, symbols, ideas, and goals that are inclusive and sensitive to the unique needs of GLBT individuals. These considerations obviate the need to change pronouns, to extrapolate from irrelevant theory and research to GLBT people, or to change in any way the activities presented so that they "fit" for GLBT clients. As clinicians who have often had to utilize material written for heterosexuals and modify it to work with GLBT clients, having activities written specifically for GLBT clients is a relief. We hope that clinicians using this book will feel similarly. Because of the plethora of concerns with which GLBT individuals present clinically, it is impossible to address and include all of them in one book. We chose to include issues that are frequently presented and that are often overlooked in clinical practice. Although we expect that many readers will find chapters that speak to the issues their clients present in treatment, it is our hope that when this is not the case, the resources suggested in each chapter will lead clinicians to a reading that could spark their own creativity.

The book is organized into four content areas: (1) coming-out issues and the management of homophobia and heterosexism; (2) relationship issues; (3) the intersection of gender, ethnic, and sexual identities; and (4) specific issues such as substance abuse and spirituality. Each content area offers a variety of activities that respond to the issues in ways that are inventive and respectful. Although the chapters are separated and categorized to lend some organization to complex issues, we recognize that most issues are multidimensional. For this reason, the chapters can easily be combined to address multiple issues for any one client or the same activity can be applied to work with several clients in different manners. For example, since coming-out issues and heterosexism are threads that are woven into nearly all of the issues included in this book, we encourage clinicians to borrow from any and all of the activities in ways that are meaningful to their work with clients who are struggling to define themselves in the face of oppression.

Finally, we believe that this book will speak to all clinicians working with GLBT clients. For those who are new to treating GLBT clients, the activities in this book offer rich material, based on the current literature, to guide your work. It also provides you and your clients with a variety of readings to enhance learning. For the seasoned clinician who has worked extensively with GLBT clients, the activities in this book can expand and invigorate the work you do by sharing fresh and innovative strategies. For professors and trainers who teach students and colleagues how to work with GLBT clients, the activities can be incorporated into the subject matter of your curriculum as a way to illustrate a particular issue. The resource lists are also useful as adjuncts to the required reading for a course or workshop.

We hope that this book inspires others to creatively and respectfully treat gay, lesbian, bisexual, and transgendered clients. It has certainly inspired our clinical and academic work.

Acknowledgments

Foremost, we would like to thank Lorna Hecker for inviting us to contribute to this series and for her vision. Her belief that a book of this nature would be important and useful for clinicians working with GLBT clients was clear and motivating. We thank her for that vision and for her understanding of the complexities of sexual identity.

We would like to extend our immense gratitude to all of the contributors to this book. Their imagination, resourcefulness, and dedication to the GLBT community come through in every chapter.

Our last acknowledgment is to the GLBT community. We are inspired by the courage and pride with which you live your lives in spite of oppression. This book is for you.

SECTION I:
HOMEWORK, HANDOUTS, AND ACTIVITIES FOR COMING OUT AND MANAGING HOMOPHOBIA AND HETEROSEXISM

Conflicts in Self-Perceptions
in the Coming-Out Process

Michael Barbee

Type of Contribution: Activity/Homework

Objective

The objective of this activity is to develop a greater awareness of self-concept and awareness of others' perceptions during the coming-out process. The experiences of self and others are often a source of conflict for the client, both internally and interpersonally. This activity can give both therapist and client an idea of the role of homophobia, internalized homophobia, ego strength, support system, and reality testing in the process of a developing identity.

Rationale for Use

This activity is designed to help the client look at self-perceptions during the emergence and claiming of an identity as a member of a sexual minority. The client is able to compare his or her present sense of self with others' perceptions, as well as with his or her sense of an ideal self. This is especially important in the development of an identity experienced as conflictual to the client, and one for which he or she may have no role models. The images created allow the client to hold conflicting points of view, as well as to imagine a resolution of the conflict.

This activity can be used with individuals or groups (if all members are confronting gay, lesbian, or bisexual [GLB] identity development), and can be done in session or assigned as homework.

Materials

Ideally, large white drawing paper (e.g., 18" × 24") and a variety of watercolor markers, or any similar materials may be used.

Instructions

The therapist may introduce the exercise in the following manner:

> As people develop a sense of being GLB, they are often confronted with conflicts between how they are coming to see themselves and the heterosexual image of adulthood they were taught, as well as conflicts between how other people may see them and how this might change if they come out. This exercise will help us look at where you are with these conflicts, the progress you have made so far in resolving them, and how you would ideally want to identify regarding sexual orientation. We will use the drawings that you create in

future sessions to look at the hopes, fears, myths, and stereotypes you hold about being GLB, as well as your own notions, who will support you, and the role that sexual orientation plays in your overall identity.

The therapist then instructs the client to complete three drawings:

1. How I see myself
2. How others see me
3. My ideal self

These instructions should be interpreted by the client, who is encouraged to be spontaneous and creative, using symbols of various colors and shapes. (Encourage the client not to be preoccupied with realistic figure drawings.)

The therapist may use the following questions to guide the client in interacting around specific drawings, as appropriate:

- How does sexual orientation fit into your overall sense of identity?
- How do other people see you in comparison to how you see yourself?
- How do specific others (e.g., parents, friends, boss, etc.) see you, and whose perceptions matter most?
- Are your self-perceptions realistic? Are they influenced by shame, guilt, or stereotypes?
- How does homophobia impact your self-concept?
- What stereotypes are you aware of or afraid of as you develop your identity?
- How would your ideal self be different and what role would sexual orientation play?
- How would others' perceptions change or remain the same if you came out?
- What do you hear others say about homosexuals (jokes, stereotypes)?

Suggestions for Follow-Up

The drawings produced by this exercise can be used as an ongoing measure of the client's progress in developing identity as they are taken out and reexamined over time. The exercise can be done again a few months following the initial exercise, and the results compared, to give the client a sense of progress and changing perceptions of self and others. More specific exercises can follow, such as: how my mother/father sees me; how society sees homosexuals (stereotypes and media presentations); how I see the gay "community"; or how gays, lesbians, and bisexuals portray themselves to the public.

Contraindications

This exercise requires maturity of thought and the ability for self-reflection, as well as symbolic capability. It should be utilized when it will provide affirmation and increased insight, rather than during times of instability (i.e., when experiencing suicidal ideation or other vulnerable periods). Caution: Some clients, especially members of ethnic or cultural minorities, may not develop a Western "gay" identity, and may never "come out" in their family or community. All clients should be encouraged to develop a sense of identity that works for them individually.

Readings and Resources for the Professional

Berger, R. and Kelly, J. (1996). *Textbook of homosexuality and mental health*. Washington, DC: American Psychiatric Press.

D'augelli, A. and Patterson, C. (Eds.) (1996). *Lesbian, gay, and bisexual lives over the lifespan*. New York: Oxford University Press.

Hancock, G., Cochran, S., Goodchilds, J., and Peplau, L. (1991). Issues in psychotherapy with lesbians and gay men. *American Psychologist, 46*(9), 964-972.

Klein, F., Sepekof, B., and Wolf, T. (1985). Sexual orientation: A multi-variable dynamic process. *Journal of Homosexuality, 11*(2), 35-49.

Bibliotherapy Sources for the Client

Eichberg, R. (1991). *Coming out: An act of love*. New York: Plume.

Isay, R. (1997). *Becoming gay: The journey to self-acceptance*. New York: Henry Holt.

Johnson, B. (1997). *Coming out every day: A gay, bisexual, and questioning man's guide*. San Francisco: New Harbinger.

Mohler, M. (1999). *Homosexual rites of passage: A road to visibility and validation*. Binghamton, NY: The Haworth Press.

2

Hurdles

Andrew Walters

Type of Contribution: Activity

Objectives

This activity, most successfully used in a group context, has two central objectives. A primary objective is for clients to describe and personify the multiple psychological and psychosocial stresses associated with coming out. They are asked to narrate dimensions of intrapersonal conflict and difficulty (or, more rarely, ease) that they have experienced, or that they could foresee experiencing, in the process of acknowledging to self or to others their bisexuality or homosexuality. A second objective, demonstrated both visually and through narrative, is for clients to recognize and respect the individual differences that characterize the coming-out process. That is, what is described as overwhelmingly difficult for one person may be seen as negligible or inconsequential for another. Although some sources of difficulty are reported similarly by most individuals adopting a gay, lesbian, or bisexual identity, substantial variation is normative in decisions about to whom one will come out, the timing of these disclosures, and the degree of perceived difficulty associated with *each* disclosure. This activity illustrates the variability of coming out among individuals.

Rationale for Use

Coming out—the process of identifying to self and to others one's homosexuality or bisexuality—continues to be identified as an intense, sometimes chronic stressor, but also one that is believed to be critical to the development of a positive self-identity. Developmental research across disciplines (e.g., psychology, social work, medicine, and public health) suggests that, although coming out may occur at any age, for most individuals it happens in adolescence or young adulthood. Many gay youth groups have been formed in schools, through outreach programs, and on the Internet. However, it would be a mistake to assume that membership to a gay youth group (or access to an on-line chat room or listserv) serves as an indicant of an individual's adjustment and comfort to new (and often frightening) feelings of being gay, lesbian, or bisexual. There are strong empirical data to suggest that gay youth are at increased risk for disturbances of mental health (D'Augelli, Hershberger, and Pilkington, 1998; see also Hershberger and D'Augelli, 1995) and increased risk of suicide (Fergusson, Horwood, and Beautrais, 1999; Schneider, Farberow, and Kruks, 1989), and that, more generally, individuals who conceal a homoerotic identity may be at increased risk for physical illnesses (Cole et al., 1996).

A body of research suggests wide variability in others' reactions upon learning that someone they know is gay, lesbian, or bisexual or from direct coming-out disclosures (Savin-Williams, 1989; see also Rotheram-Borus, Hunter, and Rosario, 1995). Thus, it is often wise to consider quite carefully both the individuals to whom one may want to come out and the timing of these disclosures. Counselors and therapists have demonstrated remarkable skill in helping clients think through the sequelae of their coming out to friends, family, and co-workers (Hunter et al., 1998). For example, therapists associated with a college or university counseling center may understand and appreciate a client's perception that a college environment is infinitely more liberal and accepting of differences than was the client's hometown or family. More often than not, however, the therapist also recognizes that disclosures of gay, lesbian, or bisexual sexual orientations are likely to result in different consequences when directed at one's family versus one's new circle of college friends.

In human sexuality courses, supervised practica, and professional-training seminars, students, clients, and professionals alike often assume that coming out is an inevitable process and it occurs as a one-time, all-or-nothing life event. In addition, there appears to be an assumption among some individuals that the consequences of coming out are equal across situations. Clearly, these assumptions are faulty. In the first place, coming out is *not* an inevitable process. Unless someone is "outed" by others, he or she has the potential to control (e.g., by demeanor, deliberate conversational choices) the assumptions or inferences others might make about him or her. Even in circumstances where someone's eroticism is directed at his or her own sex (e.g., a man is turned on sexually by other men), "coming out," as it is understood within the larger cultural context, refers to the acknowledgment to self, as well as to others, that one wishes to establish an identity that corresponds to an erotic map. Although homoeroticism and the adoption of a gay, lesbian, or bisexual identity are related (and sometimes parallel processes), it is important to understand that these are conceptually distinct qualities. Further, coming out is reported by many gay, lesbian, and bisexual persons as difficult precisely because it is not a one-time event. Individuals must constantly weigh the consequences of coming out to others.

The activity described here, referred to as "Hurdles," was designed to demonstrate the multiple stresses and consequences of identifying oneself as gay, lesbian, or bisexual. It has been used successfully with many constituencies, but it may be especially helpful for homosexual and bisexual youth ("youth" is currently defined as lasting through ages twenty-one to twenty-two). The metaphor of a hurdle captures the experiences that many homosexual and bisexual clients report during their coming-out process. In a running meet, a runner may vault a hurdle of a particular height, but successive hurdles may be higher or lower than the first or, alternatively, they may be easier to master given where a runner is in terms of speed and direction. Individual differences in coming out show a similar tendency. For some clients, once they have cleared their first hurdle they have more self-confidence to face subsequent obstacles, which often seem less threatening. For others, it may appear that the hurdles with which they are confronted become increasingly more difficult and daunting. Central to this activity is the fact that coming out is an individual process. Although the majority of individuals who do come out report dimensions of the process as inherently difficult, in this activity it is presumed that each client is on her or his own path of development; no paths are guaranteed to be easier than others.

Materials

In keeping with the imagery of jumping hurdles on a running track, the hurdles used for this activity are seven pieces of lumber, each two by six inches. Each hurdle lists one of seven obstacles someone must negotiate when coming out: self, family, religion, career, friends, politics, and other. Hurdles can be painted and decorated as preferred. Vinyl lettering (available at any paper supply store) usually provides a neater appearance than does painting. Additional hurdles can be made and used depending on the client's (or group's) needs. However, the "other" hurdle is usually sufficient to meet individual needs.

Instructions

Although this activity can work successfully with individual clients, it was designed to be used with groups. It works most effectively with larger groups (i.e., fourteen to eighteen persons, and including classes of thirty to thirty-five), primarily because of the richer discussion that follows the activity. Thus, it may work most successfully for coming-out support groups and clients in a group therapy addressing primarily coming-out issues. In addition, many counselors and therapists are called upon to facilitate educational programs for nonclient populations (e.g., parents in a community setting or on-campus students attending an evening program in their residence hall). "Hurdles" has been and can be used successfully in these and other settings.

The activity begins with the solicitation of a volunteer who is asked to come forward (that is, to an open area of the room). It is explained to the volunteer (and to other members of the group) that the volunteer will be asked to share real or perceived experiences associated with coming out as lesbian, gay, or bisexual. If this activity is being used with clients who identify themselves as "questioning" (their identity), it is important to make clear that a volunteer's sexual orientation is of no consequence to the activity nor does volunteering implicate one as being homosexual. In fact, some of the most poignant experiences have been from heterosexually identified volunteers who, with empathy, share with a group how difficult it would be for them to negotiate the hurdles that they have seen their gay and lesbian friends confront. The activity is designed to confront and challenge individuals' understanding of and empathy for coming out. In this context, it should be informative to all group members, regardless of sexual or affinity orientation.

In order to increase the number of active participants in the activity, seven additional volunteers are sought; each will be asked to hold one hurdle. These volunteers move to the front of the room and are handed a hurdle at random. They are asked to stand in a singular line such that the hurdles are visible to the rest of the group and to the first volunteer. The therapist or facilitator should structure the activity so that participants can envision the first volunteer (i.e., the woman or man about to describe the coming-out process) as at the beginning of a racetrack, looking forward at the various hurdles she or he has to confront and vault.

Participants may define the hurdles personally. For example, an individual may choose to identify the career hurdle not in terms of a current job, but for one that she or he hopes to obtain in subsequent years. Or to provide another example, family may be identified as including both biological family and very intimate friends. The hurdle labeled other allows participants to choose an aspect of their own lives (but one that may not be represented by the other defined hurdles) that they perceive to be particularly salient in coming out and in establishing a gay identity. Over the course of many years, this hurdle has been used to describe membership to civic organizations, the military, one's children (who some individuals prefer to separate from the family hurdle), and to racial and ethnic heritages (e.g., I'm black and I'm pretty heavily involved in my church, and the community I'm involved in doesn't accept homosexuality. For a long time, I tried to separate my sexuality out of me, but I can't. So, I have to ask myself, "Am I black first and then gay, or do I think being a person of color is a whole other set of issues?").

Next, the volunteer is asked to begin the coming-out process by selecting the first hurdle that she or he wishes to face. The volunteer shares with the group why this particular obstacle was chosen and what consequences or dynamics she or he anticipates in confronting this hurdle. The person holding the selected hurdle steps forward and adjusts the height of the hurdle to the volunteer's specifications. Thus, the volunteer—the person coming out—chooses both the order of hurdles and the degree of difficulty perceived with each. For example, a volunteer might first select the hurdle labeled family. If the person feels that coming out to her or his family would be very easy, she or he could ask the volunteer holding that hurdle to place it near the floor, indicating that she or he could negotiate that hurdle with little difficulty, literally by stepping over it.

Alternatively, the volunteer could instruct the person holding the hurdle to adjust it at knee, waist, or shoulder height, indicating greater difficulties associated with disclosing one's sexual orientation to family. The volunteer is asked to share with the group why she or he perceives it would be easy (or difficult) to come out to members of one's family.

After having mastered the first hurdle, the volunteer is asked to select a second (i.e., "To whom would you come out next?"). This procedure is repeated for the remaining hurdles, allowing time for the client to discuss the processes by which the order of hurdles was selected, and the degree of difficulty associated with each. When finished, a visual, metaphoric running track has been created that illustrates how one participant would approach the process of coming out. If the interpersonal dynamics of the group are such that group members are free to ask questions, it takes approximately fifteen to twenty minutes for an individual to share the coming-out experience using hurdles. Because the success of this activity rests on the trust of self-disclosure, it is important that enough time be structured into the activity so that participants do not feel rushed or cut off and, as described in the following, so that the group has the chance to see at least one other individual reenact the running track analogy.

A second volunteer is asked to assume the coming-out role. If group size permits, different volunteers are recruited to hold the hurdles as well. This allows the involvement of as many participants as possible in the learning experience. The same procedure, as previously described, is repeated. To meet the second objective of this activity, it is important that at least two persons role-play (or share from direct, personal experience) the hurdles that they would place and confront on the running track. Over the course of many years and dozens of sessions in which this activity has been used, no two individuals have selected the hurdles in the same order, attributed the same degree of difficulty to them, or cited the same reasons for why any dimension of coming out is perceived as interpersonally stressful.

These individual differences, as aptly demonstrated by two peers in a group, both of whom have shared their experience, are critical dimensions to the educational and therapeutic foci of this activity. Although the activity can be used as a role-play or as a narration of current experience, the choices participants make in arranging their hurdles and the rationales they provide for these choices illuminate and exemplify the diversity among gay, lesbian, or bisexual individuals as they consider coming out to others. For example, some participants will select one hurdle (typically self or family) and ask the person holding that hurdle to stand on a chair and hold the hurdle as high above her or his head as possible, illustrating the extreme difficulty this person perceives associated with facing this hurdle. Her or his explanation details the distress and challenges associated with this obstacle. But then, remarkably, the participant may say to the volunteers holding the remaining hurdles, "All of you can just put the hurdles you're holding right on the floor. After I've blown through that top one, I can just breeze through the rest of the hurdles. If I can get through that first hurdle, my family, I'd be okay and wouldn't worry about any of the others." In other cases, a participant may ask that a hurdle be removed from the running track; the stresses associated with a particular hurdle may evoke so much challenge that the person simply elects not to confront it. For example, individuals who were raised in and/or who currently subscribe to religious orthodoxies that proscribe homosexuality may choose not to come out in that dimension of their life. These role-play experiences become meaningful for participants when they learn (through the therapist or from one another) that many lesbian, bisexual, and gay individuals approach the process of coming out with precisely this much variability. After at least two trials, discussion is opened to the group.

Suggestions for Follow-Up

Regardless of group composition, it is important for the counselor or therapist to support the struggles, real or perceived, that participants cite as difficult dimensions of coming out. In addition, it is important that the professional provide a supportive and not overly challenging environment in which individuals feel comfortable to express themselves, to ask questions, and to take personal risks (risks that, in reality, are likely to not always be associated with favorable outcomes). The strength of this activity rests on the trust and support of group members. The therapist, if facilitating the activity, must honor the directions that are provided to describe the activity's goals and procedures. If participants are instructed that they can select the hurdles that they want to face in any particular order, and are also told that they can elect to disregard one or more hurdles, then those directions should be honored. If participants perceive that the therapist disagrees or finds fault with their choice, a critical educational or therapeutic moment may be lost.

Support groups or interventions for gay youth, even those who choose to remain silent during the meeting, are of critical importance. "Hurdles" may serve as a conversational springboard for these clients. In some cases, discussion can be complemented by guest speakers who can attest to the fact that coming out can be, and typically is, stressful, but that it is a manageable dimension of development, and one for which persons can obtain social support.

Contraindications

Clients must be able to work in metaphor. If therapists are performing family therapy, it may be helpful to present the exercise to the family member questioning sexual orientation first (e.g., in a group session or in an individual session where the client can visualize the various hurdles), prior to involving the family system into a larger discussion. All family members should be informed about the nature of the activity. The activity should not be used if the therapist has any reason to suspect that frank and open discussions about homosexuality and coming out will exacerbate family conflict.

Readings and Resources for the Professional

Professional Literature

D'Augelli, A. R. and Patterson, C. (Eds.) (1995). *Lesbian, gay, and bisexual identities over the lifespan: Psychological perspectives.* New York: Oxford University Press.
Gonsiorek, J. (Ed.) (1995). *Homosexuality and psychotherapy: A practitioner's handbook of affirmative models.* Binghamton, NY: The Haworth Press.
Greene, B. (1994). Ethnic-minority lesbians and gay men: Mental health and treatment issues. *Journal of Consulting and Clinical Psychology, 62,* 243-251.
Hunter, S., Shannon, C., Knox, J., and Martin, J. I. (1998). *Lesbian, gay, and bisexual youths and adults: Knowledge for human service practice.* Thousand Oaks, CA: Sage Publications.
Ryan, C. and Futterman, D. (1998). *Lesbian and gay youth: Care and counseling.* New York: Columbia University Press.
Weinberg, M., Williams, C., and Pryor, D. (1994). *Dual attraction: Understanding bisexuality.* New York: Oxford University Press.

Organizations

American Association of Sex Educators, Counselors, and Therapists (AASECT)
PO Box 5488
Richmond, VA 23220-0488
www.aasect.org

The American Board of Sexology
PO Box 1166
Winter Park, FL 32790
(407) 645-1641
www.sexologist.org

American Psychological Association (APA)
Office of Lesbian, Gay, and Bisexual Concerns
750 First Street NE, Washington, DC 20002-4242
(202) 336-6041
www.apa.org/pi/lgbc

Association of Gay and Lesbian Psychiatrists (AGLP)
4514 Chester Avenue, Philadelphia, PA 19143-3707
(215) 222-2800
www.aglp.org

The Interfaith Alliance
1012 14th Street NW, Suite 700, Washington, DC 20005
(202) 639-6370
www.tialliance.org

National Association of School Psychologists (NASP)
4340 East West Highway, Suite 402, Bethesda, MD 20814
(301) 657-0270
www.naspweb.org

National Association of Social Workers (NASW)
National Committee on Lesbian, Gay, and Bisexual Issues
750 First Street NE, Suite 700, Washington, DC 20002-4241
(202) 408-8600 or (800) 638-8799
www.socialworkers.org

National Gay and Lesbian Task Force (NGLTF)
1700 Kalorama Road NW, Washington, DC 20009-2624
(202) 332-6483
www.ngltf.org

The Sexuality Information and Education Council of the United States (SIECUS)
Executive Director, 130 W. 42nd Street, Suite 350, New York, NY 10036-7802
(212) 819-9770
www.siecus.org

The Society for the Scientific Study of Sexuality
Executive Director, P.O. Box 416, Allentown, PA 18105-0416
(610) 530-2483
www.ssc.wisc.edu/ssss

Society for Sex Therapy and Research (SSTAR)
409 12th Street SW, Washington, DC 20024-2188
(202) 863-1645
www.sstarnet.org

Bibliotherapy Sources for the Client

Readings

Bass, E. and Kaufman, K. (1996). *Free your mind: The book for gay, lesbian, and bisexual youth—And their allies*. New York: HarperCollins.

Borhek, M. V. (1993). *Coming out to parents: A two-way survival guide for lesbians and gay men and their parents*. Cleveland, OH: Pilgrim Press.

Griffin, C. W., Wirth, M. J., and Wirth, A. G. (1997). *Beyond acceptance: Parents of lesbians and gays talk about their experiences*. New York: St. Martin's Press.

Whitehead, S. L. (1997). *The truth shall set you free: A family's passage from fundamentalism to a new understanding of faith, love, and sexual identity*. Lexington, KY: Westminster John Knox Press.

Organizations

Lavender Youth Recreation Information Center (LYRIC)
127 Collingwood Street, San Francisco, CA 94114
(415) 703-6150
www.lyric.org

National Gay and Lesbian Task Force (NGLTF)
1700 Kalorama Road NW, Washington, DC 20009-2624
(202) 332-6483
www.ngltf.org

Parents, Families and Friends of Lesbians and Gays (PFLAG)
1726 M Street NW, Suite 400, Washington, DC 20036
(202) 467-8180
www.pflag.org

The Sexuality Information and Education Council of the United States (SIECUS)
Executive Director, 130 W. 42nd Street, Suite 350, New York, NY 10036-7802
(212) 819-9770
www.siecus.org

The Trevor Project
Twenty-Four Hour Suicide Hotline For Gay Youth
(800) 850-8078
www.thetrevorproject.org

References

Cole, S. W., Kemeny, M. E., Taylor, S. E., and Visscher, B. R. (1996). Elevated physical health risk among gay men who conceal their homosexuality identity. *Health Psychology, 15,* 243-251.

D'Augelli, A. R., Hershberger, S. L., and Pilkington, N. W. (1998). Lesbian, gay, and bisexual youth and their families: Disclosure of sexual orientation and its consequences. *American Journal of Orthopsychiatry, 68*(3), 361-371.

Fergusson, D. M., Horwood, J., and Beautrais, A. L. (1999). Is sexual orientation related to mental health and suicidality in young people? *Archives of General Psychiatry, 56,* 876-880.

Hershberger, S. L. and D'Augelli, A. R. (1995). The impact of victimization on the mental health and suicidality of lesbian, gay, and bisexual youths. *Developmental Psychology, 31,* 65-74.

Hunter, S., Shannon, C., Knox, J., and Martin, J. I. (1998). *Lesbian, gay, and bisexual youths and adults: Knowledge for human service practice.* Thousand Oaks, CA: Sage Publications.

Rotheram-Borus, M. J., Hunter, J., and Rosario, M. (1995). Coming out as a lesbian or gay in the era of AIDS. In G. M. Herek and B. Greene (Eds.), *AIDS, identity, and community: The HIV epidemic and lesbians and gay men* (pp. 150-168). Thousand Oaks, CA: Sage Publications.

Savin-Williams, R. C. (1989). Coming out to your parents and self-esteem among gay and lesbian youths. *Journal of Homosexuality, 18,* 1-35.

Schneider, S. G., Farberow, N. L., and Kruks, G. N. (1989). Suicidal behavior in adolescent and young adult gay men. *Suicide and Life-Threatening Behavior, 19,* 381-389.

3

Homosexual Identity Formation: Identifying Obstacles to Growth

Marie Mohler

Type of Contribution: Activity/Homework/Handout

Objective

The objective of this activity, homework assignment, or handout is to assist the therapist in identifying the client's current stage of homosexual identity development. Identifying the client's stage of identity formation provides an essential language that can be used to facilitate progression through gay or lesbian developmental stages, en route to the client's creation of his or her positive, whole, authentic, and congruent homosexual identity.

Rationale for Use

The majority of gays and lesbians are born into heterosexual households, and are influenced at an early age by their heterosexual parents and other societal factors such as teachers, church members, and peers. Thus, it is not surprising that most people ingest the faulty societal notion that all human beings are born heterosexual. This often leads the homosexual to adopt a false heterosexual identity.

Because many homosexual children are not given the opportunity to fully develop a gay identity, it is the task of the therapist and the client to uncover which stage of the homosexual identity-formation process the client is in. Once identified, the client can then explore his or her identity, assess what he or she wants to change or maintain, and acknowledge and accept the benefits and limitations of his or her current stage of identity development.

The homework exercises provided are based on material from Mohler's (2000) book, *Homosexual Rites of Passage: A Road to Visibility and Validation,* as well as the teachings of Erik Erikson (Steinberg and Belsky, 1991) and V. C. Cass (1979). Erikson's psychosocial developmental stage of identity versus role confusion correlates to adolescence, where teenagers face the question, "Who am I?" During this life stage, teenagers experiment with different roles and identities with the goal of integrating them into one authentic identity. However, in the wake of homophobia and other negative societal issues, gay and lesbian teenagers are not always given the opportunity to truly explore their sexual orientation; consequently, they are often prevented from integrating their true gay identity into their whole sense of self. These teenagers, who have unformed, shamed, or false identities, often grow up to become wounded adults. V. C. Cass (1979) developed a homosexual identity formation model in order to provide a medium through which individuals can grow to understand the common experiences of homosexuals who are coming to terms with their sexual identity. The exercises provided are based on the Cass model.

Instructions

The therapist can use these exercises as a homework assignment, handout, or activity with individuals or couples. The client's responses may expose deeper issues such as internalized homophobia, shame, low self-esteem, substance abuse (as a coping mechanism), and/or barriers to commitment or intimacy—all stemming from an unformed or wounded identity.

The therapist instructs the client(s) to answer the questions as honestly as possible, responding with their initial "gut" reaction. Clients will either circle true or false, or choose the most accurate descriptor.

The clients can either complete the worksheet as a homework assignment or as an in-session activity. They should fill in their responses to each section sequentially, continuing on or stopping as instructed. The therapist will then process the clients' responses, in terms of their emotive and cognitive qualities, giving the therapist a window into the clients' stages of homosexual identity development. If a client gets to a point in which a response instructs him or her to stop, this indicates that the client may be "stuck" in a particular stage. The stages, in progressive order, are as follows:

Worksheet Section	Stage Task
A = Identity Confusion	To question one's sexuality
B = Identity Comparison	To address one's sense of social isolation
C = Identity Tolerance	To decrease loneliness by increasing gay and lesbian contacts
D = Identity Acceptance	To process conflict between one's self-perception and society's perceptions and views
E = Identity Pride	To deal with the incongruence between one's belief that homosexuality is acceptable and society's condemnation and disapproval of gays and lesbians
F = Identity Synthesis	To integrate one's homosexual identity into one's overall identity, so that it may be one aspect of the self rather than the whole self

If a client appears to be "stuck" in a particular stage, his or her responses in that particular section (as well as those from previous sections) provide rich material to process the how and why of his or her immobility. Much can be learned from not only what a client *is* doing, but what a client is *not* doing.

Suggestions for Follow-Up

Once the client's current stage of homosexual identity formation is identified, the therapist can explore with the client the potential fears, issues, or obstacles that prevent him or her from evolving through the growth process. The therapist can educate the client about the many choices available to him or her, and the consequence of such choices, which can either liberate or limit the client's forward progression. It will be very important to educate the client about the specific issues of fear, shame, and internalized homophobia, and how these issues have the potential to shape or impact his or her current identity and way of being in the world. At this juncture, the therapist and client may wish to reevaluate treatment goals based on the client's individual needs and circumstances. The therapist can assist the client's exploration of the limitations, benefits, and consequences of remaining in an early stage of identity development, or he or she can use additional therapeutic tools to facilitate the client's resolution of such issues, and transformation into a whole, integrated, empowered person.

Contraindications

As with all types of therapy, a client's steadfast commitment to self-exploration and personal growth will be an essential ingredient in this exercise's ability to enhance his or her positive identity development and acceptance of his or her place in the world. If a client is not committed to admitting true feelings and experiencing personal vulnerability during these discussions, and is therefore not ready to expose raw feelings, fears, and issues, this exercise may not be effective. Ultimately, this exercise was designed for the client who is motivated to do "whatever it takes" in order to clarify, perhaps for the first time, who he or she is, how he or she operates in the world, and how he or she can attain true self-empowerment through identity integration.

Readings and Resources for the Professional

Margolies, L., Becker, M., and Jackson-Brewer, K. (1987). Internalized homophobia: Identifying and treating the oppressor within. In The Boston Lesbian Psychologies Collective (Eds.), *Lesbian psychologies: Explorations and challenges* (pp. 229-241). Urbana, IL: University of Illinois Press.

Morrison, A. P. (1996). *The culture of shame*. New York: Ballantine Books.

Neisen, J. H. (1993). Healing from cultural victimization: Recovery from shame due to heterosexism. *Journal of Gay and Lesbian Psychotherapy, 2*(1), 49-63.

Bibliotherapy Sources for the Client

Berzon, B. (1992). *Positively gay: New approaches to gay and lesbian life*. Berkeley, CA: Celestial Arts.

Kaufman, G. and Raphael, L. (1996). *Coming out of shame: Transforming gay and lesbian lives*. New York: Bantam Doubleday Dell Publishing Group, Inc.

Sutton, R. (1994). *Hearing us out: Voices from the gay and lesbian community*. Boston, MA: Little, Brown and Company.

References

Cass, V. C. (1979). Homosexual identity formation: A theoretical model. *Journal of Homosexuality, 4*(3), 219-235.

Mohler, M. (2000). *Homosexual rites of passage: A road to visibility and validation*. Binghamton, NY: The Haworth Press.

Steinberg, L. and Belsky, J. (1991). *Infancy, childhood, and adolescence: Development in context*. New York: McGraw-Hill, Inc.

Homosexual Identity Formation Assessment

Section A

1. I question (or have questioned) my sexual orientation.   True   False

2. I have had intimate homosexual thoughts or feelings.   True   False

3. I feel I cannot tell anyone about these feelings and attractions to someone of the same sex.   True   False

4. I question whether these homosexual thoughts, behaviors, and feelings are the "real me."   True   False

5. I engage in heterosexual relationships because I do not want to be different or gay.   True   False

6. I sometimes hang out with intolerant, judgmental people who hold antigay beliefs, hoping to convince myself that being gay is unacceptable.   True   False

7. I try to deny that I have homosexual thoughts or feelings.   True   False

8. Choose the statement that best describes your current beliefs:

   A. My thoughts, feelings, and behaviors are homosexual in nature, and I accept them as true and irrefutable.
   (Proceed to Section B.)

   B. My thoughts, feelings, and behaviors are homosexual in nature, and although true, they are unacceptable to me.
   (Stop here.)

Section B

1. I know a homosexual.   True   False

2. I am friends with a homosexual.   True   False

3. I recognize that I may be (or I am) a homosexual.   True   False

4. I feel isolated and different from mainstream society.   True   False

5. I am afraid that my family, peers, and others will not understand or accept my homosexuality.   True   False

6. If I am homosexual, I do not know what that means or how it will change my life.   True   False

7. I have a good support system, including open-minded friends and family.   True   False

8. Choose the statement that best describes your current beliefs:

   A. I may be different and although that's OK with me, I am not ready to come out to anyone else.
   (Proceed to Section C.)

   B. The possibility that I am different is not OK. It's just a phase I'm going through.
   (Stop here.)

   C. Being different is not acceptable. Maybe someone can help me transform into a heterosexual.
   (Stop here.)

   D. Nothing is acceptable about who I am.
   (Stop here.)

Section C

1. I am ready to meet more people like me; people who are gay, lesbian, or bisexual.　　True　False

2. I have had positive contacts with members of the gay community.　　True　False

3. When I am around other homosexuals, I feel less isolated.　　True　False

4. My positive interactions and friendships with other homosexuals make me want to come out to them.　　True　False

5. I fear disclosing my homosexual identity to anyone.　　True　False

6. I had a bad interaction/experience with a homosexual, and I question whether exploring my sexual identity is something I want to do.　　True　False

7. Choose the statement that best describes your current beliefs:

   A. Positive contacts and experiences with other homosexuals have decreased my feelings of aloneness, and increased my desire to find my place in the homosexual community.
   (Proceed to Section D.)

   B. Negative contacts and experience with other homosexuals leave me wanting to degrade homosexuals, decrease my level of contact with the community, and/or stop exploring my homosexual identity.
   (Stop here.)

Section D

1. I am becoming increasingly OK with my own sense of being homosexual; however I am still trying to integrate and resolve how society views homosexuals.　　True　False

2. I continue to have positive contacts with the homosexual community, which affirms my desire to accept the trueness of my homosexual identity.　　True　False

3. Despite both positive and negative interactions with homosexuals, I continue to seek validation for my homosexual identity and lifestyle.　　True　False

4. Negative interactions with homosexuals leave me wanting to just tolerate my homosexual identity, and to cease this growth process.　　True　False

5. I feel safer when I adorn a "heterosexual mask," and try to blend into the heterosexual world.　　True　False

6. I spend the majority of my time with: heterosexuals or homosexuals.　　Circle one.

7. Choose the statement that best describes your current beliefs:

   A. I am committed to trying to pass as a heterosexual (to reduce my experience of confrontation and judgment).
   (Stop here.)

   B. I find myself limiting contact with heterosexuals and increasing my contact with homosexuals.
   (Proceed to Section E.)

   C. I am beginning to come out to selected homosexuals.
   (Proceed to Section E.)

Section E

1.	I believe that my homosexual identity is fully acceptable, yet I am still grappling with society's condemnation or intolerance.	True	False
2.	I continue to increase my commitment to the homosexual community.	True	False
3.	I feel frustrated with society's perception of homosexuals.	True	False
4.	I devalue heterosexuality and heterosexuals.	True	False
5.	I feel a great sense of pride.	True	False
6.	My feelings of pride lead me to activism.	True	False
7.	I am less protective of concealing my homosexual identity, and I am "out" a majority of the time.	True	False

8. Choose the statement that best describes your current beliefs:

A. I have disclosed my homosexual identity to others and because I believe their reactions were positive, I feel confident in moving forward to affirm, accept, and complete/integrate my homosexual identity.
(Proceed to Section F.)

B. I have disclosed my homosexual identity to others and because I believe their responses were negative, I *question* whether I desire to pursue complete acceptance of my homosexuality as an integral part of my identity.
(Stop here.)

Section F

1.	I recognize and accept that my homosexual identity is an integral part of who I am; combined with many other strengths and a few flaws, it adds to my completeness.	True	False
2.	I am able to trust the supportive heterosexuals in my life.	True	False
3.	I limit contact with unsupportive or intolerant heterosexuals (and recognize that their intolerance is their issue to contend with).	True	False
4.	I recognize that there are positive *and* negative people within both the homosexual *and* heterosexual populations. (Thus, people need to be evaluated on an individual basis.)	True	False
5.	I have the same personal and public identity.	True	False

6. Choose the statement that best describes your current beliefs:

A. I have found an unsupportive environment, which leaves me unable or unwilling to integrate all aspects of my identity. Consequently, I find myself returning to an earlier stage of identity development/acceptance.
(Stop here, and discuss with therapist.)

B. I have found a supportive environment in which I am able to integrate all aspects of my identity, so that I live authentically, positively, and congruently on a daily basis.
(Congratulations!)

4

Semihypnotic Visualization: Treating Internalized Homophobia in Sexual and Gender Minorities

Randolph Bowers

Type of Contribution: Activity

Objective

The goal of this activity is to create an environment for exploration and healing of internalized homophobia.

Rationale for Use

Homophobia is a cultural phenomenon that begins in elementary school and is manifested predominantly among boys (Plummer, 1999). Behaviors associated with homophobia at this age are name calling, aggressiveness, and other stigmatizing gestures such as joking, socially isolating individuals seen to be different, and violence (Plummer, 1999).

Plummer (1999) suggests that although homophobic behaviors tend to taper off during the mid to late teen years, the power of internalized socialization remains. As such, homophobia is said to pervade mainstream society, but is most felt by gay, lesbian, bisexual, and transgendered people.

Semihypnotic visualization is suggested as a way to begin defusing the damage done by homophobia and to begin the healing process. Semihypnotic visualization for internalized homophobia is a strategy developed in part by the application of principles from clinical hypnosis (Erickson and Rossi, 1979; Rossi and Ryan, 1985) and neurolinguistic programming (Dilts, 1976, 1980). Visualization has long been a favored exercise for stress reduction, self-esteem building, and creativity enhancement (Andreas and Andreas, 1987, 1994). Use of visualization in therapy is a dynamic tool, as many clients will use their visual sense system along with auditory and kinetic systems in the midst of the communication process (Rossi, 1986).

This approach combines relaxation, slow breathing, and use of creative metaphorical and visual language. It also includes awareness of multiple levels of meaning and precise matching of language to the client's communication systems and underlying issues, with the intention of facilitating change at unconscious levels.

Instructions

The following example is a basic template on which you, the therapist, can elaborate, depending on the particular needs of each client. Take time with the process, exploring each facet of meaning that emerges. When the client is relaxed, maintain a continual and slow dialogue between you and the client. Pace the relaxation and lead the client through the process.

It may be helpful to keep notes during the process, which is not intrusive to the session because the client is relaxed and usually has his or her eyes closed. Simple notes on the client's meanings or images can help you remember to weave those words into your strategy as the process unfolds. Some therapists choose to use soft music, but following the tradition of Milton Erickson (Erickson and Rossi, 1979; Rossi and Ryan, 1985), your voice is enough to offer a quality of sustained engagement along with a simplicity and elegance that permeates the process.

The client should always be given choices. With sexual and gender minorities, choices to engage, to disengage, to open up, to wait to open up, or to leave and call it a day are all crucial to building authentic trust. Dealing with such a sensitive issue as homophobia is in certain respects similar to working with abuse recovery or posttraumatic stress. Homophobia is even more sensitive of an issue in the sense that its social mechanics are pervasive, but recognition of it is rare (Plummer, 1999).

Once you have gained initial consent and have explained the outline of the strategy for the client's cognitive understanding, gently change your tone of voice and your delivery, becoming slower in your speech. You might say, "I invite you to relax in your chair. While this experience is safe and allows us to explore many things together, if you feel uncomfortable we can pause. All you need to tell me is pause, and we will stop and look at whatever is happening or change direction as you need. How does that sound to you?"

Continue using semihypnotic language. "Comfort and safety is the environment we can create for ourselves when we do inner work. We create that safety by relaxing and exploring one area that is guarded by boundaries. Similar to our skin which forms a boundary of safety between the world and us, we can communicate with the world. So our inner mind has pathways we can explore and understand."

Then say, "If perchance you feel uncomfortable, we can stop anytime you need to stop. We can move out of this experience and go into a place that is more comfortable, or we can talk about your experience. You may touch upon something valuable to you; an insight, a feeling, or a question may arise. We do not know which particular something is valuable to you. But in the wisdom of your unconscious and self, that valuable insight will come up when you are ready, as tomorrow becomes today and the past is transformed in the present moment."

At this stage, several layers of consent have been gained. You have assessed any hesitations and can proceed with the strategy. Setting up the context is just as important as the work itself. Moving step by step ensures that the client will not feel threatened and you will have a longer period of time to build rapport, safety, and gain knowledge about the client's beliefs and needs.

It may take ten to fifteen minutes to begin a session and set up a relaxing context for the strategy. The strategy will take about twenty minutes. Debriefing will take another fifteen or twenty minutes, for a total of about fifty to fifty-five minutes.

The Exercise

You may say, "Become aware of your breathing. Find a comfortable position, sense your body now, and slowly become aware of your feet on the floor. . . ." Slowly continue up through each part of the body, from the toes to the tip of the head, suggesting deeper and deeper layers of successive relaxation.

The exercise begins with visualizing other people. This is done strategically to allow the client time to explore sensitive issues in safety. It also allows you time to understand the client's experience, setting up a context of mutual safety and rapport.

Continue with, "Open your mind now to imagine two [men or women] together who are in an intimate relationship with each other. They are lovers, and they live together and share daily life. They eat breakfast together, and on the weekends they have bacon and eggs with all the fixings.

At night they watch TV and relax together, sometimes enjoying a special dessert of ice cream. Their lovemaking is intimate, vulnerable, and passionate. They talk for long hours after they have sex and hold each other tenderly."

After painting the picture, ask, "What do you feel as you watch this couple share their lives so intimately?" Discuss the feelings that come up, maintaining a gentle and relaxing atmosphere and allowing space for exploration. Other questions that could be asked include, "Do any uncomfortable feelings come up for you as you see a homosexual couple living together?" or "Can you imagine yourself living that life? Why or why not?"

Explore the client's belief system about same-sex relationships with questions such as, "What is it about them that gives you the feeling they are not happy? Is that unhappiness at all a part of your world?" The client may be in a relationship, and the images of the couple may bring up problems in his or her own partnership. Explore these issues within a meditative framework, gently coming back to relaxing phrases and images. For example, "I understand that you are upset, since your partnership now has some problems for you. I invite you to think of those problems now, and with each outward breath, imagine those problems flowing away. Of course they do not just flow away, but over time, in the mystery of how life works, those problems inevitably become transformed. So that, with each breath inward and outward . . . , the answers we sought yesterday become the realizations of today and change into the dreams we have for tomorrow. The important thing is to breathe, and begin to recognize that you are precious to the stars and skies, just as you are, with each precious breath."

Continue with, "Now if you could speak directly with the couple who are living together, what would you say to them?" Explore the meanings of the client's communication to the couple. They are symbolically a part of the client's internalized relationship beliefs, values, and experiences. Stay attuned to possible cues of internalized homophobia.

You may suggest, "Watch them now, as they move closer to each other, and begin to touch each other's hands and gently caress each other's faces." A number of questions could be asked here, depending on your assessment of the client's comfort. For instance, "What do you feel when you see their affection? Does their love feel natural for you? Why or why not? Are you comfortable living out your desire for same-sex love? What does that mean for you?"

As these images are creatively explored, they could lead into several sessions of rich discussion. Much information is gained that can help unravel the complex tapestry of internalized shame, guilt, low self-esteem, and homophobia. Although the strategy is not the place for any in-depth cognitive discussion of responses, those responses can be used later on during debrief and in subsequent sessions.

You can end the strategy by coming back to breathing, the focal point for body-mind awareness. "Accept all that you have said and felt, all the expressed words and especially the silent words and gestures and the feelings that lay beneath the surface. They can all be accepted, yes, with each breath. Feel the breath enter your body . . . and leave your body. You are suspended in that cycle of life that gives birth to new ideas of tomorrow, and the past is transformed in the present breath—even our fears, anxieties, and hurts."

Continue with, "When you were a child and you cut your hand, it hurt a lot all at once and then slowly began to heal. It healed with each moment, and didn't they go by quickly? And suddenly, when your body was ready, in its own wisdom, the cut was healed and the scar disappeared. . . . With each breath, bring your mind back to this room . . . so that in a few breaths you will be fully present in mind in this chair, in body in this chair, and in the office where we sit together."

Gently make a transition to cognitive processing by giving the client time to adjust, and when he or she is ready, begin the debrief by asking, "How was that for you?"

Suggestions for Follow-Up

Using notes taken during the strategy as memory anchors, the therapist can more readily recall feelings, impressions, images, beliefs, and values. Therapist and client can explore together the link between these impressions and possible internalized homophobia. Discussion may lead into family-of-origin work, traumatic experiences during school years, and present-day challenges faced because of being homosexual in a heteronormative society.

To enhance the potency of follow-up, keeping an audiotape of the session is recommended. The client can listen to it between sessions, reflecting on the experience more directly. The client may choose to share the tape with his or her partner between sessions. This can bring the experience of understanding homophobia and healing from homophobia into their relationship, and thus become a tool for building intimacy and combating the social isolation homophobia creates.

Although the strategy fits well within one session, the issues it raises demand sensitivity and safety built over several sessions. The stronger the rapport with the client, the more likely that exploring internalized homophobia will be productive and healing, and not harmful.

Contraindications

The exercise is extremely evocative and can bring up incredibly rich information and materials, memories and insights, and feelings and beliefs. At minimum, the therapist must be highly skilled in the core dimensions of counseling, including empathy, positive regard, listening, genuineness, and respect. Further training in precise use of language, in gaining sensory acuity, and in use of semihypnotic strategies is recommended. If tailored to each client in appropriate ways and with knowledge of gay and lesbian differences, this strategy bears only one cautionary note: it is not recommended for use with clients who have just lost a loved one.

Homophobia is found to be a significant factor across many counseling disciplines (Berkman and Zinberg, 1997; Griffin, 1998; Johnson, 1999). It influences both therapist *and* client. This exercise focuses on client transformation, but to gain therapeutic success, awareness on the part of the therapist is necessary. Therapists need to understand and to uncover their own homophobia before attempting to treat others.

Readings and Resources for the Professional

Berkman, C. and Zinberg, G. (1997). Homophobia and heterosexism in social workers. *Social Work, 42*(4), 319-332.

Dilts, R., Hallbom, T., and Smith, S. (1990). *Beliefs: Pathways to health and wellness.* Capitola, CA: Meta Press.

Gelso, C., Fassinger, R., Gomez, M., and Latts, M. (1995). Countertransference reactions to lesbian clients: The role of homophobia, counselor gender, and countertransference management. *Journal of Counseling Psychology, 42*(3), 356-364.

Griffin, G. (1998). Understanding heterosexism: The subtle continuum of homophobia. *Women and Language, 21*(1), 33-37.

Johnson, E. (1999). Internalized homophobia and therapeutic efficacy. In L. Pardie and T. Luchetta (Eds.), *The construction of attitudes toward lesbians and gay men* (pp. 65-87). Binghamton, NY: The Haworth Press.

Pardie, L. (1999). Heterosexist ideologies and identity development: A transpersonal view. In L. Pardie and T. Luchetta (Eds.), *The construction of attitudes toward lesbians and gay men* (pp. 89-109). Binghamton, NY: The Haworth Press.

Plummer, D. (1999). *One of the boys: Masculinity, homophobia, and modern manhood.* Binghamton, NY: The Haworth Press.

Rossi, E. and Ryan, M. (Eds.) (1985). *Life reframing in hypnosis: The seminars, workshops, and lectures of Milton H. Erickson* (Vol. 2). New York: Irvington Publishers, Inc.

Bibliotherapy Sources for the Client

Cornett, G. (1995). *Reclaiming the authentic self: Dynamic psychotherapy with gay men.* Northvale, NJ: Jason Aronson, Inc.

Jordon, K. and Deluty, R. (1998). Coming out for lesbian women: Its relation to anxiety, positive affectivity, self-esteem, and social support. *Journal of Homosexuality, 35*(2), 41-63.

Kaufman, G. and Raphael, L. (1996). *Coming out of shame: Transforming gay and lesbian lives.* New York: Doubleday.

Morris, J. (1997). Lesbian coming out as a multidimensional process. *Journal of Homosexuality, 33*(2), 1-21.

Savin-Williams, R. (1998). *". . . And then I became gay": Young men's stories.* New York: Routledge.

References

Andreas, C. and Andreas, T. (1994). *Core transformation: Reaching the wellspring within.* Moab, UT: Real People Press.

Andreas, S. and Andreas, C. (1987). *Change your mind and keep the change.* Moab, UT: Real People Press.

Bandler, R. and Grinder, J. (1981). *Trance-formations: Neuro-linguistic programming and the structure of hypnosis.* Moab, UT: Real People Press.

Berkman, C. and Zinberg, G. (1997). Homophobia and heterosexism in social workers. *Social Work, 42*(4), 319-332.

Dilts, R. (1976). *Roots of neuro-linguistic programming.* Capitola, CA: Meta Publications.

Dilts, R. (1980). *Neuro-linguistic programming: The study of the structure of subjective experience.* Capitola, CA: Meta Publications.

Erickson, M. and Rossi, L. (1979). *Hypnotherapy: An exploratory casebook.* New York: Irvington Publishers, Inc.

Griffin, G. (1998). Understanding heterosexism: The subtle continuum of homophobia. *Women and Language, 21*(1), 33-37.

Johnson, E. (1999). Internalized homophobia and therapeutic efficacy. In L. Pardie and T. Luchetta (Eds.), *The construction of attitudes toward lesbians and gay men* (pp. 65-87). Binghamton, NY: The Haworth Press.

Plummer, D. (1999). *One of the boys: Masculinity, homophobia, and modern manhood.* Binghamton, NY: The Haworth Press.

Rossi, E. and Ryan, M. (Eds.) (1985). *Life reframing in hypnosis: The seminars, workshops, and lectures of Milton H. Erickson.* (Vol. 2), New York: Irvington Publishers, Inc.

Rossi, L. (1986). *The psychobiology of mind-body healing.* New York: W. W. Norton and Company.

5

Queer Space:
Empowering Realizations of Sacred Sexuality

Randolph Bowers

Type of Contribution: Activity

Objective

The objective of this activity is to create experiences of personal transformation. These experiences may act to empower sexual and gender minority persons to access and feel within their bodies the goodness and sacredness of their lives. By opening space in which ritual acts can be performed in safety, possibilities may emerge for acknowledging the sacredness of sexual and gender differences. With these realizations may come deeper possibilities for healing and integration of the self.

Rationale for Use

Growing up gay, lesbian, or bisexual often includes an experience of being cut off from the body, isolated within the mind, and isolated socially (Plummer, 1999). Isolation can often include intense and chronic experiences of loss, fear, powerlessness, shame, guilt, remorse, and regret (Kaufman and Raphael, 1996a). What seems to pervade these experiences is a high level of negative affect directly associated with shame for the core of one's very being—one's sexual embodiment (Kaufman and Raphael, 1996a).

If you can imagine denying your physical and sexual feelings most of your life, you might realize that intellectualization becomes a means for survival. Entering the levels of unconscious processing may give a client a new experience of acceptance, joy, peace, or wonderment (Rossi and Ryan, 1985). Likewise, unconscious work may increase the sense of safety to feel sorrow, shame, and loss that is stored for decades (Rossi, 1986).

The phrase "sacred space" is used as a metaphor for facilitating personal empowerment with sexual and gender minority clients (Kaufman and Raphael, 1996b). Sacred space describes strategies that help facilitate this change (Dilts and MacDonald, 1997). This space includes personal exploration through creative use of physical and kinetic markers, through visualization and imagination, and through auditory feedback during the therapeutic process (Dilts, 1976).

Sacred space is primarily a safe place, similar to a sanctuary, where the client can open doors to experiences that are normally closed. For instance, many gay and lesbian clients have never had a safe place to explore their sexual feelings. They have grown up in families that disallowed their sense of being, in schools and on playgrounds where they were subjected to derision and shame, and in churches where they were not welcomed (Plummer, 1999).

Physical or kinetic markers entail the symbolic use of stones, special objects, and physical space to enter a somewhat subliminal or otherworldly space. This is the place of dreamtime and creativity, where the younger self is more accessible. Grounded in Ericksonian (Erickson and

Rossi, 1979; Ross and Ryan, 1985) and neurolinguistic programming (Andreas and Andreas, 1987; Bandler, 1985; Bandler and Grinder, 1981, 1982; Dilts, 1980) methodologies, the issues of sexual and gender minorities are brought into a space of creative reframing. This space may offer sexual and gender minority persons a place to explore the sacred aspects of human sexuality.

Imaginative processes include use of actual physical objects in a ritual that provides visual anchors. An anchor helps to ground the process by giving focus and direction as well as allowing the imagination the safety to explore. Auditory feedback entails a close interaction between the therapist and the client, such that facilitating the client's process involves accurate and detailed interpretation of cues that allow the therapist to know what is happening within the client's inner world. These cues include body language; facial coloring; muscular changes in tone around the shoulders, neck, and facial areas; and changes in voice tone, eye movements, and words spoken by the client.

Cognitive work is not the primary focus of these exercises, as the purpose of the process is to create a space of integration of mind and body. In other words, to move beyond the limitations of the conscious mind by entering the subliminal space of imagination, childlike ritual space, and perhaps even of shamanic wisdom (Andreas and Andreas, 1994; Dilts and MacDonald, 1997). The process is proactive and experiential.

Instructions

Begin this exercise by asking if your client has a special place he or she likes to visit in his or her imagination or in reality, such as a stream, a lake, or the ocean. The client may have a space in his or her bedroom that is special. Reference to this solitary space is often helpful, as the ritual space created together requires a certain degree of courage and self-disclosure. Asking the client to recall prior experiences of being alone in this special place, or of connection with the earth, can build a bridge toward learning the skills of opening personal transformative space. Ask the client to express those feelings, to see this special space, and to symbolically touch the items around him or her in that space. The idea of opening a sacred place is to consciously create a place in which healing work can be enacted in complete safety. This first preparatory visualization sets the stage for the following strategies.

Opening the Circle

Have a dozen or so medium- and small-sized stones. Special objects can also be substituted, although the groundedness, solidity, and age of stones seems most apt. Ask the client to stand and look at the area of the room where the circle will be created. Suggest that he or she breathe deeply and imagine the size of the circle. Suggest that the circle could become a space in which personal work can be done in safety and that this space and its meaning can be explored as the healing process unfolds.

Ask the client to pick stones for each of the four directions of being. These directions are symbolic of the integrity of earth, the completeness of a circle, and the fullness of life cycles. They symbolize healing as an unfolding process and acceptance of all the parts of self brought into the circle and integrated into one whole, and represent the directions north, south, east, and west. They are used in many world religions and are linked to ancient rituals of transformation and seasonal change. As you ask the client to enact each stage of the process, feel free to explain to him or her the various meanings that will make sense to the client within his or her particular worldview.

When the client has picked sufficient stones or objects, ask him or her to place the stones on the floor in each direction. You may begin with north and proceed clockwise to east, south, and west. Return to north to complete the circle. As the client places each stone, invite him or her to imagine the powers of earth or spirit that he or she would like to have help from on this journey. Invite the client to imagine he or she is building a circle of protection in which what comes in and what goes out can be controlled.

Suggest that you will remain outside the circle, as a gentle guide, while the client enacts his or her own work inside the circle of being. As the client imagines the powers he or she wishes help from, you can suggest other symbolic meanings for each direction. These may include the rising and setting of the sun in the east and west, or mention of the animals that live in the northern and southern hemispheres.

When the circle is complete, ask the client to either stand or sit within the center of being in the circle, and to feel the space with his or her hands, feeling around the circle as he or she slowly rotates. Suggest that this is a sacred space, a personal safe place he or she can go to whenever needed to do personal work. Ask the client what this feeling is like, to be in his or her own circle of power. The client will often be overwhelmed, as he or she has never known such an affirming and energetic experience. Ask the client to imagine carrying this feeling with him or her through life, and suggest how wonderful that would be.

Sensing Personal Power

Work with the exercise as a serious but also fun exploration. If any given strategy does not work, suggest trying something else that will. This promotes an environment for learning without the pressure of being right. Suggest that the client can expand the energy field of circle outward with the willpower of mind and body. Ask the client to just try. Extending his or her hands to the edge of the circle, direct the client to feel the space and push the energy outward another two feet. Ask the client to fill the room with this energy by extending his or her hands and vocalizing the word "power!" Share with the client how you feel his or her energy now, and then ask the client to bring this energy into the original circle now, feeling it return to that secure and peacefully grounded space. Suggest again that the client can feel in his or her body a connection to the earth, the ocean, or the lake where the client has enjoyed a peaceful day.

Summarize what has happened with the client. You might say, "You may sense your energy shifting as you remember your time at the ocean. The personal sense of connection with the earth is part of you now, in your own circle of power—a place of healing for you. A time of safety and calm, as you breathe in and breathe out. The movement of natural processes unfolds as the unconscious mind flows more deeply into that space of sacred life and energy. Reach out your hands to feel your own space, the space of your own body and energy. Every part of the tree of life from its roots and trunk to the highest branches is sacred. Breathe the life of the tree and acknowledge your own sacredness: I am the tree. I am the ocean. I am the stars. This is my life. I have a right to be here."

Now ask the client to look at the stones around the circle and trace the circle with his or her eyes. Ask if he or she is willing to step outside the circle now, leaving its power for a moment, but emphasize that he or she will return soon. Suggest that the client motion as if he or she were opening a door, and have him or her step through that door and out of the circle, then turn and close the door.

Finding a Core Need

Ask the client to choose one major issue to work on within the circle. Then ask him or her focusing questions to make the change desired more concrete. This works for general and specific issues. A general issue might be self-esteem, and a specific issue might be the client's acceptance of parents' attitudes toward him or her. Using self-esteem as an example, ask the client, "If you could have the fullness of self-esteem in you now, at this moment, what would that do for you?"

Unconsciously, the question asks the client to feel and experience the desired event, and to acknowledge the experience and then to realize something consciously from it. The client might answer, "It would give me assurance." Then ask, "If you had all the assurance you would ever need now, feeling that assurance within you in the fullness of your being, what would that do for you?" The client will go a level deeper and may answer, "Security, it would give me security." As you ask similar focusing questions, the client will eventually get to a core need. You know you are at a core need or state of being when the client can go no further and the state he or she has reached has a quality of fullness or completeness. It may include love, freedom, acceptance, community, oneness, or some other need (Andreas and Andreas, 1994).

Answering the Core Need

When the core need and state of being is identified, ask the client to sense where this core need is within his or her body. Ask the client to describe what it looks like. Explore the significance of the insight briefly, and then ask the client to return to the circle carrying with him or her this core need and state of being. When in the circle, ask the client what if feels like having all the resources of the circle now with him or her and his or her core need and state of being together. What does he or she most want to do? Can the client feel how to meet this core need now? What are the possible changes he or she can visualize now?

New perspectives will likely emerge. Ask the client to feel that sense of difference within his or her body and mind. Maybe the client wishes to touch his or her legs and arms, holding on tenderly. Perhaps the client will become quiet and reflective, and share with you the changes he or she wishes for in his or her life. The client could become energetic and quite animated, feeling empowered to forge new paths.

Closing the Circle

Afterward, invite the client to close the circle by bringing the space into his or her body, carrying it. Invite the client to imagine walking through tomorrow with these resources, to think of a week from now when he or she will be at work or home . . . and to be able to access these inner resources and claim his or her own space at will. How does that feel? What does it look like? What does he or she hear inside when imagining that? The client may pull the stones inward, or dispel the circle while standing up with the motion of his or her hands. Afterward, the client can return the stones to their place.

Debrief by discussing the exercise back in the regular space of your office chairs. Suggest that the client can journal about the experience as the week unfolds, and that he or she can come back to learn another step in creating change within the circle. Ask the client to write in a journal about areas he or she wants to work on in the circle that are specific to his or her being gay, lesbian, or bisexual.

Working Within Sacred Space

This second exercise is for the client who already has awareness of creating sacred space. Its purpose is to reinforce the learnings of the previous exercise and go further in consciously realizing the ritual significance of the work. It is designed for the client who wants to explore his or her sexuality or gender difference in the context of ritual meaning and growth in spirituality. The following examples focus on sexuality, but the intention of the exercise can be applied to gender and to other issues.

Begin by checking in with the client on his or her experience of the last session. Ask the client impressions of what was experienced, and gain a sense of where his or her knowledge levels are. After ten or fifteen minutes, invite the client to focus on his or her sexuality. For example, John is a twenty-seven-year-old African American. He is a sensitive man who enjoys classical music and dancing. John works as a computer specialist. When he is asked to focus on his sexuality, his cheeks flush, his muscles become tense, his breath shortens, and his face turns downward. John is experiencing all the physiological effects of shame. He is asked to express what he feels and where it is in his body. John describes a dark private place of hiding from the world. The therapist asks, "What do you want to do, John? Do you want to go into that dark place with me now, or do you want to go into the sacred circle and see what changes can be made?" John chooses the more resourceful option for him at the time, to enter the sacred circle and explore what personal changes may be made to his situation.

Invite the client to imagine holding an issue in his or her hands. What does it look like? Ask the client to place the issue on a chair, and leave it there for a moment while he or she opens the circle. Open the circle in a similar fashion as previously described. When the circle is opened, help the client to continue to amplify the resources that are needed in visual, auditory, and kinetic ways. To accomplish this, speak again of the powers in each direction as the circle is being opened. Speak of power and healing inherent in nature and in human body cycles. Gently speak of the wonder of how self-esteem grows within the child through the years of growth, hurt, and healing, and how the unconscious mind can generate healing in an instant or over time, because it is beyond time.

When you can see through body language and physiology that the client is in a state of resourcefulness, ask him or her to remember the issue that is sitting in the chair across the room. Ask if he or she wants to take that issue up now, and bring it into the circle and see what happens. You may symbolically carry the issue to the client with his or her permission, or the client may wish to go and get it.

John chose to allow the therapist to carry the issue, a dark place of hiding, to him. He allowed the therapist to hand it to him from across the divide of the circle, and he trembled as it fell into his hands. The therapist asked, "What would you like to do now?" John replied, "Fall to my knees." The strategy led into sharing years of grief and loss, and the hope of love and acceptance. The client held himself and wept in the circle, and the therapist sat just outside the circle witnessing John's coming out of the closet of shame.

Although the strategy is designed to be solution focused, it is flexible enough to stay with the client's process when necessary. After John was able to express his feelings for the first time to anyone, it was possible for him to mourn and release certain parts of his past. He could then explore changes. The strategies are designed on the presupposition that a client creates the changes he or she needs when opportunities are presented, and when faced with choices, the client will tend to choose the most resourceful option for him or her at the time.

Suggestions for Follow-Up

There are many ways to follow up with the sacred circle exercises, and perhaps one of the most valuable is narrative work with journaling and creative writing. Therapists may suggest that a client keep a journal during therapy, and that he or she record insights and questions that emerge during his or her ritual work. This material can be shared voluntarily by the client and may enrich the process of reflection and self-realization. Therapists may suggest that a client can go on to explore sexual fulfillment and healing within his or her circle, gently moving toward deeper layers of self-acceptance and love.

Some general questions that can further lead into exploration of sexual identity follow:

1. As you reflect back on the circle experience, what stands out for you as the most significant?
2. We began last week with a sense of affirming the sacredness of your sexuality. I am wondering: where are you now with that?
3. If you were to go into the circle again, what work would you most want to accomplish with your sexuality?
4. I am aware of how tender and personal this time is for you, and I am wondering, do you have a sense of how to express your truths in your daily life? How might that be safe or unsafe for you?
5. Given your experience here in our time together, what does empowerment mean for you now? In what ways can you imagine giving yourself more power to be the person you really want to be?

Contraindications

These strategies are creative, evocative, and dynamic. They engage with intensive visualization and mind-body integrative work. Generally, they should not be used with a client dealing with severe mental illness, such as clinical depression or psychosis. He or she may be unable to effectively manage the provocative experience and profound release of emotion.

Readings and Resources for the Professional

Eisler, R. (1995). *Sacred pleasure: Sex, myth, and the politics of the body—New paths to power and love*. New York: Sage Publications.

Ferrucci, P. (1982). *What we may be: Techniques for psychological and spiritual growth through psychosynthesis*. Los Angeles, CA: Tarcher.

Fox, M. (1983). *Original blessing: A primer in creation spirituality*. Oakland, CA: Bear and Company.

Helminiak, D. (1989). Self-esteem, sexual self-acceptance, and spirituality. *Journal of Sex Education and Therapy, 43*(5), 307-318.

Helminiak, D. (1995). The spiritual dimensions of the gay experience. *Pastoral Psychology, 43*(5), 307-318.

Maslow, A. (1964). *Religions, values and peak-experiences*. New York: Viking Press.

Plummer, D. (1999). *One of the boys: Masculinity, homophobia, and modern manhood*. Binghamton, NY: The Haworth Press.

Bibliotherapy Sources for the Client

Myss, C. (1996). *Anatomy of spirit: The seven stages of power and healing*. New York: Three Rivers Press.

O'Neill, C. and Ritter, K. (1992). *Coming out within: Stages of spiritual awakening for lesbians and gay men*. San Francisco, CA: Harper.

Thompson, M. (1987). *Gay spirit: Myth and meaning*. New York: St. Martin's Press.

Thompson, M. (1994). *Gay soul: Finding the heart of gay spirit and nature*. New York: St. Martin's Press.

References

Andreas, C. and Andreas, T. (1994). *Core transformation: Reaching the wellspring within.* Moab, UT: Real People Press.

Andreas, S. and Andreas, C. (1987). *Change your mind and keep the change.* Moab, UT: Real People Press.

Bandler, R. (1985). *Using your brain for a change.* Moab, UT: Real People Press.

Bandler, R. and Grinder, J. (1981). *Trance-formations: Neuro-linguistic programming and the structure of hypnosis.* Moab, UT: Real People Press.

Bandler, R. and Grinder, J. (1982). *Reframing: Neuro-linguistic programming and the transformation of meaning.* Moab, UT: Real People Press.

Dilts, R. (1976). *Roots of neuro-linguistic programming.* Capitola, CA: Meta Publications.

Dilts, R. (1980). *Neuro-linguistic programming: The study of the structure of subjective experience.* Capitola, CA: Meta Publications.

Dilts, R. and MacDonald, R. (1997). *Tools of the spirit.* Capitola, CA: Meta Publications.

Erickson, M. and Rossi, L. (1979). *Hypnotherapy: An exploratory casebook.* New York: Irvington Publishers, Inc.

Kaufman, G. and Raphael, L. (1996a). *Coming out of shame: Transforming gay and lesbian lives.* New York: Doubleday.

Kaufman, G. and Raphael, L. (1996b). *The dynamics of power: Building a competent self.* Boston, MA: Schenkman Books.

Plummer, D. (1999). *One of the boys: Masculinity, homophobia, and modern manhood.* Binghamton, NY: The Haworth Press.

Rossi, E. and Ryan, M. (Eds.) (1985). *Life reframing in hypnosis*: *The seminars, workshops, and lectures of Milton H. Erickson* (Vol. 2). New York: Irvington Publishers, Inc.

Rossi, L. (1986). *The psychobiology of mind-body healing.* New York: W. W. Norton and Company.

6

To Pass or Not to Pass:
Exploration of Conflict Splits
for Bisexual-Identified Clients

Sharon Horne
Julie Shulman
Heidi M. Levitt

Type of Contribution: Activity

Objective

The goal of this activity is to help bisexual-identified clients resolve conflicts regarding coming out in varying contexts.

Rationale for Use

Although "passing" (an individual who is gay, lesbian, or bisexual *passes* as heterosexual in an effort to ward off fear or anxiety) is not an exclusive experience for bisexual individuals, coming out as bisexual is challenging in unique ways from coming out as gay or lesbian (Dworkin, 2000). A bisexual identity may be rendered invisible or dismissed in either gay or lesbian culture or in heterosexual culture; if a bisexual individual has a same-sex partner, gays, lesbians, and heterosexuals typically assume that the person is gay or lesbian, but if a bisexual individual has an other-sex partner, typically the assumption is made that the person is heterosexual. In either case, the challenge for bisexual individuals to come out, or not to come out, is complex and places them at risk for rejection from both heterosexual society and gay and lesbian culture. However, not disclosing one's sexual identity has been shown to negatively impact psychological well-being (Herek, Gillis, and Cogan, 1999). Therefore, the goal of this exercise is to increase bisexual clients' skills and resources for making decisions about whether, when, and how to disclose their sexual identity.

A common therapeutic technique within the process-experiential psychotherapy modality involves two-chair dialogue for what are called "conflict splits" (Greenberg, Rice, and Elliott, 1993, p. 188). According to an experiential approach, people often internalize cultural and familial beliefs that conflict with their own needs. These conflicts are often out of a person's awareness, but the symptoms of this struggle often are not. This struggle, then, between two conflicting beliefs entails both a sense of confusion when one's own needs are not being met, and a decrease in self-esteem, an increase in depression, or an increase in anxiety when one is not meeting others' expectations. In a conflict split, a person integrates these self-evaluations and her or his own feelings and needs.

Although many counselors may be tempted to discuss with bisexual-identified clients the pros and cons of each potential path (passing or coming out), the two-chair dialogue instead is a process that entails a "living-through of the conflict in the present in order to forge new solutions" (Greenberg, Rice, and Elliott, 1993, p. 191). Although the former is appealing insofar as it is a rather straightforward intervention, it may serve to neglect the client's emotions regarding the decision to pass or come out. When engaging clients in a two-chair dialogue, a comprehensive reconciling and integration of the two sides of themselves is of utmost importance. Clients can reconstruct their new experience and come to a place of greater self-acceptance (Greenberg, Rice, and Elliott, 1993).

Instructions

The conflict split is introduced following a client's description of a struggle between two opposing aspects of self. A bisexual client who is struggling with wanting to be out to others as bisexual, but is feeling pressured to pass as either heterosexual or gay or lesbian, may benefit from such a technique. Indeed, the two-chair dialogue technique for conflict splits is designed to assist in processing through such opposing, confusing, and often difficult decisions.

The differing sides of the conflict may also be different for each client. For example, for one bisexual woman, she may feel quite pressured to pass as lesbian. She may have heard repeated messages from her lesbian community that she should not "admit" to being bisexual, as being attracted to men might be devalued. Another woman may have heard messages suggesting that she should be herself, including acknowledging and disclosing her bisexuality. Although the former scenario seems more likely, it is surely possible that a client may feel a desire and need to pass while simultaneously feeling pressured to be out as bisexual. The counselor working with a bisexual client must allow the client to determine which side of the conflict feels most like the side that has accepted internalized cultural beliefs and which side reflects her or his own wishes and needs.

Typically, a client will have overtly or subtly expressed an internal conflict. One part of the self is found to be condemning or criticizing the other; this part of the self is referred to as the "internal critic" (Greenberg, Rice, and Elliott, 1993, p. 189). A counselor should propose trying the technique with the client. The counselor should be aware that this exercise typically takes up the majority of a fifty-minute session. The counselor must "establish task collaboration" (p. 197) with the client as well as structure the exercise. This means that the counselor asks the client if she or he would like to focus on this split, briefly explains its purpose, and gets the client's agreement to try it out. Then, the counselor introduces the exercise, explaining that the two different parts of the self will be in two chairs, helping the client to determine which side feels most aligned with his or her own needs and keeping this side, the "experiencing self" (p. 189), in the original chair. Hence, the two chairs are to be occupied by the critical self and the experiencing self.

The counselor uses a great deal of reflection during this exercise, making sure to follow both sides of the client, but also emphasizing the affective reactions of both. Greenberg, Rice, and Elliott (1993) outline three central stages involved in this two-chair dialogue: opposition, identification and contact, and integration (as well as a final meaning-making stage).

Opposition Stage

1. Encourage harsh and specific criticisms from the critical side as well as affective reactions from the experiencing part of the self.
2. Help to identify as clearly as possible the two aspects of the self. The goal is to emphasize and clarify the criticisms from the critical chair as well as the felt reactions from the other chair.

3. Assist the experiencing side of the client in attending to her or his emotional reactions, in lieu of coming up with counterarguments to the critic.
4. Separate and create contact between the two sides, asking the client to express herself or himself directly to the other chair. The process of switching chairs from one aspect of self to the other also assists in this goal.
5. Encourage each side to take responsibility only for her or his side. Encouraging the experiencing side to use "I" statements to express feelings and the critical side to use "you" statements to reveal its blaming characteristic helps to build this responsibility.

Identification and Contact Stage

1. Direct the client to repeatedly alternate between the chairs, in order to create contact between the critical and the experiencing sides. The goal at this stage is to help the client build greater differentiation between the two sides.
2. Encourage the client's experiential side to assert its desires and needs to the critical chair.
3. Encourage the critical side to blame the experiencing side with specific assertions, while helping to "increase awareness of values and standards" (Greenberg, Rice, and Elliott, 1993, p. 197) of this critical side.
4. When the blaming has discontinued, the unexpressed needs and wants (from the experiencing side) have been voiced, and the values and standards (from the critical side) have begun to be expressed, the integration begins.

Integration Stage

1. When the critic appears to be softening her or his harshness, the counselor must focus her or him on her or his inner experience, fostering expression.
2. Assist the two sides in negotiation or integration by allowing both to express their perspectives, often continuously switching the client back and forth between the chairs.
3. The client will often experience a coming-together of the two sides. When this occurs, it is appropriate to ask the client to exit the dialogue.

Final Stage

1. When the client is seated in her or his original chair, the counselor implements the final "postdialogue stage," wherein meaning is made.
2. Discuss with the client her or his experience of the exercise, allowing and encouraging the client to assimilate and integrate the new experience of self.
3. If a resolution has not been reached, Greenberg, Rice, and Elliott (1993) suggest that the counselor summarize what occurred and assign homework involving making note of new awareness and discoveries from the dialogue. Again, this dialogue need not be abandoned at the end of a single session. The counselor may return to the same or slightly different two-chair dialogue in future sessions.

Suggestions for Follow-Up

As counselors, it is important to keep in mind that this decision is rarely resolved in a single exercise. Rather, the conflict can arise in multiple contexts and settings, often changing over time. For instance, a bisexual client may choose to pass as heterosexual at work and with her or his family of origin, may later decide to pass as lesbian or gay within her or his social community and still, with her or his partner, identify openly as bisexual. In time, she or he may choose to come out to her or his family of origin as bisexual. A counselor must be aware that the particular conflict may need to be addressed with respect to varying contexts and may need to be revisited as necessary. As such, when incorporating the two-chair dialogue to resolve conflict splits, the counselor remains willing to return to the technique as many times as necessary throughout the counseling process.

Contraindications

Although this activity has been adapted for use with bisexual clients, it does not rule out application with a variety of clients who are struggling with coming out. It should be employed with clients who are comfortable with experiential exercises and who have identified a clear struggle.

Readings and Resources for the Professional

Firestein, B. A. (Ed.) (1996). *Bisexuality: The psychology and politics of an invisible minority.* Thousand Oaks, CA: Sage Publications.

Fox, R. C. (1993). Bisexual identities. In A. R. D'Augelli and C. J. Patterson (Eds.), *Lesbian, gay, and bisexual identities over the lifespan: Psychological perspectives* (pp. 48-86). New York: Oxford University Press.

Paul, J. P. (1996). Bisexuality: Exploring/exploding the boundaries. In R. C. Savin Williams and K. M. Cohen (Eds.), *The lives of lesbians, gays, and bisexuals: Children to adults* (pp. 436-461). Orlando, FL: Harcourt Brace.

Rust, P. C. (1992). The politics of sexual identity: Sexual attraction and behavior among lesbian and bisexual women. *Social Problems, 39,* 366-386.

Rust, P. (1996). Managing multiple identities: Diversity among bisexual women and men. In B. A. Firestein (Ed.), *Bisexuality: The psychology and politics of an invisible minority* (pp. 55-83). Thousand Oaks, CA: Sage Publications.

Bibliotherapy Sources for the Client

Garber, M. (2000). *Bisexuality and the eroticism of everyday life.* New York: Routledge.

Hutchins, L. (1991). *By any other name: Bisexual people speak out.* Los Angeles, CA: Alyson Publications.

Larkin, J. (2000). *A woman like that: Lesbian and bisexual writers tell their coming out stories.* New York: Harperperennial Library.

Orndoff, K. (1998). *Bi lives: Bisexual women tell their stories.* Tucson, AZ: Sharp Press.

Storr, M. (1999). *Bisexuality: A critical reader.* New York: Routledge.

Weinberg, M. (1995). *Dual attraction: Understanding bisexuality.* New York: Oxford University Press.

References

Dworkin, S. H. (2000). Individual therapy with lesbian, gay, and bisexual clients. In R. M. Perez, K. A. DeBord, and K. J. Bieschke (Eds.), *Handbook of counseling and psychotherapy with lesbian, gay, and bisexual clients* (pp. 157- 81). Washington, DC: American Psychological Association.

Greenberg, L. S., Rice, L. N., and Elliott, R. (1993). *Facilitating emotional change: The moment-by-moment process.* New York: Guilford Publications.

Herek, G. M., Gillis, J. R., and Cogan, J. C. (1999). Psychological sequelae of hate-crime victimization among lesbian, gay, and bisexual adults. *Journal of Consulting and Clinical Psychology, 67*(6), 945-951.

7

Homosexual Rites of Passage: A Path to Validation

Marie Mohler

Type of Contribution: Activity/Homework/Handout

Objective

The objective of this activity is to assist the therapist in affirming a gay or lesbian client's personal growth and development, and overcoming his or her shame, fear, or internalized homophobia through the celebration of developmental milestones or rites of passage. This activity will facilitate the client's personalization of homosexual rituals and rites of passage in his or her life, which will ultimately promote the client's sense of connectedness to the larger gay, lesbian, and bisexual community, and to his or her own gay or lesbian identity.

Rationale for Use

Rites of passage may be defined as notable transitions in a person's life. These significant transitions are celebrated through a ritual of behaviors that create meaning and interpersonal connection in our lives. It is the celebration of rituals over time that establishes their significance within a community. Common heterosexual rites of passage include engagements, weddings, childbirth, and anniversaries. Homosexuals often are not granted these same rites with equal importance and enthusiasm. As we come to understand the destructive and hurtful nature of fear, shame, society's promotion of conformity (and intolerance of diversity), and the subsequent encouragement of homosexual silence and invisibility, it is clear that the gay and lesbian community needs to create its own source of positive reinforcement and validation. Rites of passage provide a way to overcome and transcend shame, homophobia, invisibility, insignificance, and silence. They provide a source of empowerment.

These exercises, which are based on material from Mohler's (2000) book, *Homosexual Rites of Passage: A Road to Visibility and Validation,* include a listing of significant homosexual rites of passage, and pertinent questions to facilitate the client's personalization of each milestone, in order to encourage gay men and lesbian women to use these growth markers as a means to validate their right to community, societal recognition, and support.

Instructions

The therapist can use these exercises as a homework assignment, handout, or activity with individuals or couples. The results may expose deeper issues such as shamed or wounded homosexual identities, internalized or societal homophobia, "unfinished business," and commitment or intimacy issues.

The therapist instructs the client to answer the questions as honestly as possible, responding with his or her initial "gut" reaction. It would be optimal if the client could write responses in a journal to allow full disclosure and exploration of feelings. However, if this is not appropriate, a thorough discussion of the client's thoughts and emotions surrounding the particular rite of passage can be beneficial as well.

If a client reports a developmental milestone that is painful and has left him or her wounded in some way, the therapist can help the client to release the shame or pain, and find ways to identify the significance of the growth marker and to celebrate its meaning in order to facilitate healing and validation.

The proposed rites of passage are described in terms of a typical life sequence from birth until death simply for the ease of organization. The therapist can focus on whichever growth marker appears pertinent to the client and the healing he or she seeks. Therefore, the exercises do not have to be conducted in any particular order; simply select the pertinent exercises that are relevant to each individual client's needs.

Suggestions for Follow-Up

In order to succeed in the meaning-making potential of homosexual rites of passage, it is essential to process the client's responses in the context of the healing he or she seeks. Some may want to simply acknowledge, attend to, and celebrate past identity-shaping, previously overlooked milestones, and others may need to explore deeper wounds, feelings of insignificance, internalized homophobia, shame, and their subsequent effects on his or her self-esteem and self-concept. The therapist may suggest a reevaluation of treatment goals at this point. If deeper healing is needed, the therapist can use additional therapeutic resources to address these clinical issues. If a client seeks a sense of healing and validation through the celebration of current milestones or those deemed insignificant in years past, the therapist can facilitate the creative development of appropriate rituals to affirm and celebrate each rite of passage.

Contraindications

Although this exercise may be used as a way to create a simple dialogue with individuals and/or couples, regarding their attunement with and celebration of their homosexual identity, the therapist should be prepared for positive and painful emotions to surface. Thus, although these exercises may facilitate a sense of welcomed affirmation, validation, and empowerment for some through the establishment and practice of homosexual rites of passage, others may experience memories of past traumas, wounds, or negative feelings that will need special attention. Ultimately, the client who has a true commitment to heal old wounds or to validate and empower his or her current identity will benefit the most from this therapeutic tool.

Readings and Resources for the Professional

Imber-Black, E. and Roberts, J. (1992). *Rituals for our times: Celebrating, healing, and changing our lives and our relationships.* New York: HarperCollins Publishers.

Mohler, M. and Frazer, L. (2002). *A donor insemination guide: Written by and for lesbian women.* Binghamton, NY: The Haworth Press.

Slater, S. (1995). *The lesbian family life cycle.* New York: The Free Press.

Thompson, M. (1992). Coming out inside. In B. Berzon (Ed.), *Positively gay: New approaches to gay and lesbian life* (pp. 16-20). Berkeley, CA: Celestial Arts.

Bibliotherapy Sources for the Client

Berzon, B. (1996). *Positively gay: New approaches to gay and lesbian life*. Berkeley, CA: Celestial Arts.

Clunis, D. M. and Green, G. D. (1995). *The lesbian parenting book: A guide to creating families and raising children*. Seattle, WA: Seal Press.

Noble, E. (1987). *Having your baby by donor insemination: A complete resource guide*. Boston, MA: Houghton-Mifflin Company.

Reference

Mohler, M. (2000). *Homosexual rites of passage: A road to visibility and validation*. Binghamton, NY: The Haworth Press.

Homosexual Rites of Passage

Acknowledging Homosexual Feelings: The Importance of Firsts

Exercise 1: Establishing the Significance of Early Childhood Memories

- What is the first childhood memory you can recall?
- Allow your memories to enter your stream of consciousness. (Focus on the earliest memory that appears strongest.)
- What feelings do you associate with that recollection?
- What images, sounds, and/or smells do you recall?

Whatever memory came into awareness when pondering your earliest recollection probably left a lasting impression on you for some reason. Because you remembered that particular event or feeling and not some other moment in time, your earliest memory is significant in your life in some way. It likely influenced your identity development due to its significance.

Exercise 2: First Awareness of Differentness

- Did you ever have inklings of differentness?
- At what age did you first have these feelings?
- Was there a specific trigger of your awareness of these feelings?
- Did you have a keen sense early on that you were somehow inherently different?
- Were those feelings peaceful for you or anxiety provoking? Why?

Exercise 3: First Childhood Crush on Individual of the Same Sex

Take a moment and think back to your first childhood crush on a same-sex individual.

- What about your first crush captivated you?
- How did you meet? What made you first notice this person?
- What were those first-crush feelings like for you?
- Did you feel butterflies in your stomach or feel yourself getting tongue-tied?
- Did this person ever know that you felt this way about him or her?
- Did you ever share these feelings with anyone? If so, how was it received?

Exercise 4: First Awareness of Lasting Same-Sex Feelings

- What was it like for you when your first-crush feelings and awareness of differentness did not subside or disappear?
- How did you feel when the *phase,* as many parents like to call it, did not pass?
- How did you feel inside?
- How did you feel about yourself in light of this new information?
- Was this something that you wanted to hide or deny?
- Was this something that intrigued you and warranted further exploration? Or was this consistent with a sense of always knowing that you were different in this way, and in its discovery, you found further resolution and peace?

Exercise 5: First Kiss or Experimentation with the Erotic Areas of Same-Sex Partner

- Who is the first same-sex person you kissed?
- How did your body react to his or her touch?
- What was it like, that "I'm kissing a GIRL!" feeling? (For women) Or "I'm kissing a BOY!" feeling? (For men)
- Did you know what to do? Did you know what to do next?
- Did it feel natural?
- Did you want to do it again?

Coming Out

Exercise 6: Personalizing the Coming-Out Process/Milestone

- Where do you think you are in the identity-development/coming-out process?
- How might coming out affect your life? Or how has it already affected your life? In what ways?
- When did you first come out to yourself?
- How old were you?
- What was that experience like for you?

- What are/were your fears about disclosing your sexual identity to yourself and others?
- How did you decide whom to tell first?
- What qualities of that person led (or will lead) you to disclose that private part of your self?
- How did or would you disclose your identity to this person?
- What was his or her reaction?
- What did you expect his or her reaction to be?
- How did this reaction affect you?
- Has anyone's reaction affected your ability to complete the coming-out or homosexual identity-formation process? If so, what do you think created the stumbling block?
- How might you overcome similar obstacles in the future, en route to a healthier and happier identity?

Relationships

Exercise 7: First Dating Experiences

- Was your first dating experience an event you associate with excitement? With trepidation? Or somewhere in between?
- What about dating do you associate with those feelings?
- How did you approach the experience? With a willingness to learn? To change? To communicate? To listen?
- If you reflect on one of your initial dating experiences, what can you say you learned about yourself through that experience?
- What stands out as memorable about the experience?
- How can that memory make meaning for you in your life? What insights about yourself can you take from this learning experience that can help you grow as a person and as a partner?

Exercise 8: Identifying Partner Attributes and Compatibility

Think about the following questions in an attempt to explore the kind of partner you think you are or could be.

- How well do you know yourself?
- What are your likes? Dislikes? Please list them.
- What are your favorite things to eat? Your pet peeves?
- What life situations do you find challenging? Frustrating?
- Are you willing to change? Compromise?
- What personal qualities have you previously thought about changing?
- Do you have any experience with making personal growth changes, which became stable and consistent over time?
- How have you resolved conflicts in the past?
- What was your parents' marriage like?
- What positive and negative behaviors did you learn from them that you engage in on a regular basis?
- How might these behaviors affect a partnership?
- How effective are you as a communicator?
- What is your general style of communicating your needs? How is it generally received?

Think about the following questions in order to explore the traits that you seek in a partner.

- What attracts you to a prospective partner?
- What hobbies or activities do you enjoy as shared activities?
- How might another individual's upbringing and patterns join with yours?
- What kinds of communication skills does the potential partner have?
- What are the person's short- and long-term goals?
- Is the potential partner progressing in a similar direction with you in terms of growth and goals? If not, can mutual compromise and commitment to work on the relationship allow your relationship to grow?
- What qualities are you willing to accept as a lovable part of that person that is different from you?
- What qualities are you unwilling to accept or work through?
- What stage of homosexual identity development are you each in?
- Are you able to discuss your awareness of your gay or lesbian identity and the degree to which you are comfortable being out to others?

Exercise 9: First Relationships: Lesson Learning and Meaning Making

- What was your first relationship based on? Trust? Mutual respect? Physical chemistry? Distrust? Love?
- What was exciting about the prospect of your first homosexual relationship?
- Was it intense? Validating? Fun? Scary?
- What was it like to share yourself with someone else?
- Did you discover new things about yourself? If so, what?
- How did you communicate your respect for him or her?
- How did he or she communicate respect for you?
- What was it that was found to be insurmountable, if your first relationship did not work out?
- What personal qualities, identified in Exercise 8, enhanced your relationship? What qualities enhanced your division?
- What lessons can be learned from your first relationships to provide greater insight about the partner you were and the partner you would like to be?

Commitment Rituals

Exercise 10: Engagement, Commitment Ceremonies, Honeymoons, and Anniversaries

- At this point in your life, how prepared are you to commit yourself to someone?
- Are you currently in a long-term relationship?
- Have you ever considered engagement or a commitment ceremony?
- How might a commitment ritual add meaning to your life and relationship?
- What is your fantasy about your commitment ceremony or ritual? What would it look and feel like? Who would attend?
- If you have already committed to a life partner, what was that experience like for you?
- Would you consider a renewal of vows to each other, to reaffirm your feelings, love, and commitment?
- If you are single or dating at this point, is a monogamous, committed relationship a goal for you?
- What might a long-term life commitment mean for you?
- How would your current standard of living change if you invited someone into your inner sanctuary for a lifetime of love and commitment?
- How would you want to celebrate and affirm these important commitment rites of passage in your life?

Family Planning

Exercise 11: Making the Decision to Parent

- What qualities do you think make someone a good parent?
- Do you think your homosexuality limits your options in terms of parenting? If so, how? In what ways?
- How do you define "parent" or "parenting"?
- If you think back to your own childhood, what qualities of your parents, guardians, or mentors earned your respect and love?
- What qualities or behaviors instilled discipline and taught you responsibility?
- Which of your own personal qualities do you think you inherited from your parents? Of those, which ones would you like to pass on to your own children?
- Do these questions about parenting trigger or confirm your own desire to become a parent?
- What appeals to you about raising a child and creating a family? What is less than appealing?
- How might your current stage of gay or lesbian identity development or coming out affect your desire or ability to parent?
- How might you handle or combat society's homophobia regarding gay parents raising children?
- Do you have the ability to sacrifice your own needs and devote the necessary energy to shape a child's whole and healthy identity?
- If you find yourself answering in the affirmative to many of these questions, have you considered how you would translate the concept of parenting into a reality?
- If so, what appeals most to you? Adoption? Donor insemination? Surrogate motherhood? Foster parenting?
- What are the challenges or obstacles between where you are now and where you need to be in order to make parenting a reality for you?
- How can you find resolution with these issues in order to move forward?

Aging Rites

Exercise 12: Retirement

- What issues do you foresee affecting you regarding retirement?
- At what age do you believe you will retire? Or have you already?
- What will retirement be like for you?
- How will you restructure your days when there is no sense of "having" to be anywhere?
- Will you embrace the freedom or will you seek another form of structure?
- What social activities will you continue or become involved in?
- What hobbies will you pursue when you finally have the time to actively devote your attention to this area?
- How might your relationship change as a result of retirement?
- Are your spouse, significant others, and/or friends retired as well?
- How might that affect your enjoyment of retirement?
- How will your identity be affected by your new title of "retiree"?
- Will your gay or lesbian identity change as a result of your transition into retirement?
- Do you think that you will continue living in your current dwelling, or will you make a home in a retirement community?
- What rituals will you continue to employ to affirm your homosexual identity?

Exercise 13: Grandchildren

- What will it be like to be a gay or lesbian grandparent?
- What do you want your grandchildren to know about your sexual identity?
- What will your role be as a grandparent?
- What kind of rapport do you have with your own children?
- How will the grandchildren be taught about the special gift of having two grandmothers or grandfathers?
- How might you teach them about the importance of accepting diversity?
- What could they learn from you that would be different from society's homophobia?
- How might you affirm their developing identities?
- How would you celebrate being a grandparent?

8

The Experiential Ecomap Exercise: Creating Client-Based Narratives of the Influence of Ecosystemic Environments on the Coming-Out Process

Michelle M. Crooks-Yared

Type of Contribution: Activity

Objectives

In a broad sense, this activity is designed to help gay and lesbian clients identify the implications of their gay or lesbian identity in relation to the various ecosystemic environments in which they are embedded. It will also help them explore the influences of those environments on their coming-out process. More specifically, this activity will help the client to:

- Verbalize his or her feelings about being gay or lesbian in relation to each significant environment in which the client interacts;
- Identify environments that elicit the most anxiety for the client in terms of being gay or lesbian;
- Identify strengths in the ecosystemic environment that will assist the client in maximizing positive resources for support;
- Create personal narratives around the client's coming-out process in relation to his or her environments; and
- Develop alternate ways of interacting in problematic personal relationships.

Rationale for Use

Several authors (Cass, 1984; Coleman, 1982; Troiden, 1988) have conceptualized a coming-out process that includes a series of stages which span from early suspicion of one's gay or lesbian sexual orientation to eventual full acceptance and integration of a gay or lesbian identity. Although these models offer linear stages for acquiring a gay or lesbian identity, progression through them does not necessarily follow a linear pattern. Often, previously navigated stages will need to be renegotiated as the gay or lesbian person reaches transitional stages in the life cycle or encounters new domains. In addition, the individual may exhibit varying levels of being "out" depending upon the environment in which he or she is interacting.

An ecosystemic perspective is especially germane to clinical work with gay and lesbian clients. An ecosystemic approach emphasizes the reciprocal nature of the relationship between human beings and their environments (Bristor, 1990). These relationships are especially important to gays and lesbians as their interaction in each environment may potentially be affected by the broad societal processes of heterosexism and homophobia. Heterosexism may be defined as the assumption that heterosexual relationships are the only "correct" or "normal" manifestations of human sexuality and therefore the only relationships worthy of recognition or legitimization by society. Homophobia refers to the irrational fear or hatred of gays or lesbians. This definition is often extended to include discrimination and violence toward gay and lesbian individuals brought on by this fear (Blumenfeld, 1992). Gay and lesbian individuals may internalize these concepts themselves as they are inundated with negative societal messages concerning their sexual orientation.

The ecomap emerged in the late 1970s as a tool to help in the assessment of families involved in the child welfare system (Hartman, 1978). It continues to be used in clinical settings to create a pictorial synthesis of the relationship between families and their environments. It is especially useful in helping the therapist assess the nature of relationships between individuals and their environments by creating a visual representation that illustrates the nature of the client's interactions. A very helpful way to construct an ecomap is to begin with the individual's family as a genogram in the center of the page. Next, several circles are drawn surrounding the genogram and labeled as external systems in the environment such as work, friends, or school. The external circles may be drawn in such a way that the spatial distance between the circle and the genogram represents the amount of significance the system has for a particular family. Various connecting lines (e.g., bold, weak, broken) can also be used to convey information about the nature of the relationships between family members and outside systems (Harold, Mercier, and Colarossi, 1997).

This exercise utilizes an integrative approach that will serve as both an assessment tool for the therapist and a therapeutic intervention for the client. The exercise draws upon several prominent family therapy theoretical frameworks to inform its use. Nichols and Schwartz (1995) include several theories relevant to this exercise, such as contextual family therapy, experiential family therapy, bowenian family therapy, narrative therapy, and solution-focused therapy. The questions used in the exercise, however, can be reformulated and fashioned to fit alternate theoretical concepts practiced by individual therapists. This exercise is intended to be organized, yet it allows for eclecticism in theoretical practice.

The theories previously mentioned were chosen for various reasons. The experiential nature of the exercise is intended to increase individual awareness, expression, and growth related to the client's gay or lesbian identity. The focus of experiential therapy is on living in the moment rather than developing insight. The aim is to identify places where clients are "stuck," to identify strengths, and to help clients experience their emotional life in a more robust manner (Nichols and Schwartz, 1995). In doing so, clients will complete relational transactions, interpret hostility, see how others see them, see how they see themselves, disagree, make choices, learn through practice, free themselves from the harmful effects of past models, and give congruent messages. This form of therapy is especially appropriate for work with gays and lesbians because the propensity to hide their sexual orientation in response to hostile environments is very common and effectively robs them of a significant portion of their emotional life. Hiding this aspect of themselves becomes second nature and encourages gays and lesbians to deny their feelings surrounding a core part of their identity. This may also result in maladaptive attempts to escape the pain of isolation through drug and alcohol abuse or suicide. Helping gay and lesbian clients address their feelings in a safe environment will propel them toward connecting with themselves and others in healthy and productive ways. The remaining theoretical underpinnings of the exercise will be briefly addressed in the following section as they relate to portions of the activity.

Materials

Cut several circles from construction paper (approximately ten to twelve inches in diameter), and label them with external systems with which people are typically involved, such as extended family, education, social or cultural, work, health care, religion, and legal. Cut three or four additional circles and leave them blank. These circles may be laminated to protect their condition for future use.

Cut several smaller circles (two to three inches in diameter) that are identical to the set of larger ones. Label two additional circles "most comfortable environment" and "least comfortable environment."

Label the front of large index cards with four different categories, including "coming out," "others," "homophobia," and "action." On the back of each card a small number of questions should appear. The questions for each category follow:

- *Coming out:* How out are you able to be when you are in this environment? What makes it easy for you to be out here? (if client is more out) What makes it difficult for you to be out here? What would happen if you were to be more out? What do you think would have to happen to enable you to be more out here? When do you think you might be able to be more out here? (if client is less out)
- *Others:* Who is the most accepting of your gay or lesbian sexual identity in this environment? What would this person say is the reason he or she is supportive? What does this person do to show you that he or she is supportive? Who is the least accepting of your gay or lesbian identity in this environment? What would this person say is the reason that he or she is not accepting? What does this person do or say that shows you he or she is not accepting?

Note: These questions are based on some of the theoretical concepts related to contextual family therapy (Boszormenyi-Nagy, Grunebaum, and Ulrich, 1991). Equity in relationships is a key component of contextual theory, as well as the concept of multilateral partiality, in which everybody's interests are taken into consideration. These questions are intended, in part, to help the client attend to issues of fairness and balance in relationships with others in regard to his or her sexual identity. Asking the client to answer questions from another person's perspective may help build empathy (not necessarily agreement) for another person's position. It may also help the client understand the limitations of others, exonerate people in certain instances, and appreciate the imperfection of human relationships. Therapists who are proponents of this theoretical approach will be able to expand upon these concepts in future sessions with the client.

- *Homophobia:* How is homophobia able to recruit you into negative feelings about your sexual orientation? When are you most vulnerable to the influence of homophobia? When are you most able to resist the strength of homophobia? How does homophobia recruit others in this environment? How would this system look different if homophobia were conquered and abolished? How might this happen?

Note: These questions were developed in relation to concepts posited by narrative therapy (White and Epston, 1990). Narrative therapy is intended to help make the client the expert of his or her own experience, thereby reducing the power differential between the client and therapist. These questions will help the client externalize the problem of homophobia and identify its practice of power. They will also help the client anticipate future patterns of recruitment and devise plans to mobilize support systems to reduce the power of negative influences.

- *Action:* What is one small goal you have that will help you integrate your sexual identity with this environment? What do you do now that may prevent this? What would you like to be doing instead? How will you start to do this? How will you know when you are making progress toward this goal? What will you be doing/thinking/feeling that is different from now?

Note: These questions are solution focused in nature. They are based upon the idea that a negotiable goal is achievable without the therapist's preconceived idea of what underlies the problem (de Shazer, 1985).

Instructions

1. Ask the client to stand in the middle of the room. Say something such as, "Imagine that you are in a place where you are able to be yourself. You are content with your sexual identity. The people around you are supportive. This is a peaceful and comfortable place for you . . ."
2. Give the client the set of large circles and ask him or her to arrange the circles in proximity to the "comfortable" place in the center of the room. Environments that are more comfortable would be closer to the center spot. The less comfortable the environment, the further it should be from the center. Ideally, a large open floor space is best for this activity; however, therapists can improvise and tailor the exercise to their office. If the client is not involved with a particular system, she or he will turn those circles upside down. If there are systems that the client is involved in that are not labeled, she or he will label the system on a blank circle and place it among the others.
3. Place the smaller circles in a small box. Ask the client to draw a circle from the box. Then ask the client to go to that space and think about how she or he feels while walking to the space. When the client is standing in the space, ask him or her to talk about what it is like when she or he is in this environment. How does the client usually feel in this environment? Ask the client to verbalize the physical manifestations of his or her emotions in this environment. Use some experiential techniques such as asking the client to sculpt his or her body into a position that illustrates his or her feelings in this environment.
4. The first time the client is standing on a particular circle, ask him or her the questions on the "coming out" card. The client should eventually progress through the four cards for each environment. When the client draws this environment the second time, she or he should answer the "others" card. The third time, the client should answer the "homophobia" card and finally the "action" card on the fourth time. Experiential techniques can also be used in conjunction with the cards. Examples might include role-playing a negative interaction with a person who is not perceived by the client as being supportive or drawing a picture of "homophobia."
5. The client should then draw a circle from the box again and go to (or stay at) that place. The circles should be returned to the box each time until the client has been to that environment four times and has exhausted all of the cards.
6. Ask the client to pay attention to his or her feelings as she or he journeys to the environment. (The aim is to train the client to exercise self-awareness rather than becoming anesthetized to his or her feelings.) Encourage the client to practice this outside of therapy.
7. The client should continue through these steps until the cards in all of the environments have been addressed.

A two-hour session would be most desirable for this activity; however, it could potentially take more than one session. This activity is structured in such a way as to reduce linearity (steps four and five) and emphasize the nature of modulating expressions of identity as the client moves in and out of several environments on a regular basis.

Suggestions for Follow-Up

The therapist should spend time processing this activity with the client at the end of the session to find out what the client found to be helpful or not as helpful. The client may be asked if there were certain environments that would be useful as a primary focus for subsequent sessions (e.g., coming out to a particular person). The therapist should leave enough time following the session to make notes about significant areas of concern for the client in each environment, as well as sources of strength and support. It may be helpful for the therapist to diagram the position of the circles on a piece of paper. After the therapist and client have established mutual goals, the therapist may continue to explore previous questions more deeply with the client. For example, this exercise may reveal that the client's sexual identity provokes anxiety in many personal relationships. In Bowenian therapy, the amount of anxiety in relationships is a function of differentiation, both in actual relating and in one's fear of being different than what significant others want the person to be (Kerr and Bowen, 1988). The therapist may explore with clients whether they are able to be themselves in terms of their gay or lesbian identity, or if they feel hostage to others' expectations regarding their selfhood. If this is a significant problem, a Bowenian approach could be helpful to help the client maintain relationships without being reflexively shaped by other people. The therapist, however, has the option of using any number of theoretical concepts in connection with this activity. The therapist may also repeat the activity at a later date to assess changes in clients' perceptions of their ecosystemic environment.

Contraindications

The activity itself does not have any specific contraindications; however, it is geared more toward individuals specifically concerned with issues involving coming out. Although the ecosystemic environment is significant to all individuals, and perhaps even more so to gays and lesbians because of limitations imposed simply by virtue of their sexual orientation, some clients may be seeking assistance for specific issues that do not relate specifically to their sexual orientation. In these cases, this activity may not suit the goals of what they would like to achieve in therapy. Other clients may not be comfortable with an experiential approach. This activity should be congruent with clients' therapeutic needs and should not be forced on clients who are uncomfortable with being active in the way in which the activity requires.

This activity requires the use of the therapist's personality. Therapists who are not comfortable with spontaneity and active use of self may be less effective using this activity. The therapist should also examine his or her own level of homophobia and work through issues concerning this (whether the therapist is gay, lesbian, or heterosexual). Therapists who harbor significant homophobic feelings themselves will not be able to help the client. Finally, it would be extremely beneficial for the therapist to have a solid understanding of the coming-out process, systems theory, and potential limitations of each environment for gays and lesbians. For example, when thinking about the legal system, with the recent exception of the state of Vermont, the balance of the forty-nine states do not recognize gay marriage. Thus, there is an absence of many benefits to gay couples that are afforded to heterosexual couples. Limited understanding of these concepts will likely limit the effectiveness of the therapist.

Readings and Resources for the Professional

Blumenfeld, W. (1992). *Homophobia: How we all pay the price*. Boston, MA: Beacon Press.
Boszormenyi-Nagy, I., Grunebaum, J., and Ulrich, D. (1991). Contextual therapy. In A. Gurman and D. P. Kniskern (Eds.), *Handbook of family therapy*, Volume II (pp. 200-238). New York: Brunner/Mazel.

Bristor, M. (1990). *Individuals, families, and environments*. Dubuque, IA: Kendall Hunt.

Cass, V. C. (1984). Homosexual identity formation: Testing a theoretical model. *The Journal of Sex Research, 20,* 143-167.

Coleman, E. (1982). Developmental stages of the coming out process. In W. Paul, J. D. Weinrich, J. C. Gonsiorek, and M. E. Hotvedt (Eds.), *Homosexuality: Social, psychological, and biological issues* (pp. 149-158). Thousand Oaks, CA: Sage Publications.

de Shazer, S. (1985). *Keys to solutions in brief therapy*. New York: W. W. Norton and Company.

Harold, R., Mercier, L., and Colarossi, L. (1997). Ecomaps: A tool to bridge the practice research gap. *Journal of Sociology and Social Welfare, 24*(4), 29-44.

Hartman, A. (1978). Diagrammatic assessment of family relationships. *Social Casework, 59,* 465-476.

Kerr, M. and Bowen, M. (1988). *Family evaluation*. New York: W. W. Norton and Company.

Nichols, M. and Schwartz, R. (1995). *Family therapy*. Boston, MA: Allyn and Bacon.

Troiden, R. R. (1988). *Gay and lesbian identity*. Dix Hills, NY: General Hall, Inc.

White, M. and Epston, D. (1990). *Narrative means to therapeutic ends*. New York: W. W. Norton and Company.

Bibliotherapy Sources for the Client

Berzon, B. (Ed.) (1992). *Positively gay*. Berkeley, CA: Celestial Arts.

Handel, L. (1998). *Now that you're out of the closet, what about the rest of the house?* Cleveland, OH: The Pilgrim Press.

O' Neill, C. and Ritter, K. (1992). *Coming Out Within*. San Francisco, CA: HarperCollins.

References

Blumenfeld, W. (1992). *Homophobia: How we all pay the price*. Boston, MA: Beacon Press.

Boszormenyi-Nagy, I., Grunebaum, J., and Ulrich, D. (1991). Contextual therapy. In A. Gurman and D. P. Kniskern (Eds.), *Handbook of family therapy,* Volume II (pp. 200-238). New York: Brunner/Mazel.

Bristor, M. (1990). *Individuals, families, and environments*. Dubuque, IA: Kendall Hunt.

Cass, V. C. (1984). Homosexual identity formation: Testing a theoretical model. *The Journal of Sex Research, 20,* 143-167.

Coleman, E. (1982). Developmental stages of the coming out process. In W. Paul, J. D. Weinrich, J. C. Gonsiorek, and M. E. Hotvedt (Eds.), *Homosexuality: Social, psychological, and biological issues* (pp. 149-158). Thousand Oaks, CA: Sage Publications.

de Shazer, S. (1985). *Keys to solutions in brief therapy*. New York: W. W. Norton and Company.

Harold, R., Mercier, L., and Colarossi, L. (1997). Ecomaps: A tool to bridge the practice research gap. *Journal of Sociology and Social Welfare, 24*(4), 29-44.

Hartman, A. (1978). Diagrammatic assessment of family relationships. *Social Casework, 59,* 465-476.

Kerr, M. and Bowen, M. (1988). *Family evaluation*. New York: W. W. Norton and Company.

Nichols, M. and Schwartz, R. (1995). *Family therapy*. Boston, MA: Allyn and Bacon.

Troiden, R. R. (1988). *Gay and lesbian identity*. Dix Hills, NY: General Hall, Inc.

White, M. and Epston, D. (1990). *Narrative means to therapeutic ends*. New York: W. W. Norton and Company.

9

Coming Out of Marriage: Developing an Emerging Gay, Lesbian, or Bisexual Identity

Mary J. Didelot
Lisa A. Hollingsworth

Type of Contribution: Activity/Homework

Objective

This activity can be used with a client who terminates a heterosexual marriage because of an emerging gay, lesbian, or bisexual identity, and who now may find himself or herself revisiting intense internal struggles similar to the identity struggles he or she experienced during adolescence. This activity will help the client not only to normalize his or her feelings, but also to gain control of a perceived chaotic life transition.

Rationale for Use

Women and men who go through a metamorphosis from a married heterosexual to a single gay, lesbian, or bisexual (GLB) identity may find that this transition is one that manifests itself as a delayed adolescence. Because sexual orientation is a significant part of identity formation (Kimmel, 2000), delayed identity development is a crucial concept in GLB psychology (Hancock, 2000). For many, this GLB identity does not fully form until adulthood (Hunter and Mallon, 2000). Just as adolescents go through the struggles of searching for identity, intimacy, and values, these individuals go through the same struggles, but now within the context of homosexuality rather than the experienced heterosexuality. Because these are adults who are again going through this stage, their confusion and frustration may be exacerbated. These adults do not expect to revisit these issues again. Therefore, because they are now faced with developing an emerging homosexual identity, they might need support as they work through the Eriksonian (1968) themes of self-evaluation, decision making, and commitment to their own decisions to move toward this identity. This is a transition that is both exhilarating and painful because it is one of loss and gain: the pain of loss of the "old" self, and the exhilaration of discovering the new, ideal self. Unfortunately, the psychic dichotomy of this transition can manifest itself in a perceived lack of control.

Following an Eriksonian (1968) model of identity formation, adolescents must begin creating their identity to initiate movement toward the ideal self. For the newly identified GLB adult, there is a sudden shift from the past to a world of new possibilities: "Who am I now?" and "What is my reality within my new identity?" When these adults fail to take a critical look at their emerging identity, the result will be identity confusion. This, then, may cause both poor and inconsistent evaluation and decision making, which permeate all aspects of life.

Using that same Eriksonian (1968) model, a true identity is necessary to nurture healthy, intimate relationships and commitments. For women, there is a further issue with intimacy: many women obtain their identity through relationships (Muus, 1996). Using Gilligan's (1982) model of identity development for girls, we may extrapolate that lesbian and bisexual women going through this transition may experience the added struggle between selflessness (i.e., putting others' needs before self) and selfishness (i.e., recognizing and meeting the needs of self first while meeting the needs of others if possible). This makes lesbians and bisexual women even more susceptible to losing their true identity in a relationship, thus risking their own movement toward the ideal self.

Also, within this context of the search for intimacy is the confusion between intimacy and sex that some gays, lesbians, and bisexuals experience. The emphasis upon "sex" in sexual orientation may cause many individuals to initially become confused by the subtle differences between satisfying their sexual needs and satisfying their need for intimacy (Hancock, 2000; Kimmel, 2000). In their fervor to discover the real self, there is also a tendency to explore sexual limits with many different partners without regard to intimacy (Hancock, 2000; Kimmel, 2000). Although this conduct can be a part of the natural growth process, it can also be physically dangerous, e.g., abuse, placement in unsafe environments, sexually transmitted diseases, etc., may be the consequences. Thus, it warrants discussion as part of a responsible therapeutic process.

This rule and limit testing may also extend to other areas of everyday living, especially for lesbians and bisexual women. Going back to Gilligan's (1982) schema, an adolescent girl faces the selfless versus selfish struggle. This struggle, therefore, may make identity development more difficult for women. As young women engage in this struggle, they become less confident and more self-doubting. This lack of confidence may also be seen within this particular population of lesbians. Thus, applying and extending Gilligan's (1982) care perspective to lesbians and bisexual women, a strong desire for connectedness with other lesbians may cause a woman to sacrifice her own voice and values for a relationship, no matter how good or bad that relationship may be.

By using this intervention, the therapist can help the lesbian client examine three crucial areas of transition (i.e., self-evaluation, decision making, and commitment). These areas translate into such questions as the following:

- Am I still a good person?
- Am I the same person I was when I was married?
- Will my family still love me?
- Did I make the right decision?
- How has this decision affected others in my life?
- Will I be comfortable with a lesbian/gay/bisexual identity?
- Am I truly committed to follow through on the decisions I have made?

This will also help the client to concretely follow her progress as she moves toward control and psychic peace. With appropriate intervention from the therapist, the struggle can be lessened.

Instructions

At the first session, the therapist should place emphasis on the transitional nature of this particular event in the client's life and emphasize that the feelings and thoughts he or she is experiencing are normal for his or her situation. Without articulating these important ideas, the therapist will be allowing feelings of confusion and chaos to continue and grow. Once these words are articulated, the therapist should introduce the GLB Identity Formation Chart in the following manner:

I am now going to show you a GLB Identity Formation Chart. I'd like for you to think back to when you were going through adolescence. Remember how your thoughts were consumed with finding a significant other, having friends who had similar interests, and fantasizing about intimate and sexual interactions with another person? During this time, you likely experienced one of a few thoughts: (1) you were interested in the opposite sex, (2) you thought you were interested in the opposite sex, (3) you thought you were interested in both sexes, or (4) you were interested in the same sex but did not feel okay to act on your feelings. In any case, you probably never had the opportunity to experience adolescence as a gay, lesbian, or bisexual. Now that you have identified your sexual orientation, you can go back and revisit the process. I know that you are feeling frustrated and confused in your search for identity and partnership. I also know that you may not be feeling happy or comfortable with choices you have made and are making in your personal life. Sometimes the pain of going through this transition causes you to be depressed, angry, and doubtful about your choice to pursue your emerging identity as you wish to.

Sometimes, though, you probably feel better about yourself than you ever have before. It's hard bouncing back and forth between these feelings. I know it's fatiguing at times, and you wonder what you are really doing. However, you may experience a sense of relief after we look at the chart together, and a sense of control once you understand where you are in this scheme of things and where you may want to go.

Using the stage design of the American Academy of Child and Adolescent Psychology (2000) as a guide, a flow paradigm based upon this AACAP adolescent development model was adapted and modified by Didelot and Hollingsworth. The AACAP model includes the stages of confusion (rejection of a new or modified identity), emergence (instability and fragility of identity based in fear), and ideal (a healthy, stable identity) indicating progress toward a sound sense of identity. The three areas of movement, i.e., realistic self-evaluation, sound decision making, and healthy relationships, are identified by AACAP as the core areas for the maturation of identity. The germane traits listed under each area of movement have been modified for GLB adults who are experiencing the ramifications of delayed adolescence. The therapist may begin the discussion with the following introduction:

As we go through this chart the first time, I'm going to explain each of these areas to you. Let's pay particular attention to the formulations in Stage III. These are descriptors of a sound identity within the general culture of our country, but they may not be indicators of a healthy identity for you personally. And that is just fine. If you feel this way, then let's change the ideal goal together to fit you and the person you wish to become.

Then, I'm going to give you a copy of this chart to fill out for your homework. All you have to do is mark the feelings or experiences you have had with a P for past. Mark the feelings or experiences you are having now with an N for now. During the next session, we will discuss each of these, take a look at how each of them impacts you now, and see what we need to do to help you move through this difficult transition. The goal is to help you become the person you wish to be by giving you a basis for evaluation and points of reference. This is constructed to help you make sense of this transition period. Now, let's look at the GLB Identity Formation chart.

Suggestions for Follow-Up

It is highly suggested that because this is a dynamic process, this paradigm should serve not only as an initiator of discussion and focus but also as a guide for personal development and a measure of progress.

Some follow-up questions might include the following:

1. In what area(s) do you feel you are most comfortable? Why do you think that is?
2. In what area(s) do you think you have just recently made the most progress? Why? What experiences have led to this feeling?
3. Is there any area(s) where you feel stuck? Please elaborate. Let's look at some options that may help you start to move toward your goal(s).
4. Is there any particular area(s) that you feel we need to work on next?

Contraindications

As in all counseling activities, if the client is not willing to accept that he or she may need to explore his or her developmental process, this will not be successful. However, most clients seem to be relieved to have both a logical explanation for their feelings and the hope that this frustrating transitional period is temporary.

Readings and Resources for the Professional

Abbott, D. and Farmer, E. (1995). *From wedded wife to lesbian life: Stories of transformation.* Santa Cruz, CA: Crossing Press.

Signorile, M. (1996). *Outing yourself.* New York: Simon and Schuster.

Strock, C. (2000). *Married women who love women.* New York: Alyson Publications.

Vargo, M. (2000). *Acts of disclosure: The coming-out process of contemporary gay men.* Binghamton, NY: The Haworth Press.

Bibliotherapy Sources for the Client

Abbott, D. and Farmer, E. (1995). *From wedded wife to lesbian life: Stories of transformation.* Santa Cruz, CA: Crossing Press.

George, K. (2000). *Mr. Right is out there: The gay man's guide to finding and maintaining love.* Los Angeles, CA: Alyson Publications.

Johnson, B. (1997). *Coming out every day: A gay, bisexual, and questioning man's guide.* Oakland, CA: New Harbinger Publications.

Strock, C. (2000). *Married women who love women.* Los Angeles, CA: Alyson Publications.

Vargo, M. (2000). *Acts of disclosure: The coming-out process of contemporary gay men.* Binghamton, NY: The Haworth Press.

References

American Academy of Child and Adolescent Psychology (2000). Normal adolescent development. ADOL. [On-line]. Retrieved from <http://education.indiana.edu/cas/adol/development.html>.

Erikson, E. (1968). *Identity: Youth and crisis.* New York: W. W. Norton and Company.

Gilligan, C. (1982). *In a different voice.* Cambridge, MA: Harvard University Press.

Hancock, K. A. (2000). Lesbian, gay, and bisexual lives: Basic issues in psychotherapy training and practice. In B. Greene and G. L. Croom (Eds.), *Education, research, and practice in lesbian, gay, bisexual, and transgendered psychology* (pp. 91-130). Thousand Oaks, CA: Sage Publications.

Hunter, J. and Mallon, G. P. (2000). Lesbian, gay, and bisexual adolescent development: Dancing with your feet tied together. In B. Greene and G. L. Croom (Eds.), *Education, re-

search, and practice in lesbian, gay, bisexual, and transgendered psychology (pp. 226-243). Thousand Oaks, CA: Sage Publications.

Kimmel, D. C. (2000). Including sexual orientation in lifespan developmental psychology. In B. Greene and G. L. Croom (Eds.), *Education, research, and practice in lesbian, gay, bisexual, and transgendered psychology* (pp. 59-73). Thousand Oaks, CA: Sage Publications.

Muus, R. (1996). *Theories of adolescence*. New York: McGraw-Hill.

GLB Identity Formation Chart

STAGE I	STAGE II	STAGE III
Confusion	*Emergence*	*Ideal*

Movement Toward Realistic Self-Evaluation

__ Struggle with identity	__ Alternating between high expectations and low self-esteem	__ Solid identity
__ Moodiness	__ Periods of sadness	__ Emotional stability
__ Many GLB acquaintances important	__ Making new friends important	__ Stable friendships (GLB or straight)
__ Peer group influence	__ Emphasis on group superiority	__ Self-reliance and self-esteem
__ Homophobia	__ Withdrawal of emotions	__ Self-love
__ Immediate gratification expected	__ Some delayed gratification tolerated	__ More tolerance for delayed gratification
__ Sexual orientation defines dress for acceptance in the GLB community	__ Extreme concern with appearance, to stand out in the GLB community	__ Moderate concern about appearance to please self
__ Inability to laugh at self	__ Sarcasm about self	__ Sense of humor about self
__ Perceives no decision skills	__ Perceives poor decision skills	__ Perceives logical skills
__ GLB peer group defines interests	__ Honing own interests within GLB community	__ Stable interests within all communities
__ Finding faults in self	__ Finding faults in others	__ Ameliorating faults in self

Movement Toward Sound Decision Making

__ Rule and limit testing	__ Some demonstration of conscience	__ Personal dignity
__ No goals	__ Some demonstration of goal setting	__ Set and reach goals
__ Denial of values	__ Interest in values	__ Values developed and set
__ No insights into conduct	__ Contrived or poor insight into conduct	__ Sound and true insight into conduct

Movement Toward Healthy Relationships

__ GLB group activities only	__ Constantly changing GLB interpersonal relationships	__ Serious relationships, GLB or straight
__ Shyness	__ Emphasis on sexual attractions	__ Capacity for love
__ Modesty	__ Experimentation	__ Passion
__ Rejection of GLB identity	__ Fears associated with GLB identity	__ Clear GLB identity

10

Who Told Me That?
Challenging Internalized Homophobic Messages

Cyndy J. Boyd
Joy S. Whitman

Type of Contribution: Activity/Handout

Objectives

This activity is designed to help gay, lesbian, or bisexual (GLB) clients increase their awareness of the homophobic, heterosexist, and otherwise discriminatory societal messages that they have internalized, to understand the messages as stereotypes rather than as realistic descriptions, and to examine the impact that these stereotypes have both on the demographic groups in which the clients hold membership and on the individual clients. When clients have integrated this information, it can be used to reevaluate and rewrite the messages, as a way to increase self-esteem and improve the quality of their relationships.

Rationale for Use

Internalized homophobia is extremely destructive for GLB persons. The possible consequences include the tolerance of discriminatory or abusive treatment from others; the sabotaging of career goals by blaming external homophobia on the part of colleagues (Gonsoriek, 1988); distrust and loneliness (Finnegan and Cook, 1984); impaired sexual functioning (Brown, 1986); unsafe sex (Waldo et al., 2000); domestic violence (Pharr, 1988); substance abuse (Glaus, 1988); eating disorders (Brown, 1987); a lack of self-worth, especially with regard to giving and receiving love; projecting this devalued self-worth onto one's romantic partner (Friedman, 1991); and suicide (Remafedi et al., 1998). Its effects are pervasive and are especially egregious in the areas of intra- and interpersonal functioning (Shidlo, 1994).

The etiology of internalized homophobia lies in the acceptance of harmful societal messages about GLB individuals that are disseminated through the media, family, religion, schools, and other social avenues. The literature has demonstrated that members of any minority group who are not able to recognize such negative messages as the outgrowth of an oppressive society, and instead blame themselves for the discrimination they endure, tend to have lower self-esteem (Crocker and Major, 1989). Therefore, it is clear that the task of helping GLB clients to deconstruct these messages and reject them as accurate reflections of who they are as individuals is an important one in building self-esteem.

Instructions

This list of questions can be used as a vehicle for discussion in individual, couple, or group therapy. It can also be distributed to clients as a homework assignment to be discussed in a later therapy session.

This exercise should be introduced to the GLB client who is struggling with self-esteem issues that are connected to shame or devaluation of his or her sexual orientation. The client should be informed of the connection between his or her self-perceptions and the messages that he or she has internalized from various sources. Then, the purpose of the exercise, which is to aid the client in the understanding of both the origin and impact of these messages on his or her self-image and relationships, should be communicated. The client should be informed that the exercise is designed to help him or her to depersonalize these messages, to fully explore the ways in which these messages have interfered with his or her functioning, and to use these insights to make new choices about how to best take care of himself or herself in the face of an oppressive culture.

The therapist and client should generate at least one identity to use as the focus of this exercise. The exercise could be completed multiple times, using several different group memberships, if they apply to the client. For instance, an African-American lesbian might benefit from looking at three minority identities that affect her life: her racial, sexual, and gender identities. A white bisexual male with a disability might want to explore the stereotypes and their effects on his self-image regarding sexual orientation and disability. It may also be helpful to look at his racial and gender identities. Although they are majority group identities, important and sometimes hurtful messages about being part of a majority culture, or not assimilating well enough to the majority culture, are oftentimes internalized and contribute to low self-esteem.

Suggestions for Follow-Up

This exercise should be incorporated into therapy as the beginning of an in-depth exploration of the construction of the client's identity and self-talk. It can be used as a point of reference as the therapist and client continue to work on understanding the ways in which the client has formed his or her current self-image. Ideally, it is a springboard from which to empower the client to recognize that his or her low self-esteem is neither immutable nor an accurate reflection and, therefore, can be adjusted and improved.

As the client undertakes this in-depth look at the stereotypes he or she has held about sexual orientation, the therapist can begin exploring with the client new statements he or she can make about the multiple identities. For each stereotype the client recognizes, ask him or her to debunk it in some way. For example, if one of the stereotypes a lesbian isolates is "lesbians are not feminine," ask her to identify someone she knows who does not ascribe to that idea, to look at lesbian magazines to find pictures or stories that do not fit into that stereotype, or to talk with other lesbians and find out what their thoughts are about that belief. In some way, follow up with each stereotype so that the client can change prevailing beliefs as he or she integrates different aspects of identity.

Contraindications

This exercise requires some skill on the part of the client for self-observation and for discussion of abstract concepts with regard to the connection between broad societal messages and his or her experiences. Therefore, a client whose cognitive capacity for abstraction is limited may not find this exercise to be helpful.

For the client who identifies as having a multiple minority status, the therapist should assess whether the client can tolerate exploring the effects of all group memberships on his or her self-esteem. In order to ensure that the client will not be overwhelmed by this exercise, the client's stage of identity development with regard to all minority identities should be considered. In all cases, the client's emotional state must be such that he or she will not experience a sudden awareness of these issues as debilitating. In instances where the client's emotional state is fragile and/or the client has little prior insight into these issues, it is recommended the therapist pace this work accordingly.

Readings and Resources for the Professional

Greene, B. (1997). *Ethnic and cultural diversity among lesbians and gay men*. Thousand Oaks, CA: Sage Publications.

Herek, G. M. (1998). *Stigma and sexual orientation: Understanding prejudice against lesbians, gay men, and bisexuals*. Thousand Oaks, CA: Sage Publications.

Rothblum, D. and Bond, L. A. (1996). *Preventing heterosexism and homophobia*. Thousand Oaks, CA: Sage Publications.

Sears, J. T. and Williams, W. L. (1997). *Overcoming heterosexism and homophobia*. New York: Columbia University Press.

Bibliotherapy Sources for the Client

Berzon, B. (2001). *Positively gay*. Berkeley, CA: Celestial Arts.

Mohler, M. (1999). *Homosexual rites of passage: A road to visibility and validation*. Binghamton, NY: The Haworth Press.

Plummer, D. (1999). *One of the boys: Masculinity, homophobia, and modern manhood*. Binghamton, NY: The Haworth Press.

Rose, S. M. (2002). *Lesbian love and relationships*. Binghamton, NY: The Haworth Press.

References

Brown, L. S. (1986). Confronting internalized oppression in sex therapy with lesbians. *Journal of Homosexuality, 12*, 99-107.

Brown, L. S. (1987). Lesbians, weight, and eating: New analyses and perspectives. In The Boston Lesbian Psychologies Collective (Ed.), *Lesbian psychologies: Explorations and challenges* (pp. 294-309). Urbana: University of Illinois.

Crocker, J. and Major, B. (1989). Social stigma and self-esteem: The self-protective properties of stigma. *Psychological Review, 96*, 608-630.

Finnegan, D. G. and Cook, D. (1984). Special issues affecting the treatment of male and lesbian alcoholics. *Alcoholism Treatment Quarterly, 1*, 85-98.

Friedman, R. C. (1991). Couple therapy with gay couples. *Psychiatric Annals, 18*, 33-36.

Glaus, O. K. (1988). Alcoholism, chemical dependency and the lesbian client. *Women and Therapy, 8*, 131-144.

Gonsoriek, J. C. (1988). Mental health issues of gay and lesbian adolescents. *Journal of Adolescent Health Care, 9*, 114-122.

Pharr, S. (1988). *Homophobia: A weapon of sexism*. Little Rock, AR: Chardon.

Remafedi, G., French, S., Story, M., Resnick, M. D., and Blum, R. (1998). The relationship between suicide risk and sexual orientation: Results of a population-based study. *American Journal of Public Health, 88*, 57-60.

Shidlo, A. (1994). Internalized homophobia: Conceptual and empirical issues in measurement. In B. Greene and G. M. Herek (Eds.), *Lesbian and gay psychology: Theory, research, and clinical applications. Psychological perspectives on lesbian and gay issues* (pp. 176-205). Thousand Oaks, CA: Sage Publications.

Waldo, C. R., McFarland, W., Katz, M. H., MacKellar, D., and Valleroy, L. A. (2000). Very young gay and bisexual men are at risk for HIV infection: The San Francisco Bay Area Young Men's Survey II. *Journal of Acquired Immune Deficiency Syndromes, 24*(2), 168-174.

Minority Group: _____

1. List eight stereotypes often connected with this group.

2. How are members of this group impacted by these stereotypes?

3. How are nonmembers of this group impacted by these stereotypes—how do they perceive or treat members of this group?

4. How do members of this group perceive or treat one another?

5. How did you learn about the stereotypes in question 1?

6. How were these stereotypes communicated to you?

11

Surviving Trauma and Anxiety
As a Result of Events of Discrimination

Jackie Mascher

Type of Contribution: Activity/Handout

Objectives

1. To increase a client's awareness that discrimination is a traumatic event
2. To help a client recognize the role of discrimination and trauma in his or her life
3. To validate and normalize client responses to discrimination and trauma
4. To increase a client's awareness of his or her response patterns to discrimination and trauma

Rationale for Use

Trauma is broadly defined to include not only the most obvious acts of emotional, physical, and psychological violence but any act of emotional, physical, or psychological injustice. Unfortunately, trauma is far more common than most diagnostic categories and psychological literature would indicate; in fact, trauma responses among people of marginalized social groups, including gays, lesbians, and bisexuals, are not at all unusual (Brown, 1994; Root, 1992a,b). Social discrimination can produce trauma responses in individuals regardless of whether such individuals have other stories of trauma in their lives.

Heterosexist discrimination, or any discrimination, can be a single, blatant event or a subtle, ongoing circumstance. For a gay, lesbian, bisexual, or transgendered person, everyday heterosexist environments can be hostile and threatening. Heterosexist environments can lead to normal trauma responses such as hypervigilance, difficulty engaging in relationships, fear, anxiety, and so on. The effects of trauma can be long-lasting, and often survivors of trauma have little awareness that past trauma can be so intimately connected with their current feelings, thoughts, and behaviors. In addition, the effects of trauma and of discrimination can be exacerbated by *secondary injuries*. These secondary injuries include the harmful reactions of others in the social environment when victims choose to retell their stories of discrimination, are prompted or feel pressured to retell stories of trauma, or when survivors reexperience the effects of their trauma for various reasons (Lowe and Mascher, 1999).

Clients can become aware of the role of discrimination and trauma in their lives. Individuals who learn to recognize the patterns of their responses to traumatic discrimination will have an increased awareness of their hostile environments, the effects of their responses to such environments, and will also gain a language to talk about heterosexism. Awareness will help clients begin to gain control over the effects that a traumatic relationship, event, or environment has on their lives. The following handouts and exercises are used to help clients recognize that there has been trauma, and that indicators of trauma can come in the form of various cognitive, behavioral, and emotional responses that may cause changes in their interpersonal relationships. Clients will come to understand how various trauma responses can be worked through with the help of others and with the help of internal resources. Moreover, clients can better learn what to expect from their interpersonal supports, and can learn how to maximize these supports.

Instructions

Give the client a copy of the handout Normal Reactions to Events of Discrimination. Orient him or her to the broad range of normal responses that exist. Discuss whether the client recognizes any of these behaviors as his or her own, and how the magnitude of these responses may vary. Explore how these normal reactions of your client might be ongoing and continuous, sudden and intermittent, and traceable to one event or to many events.

The Awareness Journal is particularly useful to document everyday reactions to an environment when the precipitating discriminatory event is unknown. The journal should be photocopied so that it might be used on numerous occasions. Ask a client to complete the Awareness Journal, which may also be completed for the first time in a session with the aid of the therapist. Using the handout Normal Reactions to Events of Discrimination, the client first documents his or her physical reactions, emotions, thoughts, and behaviors, along with the date and time of these reactions. Last, or with the help of the therapist, the client describes the situation that may have coincided with or preceded these reactions, or reminds the client of these reactions.

The therapist validates and normalizes all of the client's trauma reactions as much as possible. Often clients will wonder if a seemingly minor event of discrimination warrants all of her or his documented reactions; therapists should validate that any event of discrimination is a harmful and threatening occurrence. Often, therapists and clients will find that a traumatic situation is unidentifiable, undefinable, or cumulative and complex. The discussion may not center around the trauma event per se; rather, it is a client's experience that is important, even if the trauma reactions are the only data that come to light. For example, it is possible to feel discriminated against by an overriding heterosexist climate in a social environment or situation. Validate these possibilities.

Then, with the client, review the handout Helpful Reactions to Events of Discrimination as well as the handout Unexpected Injuries: When Caring People Make Things Worse. The first handout is a list of what your client may find most helpful when he or she seeks support from others about an experience of discrimination. The therapist should model these responses but should also inquire about the support system of the client. The second handout is a list of secondary injuries, or the harmful responses of well-intentioned people who are trying to be supportive. Help the client process the differences between the two lists. Discuss whether the client has considered seeking support from others concerning his or her experiences. Inquire how people in the client's support system have responded to his or her stories, and whether these responses have been helpful or harmful.

Use the Interpersonal Reactions to Events of Discrimination activity questions to help the client process one particular story of traumatic discrimination. Give a copy of these questions to the client, so that he or she can learn to identify traumatic events, identify secondary injuries, and take steps toward building more comprehensive support systems. As your client becomes familiar with the nature or his or her support system, discuss ways he or she can increase the support received from others. For example, your client can have conversations with loved ones about discrimination and, in doing so, it may be helpful for your client to understand what he or she is seeking from another, and to communicate these needs (e.g., "I just need you to listen right now" or "I need you to let me be angry").

Suggestions for Follow-Up

Emphasize the process of trauma responses, and that these can be cyclical response patterns. A client's reactions to discrimination could represent several discriminations lumped together, vestiges of prior unrecognizable injustices, or other maltreatment unassociated with the client's sexuality. Assess these possibilities. Above all, emphasize that these discriminations and traumas originate as external environmental stressors, in order to counteract one particularly harmful effect of discrimination on your client, internalized oppression. Use the exercises in "Managing Heterosexism at Work or School" as follow-up exercises (see Chapter 12). Discuss the ways in which heterosexist discrimination parallels racism, sexism, ableism, and other isms.

The client's normal responses to discrimination are often debilitating, and the feelings of victimization often pervade other contexts in the client's life. Help a client to evaluate the reality and safety of his or her current situation. Validate the very real threats that exist for the client, then help him or her to assess the relative safety and threat of these various contexts. Assess the nature of the client's support system, in particular, and how events of discrimination may be affecting his or her relationships. Be familiar with gay-friendly attorneys in your area so that you might make a referral should your client be interested in legally pursuing matters of discrimination.

Contraindications

The therapist must be familiar with basic trauma literature and be prepared to incorporate the exercises in this chapter into basic trauma treatment. Clients might first need to be introduced to the idea of heterosexism, that heterosexism is pervasive in everyday contexts, and that heterosexism constitutes a social abuse of power. For some clients who are just coming to terms with being nonheterosexual, these ideas themselves can be threatening, and so these exercises may not be appropriate for such clients. Moreover, clients might first need to be oriented to the idea of trauma and recovery.

Readings and Resources for the Professional

Brown, L. S. (1994). *Subversive dialogues: Theory in feminist therapy.* New York: Basic Books.

Gay and Lesbian Alliance Against Defamation (2001). Retrieved online August 2, 2002, from <www.glaad.org>.

Herman, J. L. (1992). *Trauma and recovery.* New York: Basic Books.

Herman, J. L. (1993). Sequelae of prolonged and repeated trauma: Evidence for a complex post-traumatic syndrome (DESNOS). In J. R. T. Davidson and E. B. Foa (Eds.), *Post-traumatic stress disorder: DSM IV and beyond* (pp. 213-228). Washington, DC: American Psychological Association.

Root, M. P. P. (Ed.) (1992a). *Racially mixed people in America.* Thousand Oaks, CA: Sage Publications.

Root, M. P. P. (1992b). Reconstructing the impact of trauma on personality. In L. S. Brown and M. Ballou (Eds.), *Personality and psychotherapy: Feminist reappraisals* (pp. 229-266). New York: Guilford.

Bibliotherapy Sources for the Client

Allen, J. (1995). *Coping with trauma: A guide to self-understanding.* Washington, DC: American Psychological Association.

Gay and Lesbian Alliance Against Defamation (2001). Retrieved online August 2, 2002, from <www.glaad.org>.

Herman, J. L. (1992). *Trauma and recovery*. New York: Basic Books.

References

Brown, L. S. (1994). *Subversive dialogues: Theory in feminist therapy*. New York: Basic Books.

Lowe, S. M. and Mascher, J. (1999). *Forming alliances: An intervention to combat racism and other "isms."* Interactive session presented at the Annual Conference of the Asian American Psychological Association, Boston, MA.

Root, M. P. P. (Ed.) (1992a). *Racially mixed people in America*. Thousand Oaks, CA: Sage Publications.

Root, M. P. P. (1992b). Reconstructing the impact of trauma on personality. In L. S. Brown and M. Ballou (Eds.), *Personality and psychotherapy: Feminist reappraisals* (pp. 229-266). New York: Guilford.

Normal Reactions to Events of Discrimination

Events of discrimination can be single, blatant events or subtle, ongoing circumstances. The following are normal responses to all kinds of victimization. Get to know your response patterns. They can be clues to you that discrimination is occurring.

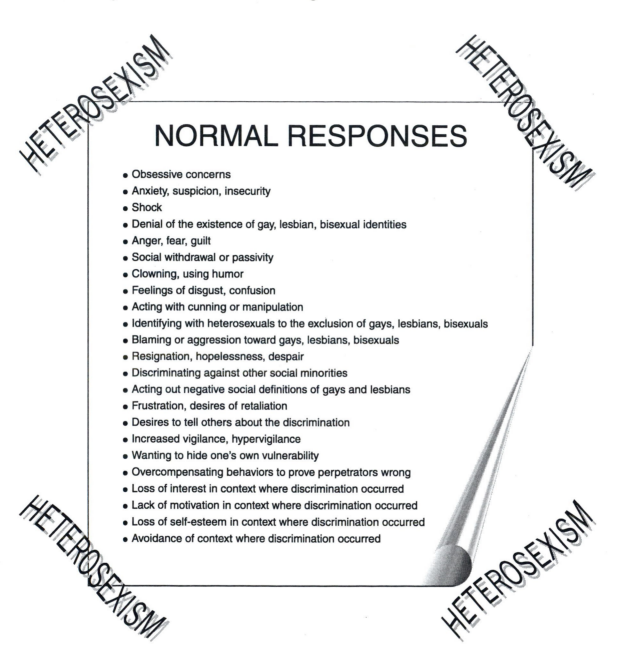

NORMAL RESPONSES

- Obsessive concerns
- Anxiety, suspicion, insecurity
- Shock
- Denial of the existence of gay, lesbian, bisexual identities
- Anger, fear, guilt
- Social withdrawal or passivity
- Clowning, using humor
- Feelings of disgust, confusion
- Acting with cunning or manipulation
- Identifying with heterosexuals to the exclusion of gays, lesbians, bisexuals
- Blaming or aggression toward gays, lesbians, bisexuals
- Resignation, hopelessness, despair
- Discriminating against other social minorities
- Acting out negative social definitions of gays and lesbians
- Frustration, desires of retaliation
- Desires to tell others about the discrimination
- Increased vigilance, hypervigilance
- Wanting to hide one's own vulnerability
- Overcompensating behaviors to prove perpetrators wrong
- Loss of interest in context where discrimination occurred
- Lack of motivation in context where discrimination occurred
- Loss of self-esteem in context where discrimination occurred
- Avoidance of context where discrimination occurred

HETEROSEXISM HETEROSEXISM HETEROSEXISM HETEROSEXISM

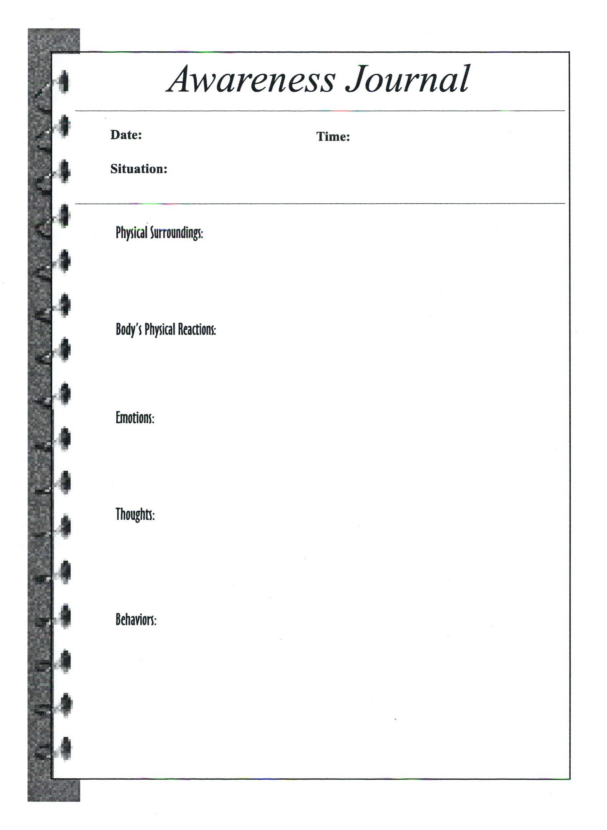

Awareness Journal

Date: **Time:**

Situation:

Physical Surroundings:

Body's Physical Reactions:

Emotions:

Thoughts:

Behaviors:

Helpful Reactions to Events of Discrimination

1. **Inquire:** "Are you all right? I'm interested in hearing about what happened."

   Sometimes, due to shock, shyness, fear, or other reasons, retelling a story of discrimination can be difficult. Show interest by inquiring about an incident, and make it clear that you are available to listen should the victim choose to tell his or her story.

2. **Listen:** "What happened? Tell me more."

   Active listening includes paraphrasing, paralinguistic reflections ("uh-huh"), and open-ended questions. It also includes open body language, good eye contact, and a posture that demonstrates genuine interest.

3. **Believe:** "I believe you."

   The story may be conveyed to you in a way that is muddled or not chronological. Victims often second guess their own experiences, dissociate from their injuries, or downplay the incident. Demonstrate your belief in their experience.

4. **Validate:** "That was such a homophobic comment!"

   Unconditional validation is critical and is a key ingredient to good support. Define the incident as one of discrimination.

5. **Empathize:** "I'm sorry that this happened to you."

   It is helpful for victims of discrimination to know that they are not alone. Communicate caring.

6. **Affirm Emotions:** "You have a right to be outraged."

   Help to name the emotions that are expressed, and validate them. Victims often feel outrage, fear, sadness, anger, hopelessness, and guilt, or a combination of these. Whatever the initial response of the victim, it is appropriate.

7. **Share in the experience:** "I'm outraged and saddened hearing your story."

   It should not be a high priority for you to share a similar victimization story of your own, as this may detract from the emotional response the victim is carrying. However, communicate how you feel when you hear the story.

8. **Empower:** "Is there something we can do about this? What do you need right now?"

   At moments of vulnerability (such as after having been discriminated against), most people welcome a sense of power.

9. **Intervene/Advocate:** "Do you want to file a report? I'll go with you."

   Taking action on behalf of a person without their consent may result in further victimization. On the other hand, it is difficult to be a victim and an advocate for oneself simultaneously. A collaborative effort, if indicated, is usually most helpful.

10. **Follow up:** "I was thinking about what happened to you last week. How are you feeling now?"

    Because trauma response is a process, it is important to follow up what may be a very difficult conversation. The victim may feel vulnerable or embarrassed at having shared a story with you, and so it is necessary for you to take initiative in recognizing the severity of the experience.

Unexpected Injuries: When Caring People Make Things Worse

1. **Disbelief:** "Are you sure?"

   Don't initially ask a victim to clarify or prove that discrimination has occurred. Don't ask questions that imply judgment. Instead, say that you'd like to hear more about the incident.

2. **Denial:** "That sort of thing usually doesn't happen around here."

   Refusing to believe in a story of discrimination doesn't help the reality of the victim's thoughts and emotions. Instead, validate the victim's experiences.

3. **Dismissiveness:** "Don't take it too seriously."

   A victim may or may not appear to take an experience seriously. Either way, validate and confirm the nature of the discrimination.

4. **Defensiveness:** "What are you saying, exactly?"

   It's hard not to feel defensive when we are witnesses to someone else's injuries, but our defensiveness shifts the attention away from the primary event of discrimination. Stories often do not get told out of concern for another person's defensive reactions.

5. **Intellectualization:** "The problem with society these days is . . ."

   In retelling a story of discrimination, victims are not initially looking for an injury to be explained. Instead, focus on the emotional meaning of the event.

6. **Rationalization:** "I'm positive he didn't mean anything by it."

   There may be good reasons why an event of discrimination has happened, but such explanations tend to minimize the unjust incident.

7. **Refocusing:** "A similar thing happened to me this morning . . ."

   In an effort to connect with the victim's story, or to rescue the victim from uncomfortable emotions, some listeners change the subject too early. This places the victim in a role of listener after you've expressed interest in helping him or her.

8. **Fixing it:** "Show me the graffiti! I'm going to go report this incident."

   Jumping to action prematurely, without the consent of the victim, communicates an inability to sit with the victim's strong emotions and it also disempowers the victim.

9. **Squashing feelings:** "Oh no! Please don't cry . . ."

   Negative emotions can be uncomfortable, but emotions that go unvalidated tend to surface in other ways. Instead, stay with the victim's intense range of emotions which, if expressed, will be expended.

10. **Blaming the victim:** "Why did you have to mention that you were gay?"

    At all costs, avoid connecting the discrimination or trauma with the intrinsic identity of the victim.

Interpersonal Reactions to Events of Discrimination

1. Find a safe place. This place might be in the presence of someone close to you, or somewhere that is positively special and meaningful to you. Choose a place where you will not be disturbed. When you feel relaxed and safe, recall an event of discrimination that you have suffered from in the recent past.

2. Whom did you tell afterward?

3. How did that person respond to your story, specifically? What were his or her exact words, if you can remember them?

4. Using the Helpful Reactions list, identify the ways this person was most helpful in responding to you.

5. Using the Unexpected Injuries list, identify the ways this person was least helpful or injurious in responding to you.

6. Sometimes when people tell others about a story of discrimination, they reexperience some of their original reactions to the event. Look at the Normal Reactions to Events of Discrimination list. How did you feel during and after telling your story of discrimination to the other person?

7. How has your relationship with the other person been changed after telling him or her your story?

8. Are you likely to seek support from the same person again in the future? Why or why not?

12

Managing Heterosexism at Work or School

Jackie Mascher

Type of Contribution: Activities/Handouts

Objectives

1. To help a client recognize and admit his or her own heterosexism
2. To help a client understand the pervasiveness and the effects of heterosexism on life and relationships
3. To help a client acknowledge that his or her discomfort is the result of an "ism" and not the result of his or her sexuality
4. To normalize all sexualities
5. To identify heterosexist stressors in a client's environment
6. To orient a client to his or her basic human rights
7. To provide a client with a resource that is humorous, readily accessible, and functions as a way to externalize the problems in a heterosexist environment

Rationale for Use

Heterosexist harassment can be explicit or implicit. It can be the indescribable feeling in the air (Steele, 1997) which communicates a supposed superiority of heterosexuality, or that heterosexuality is the only socially sanctioned and acceptable orientation. Heterosexism can be either intentional or unintentional on the part of others, and it can be expressed in the form of a single specific act or more subtle, ongoing attitudes and behaviors (Atkinson and Hackett, 1998). Discrimination and harassment that target gay, lesbian, and bisexual (GLB) people occur daily. Because of the heterosexism in most professional environments, GLB people at work or at school might not be able to access retribution immediately, to obtain the support of their loved ones, to develop support systems, and for other reasons may not be able to confront the heterosexism in a professional environment (Cain, 1991). Due to heterosexism, GLB people carry with them the very real fear that success at work or school will be obstructed, that they will be fired and unable to find another job, that they will be mistreated or lose access to major resources, and that they will otherwise be objects of social derision.

One of the most harmful effects of discrimination for lesbians, gays, and bisexuals is internalized heterosexism (Atkinson and Hackett, 1998). That is, the social problem of heterosexism comes to manifest itself within individuals; a person will believe the social myths and stereotypes about gays, lesbians, and bisexuals and apply these to himself or herself. Individuals come to blame themselves and feel ashamed or guilty for the acts of discrimination that are routinely perpetrated against them. Individuals may also dissociate from the heterosexism, deny that it exists, or otherwise psychologically and emotionally detach themselves from it. Individuals typically ascribe to themselves the feelings they have about the discrimination, for example, that they themselves are "wrong," "dirty," or "disgusting."

For all of these reasons, it is important for therapists to validate the pervasiveness of heterosexism along with its associated stress, and to recognize that heterosexism continues to be the dominant social and political sentiment. Whether or not a client is out at work or at school, or in a continual process of being out (Atkinson and Hackett, 1998; McCarn and Fassinger, 1996), it is important to recognize that harassment constitutes an infringement on basic human rights, and that a client's internalized heterosexism usually pervades other contexts of his or her life (e.g., intimate relationships). With the help of the activities and handouts that follow, clients can acknowledge and validate their daily stress and can assert their basic human rights without necessarily confronting their heterosexist environments. Other therapeutic strategies, such as carrying a simple reminder of worth on one's own person, can be enough to ground a client in hostile environments.

Getting rid of one's own heterosexism is as much of a process as was the acquisition of heterosexist sentiments in the first place. Challenging one's, and others', heterosexism is an ongoing struggle (Garnets and D'Augelli, 1994). Internalized heterosexism can come from misinformation, miseducation, and myths about particular identities. Heterosexism is furthered by the individual, institutional, and cultural practices that relegate gays, lesbians, and bisexuals to second-class citizenship. These same structures give heterosexuals the social, political, and economic privilege that gives them their unearned power over others. These differences in social power have profound psychological effects for heterosexuals and nonheterosexuals. Heterosexism syndrome is the persistence of thoughts, feelings, and behaviors that heterosexuality is the "normal," "standard," or "default" sexuality, despite overwhelming evidence to the contrary.

It is often the case that problems in living, in relationships, in career, and on other fronts co-occur with heterosexism syndrome. For example, self-identified heterosexuals may find themselves in need of more diverse relationships, may feel significant discomfort around gays, lesbians, and bisexuals, or may avoid situations that are not heterosexist. In addition, self-identified heterosexuals may have unrealistic expectations of themselves and others, may have an exaggerated sense of entitlement, and may approach situations and circumstances with rigidity, all of which may inhibit a heterosexual's emotional and psychological growth and development.

Of course, heterosexuals are not the only ones profoundly affected by heterosexism syndrome. In addition to surviving acts of discrimination, managing low self-esteem, and other obvious effects of social oppression, GLB clients may also suffer from heterosexism syndrome. The topic of heterosexism is still publicly taboo, and this can contribute to the isolation felt on a regular basis by so many GLB people (Lowe and Mascher, 1999). Individuals who identify as gay, lesbian, or bisexual are in need of a way to examine the link between their own negative self-thoughts, self-emotions, and self-behaviors and heterosexism. The checklist Do You Suffer from Heterosexism Syndrome? is a list of thoughts, feelings, and behaviors that are typical for a GLB person suffering from heterosexism syndrome.

Instructions

Assign the Do You Suffer from Heterosexism Syndrome? checklist to a client who wholly or partially identifies as gay, lesbian, or bisexual. Use of the checklist is indicated when a client could benefit from seeing the impact of heterosexism syndrome on his or her life, and when a client has little awareness that negative thoughts, feelings, and behaviors are linked with heterosexism. The checklist will help the therapist and client identify the heterosexist issues that are of particular salience to the client.

Using the Daily Heterosexism Stressors Checklist, ask a client to check off how many items happened during a particular time frame (e.g., today, this week, within the past month). Assess your client's knowledge of these events and whether he or she notices these events on a conscious level. Discuss the nature of heterosexism as a major life stressor. Ask how your client normally receives these events internally or comes to negotiate these events. Discuss the harm of silence after victimization, the role of isolation in cycles of abuse, and the damage of internalizing social rules instead of seeking regular interpersonal support regarding them. Assess the client's level of hopelessness and resignation about the pervasiveness of the heterosexism. Before moving on, be certain to validate any feelings (e.g., anger, sadness) that surface for the client by talking about these daily events on a conscious level.

The Basic Human Rights handout can be introduced to the client as a way to separate his or her intrinsic worth as a person from external heterosexism. Regardless of the nature of your client's sexuality or level of "outness," he or she can use Basic Human Rights as affirmations, to ground his or her humanity, or as statements of retort when discriminated against. Ask the client to check off which items he or she believes about himself or herself, and which items the client does not believe about himself or herself, with the recognition that he or she can feel different about these items at any given time. Assign some of the items to the client to be rehearsed as a daily mantra or affirmation.

It is often helpful for clients to have a tangible reminder of their rights to express themselves and to take action against heterosexism. Creating a token of safety and sanity that your client can carry with him or her in a wallet or pocket is such a reminder. Therefore, introduce The American Express Yourself Charge Card, your client's answer to the cost of living in a heterosexist world. Ask your client to sign his or her name on the bottom of the card. Cut out the card and either laminate it or tape it to a same-sized nonusable piece of plastic. Assign a meaning or affirmation to the card that applies to your client, for example, the ability to walk away from a heterosexist interaction, or the right to express a social or personal need in a heterosexist environment. Encourage your client to look at it or touch it as a reminder when needed.

Suggestions for Follow-Up

After recognizing the pervasive role of heterosexism in his or her life, the client may find it helpful to continue deconstructing these and other unrealistic or harmful social messages. The therapist might ask which people in the client's life were carriers of these harmful messages. In addition, the therapist might ask if there were other more loving messages for the client, even if these messages were not particularly dominant. The therapist can work to reengage these more positive social messages to make them dominant in the life of the client.

A useful and therapeutic activity is the process of "detoxing" the client's living space or home. In the event that a client is not out in his or her home, the living area can be made to be a safer space. Brainstorm with your client ways to rid his or her home of heterosexist material, such as magazines, paintings, and images. Brainstorm uses for heterosexist propaganda. For example, clients can use unfriendly newspapers to pick up dog waste, line a litterbox, or decoupage trash cans. Heterosexist propaganda can be converted into confetti for use at a commitment ceremony or anniversary celebration. Clients can engage in any activity that represents the conversion of internalized heterosexism into self-renewal or self-love.

Continue to assess the blatant and latent heterosexism in your client's environments. Talk about discrimination regularly in therapy to remind the client that the illness of discrimination is a social one, external to the intrinsic worth of him or her as a person. Monitor and combat the indications that your client has internalized heterosexism (e.g., blaming self for being out, using self-deprecating language or behavior). Discuss other strategies for managing your client's contextual problems, such as finding an increased support system, lodging a formal complaint to the human resources office at school or work, assertiveness training for interpersonal confrontations, or transitioning out of a harmful environment. Validate all degrees of stress that heterosexism causes in the life of the client.

Contraindications

These exercises are contraindicated for the client whose daily survival in hostile contexts depends on an ability to selectively acknowledge his or her surroundings. For example, a person who is recently coming to terms with her or his sexuality might experience such an analysis of dominant culture as devastating, traumatic, or overwhelming. For the client who has never considered the thoroughly negative impact of heterosexism in his or her life, this may be a first expression of his or her victimization, and may be overwhelming. Also, for the client with few social resources or social capital, these exercises might induce, rather than alleviate, stress, and could conceivably lead to the loss of significant relationships.

Therefore, assess a client's level of readiness to discuss these issues in his or her sexuality journey. These exercises do not assume that your client has confronted assumptive heterosexism in the past (i.e., that she or he is out), and it is not necessary that your client confront heterosexism at work or at school. Still, these exercises may be intimidating and inappropriate for someone who does not carry his or her identity publicly. A client with no substantial support system might be encouraged to seek gay-friendly supports prior to deconstructing daily heterosexist events that could conceivably lead to the loss of a critical job or relationship.

Readings and Resources for the Professional

Brown, L. S. (1994). *Subversive dialogues: Theory in feminist therapy.* New York: Basic Books.

Committee on Lesbian and Gay Concerns (1991). Avoiding heterosexual bias in language. *American Psychologist, 46,* 973-974.

Division 44/Committee on Lesbian, Gay, and Bisexual Concerns Joint Task Force on Guidelines for Psychotherapy with Lesbian, Gay, and Bisexual Clients (2000). Guidelines for psychotherapy with lesbian, gay, and bisexual clients. *American Psychologist, 55*(12), 140-145.

Freedman, J. and Combs, G. (1996). *Narrative therapy: The social construction of preferred realities.* New York: W. W. Norton and Company.

Zamarripa, M. X. (1997). A social constructionist approach for working with ethnic minority gay men and lesbians. *Family Therapy, 24*(3), pp. 167-176.

Bibliotherapy Sources for the Client

Lorde, A. (1983). *Zami: A new spelling of my name.* Freedom, CA: Crossing.

Lorde, A. (1984). *Sister outsider: Essays and speeches.* Freedom, CA: Crossing.

National Museum and Archive of Lesbian and Gay History (1996). *The gay almanac.* New York: Berkeley Books.

Internet Resources

American Psychological Association 1997 (2001). Answers to your questions about sexual orientation and homosexuality. Retrieved online August 2, 2002, from <http://helping.apa.org/daily/answers.html>.

American Psychological Association 2001 (2001). Policy statements on lesbian, gay, and bisexual concerns. Retrieved online August 2, 2002, from <http://www.apa.org/pi/lgbpolicy/orient.html>.

KP Media DBA 2001 (2001). The New England community pink pages. Retrieved online August 2, 2002, from <http://pinkweb.com>.

References

Atkinson, D. R. and Hackett, G. (1998). *Counseling diverse populations*. Boston, MA: McGraw-Hill.

Cain, R. (1991). Stigma management and gay identity development. *Social Work, 36*(1), 67-73.

Garnets, L. D. and D'Augelli, A. R. (1994). Empowering lesbian and gay communities: A call for collaboration with community psychology. *American Journal of Community Psychology, 22*(4), 447-467.

Lowe, S. M. and Mascher, J. (1999). Forming alliances: An intervention to combat racism and other "isms." Interactive session presented at the Annual Conference of the Asian American Psychological Association, Boston, MA.

McCarn, S. R. and Fassinger, R. E. (1996). Revisioning sexual minority identity formation: A new model of lesbian identity and its implications for counseling and research. *The Counseling Psychologist, 24*(3), 508-534.

Steele, C. (1997). A threat in the air: How stereotypes shape intellectual identity and performance. *American Psychologist, 52*(6), 613-629.

Do You Suffer from Heterosexism Syndrome?

☐ Sometimes I feel less deserving than others.

☐ I have thoughts and feelings of being "not normal."

☐ I feel the need to protect myself much of the time.

☐ I am often unable to assess whether a situation is or is not safe.

☐ Sometimes I feel numb in social situations.

☐ I often have feelings of not belonging.

☐ Sometimes I feel secretive.

☐ I have feelings of shame in social situations.

☐ I am not always certain that loving someone of the same sex is good.

☐ Sometimes I feel peripheral in social situations.

☐ Sometimes I feel insignificant or weak in social situations.

☐ Sometimes I feel the need to prove my trustworthiness to others.

☐ I often feel uncomfortable around children, elders, or strangers.

☐ I feel vigilant around representatives of religious, military, or government institutions.

☐ I feel the need to use labels ("gay" or "bisexual") for the benefit of others' understanding.

☐ Sometimes I have rigid expectations of myself and others in social roles.

☐ I sometimes feel defensive in social situations.

☐ I have been known to criticize gay, lesbian, or bisexual social leaders.

☐ Sometimes I think my sexuality defines me as a person.

☐ Sometimes when I think about my sexuality I feel "criminal."

☐ I often feel isolated or alone in my thoughts, emotions, and behaviors.

☐ Sometimes I feel rebellious, that being "bad" is "good."

☐ I have difficulty expressing my sexual wants and needs.

☐ I am often suspicious of people who want to get close to me.

☐ Sometimes I think GLB relationships are temporary and fragile.

☐ Sometimes I wonder if I am fully masculine or feminine.

☐ I think that my current sexuality was always and will always be what it is now.

☐ Sometimes I think I will pay for my sins or for my sexual happiness.

☐ I should only seek help from gay, lesbian, or bisexual communities.

☐ I think gays, lesbians, and bisexuals are more similar to one another than different.

☐ I do not always confront racist, heterosexist, or sexist remarks.

☐ Sometimes I feel repelled by same-sex displays of affection in public.

☐ Sometimes I fear that my thoughts, feelings, or behaviors will confirm a lesbian, gay, or bisexual stereotype.

☐ Sometimes I fear that my thoughts, feelings, or behaviors will disconfirm a lesbian, gay, or bisexual stereotype.

☐ Sometimes I am suspicious of gay, lesbian, or bisexual teachers, lawyers, or other professionals.

☐ Sometimes I fantasize about what it would be like to be heterosexual.

Daily Heterosexism Stressors Checklist

- ☐ I overheard others talk about a wedding, engagement, bachelor/ette party.
- ☐ Someone told me about their wedding, engagement, bachelor/ette party.
- ☐ I watched a heterosexual couple be affectionate (e.g., hold hands) in public.
- ☐ My life was referred to as a "lifestyle."
- ☐ Sexual orientation is not included in the antidiscrimination clause at work.
- ☐ Someone asked me if I was married yet.
- ☐ Someone asked, "Do you have a boyfriend/girlfriend (of the opposite sex)?"
- ☐ Someone showed me their new engagement/wedding ring.
- ☐ I witnessed the use of the words "husband" or "wife."
- ☐ I interacted with someone who has been, or is currently in, the military.
- ☐ My workplace or insurance policies do not offer domestic partner benefits.
- ☐ I filled out a form with "single," "married," "divorced," or "widowed" as choices.
- ☐ I saw a television show/movie/commercial with a majority of the characters in heterosexual relationships.
- ☐ I read a magazine or a book, or I saw a play, with a majority of the characters in heterosexual relationships.
- ☐ I listened to music, the majority of which were songs or stories about people in heterosexual relationships.
- ☐ I saw or heard a media representation of a gay, lesbian, or bisexual and the portrayal was that of a stereotype.
- ☐ Someone indicated an assumption that I was heterosexual.
- ☐ Someone indicated a belief that heterosexuality is normal.
- ☐ Someone was surprised to learn that I am gay, lesbian, or bisexual.
- ☐ Someone discounted or argued against my sexuality.
- ☐ Someone asked me about my weekend/leisure life, and I am not out to him or her.
- ☐ I interacted with people who did not know that I am gay, lesbian, or bisexual.
- ☐ Someone referred to a same-sex partner as "roommate," "pal," "buddy," "friend."
- ☐ Someone attributed my problems in living to my sexuality, without evidence of such a connection.
- ☐ Someone avoided me or refused to see me after knowing my sexual orientation.
- ☐ I educated someone who was ignorant about gays, lesbians, or bisexuals.
- ☐ Someone pressured me to disclose my sexuality to someone else.
- ☐ Other _____
- ☐ Other _____
- ☐ Other _____
- ☐ Other _____

Basic Human Rights

I have the right to . . .

____ say "NO."

____ be competent and proud of my accomplishments.

____ feel and express anger.

____ be treated as a capable human being.

____ make mistakes and be responsible for them.

____ change a situation.

____ say "I don't know, I don't agree, or I don't understand."

____ be treated with respect.

____ express my needs, opinions, thoughts, ideas, and feelings.

____ judge my own behavior and be responsible for it.

____ take pride in my body and define attractiveness in my own terms.

____ have a support system.

____ be myself and have my own identity.

____ request help and receive information from others.

____ ask and not assume.

____ have privacy.

____ be imperfect.

____ grow, learn, change, and value my own age and experience.

____ recognize MY needs as important.

The American Express Yourself Charge Card

Dear Cardholder:

Are everyday hassles getting you down? Tired of identifying yourself and arguing for benefits? Welcome to American Express Yourself, where you don't pay extra for your frustrations. Just pull out your new card and say "I'll charge this one," and walk away with your sanity! You have unlimited credit!

Here's how it works:

1. Cut out your new American Express Yourself card.
2. Sign your name.
3. Laminate the card, or tape it to a same-sized piece of plastic.
4. Carry it with you always! Charge away!

Signature of Cardholder

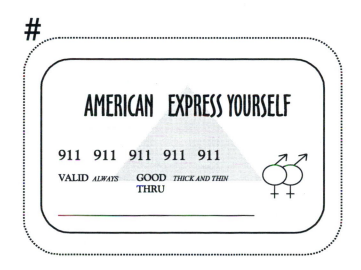

13

Overcoming Biphobia

Jackie Mascher

Type of Contribution: Activity/Handout

Objectives

1. To assess a client's understanding of bisexuality and biphobia
2. To help a client define biphobia as a social problem and not as an issue of a client's worth
3. To help a client recognize his or her own internalized phobia of sexuality or bisexuality
4. To help a client counter myths of bisexuality
5. To normalize sexual thoughts, feelings, and behaviors as similar to all other thoughts, feelings, and behaviors we use to define ourselves

Rationale for Use

Internalized oppression is the set of feelings and misinformation that bisexuals carry about themselves and other gays, lesbians, and bisexuals. Bisexuals exist in the same heterosexist environment as lesbians, gays, and heterosexuals, but biphobia represents a unique set of myths and stereotypes that apply to bisexuality as a socially marginalized group. As a social category, bisexuality is largely unrecognizable to dominant culture, and may not be as visible to gay or lesbian social groups. In addition, by not identifying as gay, lesbian, or heterosexual, bisexuals typically encounter hostility from the members of all of the other groups (Atkinson and Hackett, 1998).

Internalized biphobia has little to do with the nature of bisexuality, and everything to do with the mandatory heterosexism that surrounds us. Biphobia and discomfort with bisexuality is largely due to the social oppression of sexuality in general. Recognizing that we have internalized oppression is a critical first step toward eliminating the oppression internally and externally. There is a distinction between "acceptance" and "tolerance," and support, admiration, appreciation, and nurturance. The following exercises will help a client to rebut myths of bisexuality, recognize internalized biphobia, and define bisexuality in a healthy way.

Instructions

Have your client complete the Internalized Myths of Bisexuality checklist. This can be done during a therapy session, or it can be assigned as a homework activity. The client checks off items on the list to which he or she relates. The Internalized Myths checklist can be duplicated and reused, particularly to assess day-to-day changes in a client's internalized biphobia. Daily changes should be discussed in therapy, for instance, to ascertain what precipitating circumstances made myths salient for a client at any given time.

After the checklist has been completed, have your client complete the Saying Good-Bi to Biphobia worksheet. The questions on the worksheet can be assigned as homework or can be completed during the therapy session with the help of the therapist. The Saying Good-Bi questions are a way to challenge social myths about bisexuality by reassigning them to people of all sexualities.

Suggestions for Follow-Up

In therapy, continue the discussion about how a client defines her or his sexuality. Explore other social prescriptions about bisexuality that can be disconfirmed. Discuss the other social expectations that your client faces, and discuss how these social prescriptions are independent of sexuality. Extend your discussion of social expectations to other aspects of identity such as race, ethnicity, or gender. Inquire how your client comes to disregard these other social myths and expectations about himself or herself, and discuss how these practiced ways of disregarding social myths can apply to the ways in which your client receives messages about sexuality.

Contraindications

These exercises are designed for clients who have chosen to use the term *bisexual* to describe themselves. For clients who identify themselves otherwise, for example, as a man who has sex with men, as gay, lesbian, or as simply "sexual," these exercises may not be so appealing. However, the Internalized Myths checklist is designed to have applicability for everyone, and so some items can be adapted to externalize myths about numerous marginalized identities.

Readings and Resources for the Professional

Atkinson, D. R. and Hackett, G. (1998). *Counseling diverse populations*. Boston, MA: McGraw-Hill.

Bridges, K. L. and Croteau, J. M. (1994). Once-married lesbians: Facilitating changing life patterns. *Journal of Counseling and Development, 73*, 134-340.

Dworkin, S. H. (1992). Some ethical considerations when counseling gay, lesbian, and bisexual clients. In S. H. Dworkin and F. J. Gutierrez (Eds.), *Counseling gay men and lesbians: Journey to the end of the rainbow* (pp. 325-334). Alexandria, VA: American Association for Counseling and Development.

Gelberg, S. and Chojnacki, J.T. (1996). *Career and life planning with gay, lesbian, and bisexual persons*. Alexandria, VA: American Counseling Association.

Kauth, M. R. and Kalichman, S. C. (1998). Sexual orientation and development: An interactive approach. In D. L. Anselmi and A. L. Law (Eds.), *Questions of gender: Perspectives and paradoxes* (pp. 329-344). Boston, MA: McGraw-Hill.

Weise, E. R. (Ed.) (1992). *Closer to home: Bisexuality and feminism*. Seattle: Seal Press.

Wolf, T. J. (1992). Bisexuality: A counseling perspective. In S. H. Dworkin and F. J. Gutierrez (Eds.), *Counseling gay men and lesbians: Journey to the end of the rainbow* (pp. 175-187). Alexandria, VA: American Association for Counseling and Development.

Zinik, G. (1985). Identity conflict or adaptive flexibility: Bisexuality reconsidered. In F. Klein and T. Wolf (Eds.), *Bisexualities: Research and theory* (pp. 7-19). Binghamton, NY: The Haworth Press.

Bibliotherapy Sources for the Client

Bi.org (2001). Retrieved online August 2, 2002, from <http://bi.org>.

Bi the Way (2001). Retrieved online August 2, 2002, from <http://www.bitheway.org>.

Bisexual Insurgence (2001). Retrieved online August 2, 2002, from <http://bisexualinsurgence. org>.

Bisexual.org (2001). Retrieved online August 2, 2002, from <http://bisexual.org>.

The Bisexuality Page (2001). Retrieved online August 2, 2002, from University of California Riverside Web site: <http://lgbtrc.ucr.edu/bisexuality_page.html>.

Bisexual Resource Center (2001). Retrieved online August 2, 2002, from <http://www. biresource.org>.

Kaahumanu, L. and Hutchins, L. (Eds.) (1990). *Bi any other name*. Boston, MA: Alyson Publications.

Reference

Atkinson, D. R. and Hackett, G. (1998). *Counseling diverse populations*. Boston, MA: McGraw-Hill.

Internalized Myths of Bisexuality

The following is a list of some of the myths about bisexuality. Check the items that you feel might apply to you, then complete the questions on Saying Good-Bi to Biphobia.

- ☐ I have a fear of commitment.
- ☐ I dislike taking firm stands about issues.
- ☐ I dislike others who take firm stands about issues.
- ☐ I like to keep my options open.
- ☐ I represent a combination of masculinity and femininity.
- ☐ Sometimes I am attracted to more than one person.
- ☐ My feelings of attraction to others can depend on my mood.
- ☐ Sometimes I feel as though I don't belong.
- ☐ Sometimes I crave intimacy.
- ☐ Sometimes I am embarrassed about my attraction to others.
- ☐ I do not always fit in with gays and lesbians.
- ☐ I do not always fit in with heterosexuals.
- ☐ I must be especially careful about sexually transmitted diseases.
- ☐ I do not always understand my attractions to others.
- ☐ I fear growing older without a community.
- ☐ Sometimes I feel that my politics are trivial compared to other movements.
- ☐ It is difficult to find friends because bisexuals are so different from one another.
- ☐ I don't always agree with the beliefs of the person I am attracted to.
- ☐ There are "good" bisexuals and there are "bad" bisexuals.
- ☐ I have just not met the right woman or man.
- ☐ Sometimes I am guilty of hiding behind heterosexual privilege.
- ☐ I worry that my attractions to others are just a phase.
- ☐ Others don't know the real me.
- ☐ Sometimes I am untrustworthy, fickle, or fake.
- ☐ I don't always stand up for what I believe in.
- ☐ I don't always feel connected to other human beings.
- ☐ I have trouble feeling "at home" or feeling safe.
- ☐ I often feel alone and isolated.
- ☐ If I talk about myself, others might not understand.
- ☐ I often feel ashamed.
- ☐ Sometimes I feel greedy, selfish, or that I "want it all."
- ☐ There has been sexual tension in my friendships.

Saying Good-Bi to Biphobia

1. Consider the items you checked on the Internalized Myths of Bisexuality. How might these same items apply to heterosexuals?

   How might these same items apply to lesbians or gay men?

2. List other stereotypes you can think of about bisexuality. Can you imagine these descriptions being true of a heterosexual person?

   Can you imagine these descriptions being true of a gay or lesbian person?

3. **Sexuality** is a combination of thoughts, feelings, and behaviors. How can we account for thoughts, feelings, and behaviors changing from minute to minute, or from year to year?

   How might thoughts, feelings, and behaviors depend on one's environment?

   What is the relationship of thoughts, feelings, and behaviors to one's mood?

   Are thoughts, feelings, and behaviors predictable? Are they unpredictable? Why?

   Are your thoughts, feelings, and behaviors ever difficult to understand?

4. What items checked could also apply to your daily thoughts, feelings, and behaviors about work, school, food, or hobbies? For example:

   I dislike taking firm stands about issues (what to eat for dinner, politics).
   Others don't know the real me (what kind of food I like, my favorite color).
   I have just not found the right woman or man (line of work, furniture for my home).
   If I talk about my self (hobbies, pets), others might not understand.

5. How is **sexuality** different from the other areas of your life mentioned in question 4?

SECTION II:
HOMEWORK, HANDOUTS, AND ACTIVITIES
FOR RELATIONSHIP ISSUES

14

Assimilation, Queer Pride, and In Between: Personalizing GLBT Relationships, Sexual Practices, and Politics

Stuart F. Chen-Hayes

Type of Contribution: Activity/Homework

Objective

This activity helps gay, lesbian, bisexual, and transgendered (GLBT) clients to name and conceptualize their relationship identities, sexual practices, and political identities on a continuum. The continuum helps clients and counselors make meaning about client beliefs and values related to relationships, sexual practices, and politics within a counseling context.

Rationale for Use

Sue and Sue (1999) refer to the sociopolitical nature of counseling and its effects on clients of nondominant cultural identities, including lesbian and gay (and bisexual and transgendered) clients. James and Murphy (1998) argue that attention to multiple social contexts is essential in affirming GLBT persons in coupled relationships. Smith (1997) states that often in same-gender coupled relationships involving persons of color, partners are at different stages in the coming-out process. Rofes (1995) writes extensively on the importance of looking at the multiple personal and political meanings of the HIV pandemic on the lives of gay men and the need to re-create a gay male sexual culture and relationships based on the sociopolitical effects of HIV/AIDS. Chen-Hayes (2000, 2001a,b) argues the importance of an advocacy perspective in affirming GLBT persons in counseling. Many authors have discussed sexual practices and political variations within GLBT studies and sociopolitical contexts (Beemyn and Eliason, 1996; Califia, 1994; Lorde, 1984; Pharr, 1996; Queen and Schimel, 1997; Rofes, 1995; Rust, 2000). Professional counseling literature and activities, however, on the whole, have limited descriptions of the sexual and political value differences and identities for GLBT persons in relationships.

This exercise gives clients permission to voice their past, present, and future relationships, sexual practices, and political identities, which are often unspoken in the counseling process. Counselors and clients who are savvy to the nuances, complexities, and variations in GLBT lives have a greater knowledge to draw upon for successful counseling outcomes than persons limited to traditional medical models, or intrapsychic identity development models. Both benefit from an initial and ongoing assessment of the value differences and beliefs within relationships, sexual practices, and politics. By aligning these three variables, counselors and clients benefit from direct discussion of the variations in how GLBT clients experience themselves and others. This exercise adds to the existing identity development literature by emphasizing affirmative counseling practice and self-awareness for clients.

Instructions

Using the handouts Relationship Status Continuum, My Sexual Practices Continuum, and My Politics Continuum, ask clients to create their own continuum of values and interests by rating the importance of relationships, sexual practices, and politics, in their past, present, and future/ideal on a scale of 1 to 10 (1 = low, 10 = high). If clients are coupled, have the partner or partner(s) do the same for themselves (or do a separate one for the client's ideal partner if single).

Once clients have filled out the handouts, they are encouraged to discuss the results with the counselor as well as with their partners. This can be done as an intake with a couple for initial counseling or it may be done periodically to assess changes in the counseling process.

Brief Vignette

Reggie is a black gay man in his early thirties who has been active in progressive gay politics and HIV/AIDS education. He presents in counseling with concerns related to a recent relationship breakup. He had been dating a black gay man, also in his early thirties, who was closeted and a Baptist minister. They were in love, but Reggie could not deal with having to hide his feelings and relationship whenever members of the congregation were present, which was constantly. They frequently argued about being out, politics, and sexual differences. Reggie was committed to the relationship, but his ex wanted to have an open relationship. The sex was always "really hot," so Reggie went along with it. Although both men stated overtly that they practiced safer sex, Reggie's ex confessed to him that he did not always use condoms outside of the relationship. Reggie would prefer to keep dating black gay men, but he is not interested in going back into the closet. He wonders if he will ever find a monogamous partner who practices safer sex, and with whom he can spend his life.

The counselor asked Reggie to fill out the handouts twice—one time for himself and the other for his ex. Reggie recognized that he had been dating men who often did not share his values. He made a plan with the counselor to attempt to broaden his dating choices toward men who are more compatible with him in terms of relationship, sexual, and political issues.

Suggestions for Follow-Up

Clients are encouraged to revisit the issues periodically by revisiting the items contained on their continuums. Counselors can use discussion of the items as a way to develop counseling goals with clients and also as a measure of counseling outcome success. Counselors can gain a wealth of information to ensure that they are practicing culturally competent counseling with clients whose own values and beliefs may differ greatly from their own. Questions that counselors can use with clients to further the discussion of issues once they have filled out the handouts might include the following items:

Relationships

- What is your definition of a good relationship?
- How do you deal with sexual exclusivity or openness in a relationship?
- How do you deal with emotional exclusivity or openness in a relationship?

Sexual Practices

- How important is it to be compatible with another person in terms of sexual practices?
- What sexual practices do you enjoy most? Least?

- Have sexual differences been an issue for you in your relationships? If so, what in particular?
- What are your beliefs about safe sex and how has that or does that affect your sexual practices?

Politics

- How important is it to be around others who share your political views?
- Have political differences with others interfered or enhanced your relationships and sexual experiences?
- What effect, if any, does the coming-out process have on you or others in your dating life?
- Are you more comfortable with assimilation (GLBT persons should blend in with everyone else), or open or liberationist displays of pride (GLBT persons should be open, honest, and able to "flaunt" the differences when they choose)?
- How does the larger GLBT political climate affect your life and relationships?

Contraindications

Clients who choose not to label themselves might have discomfort with this exercise, as they might feel forced to categorize themselves. Counselors might agree with that sentiment and encourage clients to use the handouts based on past labels and beliefs, and look at how they have come to a current place of not choosing relationships, sexual practices, or political labels.

Readings and Resources for the Professional

Chen-Hayes, S. F. (2000). Social justice advocacy with lesbian, bisexual, gay, and transgendered persons. In J. Lewis and L. Bradley (Eds.), *Advocacy in counseling: Counselors, clients, and community* (pp. 89-98). Greensboro, NC: Caps Publications (ERIC/CASS).

Chen-Hayes, S. F. (2001a). Counseling and advocacy with transgendered and gender-variant persons in schools and families. *The Journal of Humanistic Counseling, Education, and Development, 40*(1), 34-48.

Chen-Hayes, S. F. (2001b). The social justice advocacy readiness questionnaire. *The Journal of Lesbian and Gay Social Services, 13*(1/2), 191-203.

James, S. E. and Murphy, B. C. (1998). Gay and lesbian relationships in a changing social context. In C. J. Patterson and A. R. D'Augelli (Eds.), *Lesbian, gay, and bisexual identities in families: Psychological perspectives* (pp. 99-121). New York: Oxford.

Laird, J. and Green, R.-J. (Eds.) (1996). *Lesbians and gays in couples and families: A handbook for therapists.* San Francisco, CA: Jossey-Bass.

Rust, P. (Ed.) (2000). *Bisexuality in the United States.* New York: Columbia University Press.

Bibliotherapy Sources for the Client

Beemyn, B. and Eliason, M. (Eds.) (1996). *Queer studies: A lesbian, gay, bisexual, and transgender anthology.* New York: New York University Press.

Califia, P. (1994). *Public sex: The culture of radical sex.* San Francisco, CA: Cleis.

Hutchins, L. and Kaahumanu, L. (Eds.) (1991). *Bi any other name: Bisexual people speak out.* Boston, MA: Alyson Publications.

Lorde, A. (1984). *Sister outsider.* Freedom, CA: The Crossing Press.

Pharr, S. (1988). *Homophobia: A weapon of sexism.* Inverness, CA: Chardon Press.

Pharr, S. (1996). *In the time of the right: Reflections on liberation*. Berkeley, CA: Chardon Press.

Queen, C. and Schimel, L. (Eds.) (1997). *Pomosexuals: Challenging assumptions about gender and sexuality*. San Francisco, CA: Cleis.

References

Beemyn, B. and Eliason, M. (Eds.) (1996). *Queer studies: A lesbian, gay, bisexual, and transgender anthology*. New York: New York University Press.

Califia, P. (1994). *Public sex: The culture of radical sex*. San Francisco, CA: Cleis.

Chen-Hayes, S. F. (2000). Social justice advocacy with lesbian, bisexual, gay, and trans-gendered persons. In J. Lewis and L. Bradley (Eds.), *Advocacy in counseling: Counselors, clients, and community* (pp. 89-98). Greensboro, NC: Caps Publications (ERIC/CASS).

Chen-Hayes, S. F. (2001a). Counseling and advocacy with transgendered and gender-variant persons in schools and families. *The Journal of Humanistic Counseling, Education, and Development, 40*(1), 34-48.

Chen-Hayes, S. F. (2001b). The social justice advocacy readiness questionnaire. *The Journal of Lesbian and Gay Social Services, 13*(1/2), 191-203.

James, S. E. and Murphy, B. C. (1998). Gay and lesbian relationships in a changing social context. In C. J. Patterson and A. R. D'Augelli (Eds.), *Lesbian, gay, and bisexual identities in families: Psychological perspectives* (pp. 99-121). New York: Oxford.

Lorde, A. (1984). *Sister outsider*. Freedom, CA: The Crossing Press.

Pharr, S. (1996). *In the time of the right: Reflections on liberation*. Berkeley, CA: Chardon Press.

Queen, C. and Schimel, L. (Eds.) (1997). *Pomosexual: Challenging assumptions about gender and sexuality*. San Francisco, CA: Cleis.

Rofes, E. (1995). *Reviving the tribe: Regenerating gay men's sexuality and culture in the on-going epidemic*. Binghamton, NY: The Haworth Press.

Rust, P. (Ed.) (2000). *Bisexuality in the United States*. New York: Columbia University Press.

Smith, A. (1997). Cultural diversity and the coming-out process: Implications for clinical practice. In B. Greene (Ed.), *Ethnic and cultural diversity among lesbians and gay men* (pp. 279-300). Thousand Oaks, CA: Sage Publications.

Sue, D. W. and Sue, D. (1999). *Counseling the culturally different* (Third edition). New York: Wiley.

Relationship Status Continuum

Create your own continuum of values and interests in terms of your relationships by rating the importance of each of these areas in your past, present, and future/ideal on a scale of 1 to 10 (1 = low, 10 = high). If you are coupled, each partner should do the same for himself or herself (or do a separate one for your ideal partner if you are single).

RELATIONSHIP STATUS	PAST	PRESENT	FUTURE/IDEAL
Single			
Dating			
Coupled, Closed Relationship			
Coupled, Open Relationship			
Multiple Partners			
Multiple Relationships			
Other: _____			

My Sexual Practices Continuum

Create your own continuum of values and interests in terms of your sexual practices by rating the importance of each of these areas in your past, present, and future/ideal on a scale of 1 to 10 (1 = low, 10 = high). If you are coupled, each partner should do the same for himself or herself (or do a separate one for your ideal partner if you are single).

MY SEXUAL PRACTICES	PAST	PRESENT	FUTURE/IDEAL
Celibacy			
Monogamy			
Serial Monogamy			
Fuckbuddy on the Side			
Three-Ways, Swapping, or Group Sex with Partner			
Nonmonogamy with One Person			
Nonmonogamy with More than One Person			
Vanilla Sex			
Kink			
A Combination of Vanilla Sex and Kink			
I **Always** Practice Safe Sex			
I **Sometimes** Practice Safe Sex			
I **Never** Practice Safe Sex			
Other: _____			

My Politics Continuum

Create your own continuum of values and interests in terms of your politics by rating the importance of each of these areas in your past, present, and future/ideal on a scale of 1 to 10 (1 = low, 10 = high). If you are coupled, each partner should do the same for himself or herself (or do a separate one for your ideal partner if you are single).

MY POLITICS	PAST	PRESENT	FUTURE/IDEAL
Conservative			
Libertarian			
Assimilationist			
Moderate			
Liberal			
Feminist/Womanist			
Progressive			
Liberationist			
Separatist			
Anarchist			
Apolitical			
Completely Closeted			
Out of the Closet to Friends			
Out of the Closet at Work			
Out of the Closet to Some Family of Origin			
Completely Out of the Closet			
Other: _____			

15

Financial Stability Within the Lesbian Relationship

Lisa A. Hollingsworth
Mary J. Didelot

Type of Contribution: Activity/Handout

Objective

This activity can be used successfully with lesbians who are entering into a new relationship or who are currently in one, as a clear prescription for financial balance and to understand the benefits of this balance within the relationship.

Rationale for Use

Many lesbian couples struggle with financial management and financial responsibility (Berzon, 1988). This struggle may result in anger, loss of trust, perceived loss of control, blame, and resentment within the relationship (Toder, 1992). Often, these are the consequence of one partner earning more money than the other. Thus, therapists can help couples with this struggle by helping them obtain financial balance.

History and experiential learning have taught lesbians that long-lasting relationships between women are, for the most part, unconfirmed (Berzon, 1988). This same history and learning has also taught them that the legalities and social acceptance that enhance the longevity of heterosexual unions are not available to their relationships. Thus, before the relationship is even initiated, it is in a precarious state. In addition, lesbian relationships are seen by society as non-procreative and exclusively sexual (Herek, 1998). This propels lesbian couples even further from the notion of "legitimate family" and a positive, healthy family environment. Exacerbating all of this is the "social invisibility [which] creates serious obstacles to forming crucial family boundaries" (Slater, 1995, p. 42). It is also significant to know that research has shown that "lesbians are more cautious, more afraid of getting ripped off, [and] less willing to trust in the durability of the relationship" (Toder, 1992, p. 55). The issue of family, therefore, is foundational to the financial challenges lesbians face.

Because this history and learning so profoundly affects lesbian relationships, there is a significant cultural difference between the lesbian and the heterosexual experience of family. Germane to this for heterosexuals are guidelines about responsibilities and expectations that are just not present for lesbians. This is particularly true in the arena of finances. In the heterosexual culture, a norm exists for the way money is shared within families. Society "prescribes the way men should relate to money—earn it, maintain control over its use . . ." (Berzon, 1988, p. 249). For lesbian couples, absolutely no social construct is available for them to follow. The singular existing gender-related financial paradigm is of no help whatsoever.

Financial management is complicated further by job discrimination against women (lesbians in particular) and common inequality in earnings (Toder, 1992). "When money is scarce, there is more stress on the relationship than when it is plentiful; the two partners are generally more tense about financial matters, and each partner, frustrated by not being able to do or buy the things she wants, tends to blame the other" (p. 54). When inequalities in earnings exist and are not addressed, the more affluent partner will likely become resentful, and the less affluent partner will gradually lose her self-esteem (Toder, 1992). This blame, frustration, and loss can then permeate every aspect of the relationship and severely weaken it.

With this intervention, the therapist may give guidelines to a lesbian couple while allowing for the couple's needs and the individuals' perceived or "felt" financial responsibilities within the relationship. Once these boundaries are fully explored and defined, they will become a sound foundation upon which the couple may build a relationship that is durable and trustworthy.

Instructions

At the conclusion of the intake session, the therapist should ask clients to bring the following to the next session: (1) all debits (bills) for the month; (2) all receipts of credits (income) for the month; and (3) individual, realistic estimates of the amount of money spent on leisure activities. If the clients do not currently share expenses, then each should bring in her own debit and credit receipts. If they do share expenses, then the collective debit and credit receipts should be brought to the next session. The following is a sample dialogue:

> It is extremely important for you to know that financial imbalance within lesbian relationships is a symptom of how we are taught by society to see our relationships. We are constantly given the message that our relationships are not real or valid—that they have no durability. I define "durability" as the capacity to withstand the day-to-day problems that occur in any relationship. Underlying any relationship, but especially lesbian relationships, is the management of finances in a logical and fair fashion. No one wants to be the partner paying for everything, or the partner who is never able to pay for anything. We can reach a state of balance of responsibilities, even though one of you may earn significantly more than the other, or one of you may have more bills than the other. The harm to the relationship comes from not addressing finances, not exploring financial responsibilities using a plan that can work, and not working together on your financial future. I am not a financial consultant, but I can help you to look critically at your situation and help you to create some guidelines for setting realistic responsibilities within your relationship. We cannot do this, however, unless each of you is willing to fully participate in this from the first activity to the last. This certainly means a willingness to bring in all your bills and discuss your income. This show of willingness also tells me that you are ready to work to strengthen and validate your relationship.

At the next session, the therapist should go through the couple's current finances and the financial structure they are using. The Discovery and Disclosure chart should be used.

This activity in itself will allow for complete disclosure and the "reality" of the current financial status of the couple and the individual. This will also clearly draw the difference between the perceived financial contributions to the relationship and the actual contribution each client is making to the financial foundation of the relationship. Thus, a foundation for truth and trust within the relationship will begin to be established.

As the therapist leads the clients through this session, and subsequent sessions if necessary, the therapist should continue to express encouragement emphasizing the strength this activity is bringing to the relationship.

Once the chart is completed, the next session should be dedicated to ways in which the couple can manage their finances. The following is a list of possible systems. It is not exhaustive so as not to exclude any different system or combination of systems that make the process comfortable for the clients. The system(s) chosen may be used with a biweekly or monthly rotation. The Systems for Payment are as follows:

1. Completely share all financial responsibilities (50 percent/50 percent). This is particularly useful when both partners earn approximately the same salary.
2. Individual financial responsibility for particular expenses (100 percent or 0 percent). This arrangement works well when one or both partners have accumulated significant individual debt.
3. Assigned percentage to each financial responsibility (0 percent through 100 percent). If there is a disparity between the income of one partner and the income of the other, this system provides an equitable balance that significantly supports the self-esteem of the lower-wage earner.
4. Any combination of the above.

The therapist should then give a sample similar to the following, which is based on a monthly schedule:

Source of Debt	Monthly Payment	Partner #1's Contribution	Partner #2's Contribution
Rent	$1,200	$600 (50%)	$600 (50%)
Water	$30	$3 (10%)	$27 (90%)
Food	$350	$105 (30%)	$245 (70%)
Credit Card	$159	$0 (0%)	$159 (100%)

Once the clients understand the concept, the therapist should again make references to the strength this equitable financial relationship will bring to their relationship. Also, the therapist should comment on how this will ameliorate blame and loss of self-esteem.

The therapist should then lead the couple in a discussion of which System for Payment will be most functional and comfortable for their relationship. After both agree to the system, their own financial chart should be completed and signed by each partner. A signature is symbolic of not only the importance of agreeing to this method but a willingness to adhere to the plan. The therapist should keep a copy of the chart in the couple's file. This act, too, will reinforce commitment to the plan. The therapist should also emphasize that this budget should be visibly posted within the home, and be present when the couple is paying bills. Since this is a couple's project, the therapist should remind the clients that paying bills is an integral part of their partnership, therefore it should be a couple's activity. It should not be one person's responsibility.

Suggestions for Follow-Up

At the conclusion of the final session, the therapist should immediately schedule a follow-up appointment for the couple to discuss the benefits of the plan and if any changes need to be made to accommodate unforeseen circumstances. This appointment should be scheduled for a few days after payday to allow the couple an opportunity to use the paradigm.

Follow-up questions may include:

1. Why do you think the system you have chosen is the best one for the relationship, as opposed to the other possible choices?

2. How does this system feel to each of you? Is it comfortable? Is it realistic for your relationship? Do you foresee any problems or challenges?
3. Let's discuss and review what your new role in the relationship will be once this system is implemented.

Contraindications

First and foremost, both partners must be willing to participate in this activity and to commit to the boundaries set by it. If there is a lack of willingness and commitment by either person, the system will fail.

Complete disclosure of each partner's financial obligations is central to the success of this intervention. If either partner refuses to disclose a debit or is embarrassed to disclose a debit, the system is rendered useless. Therefore, it is extremely important for the therapist to address any blame or hurtful feelings with immediacy as soon as those feelings are expressed, for this intervention to be successful. If, during this segment of the discussion, underlying issues surface, be well aware that these issues must be addressed first before the couple can make healthy financial decisions.

Readings and Resources for the Professional

Hertz, F. and Browning, F. (1998). *Legal affairs: Essential advice for same-sex couples*. New York: Owl Books.
Lustig, H. (1999). *4 steps to financial security for lesbian and gay couples*. New York: Fawcett Books.

Bibliotherapy Sources for the Client

Hertz, F. and Browning, F. (1998). *Legal affairs: Essential advice for same-sex couples*. New York: Owl Books.
Hughes, T. and Klein, D. (1999). *Protecting your money*. St. Paul, MN: Consortium Book Sales and Distribution.
Lustig, H. (1999). *4 steps to financial security for lesbian and gay couples*. New York: Fawcett Books.

References

Berzon, B. (1988). *Permanent partners: Building gay and lesbian relationships that last*. New York: Plume.
Herek, G. M. (1998). *Stigma and sexual orientation: Understanding prejudice against lesbians, gay men, and bisexuals*. Thousand Oaks, CA: Sage Publications.
Slater, S. (1995). *The lesbian family life cycle*. New York: The Free Press.
Toder, N. (1992). Lesbian couples in particular. In B. Berzon (Ed.), *Positively gay* (pp. 50-63). Berkeley, CA: Celestial Arts Publishing.

Discovery and Disclosure Chart

Source of Debt	Monthly Payment	Partner #1's Contribution	Partner #2's Contribution

16

Choosing a Partner

Lisa A. Hollingsworth
Mary J. Didelot

Type of Contribution: Activity/Homework

Objective

This activity will help newly out gay, lesbian, or bisexual (GLB) individuals, or those who have difficulty choosing healthy and lasting partnerships, to carefully weigh the characteristics they deem significant in a partner.

Rationale for Use

Choosing a partner can be a difficult process for GLB clients. Newly out persons, whether adolescents or adults, may feel overwhelmed, scared, and/or like kids in a candy store (Berzon, 1997). As a result, they may make poor or impulsive choices in selecting a partner. Often, they can benefit from slowing down and thinking through what they find important in a partner and in a relationship.

Instructions

The following worksheet may be utilized to help GLB individuals think through the characteristics they desire in a partner. The worksheet may be completed as a homework assignment or in session. In both approaches, the worksheet provides an avenue for initiating dialogue concerning the following: (1) which characteristics are significant in the choice of a partner, (2) which characteristics are less significant in the choice of a partner, and (3) which characteristics would greatly impede the success of a relationship. Clients can also begin to consider whether they are narrowing their scope of choices too much or if they are not making healthy choices.

Suggestions for Follow-Up

Whether filled out in session or as a homework assignment, the worksheet should be discussed thoroughly in session. It is in talking through the characteristics that clients can clarify their needs in a relationship and/or discover unhealthy patterns in their choice of partners. In addition, this worksheet can be revisited in successive sessions. Some examples of follow-up questions may include the following:

1. From the guide, do you see any patterns emerging from your answers? Or are there any characteristics that stand out for you?

2. What do these patterns or significant characteristics mean for you? What do they indicate about you?
3. If you have had previous relationships, how did these characteristics apply to those relationships?
4. From these characteristics, let's formulate a description of a person who would provide a healthy relationship for you.
5. Sometimes we all get confused about what we *want* in a relationship and what we *need*. Let's go back to that description and underline the needs. This way, we can narrow your focus to those characteristics you find essential in a partner.

Contraindications

If clients have never been in a relationship, the therapist will need to assist them in making realistic evaluations of their wants and needs in desired relationships (e.g., fantasy versus reality).

Readings and Resources for the Professional

Berzon, B. (1990). *Permanent partners: Building gay and lesbian relationships that last.* New York: Dutton/Plume.
Berzon, B. (1997). *The intimacy dance: A guide to long-term success in gay and lesbian relationships.* New York: Dutton/Plume.

Bibliotherapy Sources for the Client

Berzon, B. (1997). *The intimacy dance: A guide to long-term success in gay and lesbian relationships.* New York: Dutton/Plume.
Martinac, P. and Achtenberg, R. (1998). *The lesbian and gay book of love and marriage: Creating the stories of our lives.* New York: Broadway Books.

Reference

Berzon, B. (1997). *The intimacy dance: A guide to long-term success in gay and lesbian relationships.* New York: Dutton/Plume.

Choosing a Partner

Characteristics	Not Important				Very Important
Degree of "outness" *I want someone who is completely "out" (e.g., to family, friends, co-workers, etc.)*	1	2	3	4	5
Involvement in the GLB community *I want someone who enthusiastically participates in activities in the GLB community.*	1	2	3	4	5
Political activity *I want someone who is politically assertive in furthering GLB rights.*	1	2	3	4	5
Outgoing *I want someone who is very sociable.*	1	2	3	4	5
Sense of humor *I want someone who has a good sense of humor and likes to laugh.*	1	2	3	4	5
Monogamy *I want someone who will be absolutely monogamous.*	1	2	3	4	5
Long-term relationship *I want someone who desires a long-term, committed relationship.*	1	2	3	4	5
Type of employment *I want someone who is employed as a professional.*	1	2	3	4	5
Financial stability *I want someone who lives within his or her financial means.*	1	2	3	4	5
Financial management *I want someone who maintains his or her own finances.*	1	2	3	4	5
Physical appearance *I want someone who is physically attractive and fit.*	1	2	3	4	5
Dress *I want someone who dresses in a way I find appealing.*	1	2	3	4	5
Interested in same activities/hobbies *I want someone who is interested in participating in the same activities I do.*	1	2	3	4	5
Intimate/affectionate *I want someone who is not afraid to demonstrate his or her feelings for me physically and emotionally.*	1	2	3	4	5
Sexual attraction *I want someone who is sexually appealing and who is sexually attracted to me.*	1	2	3	4	5

Sexual behavior/interests

I want someone who is willing to explore different sexual possibilities.

| 1 | 2 | 3 | 4 | 5 |

Comfort with sexuality

I want someone who is secure in his or her sexual orientation.

| 1 | 2 | 3 | 4 | 5 |

Masculinity/Femininity

I want someone who is . . . (e.g., butch, fem, etc.).

| 1 | 2 | 3 | 4 | 5 |

Children

I want someone who wants children.

| 1 | 2 | 3 | 4 | 5 |

Living arrangements

I want someone who maintains his or her own residence.

| 1 | 2 | 3 | 4 | 5 |

Drinking

I want someone who does not drink alcohol.

| 1 | 2 | 3 | 4 | 5 |

Drug use

I want someone who does not use drugs.

| 1 | 2 | 3 | 4 | 5 |

_____

| 1 | 2 | 3 | 4 | 5 |

_____

| 1 | 2 | 3 | 4 | 5 |

_____

| 1 | 2 | 3 | 4 | 5 |

_____

| 1 | 2 | 3 | 4 | 5 |

17

Creating a Cultural and Sexual Genogram

Sheila M. Addison
Melody M. Brown

Type of Contribution: Activity

Objectives

This activity can be used with both same-race and mixed-race couples as an aid to understanding each partner's experience of culture and sexuality in her or his family. The objectives are as follows:

- To gain greater insight into each partner's family and culture of origin
- To increase the clients' and the therapist's understanding of how ethnic and sexual identities influence the couple
- To increase mutual trust and sensitivity by sharing a detailed look at each partner's family genogram

Rationale for Use

Race and sexual identity are both taboo topics in American culture; they are difficult to discuss and fraught with anxiety (Green, 1997). As a subsystem within the culture, a therapeutic relationship is not immune to these tensions. Although minority clients and therapists cannot escape the reality of the ways in which their racial identity influences their relationships, white clients and therapists frequently have difficulty seeing themselves as even having a race (McIntosh, 1998). Too often, well-meaning members of the majority culture endorse the idea of being "color-blind" as a means of reducing tension around race.

However, as J. E. Hardy (1997) writes,

> "I don't see color," some whites argue. Yeah, right. You will admire a blue sky, a burnt-orange sun, and a red rose but refuse to even *see* my brown skin? People who say they are color-blind are just blind. Acknowledge and appreciate all I am—just don't hold it against me. (p. 262)

Clearly, trying to see past race can feel similar to a kind of oppression, despite benign intentions. Therapists and clients, particularly mixed-race couples, must find ways to talk about racial and cultural differences openly; if those differences are not acknowledged and treated with respect, one or both of the partners may feel devalued or not fully accepted in either the therapeutic or the couple relationship, or in both.

Similarly, trying to ignore issues concerning sexual identity can also be hurtful. Therapists who assume that gay, lesbian, bisexual, and transgendered (GLBT) clients are more or less the same as heterosexual clients are also exhibiting a kind of blindness (Hardy, 1989). Even GLBT clients are not immune to this mistake. The same-sex couple that does not deal with the ways in which sexual identity influences them as individuals and as a couple effectively cut themselves off from a painful but potentially rich source of insight into their relationship (Brown, 1995).

Hardy and Laszloffy (1995) developed the cultural genogram activity to be used as a training tool for therapists. The scope of Hardy and Laszloffy's work has been expanded to include an in-depth look at sexuality and sexual identity, and to serve as a means to help clients think critically about how their culture and sexual identity coalesce to inform their overall identity.

For mixed-race couples, this activity gives partners the opportunity to have an in-depth look at those cultural and sexual identity characteristics that are distinctly different from their own. For same-race couples, partners can see how the culture and sexual orientation they share influence them differently. All couples can gain understanding of how their family and culture of origin influenced the development of their sexual identity and their beliefs about sexuality.

Materials

Markers, multicolored pens, and/or multicolored chalk are needed, as well as a large pad of newsprint/sketch paper or a large wipe-off board.

Instructions

In order to fully understand this exercise, therapists should familiarize themselves with the article, "The Cultural Genogram: Key to Training Culturally Competent Family Therapists" (Hardy and Laszloffy, 1995). Suggest to clients that you would like to spend time, perhaps a session for each of them, creating a genogram that will include information about cultural and sexual values in each partner's family of origin. Explain to them that you believe insight into these aspects of identity will help you as the therapist understand them better as individuals, and that you hope it will also create the opportunity for more intimacy and closeness between them as a couple as they come to know each other's history in greater detail.

Work with one client at a time, encouraging the other partner to serve as a witness to his or her partner's genogram. It will take at least one session for each genogram; you may want to schedule a slightly longer session if possible. Following the procedure for investigating and documenting cultural issues on the genogram from the Hardy and Laszloffy article, construct a three-generation genogram for one of the partners on a wipe-off board or a large drawing pad. Couples may want to take the completed genogram home, so working on paper would be ideal.

Complete the cultural genogram by following Hardy and Laszloffy's list of questions about cultural identity issues, omitting the question referring to sexual identity, as this topic will be covered in the next part of the genogram. Then proceed to the following list of questions using the same procedure for investigating and documenting sexual identity issues as you did for cultural identity issues.

- What were your family values about sexual behavior and sexual identity? Consider such topics as sex education (formal or informal), dating, marriage (including age at marriage), having children (including age at childbearing and number of children), puberty/sexual maturity, premarital sexual activity, extramarital sexual activity, different types of sexual expression, gender and sexuality, HIV/AIDS, unplanned pregnancy, contraception/abortion, civil rights for GLBT people, etc.
- Who communicated this information or these values?

- What messages did the other members of your family give you, even if they were not obvious at the time?
- Who agreed and disagreed with the "prevailing wisdom" in the family about sexual values?
- Do you know of any other GLBT people in your family? If you do, at what stage of your life did you find out about their sexual identity?
- How has their presence, or the lack thereof, influenced your development as a GLBT person?
- What were your community's values (ethnic, racial, religious, etc.) about sexual behavior and sexual identity? Consider similar topics as in the first question.
- Who in your community communicated this information or these values to you most clearly? What messages did the other members of your community give you, even if they were not obvious at the time?
- Who agreed and disagreed with the "prevailing wisdom" in the community about sexual values?
- Do you know of any other GLBT people in your community? If you do, at what stage of your life did you find out about their sexual identity?
- How has their presence, or the lack thereof, influenced your development as a GLBT person in your community?
- What are the pride or shame issues specifically related to sexuality in your family and/or community?
- What values and pride or shame issues have you kept from your family and culture(s) of origin? What values and issues have you chosen to change or discard?
- Who in your family and/or community have you come out to? In what order did you come out to other people? How did you make the decision to come out to each person or group—or was that decision made for you in some circumstances?
- Who is most supportive of your sexual identity in your family? In your community? Who is least supportive?
- How has coming out influenced your relationship with your family? With your community?
- Who knows about your relationship with your partner? Who is most supportive? Least supportive?
- How do the supportive or unsupportive people in your family and community feel about your partner's cultural identity(ies)?
- How has your culture influenced how you express your sexual orientation?
- How has your sexual identity influenced how you express facets of your culture?

Using these questions, fill in the sexual identity information on the genogram, and combine it with the information you have already gathered. Review the cultural identity genograms, and ask the clients how they think their sexual identity information should be represented on the genogram. In completing the sexual identity portion, encourage them to use creative indicators that will stand out for them just as they did in the cultural identity portion (e.g., their favorite colors or favorite shapes) to demarcate those who have been influential in their sexual identity. For example, represent an openly gay uncle by drawing a rainbow next to his representation on the genogram. For former lovers or friends who are not related but who were influential, draw a shape and color that best fits that individual. Clients can also alternatively choose one shape and color that will collectively represent people who were instrumental in their sexual identity development.

Suggestions for Follow-Up

Process the experience with the couple once the genograms have been completed. Ask them questions such as:

- What was this like for you?
- How do you see yourselves or your families differently now that you have completed the genogram?
- What have you learned about your partner?
- What are your thoughts and feelings on the intersection of your culture and your sexual identity?
- How can you use what you have learned about yourselves and each other to better your relationship?

Encourage the couple to continue learning about each other's diversity both culturally and in sexual identity. Reiterate the importance of acceptance and valuing each other as necessary tools to maintaining the couple relationship.

Contraindications

This activity is intensive and time-consuming, usually taking several sessions; therefore, it should not be used when couples are in active crisis and may need to use session time for more immediate interventions. Highly conflictual or previously violent couples should have reached a point in therapy at which they can tolerate disagreement or anxiety without acting out against each other before this activity is used.

The therapist should be prepared to deal with questions and comments about her or his cultural identity as a possible result of this process. The therapist should also be comfortable with talking about and owning his or her areas of privilege (e.g., race, class, gender, religion) in order to be able to handle questions and challenges in a therapeutic manner (McIntosh, 1998).

Readings and Resources for the Professional

Brown, L. S. (1995). Therapy with same-sex couples: An introduction. In N. S. Jacobson and A. S. Gurman (Eds.), *Clinical handbook of couple therapy* (pp. 274-291). New York: Guilford Publications.

Fukuyama, M. A. and Ferguson, A. D. (2000). Lesbian, gay, and bisexual people of color: Understanding cultural complexity and managing multiple oppressions. In R. M. Perez and K. A. DeBord (Eds.), *Handbook of counseling and psychotherapy with lesbian, gay, and bisexual clients* (pp. 81-105). Washington, DC: American Psychological Association.

Green, B. (1997). *Ethnic and cultural diversity among lesbians and gay men.* Thousand Oaks, CA: Sage Publications.

Hardy, J. E. (1997). The river of de-Nile. In M. Lowenthal (Ed.), *Gay men at the millennium: Sex, spirit, community* (pp. 260-262). New York: Jeremy P. Tarcher.

Hardy, K. V. (1989). The theoretical myth of sameness: A critical issue in family therapy training and treatment. *Journal of Psychotherapy and the Family, 6,* 17-33.

Hardy, K. V. and Laszloffy, T. A. (1995). The cultural genogram: Key to training culturally competent family therapists. *Journal of Marital and Family Therapy, 21,* 227-237.

McIntosh, P. (1998). White privilege: Unpacking the invisible knapsack. In M. McGoldrick (Ed.), *Re-visioning family therapy: Race, culture and gender in clinical practice* (pp. 147-152). New York: Guilford Publications.

Bibliotherapy Sources for the Client

Berzon, B. (1990). *Permanent partners: Building gay and lesbian relationships that last.* New York: Dutton/Plume.

Green, B. (1997). *Ethnic and cultural diversity among lesbians and gay men.* Thousand Oaks, CA: Sage Publications.

McIntosh, P. (1998). White privilege: Unpacking the invisible knapsack. In M. McGoldrick (Ed.), *Re-visioning family therapy: Race, culture and gender in clinical practice* (pp. 147-152). New York: Guilford Publications.

Williams, W. L. (1999). *The spirit and the flesh: Sexual diversity in American Indian culture.* Boston, MA: Beacon Press.

References

Brown, L. S. (1995). Therapy with same-sex couples: An introduction. In N. S. Jacobson and A. S. Gurman (Eds.), *Clinical handbook of couple therapy* (pp. 274-291). New York: Guilford Publications.

Green, B. (1997). *Ethnic and cultural diversity among lesbians and gay men.* Thousand Oaks, CA: Sage Publications.

Hardy, J. E. (1997). The river of de-Nile. In M. Lowenthal (Ed.), *Gay men at the millennium: Sex, spirit, community* (pp. 260-262). New York: Jeremy P. Tarcher.

Hardy, K. V. (1989). The theoretical myth of sameness: A critical issue in family therapy training and treatment. *Journal of Psychotherapy and the Family, 6,* 17-33.

Hardy, K. V. and Laszloffy, T. A. (1995). The cultural genogram: Key to training culturally competent family therapists. *Journal of Marital and Family Therapy, 21,* 227-237.

McIntosh, P. (1998). White privilege: Unpacking the invisible knapsack. In M. McGoldrick (Ed.), *Re-visioning family therapy: Race, culture and gender in clinical practice* (pp. 147-152). New York: Guilford Publications.

18

Knowing You, Knowing Me:
Sexual Identity and the Couple

Melody M. Brown
Sheila M. Addison

Type of Contribution: Activity

Objective

This activity is intended to highlight and reinforce positive aspects of the couple relationship.

Rationale for Use

Couples, regardless of their sexual orientation, are often so entrenched in the negative patterns in their relationship that it is difficult to see those aspects of the relationship that are valued. Particularly with same-sex couples, outside influences such as discrimination, oppression, and marginalization place an extra burden on existing relationship issues. Couples may find it difficult or impossible to successfully deal with those relationship issues along with those society imposes upon them (Berzon, 1990; DiPlacido, 1998; Morales, 1989).

The therapist can be supportive to a same-sex couple in ways society is not by encouraging them to talk openly about the dynamics of the relationship that they appreciate and value. Encouraging the couple to think this way helps them revisit the "good times" in their relationship so they can reconnect with and utilize the aspects of their partnership that worked for them (O'Hanlon Hudson and Hudson O'Hanlon, 1994; O'Hanlon and Hudson, 1996). Successfully negotiating their relationship and building a stronger bond increases the couple's resiliency in the face of an oppressive society.

Materials

Index cards.

Instructions

Write or type questions on index cards for the clients to take home as an assignment. One question per card is recommended. Since this is a take-home exercise that may be used simultaneously with more than one couple in your client caseload, you may need to have several copies of the cards available. Use the following questions:

- What do you appreciate most about your relationship?
- What was the most enjoyable experience you have ever had with your partner?
- What was the most difficult experience you have ever had with your partner?

- How did you manage to get through your first major trial together?
- What qualities do you bring to the relationship that are helpful? What qualities do you bring that are harmful?
- What do you admire most about your partner?
- Are society's heterosexist values harmful to you? How?
- What attracted you to your partner?
- Pretend you are a poet or a songwriter (you may actually possess this gift). What would you sing or write about with your partner in mind?
- What qualities about your partner have you discovered recently that you find appealing?
- What do you admire about the way your partner expresses her or his gender identity?
- What have you learned from your partner about expressing gender identity?
- How has your partner influenced the way you express your own gender identity?

Use this activity as a game that will help clients "get down to the good stuff" in their relationship. It should be introduced at the end of a session, allowing enough time for instructions and questions. Tell clients the activity is a way for you to learn more about them because you will process the experience with them during their next visit. Spend time addressing their concerns and questions regarding this activity. Be specific about the rules. Some clients may become anxious about the posture they are to assume during the game. Encourage them to make the setting as comfortable as possible, yet maintain a "barrier-free" closeness. You want them to experience the intensity of intimacy even before the game begins. Place the cards in a sealed envelope and instruct the couple not to open it until they are ready to play the game. Give the envelope to the less assertive partner and encourage the couple to set a time to play before leaving the session. The partner who has been given the envelope is to initiate the game at the designated time.

Rules

- The couple should sit facing each other—no barriers, table, etc.
- The partners should take turns picking a card from the stack of preprinted cards placed between them.
- Each partner must answer the question. The partner who picks the card answers first.
- The couple should talk to each other when answering the question. Eye contact is important.
- Only one person speaks at a time.

Suggestions for Follow-Up

Process the experience with the couple during the next session. Ask questions such as:

- What was it like?
- What did you find easy or difficult about the game?
- How do you make sense of the ease or difficulty?
- If you were to play the game again, what questions would you include that had not already been covered?
- What did you learn about yourselves through playing this game?
- What did you learn about your partner?
- How were you different or the same with each other after playing the game?

Encourage the couple to brainstorm about creative ways to foster and maintain the closeness they are building even during times when external familial or societal pressures are overwhelming. Stress the importance of taking care of themselves as individuals and then taking care of the relationship.

Contraindications

This activity is designed for clients who are near the completion of their therapeutic work. It is intended to assist them in maintaining a high level of intimacy once therapy has ended. Therefore, this activity may not be useful for clients who have not successfully worked through presenting problems. Introducing this exercise too soon could exacerbate conflict in the relationship by allowing clients to use the game to focus on the problem rather than the valued attributes of the relationship.

Readings and Resources for the Professional

Abelove, H., Aina Barale, M., and Halperin, D. M. (Eds.) (1996). *The lesbian and gay studies reader.* New York: Routledge.

Berzon, B. (1990). *Permanent partners: Building gay and lesbian relationships that last.* New York: Dutton/Plume.

Carrington, C. (1999). *No place like home: Relationships and family life among lesbians and gay men.* Chicago, IL: University of Chicago Press.

DiPlacido, J. (1998). Minority stress among lesbians, gay men, and bisexuals: A consequence of heterosexism, homophobia, and stigmatization. In G. Herek (Ed.), *Stigma and sexual orientation: Understanding prejudice against lesbians, gay men, and bisexuals* (pp. 138-186). Thousand Oaks, CA: Sage Publications.

Esterberg, K. (1997). *Lesbian and bisexual identities: Constructing communities, constructing selves.* Philadelphia, PA: Temple University Press.

Firestein, B. A. (Ed.) (1996). *Bisexuality and the psychology of politics of an invisible minority.* Thousand Oaks, CA: Sage Publications.

Jagose, A. (1997). *Queer theory.* New York: New York University Press.

Marcus, E. (1999). *Together forever: Gay and lesbian couples share their secrets for lasting happiness.* New York: Bantam Books, Inc.

Morales, E. S. (1989). Ethnic minority families and minority gays and lesbians. *Marriage and Family Review, 14,* 217-239.

O'Hanlon, B. and Hudson, P. (1996). *Stop blaming, start loving! A solution-oriented approach to improving your relationship.* New York: W. W. Norton and Company.

O'Hanlon Hudson, P. and Hudson O'Hanlon, W. (1994). *Rewriting love stories: Brief marital therapy.* New York: W. W. Norton and Company.

Bibliotherapy Sources for the Client

Berzon, B. (1990). *Permanent partners: Building gay and lesbian relationships that last.* New York: Dutton/Plume.

Berzon, B. (1997). *The intimacy dance: A guide to long-term success in gay and lesbian relationships.* New York: Dutton/Plume.

Carrington, C. (1999). *No place like home: Relationships and family life among lesbians and gay men.* Chicago, IL: University of Chicago Press.

Driggs, J. H. and Finn, S. E. (1997). *Intimacy between men: How to find and keep gay love relationships.* New York: Dutton/Plume.

Esterberg, K. (1997). *Lesbian and bisexual identities: Constructing communities, constructing selves.* Philadelphia, PA: Temple University Press.

Marcus, E. (1999). *Together forever: Gay and lesbian couples share their secrets for lasting happiness*. New York: Bantam Books, Inc.

Strongheart, A. A. S. (1997). The power to choose: We're here, we're queer, and we want to get hitched. In R. F. Goss and A. A. S. Strongheart (Eds.), *Our families, our values: Snapshots of queer kinship* (pp. 79-96). Binghamton, NY: The Haworth Press.

Sweet, M. J. (1997). Together on the path: Gay relationships in a Buddhist context. In R. F. Goss and A. A. S. Strongheart (Eds.), *Our families, our values: Snapshots of queer kinship* (pp. 115-127). Binghamton, NY: The Haworth Press.

References

Berzon, B. (1990). *Permanent partners: Building gay and lesbian relationships that last*. New York: Dutton/Plume.

DiPlacido, J. (1998). Minority stress among lesbians, gay men, and bisexuals: A consequence of heterosexism, homophobia, and stigmatization. In G. Herek (Ed.), *Stigma and sexual orientation: Understanding prejudice against lesbians, gay men, and bisexuals* (pp. 138-186). Thousand Oaks, CA: Sage Publications.

Morales, E. S. (1989). Ethnic minority families and minority gays and lesbians. *Marriage and Family Review, 14,* 217-239.

O'Hanlon, B. and Hudson, P. (1996). *Stop blaming, start loving! A solution-oriented approach to improving your relationship*. New York: W. W. Norton and Company.

O'Hanlon Hudson, P. and Hudson O'Hanlon, W. (1994). *Rewriting love stories: Brief marital therapy*. New York: W. W. Norton and Company.

19

Working with Couples on Ethnicity and Sexual Identity: The "Parts" Interview

Sheila M. Addison
Melody M. Brown

Type of Contribution: Activity

Objectives

This activity is intended to promote insight into the ways that sexual identity and ethnicity inform both partners in a couple. The objectives follow:

- Each partner will explore the ways his or her cultural identity and sexual identity affects him or her as an individual and in a relationship.
- Each partner will have the opportunity to listen and to reflect upon his or her partner's "story" of identity and the struggles that may occur between different aspects of that identity.
- The couple will have a dialogue about the previously unexplored effects of their different cultural identities on the relationship.
- The therapist will gain a greater understanding of how each partner experiences living as a member of a sexual minority, and how that identity interacts with his or her ethnic identity.

Rationale for Use

Ethnicity is a subject that many gay, lesbian, bisexual, and transgendered (GLBT) people, including therapists, are inexperienced at discussing. It is frequently considered impolite, awkward, and even threatening to comment on race directly. It is also difficult for white people to acknowledge the privilege that they receive due to their race, and thus validate the ways in which a partner of another race struggles against prejudice, discrimination, and oppression (Cerbone, 1997; Greene, 1997). Audre Lorde (1984) writes:

> Somewhere on the edge of consciousness, there is what I call a *mythical norm,* which each one of us within our hearts knows "that is not me." In America, this norm is usually defined as white, thin, male, young, heterosexual, Christian, and financially secure. It is with this mythical norm that the trappings of power reside in this society. Those of us who stand outside that power often identify one way in which we are different, and we assume that to be the primary cause of all oppression, forgetting other distortions around difference, some of which we ourselves may be practicing. (p. 116)

Especially in mixed-race relationships, partners may find themselves perpetuating a silent agreement not to talk about race and privilege. This can leave one or both partners feeling confused, frustrated, alienated, and angry. Couples may not recognize the ways in which their different cultural backgrounds influence their values and beliefs, which can lead to difficulties in resolving conflicts. Because it is impossible to escape the organizing principle of ethnicity, having a GLBT identity may be different for individuals from different cultures (Greene, 1997; Greene and Boyd-Franklin, 1996; Liu and Chan, 1996; Morales, 1996; Smith, 1997), leading to struggles over identity as individuals and as a couple. Finally, one or both partners may unwittingly be a source of oppression in the relationship based on unspoken power hierarchies that include race.

Schwartz's (1995) work with internal family systems and the hidden conversations that take place among a person's different "parts" provides a model for exploring the multiplicity of identities that queer people of color must balance. When working with a minority or mixed-race couple, it can be helpful to examine how each partner's sexual identity part(s) and ethnic identity part(s) interact and influence the couple relationship.

Instructions

Before undertaking this activity, the therapist should familiarize himself or herself with the core concepts of internal family systems theory (see Readings and Resources for the Professional).

Explain to clients that the purpose of this activity is to give both clients and therapist a clearer sense of how their sexual identity and ethnicity/cultural "parts" influence them. In particular, the focus is on how these pieces interact, how they may conflict with each other, and how they may work together as well. Explain that a person's parts can work similar to a family, where some people team up, some people do not get along, and everybody may struggle to get attention and power.

Begin with one of the partners. Ask the client to describe a time when she or he felt the influence of her or his ethnicity part very strongly. Inquire what this part wanted, how it went about trying to get what it wanted, and what messages it gave her or him to try to influence his or her behavior. If the client drew a cartoon of himself or herself talking to the ethnicity part, what would go in her or his word balloon? What would go in the part's word balloon? Who does this part remind her or him of? Find out what she or he likes about this part, and what she or he dislikes about it. What are the part's strengths and weaknesses? When is it most and least helpful? How does this part experience the relationship? How does it experience the world at large?

The therapist may also want to find out whether the client could come up with a visual image of the part or even a name for that part. After the first partner has developed a clear sense of how his or her ethnicity part works in his or her life, do the same with the other partner. The therapist should be aware that this conversation may be difficult for white clients, who typically have the privilege of not thinking consciously about ethnicity with regard to their own lives. The therapist should remain curious and encouraging; in a mixed-race couple, it may be helpful to begin with the minority partner, so she or he can model a discussion of ethnicity for the other partner.

Then the therapist should inquire about the first partner's sexual identity part, using similar questions. Once a clear picture of each client's sexual identity part has emerged, find out how the ethnicity and sexual identity parts interact. Do they get along? Do they like or dislike or just tolerate each other? When do they work as a team and when do they fight? What does the client do when the parts have conflicting needs and desires? How do the parts decide which one gets to lead at any given time? What is that like? Is one part jealous of how the other one is treated in some contexts? Do the parts have any empathy for each other's experiences? Finally, the therapist should investigate the same questions with the second partner.

Once each partner has had the chance to discuss his or her ethnicity and sexual identity parts, the therapist can expand the discussion to include both partners. One partner could have a conversation with the other partner's ethnicity part or sexual identity part and vice versa, with the second partner role-playing what her or his identified part would like to say to the other partner. Partners could also each role-play a single part and then have a conversation.

The therapist can encourage dialogue about such questions as: How does one partner's ethnicity part experience the other partner (for example, in conflict, in everyday life, in sexual situations, in discussions about money, when in a mostly gay or mostly heterosexual setting), and vice versa? Are there issues or struggles in which one or both partners are leading with a single part and ignoring other parts? What is it like for a part to feel ignored, misunderstood, or disliked by the other partner? How can one partner send loving and caring messages to all the hidden parts of the other partner? What can the couple do when one or both partners are struggling to reconcile different desires of their different parts? What should the couple do when one partner experiences oppression from the other partner around her or his ethnicity, sexual identity, or other part?

Suggestions for Follow-Up

As the couple continues to work in therapy, remind them to be attentive to each of their parts and how parts are influencing the relationship dynamic in and out of sessions. Encourage clients to speak about struggles they may have between their different parts, and to identify when one part has a too loud voice and is overshadowing the voices of other parts. Encourage them to confront oppressive forces in and out of the relationship together, and to develop solutions for improvement as a couple, rather than working as individuals or fighting against each other, so that each partner's parts feel honored and respected.

Contraindications

Partners in extreme conflict or with a risk of violence may experience too much anxiety to use this activity safely in therapy.

If one or both partners are very defensive about either or both identity parts (for example, a lesbian partner who refuses to acknowledge she is privileged within the lesbian community over her bisexual partner, or a white partner who insists that his Latino partner is overreacting about his perceptions of racism), it may be preferable to introduce this topic with individual or joint therapeutic conversations rather than this kind of activity.

If the therapist has not acknowledged or accepted the ways in which she or he is privileged around aspects of identity, this work should be done prior to attempting this kind of activity with clients (Laszloffy and Hardy, 2000; McIntosh, 1998).

Readings and Resources for the Professional

Breunlin, D. C., Schwartz, R. C., and MacKune-Karrer, B. (1992). Of mind and self: The internal family systems metaframework. In D. C. Breunlin, R. C. Schwartz, and B. MacKune-Karrer, B. (Eds.), *Metaframeworks: Transcending the models of family therapy* (pp. 57-89). San Francisco, CA: Jossey-Bass Publishers.

Cerbone, A. R. (1997). Symbol of privilege, object of derision: Dissonance and contradictions. In B. Greene (Ed.), *Ethnic and cultural diversity among lesbians and gay men* (pp. 117-131). Thousand Oaks, CA: Sage Publications.

Falicov, C. J. (1995). Cross-cultural marriages. In N. S. Jacobson and A. S. Gurman (Eds.), *Clinical handbook of couple therapy* (pp. 231-246). New York: Guilford Publications.

Greene, B. (Ed.) (1997). *Ethnic and cultural diversity among lesbians and gay men.* Thousand Oaks, CA: Sage Publications.

Greene, N. and Boyd-Franklin, N. (1996). African-American lesbians: Issues in couples therapy. In J. Laird and R. J. Green (Eds.), *Lesbians and gays in couples and families: A handbook for therapists* (pp. 251-271). San Francisco, CA: Jossey-Bass Publishers.

Laszloffy, T. A. and Hardy, K. V. (2000). Uncommon strategies for a common problem: Addressing racism in family therapy. *Family Process, 39,* 35-50.

Liu, P. and Chan, C. S. (1996). Lesbian, gay, and bisexual Asian-Americans and their families. In J. Laird and R. J. Green (Eds.), *Lesbians and gays in couples and families: A handbook for therapists* (pp. 137-152). San Francisco, CA: Jossey-Bass Publishers.

Lorde, A. (1984). Age, race, class, and sex. In A. Lorde (Ed.), *Sister outsider: Essays and speeches* (pp. 114-123). Freedom, CA: Crossing Press.

McIntosh, P. (1998). White privilege: Unpacking the invisible knapsack. In M. McGoldrick (Ed.), *Re-visioning family therapy: Race, culture and gender in clinical practice* (pp. 147-152). New York: Guilford Publications.

Morales, E. (1996). Gender roles among Latino gay and bisexual men. In J. Laird and R. J. Green (Eds.), *Lesbians and gays in couples and families: A handbook for therapists* (pp. 272-297). San Francisco, CA: Jossey-Bass Publishers.

Schwartz, R. C. (1995). *Internal family systems therapy.* New York: Guilford Publications.

Smith, A. (1997). Cultural diversity and the coming-out process: Implications for clinical practice. In B. Greene (Ed.), *Ethnic and cultural diversity among lesbians and gay men* (pp. 279-300). Thousand Oaks, CA: Sage Publications.

Bibliotherapy Sources for the Client

Collins, L. (2000). Raising Kate. *In the Family, 5*(4), 10-13, 19.

Farajaje-Jones, E. (2000). Loving "queer." *In the Family, 6*(1), 14-21.

Font, R. (1997). Making sense of pain and privilege. *In the Family, 2*(3), 9.

Greene, B. (Ed.) (1997). *Ethnic and cultural diversity among lesbians and gay men.* Thousand Oaks, CA: Sage Publications.

Griebenow, M. (2000). Looking Chinese adoption in the eyes. *In the Family, 5*(4), 6-9, 18.

Hardy, K. V. (1997). Not quite home: The psychological effects of oppression. *In the Family, 2*(3), 6-8, 26.

Hardy, K. V. and Laszloffy, T. A. (1998). The dynamics of a pro-racist ideology: Implications for family therapists. In M. McGoldrick (Ed.), *Re-visioning family therapy: Race, culture, and gender in clinical practice* (pp. 118-128), New York: Guilford Publications.

Markowitz, L. (2000). Race, culture, and adoption: An interview with Joyce Maguire Pavao. *In the Family, 5*(4), 15-17.

McIntosh, P. (1998). White privilege: Unpacking the invisible knapsack. In M. McGoldrick (Ed.), *Re-visioning family therapy: Race, culture and gender in clinical practice* (pp. 147-152). New York: Guilford Publications.

References

Cerbone, A. R. (1997). Symbol of privilege, object of derision: Dissonance and contradictions. In B. Greene (Ed.), *Ethnic and cultural diversity among lesbians and gay men* (pp. 117-131). Thousand Oaks, CA: Sage Publications.

Greene, B. (Ed.) (1997). *Ethnic and cultural diversity among lesbians and gay men.* Thousand Oaks, CA: Sage Publications.

Greene, N. and Boyd-Franklin, N. (1996). African-American lesbians: Issues in couples therapy. In J. Laird and R. J. Green (Eds.), *Lesbians and gays in couples and families: A handbook for therapists* (pp. 251-271). San Francisco, CA: Jossey-Bass Publishers.

Laszloffy, T. A. and Hardy, K. V. (2000). Uncommon strategies for a common problem: Addressing racism in family therapy. *Family Process, 39,* 35-50.

Liu, P. and Chan, C. S. (1996). Lesbian, gay, and bisexual Asian-Americans and their families. In J. Laird and R. J. Green (Eds.), *Lesbians and gays in couples and families: A handbook for therapists* (pp. 137-152). San Francisco, CA: Jossey-Bass Publishers.

Lorde, A. (1984). Age, race, class, and sex. In A. Lorde (Ed.), *Sister outsider: Essays and speeches* (pp. 114-123). Freedom, CA: Crossing Press.

McIntosh, P. (1998). White privilege: Unpacking the invisible knapsack. In M. McGoldrick (Ed.), *Re-visioning family therapy: Race, culture and gender in clinical practice* (pp. 147-152). New York: Guilford Publications.

Morales, E. (1996). Gender roles among Latino gay and bisexual men. In J. Laird and R. J. Green (Eds.), *Lesbians and gays in couples and families: A handbook for therapists* (pp. 272-297). San Francisco, CA: Jossey-Bass Publishers.

Schwartz, R. C. (1995). *Internal family systems therapy.* New York: Guilford Publications.

Smith, A. (1997). Cultural diversity and the coming-out process: Implications for clinical practice. In B. Greene (Ed.), *Ethnic and cultural diversity among lesbians and gay men* (pp. 279-300). Thousand Oaks, CA: Sage Publications.

20

Creating a "Thicker Description": Understanding Identity in Mixed-Identity Relationships

Sheila M. Addison
Melody M. Brown

Type of Contribution: Activity

Objectives

This activity has three objectives: (1) help each partner in the relationship clarify how her or his sexual identity is created and expressed; (2) help each partner understand the meaning the other has for his or her identity; and (3) open opportunities for discussing concerns, fears, or questions that each partner's identity raises for the other.

Rationale for Use

Couples in a mixed-identity relationship (heterosexual/bisexual or homosexual/bisexual) may find that assumptions or lack of information about each partner's sexual identity blocks trust and emotional and sexual intimacy. The purpose of this activity is to assist each partner in creating a "thicker description" (Epston and White, 1990) of herself or himself as a sexual being across different settings and time frames. Once one partner has described his or her identity using the Klein Sexual Orientation Grid (KSOG) (Klein, 1993), the other partner can enter into a dialogue with her or him to elicit further information or discuss the issues that are raised for the second partner.

Instructions

Provide each partner with a copy of the KSOG, and read the following instructions:

Fill out this grid as best you can with numbers from the rating scale. For example, if in the past you found yourself sexually attracted to both sexes equally, put a 4 in the Sexual Attraction, Past box. If right now, today, you feel mostly sexually attracted to the same sex, but still feel some attraction to the opposite sex, put a 6 in the Sexual Attraction, Present box. If you feel that ideally you would be sexually attracted only to the same sex, put a 7 in the Sexual Attraction, Ideal box. Do this for each of the dimensions described on the grid.

When the clients have finished, ask them to talk about the experience of filling out the grid. What was it like to try to rate their feelings as numbers? Were they nervous or anxious about putting their answers down on paper? Are they nervous or anxious about sharing their answers with their partner, or with you as the therapist? Did any of their answers, or the overall pattern of answers, surprise them? Have they ever thought about their sexual identity in this kind of multi-dimensional way before?

Ask the clients to exchange grids and look at each other's answers. What answers stand out? Are there any that are surprising or disappointing? What meaning does each client make out of his or her partner's answers? Take time for each partner to respond, with the other partner in the listening role, and then give the listening partner the chance to clarify what she or he meant by the answers brought up by the first partner. Then ask them to switch roles.

If appropriate, discuss any differences between individual ratings given to present and ideal items (i.e., a client rates her or his social attraction as being almost exclusively to the same sex, but rates her or his ideal as being equal between both sexes).

Encourage the couple to talk about how their individual sexual identities inform their identity as a couple. How important does each partner feel it is to acknowledge his or her individual identity? What are the benefits and consequences for each partner and for the couple of various degrees of openness about each partner's identity? What feelings are brought up by this exercise and conversation?

Facilitate a narrative discussion that externalizes sexual identity. What effect does sexual identity have on the couple's relationship? Are there ways that it tries to get between the partners? What tricks and techniques does it use to do this? What strengths does the couple have that sexual identity tries to undermine? When are they successful at resisting the tactics that sexual identity uses to cause trouble in their relationship?

Suggestions for Follow-Up

At the next session, ask whether the clients talked further about the exercise during their time together. Did either of them think about it privately over the intervening time? When did the subject come up? What feelings were associated with it? What effect has the discussion (in or out of session) had on the couple's relationship, and the presenting problem(s)?

Encourage the couple to talk about what it is like for each of them to be (lesbian, gay, bisexual, heterosexual). What things does each client want his or her partner to understand about being _____ ? What experiences divide them? What experiences of sexual identity are similar between both partners?

Contraindications

This exercise may be inappropriate for some couples in which one or both partners are transgendered, because it relies on a binary view of gender. It may help to modify the scale to represent a continuum of masculine and feminine gender expression or from "people whose gender is similar to mine" ranging to "people whose gender is different from mine."

Because this exercise requires trust between partners and may temporarily raise the couple's level of anxiety and insecurity, it is not recommended for couples in crisis and couples between whom violence is present.

Readings and Resources for the Professional

Epston, D. and White, M. (1990). *Narrative means to therapeutic ends*. New York: W. W. Norton and Company.

Fox, R. (2000). Therapy with bisexuals: An interview with Ron Fox. *In the Family, 6*(2), 6-9, 21.

Klein, F. (1993). *The bisexual option* (Second edition). Binghamton, NY: The Haworth Press.

Lourea, D. N. (1985). Psycho-social issues related to counseling bisexuals. *Journal of Homosexuality, 11*(1-2), 51-62.

Matteson, D. R. (1996). Counseling and psychotherapy with bisexual and exploring clients. In B. A. Firestein (Ed.), *Bisexuality: The psychology and politics of an invisible minority* (pp. 185-213). Thousand Oaks, CA: Sage Publications.

Ochs, R. (1996). Biphobia: It goes more than two ways. In B. A. Firestein (Ed.), *Bisexuality: The psychology and politics of an invisible minority* (pp. 217-239). Thousand Oaks, CA: Sage Publications.

Bibliotherapy Sources for the Client

Geller, T. (Ed.) (1990). *Bisexual identity: A reader and sourcebook*. Ojai, CA: Times Change Press.

Hutchins, L. and Kaahumanu, L. (1991). *Bi any other name: Bisexual people speak out*. New York: Alyson Publications.

Markowitz, L. (1995). Bisexuality: Challenging our either/or thinking. *In the Family, 1*(1), 6-11, 23.

Ochs, R. (1996). Biphobia: It goes more than two ways. In B.A. Firestein (Ed.), *Bisexuality: The psychology and politics of an invisible minority* (pp. 217-239). Thousand Oaks, CA: Sage Publications.

Phillips, L. (1998). I is for intersection: At the crux of black and white and gay and straight. In D. Atkins (Ed.), *Looking queer: Body image and identity in lesbian, bisexual, gay, and transgender communities* (pp. 251-258). Binghamton, NY: The Haworth Press.

References

Epston, D. and White, M. (1990). *Narrative means to therapeutic ends*. New York: W. W. Norton and Company.

Klein, F. (1993). *The bisexual option* (Second edition). Binghamton, NY: The Haworth Press.

Klein Sexual Orientation Grid

Fill out this grid as best you can with numbers from the rating scale. For example, if in the past you found yourself sexually attracted to both sexes equally, put a 4 in the Sexual Attraction, Past box. If right now, today, you feel mostly sexually attracted to the same sex, but still feel some attraction to the opposite sex, put a 6 in the Sexual Attraction, Present box. If you feel that ideally you would be sexually attracted only to the same sex, put a 7 in the Sexual Attraction, Ideal box. Do this for each of the dimensions described on the grid.

VARIABLE	PAST	PRESENT	IDEAL
A. Sexual Attraction			
B. Sexual Behavior			
C. Sexual Fantasies			
D. Emotional Preference			
E. Social Preference			
F. Hetero/Homo. Lifestyle			
G. Self-Identification			

Source: Klein, 1993, p. 19.

People rate themselves on a 7-point scale from 1 to 7 as follows:

For variables A. to E.:

1. = Other sex only

2. = Other sex mostly

3. = Other sex somewhat more

4. = Both sexes equally

5. = Same sex somewhat more

6. = Same sex mostly

7. = Same sex only

For variables F. and G.:

1. = Hetero only

2. = Hetero mostly

3. = Hetero somewhat more

4. = Hetero/gay-lesb. equally

5. = Gay-lesb. somewhat more

6. = Gay-lesb. mostly

7. = Gay-lesb. only

21

Opening the Door or Locking It Tight:
The Negotiation of a Healthy Open Relationship

Heidi M. Levitt
Karina Raina

Type of Contribution: Worksheet

Objective

This worksheet is designed to assist individuals who are currently in open relationships, or who are considering entering one, to better identify their relational needs. Clients who are considering engaging in an open relationship may find that an awareness of these needs can guide them in their decision-making process. As well, it can facilitate communication between partners and allow clients to develop relational structures that promote a healthy partnership.

Rationale for Use

Many clients enter psychotherapy to explore their intimate relationships. However, therapists may not be aware of the differences in structure that can exist within gay, lesbian, and bisexual (GLB) relationships and their accompanying issues. It is important for therapists to understand that these relationships are common in these communities and should not be pathologized. Indeed, in a study of 387 gay men, Hickson et al. (1992) found open relationships to be the most common relationship type.

Open relationships appear to be associated with gay men—as evidenced by the concentration of research within this population (e.g., Blasband and Peplau, 1985; Hickson et al., 1992; Kurdek and Schmitt, 1985-1986; O'Leary, 1997; Woolwine, 2000). Within GLB cultures, open relationships may hold meanings that are unique. For instance, they may be experienced as a way for queer individuals to express or celebrate their identities, to connect with their communities, or to explore their sexual orientations. Therapists who are outside these cultures, consequently, may be unsure how to explore these relationships.

There are no significant differences in quality of relationship when comparing gay men in open and closed relationships (Blasband and Peplau, 1985). Partners in both types of relationships have similar views of commitment, love, and relationship satisfaction. There may be differences, however, in the concerns of individuals in open and closed relationships (Blasband and Peplau, 1985; Kurdek and Schmitt, 1985-1986). Gay men in closed relationships stress the need to avoid jealousy and report less relational tension and more favorable attitudes toward their relationships. In contrast, gay men in open relationships emphasize the importance of personal independence and sexual variety. They have longer-lasting relationships and lower levels of affiliative dependency. Although clients present with the need to explore their relationship concerns, they may find it difficult to express them to therapists for a number of reasons.

Because their relationship needs are not echoed within mainstream society, GLB clients may not be able to access the terminology needed to explain their needs clearly. For instance, it may be difficult for a bisexual woman to explain to her therapist how the experience of sexual freedom at an annual women's festival can act to affirm aspects of her identity. Another client might fear judgment by the therapist at the disclosure of his or her relationship structure. The client also may worry that the therapist will not be able to envision his or her relationship within a queer cultural context and may misunderstand the meaning of the relationship. This exercise can assist clients in articulating to their therapists their concerns and can help the therapists to explore relational issues that might otherwise go unmentioned. As well, the exercise can indicate to the client a permissiveness to discuss in therapy topics that relate to open relationships and provide assurance of the therapist's receptivity.

Instructions

Identifying Appropriate Clients for This Exercise

This exercise is designed for the single client who is either considering committing to an open relationship or is in the process of identifying his or her relational needs. It is also meant for the individual or the couple who are presently in a relationship and considering altering the relationship structure. These clients may be in the process of exploring or redefining relationships that presently are either open or closed.

Presenting the Worksheet

When presenting the worksheet to an individual client, the therapist may wish to tell him or her that it outlines a variety of issues that can be important to consider when he or she is engaged in an open relationship. The therapist can suggest that the client use this sheet to help articulate and identify his or her personal preferences in relationship structure. The therapist may ask the client to contemplate or to write his or her responses to these questions, paying attention to items that are disturbing or thought-provoking. The client should be told that items on the worksheet might highlight his or her own uncertainties and that unresolved issues should be brought to the following therapy session as topics for discussion.

As well, when presenting the worksheet to a client in a relationship or to a couple, the therapist can tell the clients that the worksheet is designed to improve communication about open relationships. A couple should be asked to complete the worksheet separately and then to engage in a discussion about their responses. The therapist should ask the couple if they would prefer to initiate this discussion prior to the next session or to have the discussion facilitated by the therapist.

Clients should be cautioned that the worksheet is meant to increase their awareness of conflicts and that its purpose is to identify and clarify issues of importance for ongoing discussions. They may find the worksheet threatening because of the sensitive nature of the topics addressed, so the therapist may wish to be attentive to these fears and help to normalize them. The therapist should assure clients explicitly that he or she has no expectations regarding the outcome of the exercise. Clients may be overly attuned to judgments about their sexual orientation or relationship structure and may misinterpret the worksheet as an encouragement for or caution against an open relationship.

Suggestions for Follow-Up

After clients have identified the issues that are salient for them, the therapist might suggest selecting the item that "feels most important to discuss." He or she can guide clients to examine the emotions and meanings that arise as they contemplate the different questions. The therapist can employ a number of different interventions to deepen the process of exploration. If clients are unsure what emotions surround an issue, Gendlin's (1996) focusing would be a useful tool. By asking clients to look inward and to notice words, phrases, or images that emerge as they contemplate an issue, they can move forward in their symbolization process. If clients express puzzlement or surprise about an emotional reaction to an item, Rice's (see Greenberg, Rice, and Elliott, 1993) problematic reaction exploration, or Guidano's (1995) moviola technique could be implemented. Both these interventions ask clients to generate a slow, detailed event description and to attend to accompanying emotions. The therapist using these strategies can guide clients to experience memories or fantasies associated with items, and then to identify difficult aspects of those experiences. In any case, the therapist should conduct his or her exploration while keeping in mind that reactions might seem idiosyncratic and should be understood in the context of local GLB cultures.

Contraindications

This exercise is meant for clients who are unsure whether they wish to enter an open relationship or for clients who are in a problematic open relationship. Therapists should not implement this exercise with clients who are not interested in exploring their position on open relationships. Clients who are firm opponents or firm advocates of this relationship structure would be unlikely to benefit from this exploration. Clients who are satisfied with an open relationship may feel other issues are more pressing for them to discuss.

Abusive relational dynamics would be a contraindication for the use of this exercise. Victims of abuse might not experience the safety needed to express their desires freely, and abusive power dynamics might distort the perceptions of both victim and abuser. The issue of abuse should be the primary focus of therapy when it is present and should supercede issues of relational structure.

It is also important that therapists approach this topic with an awareness of their biases and a willingness to help individuals or couples find solutions that are appropriate within the clients' unique relationships. The topic of open relationships can create religious or moral resistance in therapists and can be experienced as threatening to their own relational beliefs. Likewise, clients who have merely begun to entertain the idea of entering an open relationship might be overwhelmed or threatened by the display of too much "open-mindedness" by their therapist. Therapists who do not feel confident in their ability to support clients' own processes of discovery should consider referring clients outward.

Readings and Resources for the Professional

Blasband, D. and Peplau, L. A. (1985). Sexual exclusivity versus openness in gay male couples. *Archives of Sexual Behavior, 14*(5), 395-412.

Gendlin, E. T. (1996). *Focusing-oriented psychotherapy: A manual of the experiential method.* New York: Guilford Publications.

Greenberg, L., Rice, L., and Elliott, R. (1993). *Facilitating emotional change: The moment-by-moment process.* New York: Guilford Publications.

Guidano, V. F. (1995). Self-observation in constructivist psychotherapy. In R. A. Neimeyer and M. J. Mahoney (Eds.), *Constructivism in psychotherapy* (pp. 155-168). Washington, DC: American Psychological Association.

Hickson, F. C., Davies, P. M., Hunt, A. J., and Weatherburn, P. (1992). Maintenance of open gay relationships: Some strategies for protection against HIV. *AIDS-Care, 4*(4), 409-419.

Kurdek, L. A. and Schmitt, J. P. (1985-1986). Relationship quality of gay men in closed or open relationships. *Journal of Homosexuality, 12*(2), 85-99.

O'Leary, J. V. (1997). A heterosexual male therapist's journey of self-discovery: Wearing a "straight" jacket in a gay men's bereavement group. In M. Blechner (Ed.), *Hope and mortality: Psychodynamic approaches to AIDS and HIV* (pp. 209-220). Hillsdale, NJ: The Analytic Press, Inc.

Woolwine, D. (2000). Community in gay male experience and moral discourse. *Journal of Homosexuality, 38*(4), 5-37.

Bibliotherapy Sources for the Client

Johnson, S. (1991). *The ship that sailed into the living room: Sex and intimacy reconsidered.* Albuquerque, NM: WildFire Books.

Mazur, R. M. (2000). *The new intimacy: Open-ended marriage and alternative lifestyles.* Boston, MA: iUniverse.com Inc.

Munson, M. and Stelboum, J. P. (Eds.) (1999). *The lesbian polyamory reader: Open relationships, non-monogamy, and casual sex.* Binghamton, NY: The Haworth Press.

O'Neill, N. and O'Neill, G. (1984). *Open marriage: A new life style for couples.* New York: M. Evans.

Schulman, S. (1999). *Girls, visions, and everything.* Seattle, WA: Seal Press.

White, E. (2000). *The married man.* New York: Alfred A. Knopf.

References

Blasband, D. and Peplau, L. A. (1985). Sexual exclusivity versus openness in gay male couples. *Archives of Sexual Behavior, 14*(5), 395-412.

Gendlin, E. T. (1996). *Focusing-oriented psychotherapy: A manual of the experiential method.* New York: Guilford Publications.

Greenberg, L., Rice, L., and Elliott, R. (1993). *Facilitating emotional change: The moment-by-moment process.* New York: Guilford Publications.

Guidano, V. F. (1995). Self-observation in constructivist psychotherapy. In R. A. Neimeyer and M. J. Mahoney (Eds.), *Constructivism in psychotherapy* (pp. 155-168). Washington, DC: American Psychological Association.

Hickson, F. C., Davies, P. M., Hunt, A. J., and Weatherburn, P. (1992). Maintenance of open gay relationships: Some strategies for protection against HIV. *AIDS-Care, 4*(4), 409-419.

Kurdek, L. A. and Schmitt, J. P. (1985-1986). Relationship quality of gay men in closed or open relationships. *Journal of Homosexuality, 12*(2), 85-99.

O'Leary, J. V. (1997). A heterosexual male therapist's journey of self-discovery: Wearing a "straight" jacket in a gay men's bereavement group. In M. Blechner (Ed.), *Hope and mortality: Psychodynamic approaches to AIDS and HIV* (pp. 209-220). Hillsdale, NJ: The Analytic Press, Inc.

Woolwine, D. (2000). Community in gay male experience and moral discourse. *Journal of Homosexuality, 38*(4), 5-37.

Identification of Relational Needs

This worksheet is designed to assist you in identifying what you would like in a relationship. Please use this as a starting place for your exploration. Feel free to adjust items so that they feel comfortable or fitting to you.

As you review the following items, please consider your present relationship desires. If items resonate with you, you may wish to further your exploration of these items in a variety of ways. You may decide to engage in some reflective writing on these themes, discuss these issues with your partner(s), or address any concerns with your therapist. If you are considering entering an open relationship, or are already in one, these are issues that you may wish to eventually discuss with your partner(s). You may find that one of the areas resonates most strongly with you, or you may find that you have concerns with items from many areas of this worksheet.

Sexuality

1. Do I wish to have a relationship that is sexually nonmonogamous?
2. How do I define being sexually nonmonogamous?
3. Are there certain restrictions I would want on sexual activity outside of my relationship?
4. How would I want to cope with issues of sexually transmitted disease and AIDS so that my relationship(s) feel safe?
5. Would it make a difference if my partner(s) or I had sexual involvement with someone of the same or opposite gender?
6. Would it be important for my partner(s) and I to be sexual with a third person only when we were all together?

Intimacy

7. Do I wish to have a relationship that is emotionally nonmonogamous?
8. How do I define being emotionally nonmonogamous?
9. Is it important for me to be the central romantic relationship in my partner's life?
10. What would define the central romantic relationship?
11. Would having an involvement with a third person make my partner feel less "special" to me or shift our level of intimacy in any way?
12. Would it make a difference if my partner or I had an emotional or romantic involvement with someone of the same or opposite gender?
13. How would I cope if either my partner's or my own extrarelational involvement evolved to hold deep emotional meaning?

Communication

14. Do I want to talk with my partner about extrarelational sexual activities?
15. Do I want to talk with my partner about extrarelational romantic involvements?
16. Do I want to talk to my extrarelational partners about my standing relationship?
17. Do I want to be open with family and friends about the "openness" of my relationship?
18. Do I need restrictions on the amount or types of contact we will have with extrarelational partners in order to respect each other?
19. If I want the freedom right now to explore my sexuality and do not want to commit to a relationship, can I communicate this clearly to my partner(s)?
20. Can I trust my partner(s) and myself to be honest with each other?

Differences in the Desiring or Acting Upon an Open Relationship

21. How does it shift the power in our relationship if only one of us desires an open relationship or only one of us acts upon this "openness"?
22. If the power does shift, how do I feel about it?
23. Is there a way that I can talk to my partner(s) about my desire/level of activity that feels safe to me?
24. Do I feel that I need to maintain the same level of desire or activity as my partner(s)?
25. Do we need to talk about our current level of commitment or relational dynamics before we have this conversation, so that we ensure our relational safety?

Possible Benefits and Needs

26. What are the advantages of being in an open relationship?
27. Are there certain needs I can more easily meet outside of my relationship?
28. Does being in an open relationship allow me to grow in certain ways as a person?
29. Do I need time to explore my sexual orientation?
30. Does being in an open relationship provide me with the opportunity to explore/maintain aspects of my queer identity?
31. Do I need a sexual or romantic intimacy with someone of a gender different than my partner's gender?
32. How much closeness do I need to feel to my partner(s) before I feel enmeshed?
33. How much distance do I need to have from my partner(s) before I feel abandoned?
34. What is the most rewarding aspect of an open relationship for me?
35. What is the most rewarding aspect of a closed relationship for me?

Possible Conflicts and Disadvantages

36. What are the disadvantages for me in being in an open relationship?
37. What are the disadvantages for me in being in a closed relationship?
38. Do I trust that our relationship is strong enough to sustain an open structure?
39. Do I feel comfortable with both my partner and I engaging in extrarelational sexual or romantic interactions?
40. How do I cope with my jealousy?
41. How do I cope with my partner's jealousy?
42. How do I cope with the jealousy of extrarelational partners?
43. Do I need a predetermined way to discuss or settle issues of jealousy should they arise?
44. What is the most frightening aspect of an open relationship for me?
45. What is the most frightening aspect of a closed relationship for me?

Long-Term Planning

46. Do I foresee openness as a temporary period or a stage of a larger relationship?
47. Do I need to have a partner who would be willing to shift to an open or closed relationship in the future?
48. If I have children, would I want the relationship structure to change at this point?
49. Do I need a way to transition into or out of "openness," if desired?
50. Are there any remaining guidelines that will be important for our long-term relationship that should be articulated?

22

Gender Roles and Intimacy for Gay Men

Diane Sobel

Type of Contribution: Activity

Objective

This two-part activity addresses gay men's difficulties establishing intimate relationships in several ways. First, it provides a new definition of intimacy, which could be applied to anyone, and that normalizes the vulnerability and anxiety in healthy relationships. Second, it focuses on the negative impact of sex-role stereotyping on gay men's ability to establish intimate relationships. It challenges gay men to move beyond simply "living out" the expectations inherent in sex-role stereotypes by increasing their awareness of the behaviors that sex-role socialization may promote. Finally, it increases the awareness of the link between stereotypically male behaviors and the ways in which men tend to avoid intimacy. It promotes alternate behaviors that are consistent with this new definition of intimacy and suggests healthier expectations for relationships.

Rationale for Use

Stereotyping and sex-role socialization have a significant impact on a number of aspects of gay men's lives (Dean, Wu, and Martin, 1992; Herek, 1986, 1992). These processes have been found to exert considerable pressures on individuals to conform to established expectations for sex-typed behavior (Basow, 1992; Franklin, 1998; Golombok and Fivush, 1994; Worrell and Remer, 1992), regardless of sexual orientation (Hancock, 2000). Sex-role socialization leads men to comply with the norms of autonomy, control, rationality, competition, and promiscuity (O'Neil, 1981). In addition, adherence to socialized sex roles prevents men from expressing feelings, showing weakness or vulnerability, or asking for help (Levant et al., 1992; O'Neil, 1981; O'Neil and Egan, 1992). Although many of these messages can be positive and advantageous for men because the characteristics are valued in our society, these features can also be limiting. Many of these ways of thinking and being can make it difficult for men to establish intimate relationships, especially with other men (Berk, 2001; Chodorow, 1999; Reid and Fine, 1992). This can be particularly problematic for gay or bisexual men since many of their friendships, as well as their romantic relationships, are likely to be with other men.

Kain (1995) describes a developmental model of intimacy that combines Schnarch's (1991) bi-level model of intimacy and Chelune, Robinson, and Krommer's (1984) notion that intimacy is the cognitive appraisal of certain behaviors. Kain (1995) suggests that one's cognitive construct of intimacy changes with psychosocial development. The first construct develops with early childhood experiences and is based on object relations theory. This "other-validated model of intimacy . . . emphasizes the expectation of reciprocity in relationships" (p. 3). For example, someone who has an other-validated model of intimacy might believe that in an intimate interaction, one's partner ought to know what one wants and feels. Therefore, there is no need to talk to each other. The self-validated model of intimacy exists when a person has "the ability to remain in a differentiated state, the ability to be a part of a relationship yet stand separate; holding on to one's sense of self when in the presence of one's partner" (p. 3). For example, in contrast with those having an other-validated model of intimacy, those with a self-validated model of intimacy believe that an interaction is intimate when one self-discloses about core aspects of oneself to another person. However, the other person's validation is not necessary in order for the interaction to be perceived as intimate.

This activity is designed to encourage development of a self-validated model of intimacy through understanding this new definition of intimacy as well as the connection between male stereotyping and avoidance of intimacy. The goal for clients is to be able to think of an experience as intimate even when it is not reciprocal. If clients were to continue utilizing the other-validated model of intimacy, they would view anxiety as an indication that something is wrong with the relationship (Kain, 1995), and they might prematurely extricate themselves from it. Once they develop a self-validated model of intimacy, they are able to experience anxiety, hurt, or pain as a "normal" and expected part of a relationship, thereby allowing them to deepen the level of connection they experience in their relationships.

Instructions

Part 1

1. In small groups of three to five members, ask the clients to fill out the worksheet on stereotypes. Have some groups work on the Males handout and other groups work on the Gay or Bisexual handout.
2. Have one member of each group report back to the larger group about the group's responses to the questions.
3. Lead a discussion about the similarities and differences between the ways the groups responded to the handouts. If no one notices the differences, point out that the gay or bisexual stereotypes are typically feminine characteristics, which tend to be devalued in our society. Male stereotypes will typically be about power and control and are the valued characteristics in our society.
4. Discuss issues of power, target and nontarget groups in an oppressive system, and how those may influence the types of stereotypes that exist about a particular group. For example, males are the nontarget group in relation to females. The majority of stereotypes about men are positive. Even though some stereotypes may be positive, they can have the same restricting and negative impact on the members of that group. Men may not think of themselves as restricted in any way because the sex-role expectations of them can result in behaviors that are valued in society. But these same sex-role expectations might contribute to the difficulties that men have in relationships (e.g., by making it difficult to express emotions).
5. Ask the group to provide examples of behavioral observations they have of themselves and of others. Point out the tendency to embody or reject the stereotypes of their group. This discussion leads to linking stereotyping with gender-role socialization and socialization into gay or bisexual culture—or rejection of both.
6. Challenge possible notions that because they are gay or bisexual, they do not do stereotypical male things. Ask for examples that provide evidence that they, as men, are socialized first as males. Point out the ways in which that plays itself out in their behavior.
7. Make a list of messages to men on a flipchart based on your discussion. It should include such things as:

Don't express emotions or feelings

Must solve own problems (on my own)

Need to be right

Don't ask for help

Be rational

Be "one up"—compete with others to win

Don't show weaknesses to others

Relationships are a lower priority

I'm nothing if I'm not providing

Be in control

Have lots of sex (with lots of partners)

Part 2

1. Using another flipchart sheet or blackboard, have the whole group brainstorm all the ways they can think of that men avoid intimacy—behaviors that they see in themselves and in other men that they know. Record their responses. Examples might include:

Multiple sex partners

Physical distance

Not expressing feelings

Humor/sarcasm

Cocky attitude/arrogance

Workaholic/no time for others

Being analytical/rational

Storytelling

Shyness

Lying

Substance use/abuse

Talking only about self

Only listening to others/talking about others

Self-involved

Superficial

Insincere/not genuine

2. Point to the list of messages to men and have the participants recall the stereotypes of men that were discussed previously. Ask them to describe the relationship between those stereotypes/sex-role messages and the ways men avoid intimacy.

3. Discuss their feelings about this, and ask for reactions. Are they surprised? How do they feel about noticing that they often do "act out" male stereotypes even in their gay relationships?

4. Normalize the ways that men avoid intimacy in the context of their socialization as males. For example, one way that a man might avoid intimacy is by developing a workaholic lifestyle. Although this keeps him from developing intimate relationships because of his lack of availability, it helps him to fit in with the gender-role expectations of high achievement, competition, etc. The group facilitator can point out that although being a workaholic may lead to a lack of intimate relationships, it is understandable that men engage in those behaviors in order to be considered men.

5. Ask the group to define intimacy. (Typically, the group will say things such as "a warm, fuzzy blanket" or "knowing what another person is thinking/feeling without having to say anything.")

6. Provide Kain's (1995) definition of self-validated intimacy as an alternative to their definition: "the ability to remain in a differentiated state; the ability to be a part of a relationship yet stand separate; holding on to one's sense of self when in the presence of one's partner" (p. 3).

7. Discuss the meaning of this new definition and clarify the role that anxiety has in an intimate interaction. Many clients will resist the notion that a certain amount of anxiety is normal in a relationship. Facilitators ought to give examples and reassurance that it is not possible to have an intimate relationship without any anxiety or vulnerability at all.

8. Normalize feelings of anxiety. Ask for clients' reaction to this new definition and what it suggests about their intimate relationships. Clients will have a mixture of reactions to this new concept. Some will feel relieved that they have not been doing things wrong, and others will be uncomfortable with the idea that an unpleasant feeling, anxiety, needs to be a part of their relationships. The facilitator's role is to validate all of these reactions.

Suggestions for Follow-Up

It is very unlikely that the clients will change from having an other-validated model of intimacy to a self-validated model of intimacy following a single group discussion. More likely, the discussion can provide a new perspective and provide a new challenge to their construct that intimacy is the same as reciprocity. Clients may begin to think about and talk about their behavior in previous relationships in this new context. This, by itself, may be anxiety provoking for clients. It would be helpful for the facilitator to provide emotional support and validation for feelings of anxiety about changing this pattern of thinking in one of two ways. If additional group sessions follow this discussion, the facilitator can encourage support from other members of the group to those struggling with the self-validated model of intimacy. If the facilitator will have individual sessions with the client, she or he can provide that support herself or himself. Clients may also be resistant to changing their construct because they are not ready to do so. Validating their feelings as well as providing information to challenge their thinking can be a helpful response in this situation. The facilitator might also engage them in a discussion of their feelings of loss about being traditionally male.

Contraindications

There are no known contraindications for using this activity. Group leaders should keep in mind, however, that helping clients progress from an other-validated model of intimacy to a self-validated model is a process. It is not a skill that can be taught or learned, but a process that can be encouraged and through which clients will progress at different rates.

Adapting This Activity for Individuals/Couples

This activity could also be done with an individual client or a couple. The main benefit of facilitating in a group format is to provide the clients with the opportunity to receive support from others who might be having some of the same experiences. If done with an individual or couple, the therapist would have to provide the majority of that support.

Readings and Resources for the Professional

Basow, S. (1992). *Gender: Stereotypes and roles* (Third edition). Pacific Grove, CA: Brooks/ Cole.

Berk, L. E. (2001). *Development through the lifespan* (Second edition). Boston, MA: Allyn and Bacon.

Chelune, G. J., Robinson, J. T., and Krommer, M. J. (1984). Cognitive interaction and intimacy. In V. J. Derlega (Ed.), *Communication, intimacy and close relationships* (pp. 11-40). New York: Academic Press.

Chodorow, N. J. (1999). *The reproduction of mothering: Psychoanalysis and the sociology of gender.* Berkeley, CA: University of California Press.

Dean, L., Wu, S., and Martin, J. L. (1992). Trends in violence and discrimination against gay men in New York City: 1984-1990. In G. M. Herek and K. T. Berrill (Eds.), *Hate crimes: Confronting violence against lesbians and gay men* (pp. 46-64). Thousand Oaks, CA: Sage Publications.

Franklin, K. (1998). Unassuming motivations: Contextualizing the narratives of antigay assailants. In G. M. Herek (Ed.), *Stigma and sexual orientation: Understanding prejudice against lesbians, gay men, and bisexuals* (pp. 1-23). Thousand Oaks, CA: Sage Publications.

Golombok, S. and Fivush, R. (1994). *Gender development*. New York: Cambridge University Press.

Hancock, K. A. (2000). Lesbian, gay and bisexual lives: Basic issues in psychotherapy training and practice. In B. Greene and G. L. Croom (Eds.), *Education, research, and practice in lesbian, gay, bisexual, and transgendered psychology* (pp. 91-130). Thousand Oaks, CA: Sage Publications.

Herek, G. M. (1986). The social psychology of homophobia: Toward a practical theory. *New York University Review of Law and Social Change, 16,* 923-934.

Herek, G. M. (1992). The social context of hate crimes: Notes on cultural hetereosexism. In G. M. Herek and K. T. Berrill (Eds.), *Hate crimes: Confronting violence against lesbians and gay men* (pp. 89-104). Thousand Oaks, CA: Sage Publications.

Kain, C. (1995, August). See me say no: Intimacy's role in AIDS-risk reduction behavior. Paper presented at the 103rd Annual Meeting of the American Psychological Association, New York.

Levant, R. F., Hirsch, L. S., Celantano, E., Cozza, T. M., Hill, S., MacEachern, M., Mary, N., Schnedeker, J. (1992). The male role: An investigation of contemporary norms. *Journal of Mental Health Counseling, 14*(3), 325-337.

O'Neil, J. M. (1981). Patterns of gender role conflict and strain: Sexism and fear of femininity in men's lives. *Personnel and Guidance Journal, 60,* 203-210.

O'Neil, J. M. and Egan, J. (1992). Men's gender role transitions over the life span: Transformation and fears of femininity. *Journal of Mental Health Counseling, 14*(3), 305-324.

Reid, H. M. and Fine, A. (1992). Self-disclosure in men's friendships: Variations associated with intimate relations. In P. M. Nardi (Ed.), *Men's friendships* (pp. 153-171). Thousand Oaks, CA: Sage Publications.

Schnarch, D. (1991). *Constructing the sexual crucible: An integration of sexual and marital therapy.* New York: W. W. Norton and Company.

Worrell, J. and Remer, P. (1992). *Feminist perspectives in therapy: An empowerment model for women.* New York: John Wiley and Sons.

Bibliotherapy Sources for the Client

Berzon, B. (1990). *Permanent partners.* New York: Penguin Putnam, Inc.

George, K. D. (2000). *Mr. right is out here: The gay man's guide to finding and maintaining love.* Los Angeles, CA: Alyson Publications.

Isensee, R. (1996). *Love between men: Enhancing intimacy and keep your relationship alive.* Los Angeles, CA: Alyson Publications.

References

Basow, S. (1992). *Gender: Stereotypes and roles* (Third edition). Pacific Grove, CA: Brooks/Cole.

Berk, L. E. (2001). *Development through the lifespan* (Second edition). Boston, MA: Allyn and Bacon.

Chelune, G. J., Robinson, J. T., and Krommer, M. J. (1984). Cognitive interaction and intimacy. In V. J. Derlega (Ed.), *Communication, intimacy and close relationships* (pp. 11-40). New York: Academic Press.

Chodorow, N. J. (1999). *The reproduction of mothering: Psychoanalysis and the sociology of gender.* Berkeley, CA: University of California Press.

Dean, L., Wu, S., and Martin, J. L. (1992). Trends in violence and discrimination against gay men in New York City: 1984-1990. In G. M. Herek and K. T. Berrill (Eds.), *Hate crimes:*

Confronting violence against lesbians and gay men (pp. 46-64). Thousand Oaks, CA: Sage Publications.

Franklin, K. (1998). Unassuming motivations: Contextualizing the narratives of antigay assailants. In G. M. Herek (Ed.), *Stigma and sexual orientation: Understanding prejudice against lesbians, gay men, and bisexuals* (pp. 1-23). Thousand Oaks, CA: Sage Publications.

Golombok, S. and Fivush, R. (1994). *Gender development.* New York: Cambridge University Press.

Hancock, K. A. (2000). Lesbian, gay and bisexual lives: Basic issues in psychotherapy training and practice. In B. Greene and G. L. Croom (Eds.), *Education, research, and practice in lesbian, gay, bisexual, and transgendered psychology* (pp. 91-130). Thousand Oaks, CA: Sage Publications.

Herek, G. M. (1986). The social psychology of homophobia: Toward a practical theory. *New York University Review of Law and Social Change, 16,* 923-934.

Herek, G. M. (1992). The social context of hate crimes: Notes on cultural heterosexism. In G. M. Herek and K. T. Berrill (Eds.), *Hate crimes: Confronting violence against lesbians and gay men* (pp. 89-104). Thousand Oaks, CA: Sage Publications.

Kain, C. (1995, August). See me say no: Intimacy's role in AIDS-risk reduction behavior. Paper presented at the 103rd Annual Meeting of the American Psychological Association, New York.

Levant, R. F., Hirsch, L. S., Celantano, E., Cozza, T. M., Hill, S., MacEachern, M., Mary, N., Schnedeker, J. (1992). The male role: An investigation of contemporary norms. *Journal of Mental Health Counseling, 14*(3), 325-337.

O'Neil, J. M. (1981). Patterns of gender role conflict and strain: Sexism and fear of femininity in men's lives. *Personnel and Guidance Journal, 60,* 203-210.

O'Neil, J. M. and Egan, J. (1992). Men's gender role transitions over the life span: Transformation and fears of femininity. *Journal of Mental Health Counseling, 14*(3), 305-324.

Reid, H. M. and Fine, A. (1992). Self-disclosure in men's friendships: Variations associated with intimate relations. In P. M. Nardi (Ed.), *Men's friendships* (pp. 153-171). Thousand Oaks, CA: Sage Publications.

Schnarch, D. (1991). *Constructing the sexual crucible: An integration of sexual and marital therapy.* New York: W. W. Norton and Company.

Worrell, J. and Remer, P. (1992). *Feminist perspectives in therapy: An empowerment model for women.* New York: John Wiley and Sons.

Gay or Bisexual

1. List eight stereotypes often connected with this group.

2. How are members of this group impacted by these stereotypes? Perceptions of self? Behaviors?

3. How are nonmembers of this group impacted by these stereotypes—how do they perceive/treat members of the group?

4. How do members of this group perceive/treat one another?

5. How did you learn about the stereotypes in question 1?

6. How did you unlearn these stereotypes?

Males

1. List eight stereotypes often connected with this group.

2. How are members of this group impacted by these stereotypes? Perceptions of self? Behaviors?

3. How are nonmembers of this group impacted by these stereotypes—how do they perceive/treat members of the group?

4. How do members of this group perceive/treat one another?

5. How did you learn about the stereotypes in question 1?

6. How did you unlearn these stereotypes?

23

Sexual Concerns/Sexual Dysfunction Assessment

Karen Fontaine

Type of Contribution: Activity/Handout

Objective

This activity is an opportunity to establish a therapeutic relationship, obtain information, note context, and develop an understanding of the sexual problem.

Rationale for Use

There is considerable incidence of sexual dysfunction among gay, lesbian, bisexual, and transgendered (GLBT) people (Nichols, 2000). If clients introduce the problem or if the therapist suspects there may be a problem, a sexual concerns/sexual dysfunction assessment is appropriate. It is particularly helpful because a wealth of information covering a broad range of topics must be gathered for a thorough understanding of the problem. For example, past and present medical history and use of medications is important as a large proportion of sexual problems are due to organic factors (Bartlik and Goldberg, 2000; Rosen, 2000). In addition, sexual performance can also be inhibited by past or present substance abuse. For these reasons, a recent comprehensive physical exam is most helpful prior to completing this assessment. Traumatic factors and past relational factors are another potential source of problems. Systemic issues within the current relationship may also play a considerable role in creating and maintaining sexual problems.

The degree to which GLBT clients have internalized society's homophobia may be a contributing factor in sexual problems, although this has declined dramatically over the past thirty years. Nichols (2000) states: "The degree to which gays and bisexuals experience 'internalized homophobia' has also diminished dramatically. When clients present with severe sexual orientation confusion or self-hatred related to sexual identity, it is often symptomatic of deeper pathology" (p. 352).

The premise of this assessment tool is, "If you never ask, you may never be told." Thus, there are many questions and in quite specific detail. The initial concern of "I don't have orgasms," can mean "I don't find my partner attractive," "I don't have orgasms with this woman, but I do with other women," "I get right to the brink and then lose it," "I'm too frightened to let go and have an orgasm," "It never gets off the ground," "I only have orgasms when I masturbate," "I only have orgasms with a vibrator," or "I'm too depressed to feel anything." Therefore, before deciding where to start—treating the relationship, treating the performance dysfunction, treating loss of desire, making a medical referral, making a referral for a twelve-step program, or providing good sex education—depends on a thorough assessment and an accurate diagnosis.

Instructions

Sex therapy is frequently indicated as an adjunct, if not primary, form of treatment where other forms of medical and psychotherapy are required. If there are no certified sex therapists who have experience with GLBT clients, other psychotherapists may need to address issues of sexual dysfunction. In any case, sex and relationship therapy are always integrated, unless there is no partner.

The content of the assessment varies according to gender and problem(s). Both content and context are significant: description of the problem, thoughts on the problem's origins and maintenance, and how connected or disconnected sex is to other aspects of the client's life. It is also important to determine if the problem is lifelong, current, or intermittent, and if it is global or situational.

The questions are meant to be guidelines and each therapist should use her or his own words or expressions. It is best to see each partner separately for the assessment process, which typically takes two hours.

Suggestions for Follow-Up

Following the assessment of both partners, the couple is encouraged to discuss their experiences with one another. During the following joint session the therapist shares her or his perceptions and treatment recommendations.

Contraindications

This assessment is inappropriate for clients who have not expressed an interest in exploring their sexuality or a concern with their sexual functioning.

Readings and Resources for the Professional

Alexander, C. J. (Ed). (1999). *Working with gay men and lesbians in private psychotherapy practice*. Binghamton, NY: The Haworth Press.

Ellison, C. R. (2000). *Women's sexualities*. Oakland, CA: New Harbinger Pub.

Leiblum, S. and Rosen, R. (Eds.) (2000). *Principles and practice of sex therapy,* Third edition. New York: Guilford Publications.

Savin-Williams, R. C. and Cohen, K. M. (1996). *The lives of lesbians, gays, and bisexuals*. Fort Worth, TX: Harcourt Brace.

Shaw, J. and Erhardt, V. (1997). *Journey toward intimacy: A handbook for lesbian couples*. Atlanta, GA: Couples Enrichment Institute.

Audiovisual Resources

Buendia Productions
P.O. Box 1869
Santa Ana, CA 92702
Therapy with GLBT clients

Bibliotherapy Sources for the Client

Atkins, D. (Ed.) (1998). *Lesbian sex scandals*. Binghamton, NY: The Haworth Press.

Daniluk, J. C. and Leiblum, S. R. (1998). *Women's sexuality across the life span*. New York: Guilford Publications.

Heiman, J. and Lopiccolo, J. (1988). *Becoming orgasmic: A sexual and personal growth program for women.* New York: Simon and Schuster.

Joannides, P. (1999). *The guide to getting it on,* Second edition. Arkansas City, KS: Goofy Foot Press.

Kay, K., Nagle, J., and Gould, B. (2000). *Male lust: Pleasure, power, and transformation.* Binghamton, NY: The Haworth Press.

Sutton, L. (1999). *Love matters: A book of lesbian romance and relationships.* Binghamton, NY: The Haworth Press.

Tejirian, E. J. (2000). *Male to male: Sexual feeling across the boundaries of identity.* Binghamton, NY: The Haworth Press.

Audiovisual Resources

Femme Productions Videos
588 Broadway, Suite 1110
New York, NY 10012
Women's erotica

Greenwood/Cooper Home Videos
P.O. Box 2575
Laguna Hills, CA 92654
Gay erotica and education

House O'Chicks
2215-R Market St., Suite 813
San Francisco, CA 94114
www.houseochicks.com
Feminist/lesbian

Mystic Fire Video
P.O. Box 422
New York, NY 10012
Spiritual/GLBT

References

Bartlik, B. and Goldberg, J. (2000). Female sexual arousal disorder. In S. Leiblum and R. Rosen (Eds.), *Principles and practice of sex therapy,* Third edition (pp. 85-117). New York: Guilford Publications.

Nichols, M. (2000). Therapy with sexual minorities. In S. Leiblum and R. Rosen (Eds.), *Principles and practice of sex therapy,* Third edition (pp. 335-367). New York: Guilford Publications.

Rosen, R. C. (2000). Medical and psychological interventions for erectile dysfunction. In S. Leiblum and R. Rosen (Eds.), *Principles and practice of sex therapy,* Third edition (pp. 276-304). New York: Guilford Publications.

Client Assessment

Personal Data

Name _____ Age _____ Date _____

Address _____

Telephone: Home _____ Work _____

Employment _____ Education _____

Job satisfaction _____

Religion _____

Current Family Structure

Name	Age	Quality of relationship with you
Partner		
Child		
Child		
Child		
Child		

Others living in the home _____

Medical History

Describe present state of health _____

Date of last physical exam _____ Results _____

HIV status _____ Symptoms _____

Medications _____ OTC _____

Alcohol/drug use _____

Significant past illnesses/surgery _____

History of mental health problems (self/family) _____

Family-of-Origin History

Siblings

Name	Age	Quality of relationship with you

Mother: age _____ If deceased, year of death/cause _____

Relationship with you growing up _____

Relationship with you now/as an adult _____

Attitude toward sex _____

Attitude toward homosexuality _____

Father: age _____ If deceased, year of death/cause _____

Relationship with you growing up _____

_____

Relationship with you now/as an adult _____

_____

Attitude toward sex _____

Attitude toward homosexuality _____

As you were growing up, what messages did you get about sex?

_____ Sex is dirty

_____ Premarital sex is sinful

_____ Good kids don't do it

_____ Sex should not be talked about

_____ Genitals are dirty and ugly

_____ Sex is mainly for procreation

_____ Sex should always be heterosexual

_____ Religious injunctions against homosexuality

_____ Masturbation is sinful or shameful

_____ Sex is OK for boys/men, but not girls/women

_____ Sex should be fun for all people

_____ Sexual thoughts and feelings are natural

_____ Anything two adults agree to is OK

_____ Other _____

Use of touch in family of origin _____

Verbal expression of affection _____

Discipline in family: by whom _____ type _____

Significant Past Relationships

What were your early sexual experiences like? _____

_____

How do you feel about these experiences? _____

_____

Have you had any sexual experiences as a child, teen, or adult that you consider to be abusive, manipulative, or in some other way negative? _____

_____

Significant partners/lovers _____

Length of relationship(s) _____

Quality of sex _____

Cause for ending the relationship(s) _____

Impact on current life _____

Current Relationship

How do you identify yourself? _____ gay _____ lesbian _____ bisexual _____ transgendered

How did you meet your partner? _____

What attracted you to her or him? _____
_____

What did she or he find attractive about you? _____

Length of dating _____ Commitment _____

Sexual activity in beginning of relationship _____
_____

Sexual activity as the relationship continued _____
_____

What are the best aspects of this relationship? _____
_____

What are the most painful aspects of this relationship? _____
_____

What qualities do you like in your partner? _____
_____

How would you like your partner to change? _____
_____

What are your goals in treatment? _____
_____

Commitment: self _____ partner _____

Couple Assessment

Social activities as a couple _____

Activities with extended family _____

How are disagreements/conflicts handled? _____
_____

What are the significant stressors in your life as a couple? _____
_____

Use of touch as a couple _____

Verbal expression of affection _____

If couple has children

Discipline of children: by whom _____ type _____

Disagreements regarding discipline _____

Sex education of children: by whom _____ topics _____

Quality/quantity of time spent with children: self _____

partner _____ satisfaction _____

How do you manage privacy away from children? _____

Social activities as a family _____

Emotional Assessment

On a continuum describe yourself: sad (1) happy (10) _____

insecure (1) secure (10) _____ anxious (1) peaceful (10) _____

unhappy with sexual identity (1) happy with sexual identity (10) _____

unhappy with your body (1) happy with your body (10) _____

How do others value you? _____
_____

What qualities do you like about yourself? _____
_____

Current Sexual Concern

Desire Concern

Do you feel that your level of sexual desire has always been low? _____

If no, when did you notice it begin to drop? _____

Were there any unusual circumstances or pressures in your life at that time? _____
_____

Are there times when your level of desire seems more intense than others? _____

If yes, when and/or under what circumstances? _____

How often do you desire sex? _____

How often does your partner desire sex? _____

Do you feel your partner's sex drive is greater than yours? _____

What can you identify as "turn-ons?" _____
_____

What can you identify as "turn-offs?" _____
_____

How is self-stimulation for you? _____

Sexual fantasies _____

Do you sometimes attempt sexual activity even though you have no desire to be sexual? _____
If yes, why?

_____ Because it had been a while since the last time

_____ Because my partner demanded it

_____ Because I hoped it would work

_____ Because I knew my partner wanted it

_____ Because I just wanted to be close

_____ Other _____

Erectile Concerns

Percent of time you are unable to get an erection _____

Percent of time an erection is obtained but lost before penetration or ejaculation _____

Percent of time your erection is firm enough and penetration is successful _____

When, approximately, did you become aware of the problem with erections? _____
_____

Did the problem start suddenly, or did it seem to develop over time? _____
_____

Do you sometimes desire sexual activity but then consciously avoid it? _____
If yes, why?

_____ Because I am afraid of failure

_____ Because I am too tired

_____ Because there is no time

_____ Because I am too stressed

_____ Because my partner is not attractive to me

_____ Because my partner is not interested

_____ Because sex is no longer important to me

_____ Other _____

Orgasmic Concerns

Do you experience sexual arousal (turned on, lubrication)? _____

Have you ever had an orgasm? _____ yes _____ no _____ not sure

If yes, under what circumstances? _____ manual masturbation _____ with vibrator

   with partner stimulation _____ with oral stimulation _____ while sleeping

How would you describe the differences between the times you did orgasm and the times you did not _____

What have you tried in the past to reach orgasm? _____

Do you think you are trying too hard to have an orgasm? _____

Is your partner pushing you too hard to have an orgasm? _____

The part of your body you are most proud of _____

The part of your body you are most disappointed by _____

Current Sexual Relationship

Use of touch with one another _____

Verbal expression of affection _____

Who initiates sexual activity? _____

How is sexual activity initiated? _____

Who controls the frequency of sexual activity? _____

Who decides on the type of sexual activities? _____

How does this get decided? _____

How do you request specific activities? _____

How do you know what your partner wants? _____

How do you/partner refuse requests? _____

Length of lovemaking _____

Satisfaction _____

Verbal expression of affection: during _____ after _____

What areas of sex are most difficult to talk about with your partner? _____

_____

Is this relationship mutually: _____ sexually nonexclusive _____ sexually exclusive

How was this negotiated? _____

Do you have more than one sexual partner at present?_____

If sexually exclusive:

   While in this relationship have you had other partners? _____

   Is your partner aware of this? _____

   Has your partner had (has currently) other partners? _____

   How did you arrive at this knowledge? _____

Do you feel that problems within your relationship are contributing to your sexual problems? _____

_____

Discuss the following activities according to the categories

Activity	Do/like	Do/don't like	Don't do/ like to try	Don't do/ don't want to try
Kissing				
Nudity				
Total body touching apart from genitals				
Caressing breasts				
Touching partner's genitals				
Touching own genitals				
Partner touching your genitals				
Manual stimulation to orgasm:				
done to you				
done by you				
Oral sex:				
done to you				
done by you				
Anal stimulation/sex				
Use of erotic materials				
Vibrator				
Sex toys				
Sex games				
S&M techniques				
Group sex				
Other activities				

24

Sexual Pleasuring Sessions

Karen Fontaine

Type of Contribution: Activity/Handout/Homeplay

Objective

The goal of sexual pleasuring sessions is to help couples shift their focus from genital sex and demands for orgasm to relaxing and enjoying the erotic/sensual process.

Rationale for Use

When couples have been in a relationship for a period of time, sex often becomes an "all-or-nothing" goal-fixated approach. The most common sexual problem for lesbian couples is desire discrepancy/inhibited sexual desire, for which this exercise is especially helpful. Gay men may also find the experience helpful as they negotiate mutual sexual activities. Participating in sexual pleasuring sessions demonstrates the importance of making time for physical intimacy in relationships.

Instructions

The therapist gives the couple the Pleasuring Sessions handout. Most couples begin at Stage One for several weeks and then move on to Stage Two, and finally Stage Three. When breasts and genitals are off limits, arousal and orgasm are no longer required and should not be expected. The pressure to respond is reduced and clients no longer need to monitor their own or their partner's performance. The emphasis shifts from trying to be sexual to learning to be sensual.

Suggestions for Follow-Up

The process of these sessions should be discussed in therapy weekly. The therapist makes suggestions or modifications based on the couple's responses to the homeplay. For example, if roles in the bedroom are rigid, suggestions may be given on how to shift the roles to a more variable style. If the therapist discovers that verbal exchange during lovemaking is nonexistent, the focus may change to improving interpersonal communication.

Contraindications

Not appropriate for persons who have an aversion to being touched, which is related to a past history of trauma.

Readings and Resources for the Professional

Alexander, C. J. (Ed.) (1999). *Working with gay men and lesbians in private psychotherapy practice*. Binghamton, NY: The Haworth Press.

Ellison, C. R. (2000). *Women's sexualities*. Oakland, CA: New Harbinger Pub.

Leiblum, S. and Rosen, R. (Eds.) (2000). *Principles and practice of sex therapy,* Third edition. New York: Guilford Publications.

Savin-Williams, R. C. and Cohen, K. M. (1996). *The lives of lesbians, gays, and bisexuals*. Fort Worth, TX: Harcourt Brace.

Shaw, J. and Erhardt, V. (1997). *Journey toward intimacy: A handbook for lesbian couples*. Atlanta, GA: Couples Enrichment Institute.

Bibliotherapy Sources for the Client

Atkins, D. (Ed.) (1998). *Lesbian sex scandals*. Binghamton, NY: The Haworth Press.

Daniluk, J. C. and Leiblum, S. R. (1998). *Women's sexuality across the life span*. New York: Guilford Publications.

Heiman, J. and Lopiccolo, J. (1988). *Becoming orgasmic: A sexual and personal growth program for women*. New York: Simon and Schuster.

Joannides, P. (1999). *The guide to getting it on,* Second edition. Arkansas City, KS: Goofy Foot Press.

Kay, K., Nagle, J., and Gould, B. (2000). *Male lust: Pleasure, power, and transformation*. Binghamton, NY: The Haworth Press.

Sommers, R. (1989). *Pleasures*. Tallahassee, FL: Naiad Press.

Sutton, L. (1999). *Love matters: A book of lesbian romance and relationships*. Binghamton, NY: The Haworth Press.

Tejirian, E. J. (2000). *Male to male: Sexual feeling across the boundaries of identity*. Binghamton, NY: The Haworth Press.

Pleasuring Sessions

Basic to pleasuring sessions is the recognition that touch is a vital part of personal communication, which gives meaning to sexual responsiveness and satisfaction for both women and men. People must touch each other in a communicative way to achieve the fullness of sexual expression. This is the most important source of sexual stimulation, and thus full awareness of the sense of touch is extremely important.

Pleasuring sessions are to be conducted for thirty minutes, usually three times a week. Times of fatigue, stress, or tension should be avoided. One partner begins the experience of giving pleasurable touching to the other. The "giving" person should respond to verbal and nonverbal directions from the "receiving" partner about preferences for locations and intensity of touch. The idea is for the giving partner to provide pleasure and to discover what touching experiences are the most gratifying for the receiving partner. The giving person, in addition to providing pleasure, is to explore at the same time her or his own enjoyment in the pleasuring process. After fifteen minutes, change roles and repeat the experience.

It is important that both partners actively communicate during these sessions. It is impossible to mind read and it does not allow for each partner to communicate his or her desires and needs. Use "I" language to communicate desires and experiences, such as, "I like . . . ," "I don't like . . . ," or "I would like you to try. . . ."

Begin slowly and progressively through each of the following stages. Be sure to continue to communicate actively at each stage.

Stage One   Start with total body touching *except* no breast touching, no genital touching, and no genital interaction.
Stage Two   Progress to total body touching *including* breast and genital touching. Do not engage in any further genital interaction.
Stage Three   Continue total body touching *including* breast and genital touching. Genital interaction is now OK.

Be creative; try lotions, powders, massage oil, body paints, various fabrics, feathers, vibrators, or whatever. Broaden your horizons by experiencing and appreciating the sensuous dimensions of hard and soft, smooth and rough, warm and cool, and qualities of texture. The first try at pleasuring activities and verbal sharing may seem awkward and artificial, but most people quickly move to mutual pleasure and increased intimacy.

Two common problems are goal orientation and time. Lovemaking is best done leisurely. You cannot enjoy your partner if you rush to end sex as soon as it begins. When you have time to spend showing love, be as romantic as possible. Enjoy a sensual dining experience, for example. When you move from food to lovemaking, do it slowly. Do not attack your partner's genitals as if the rest of the body does not count. When you make love, every touch and caress should be pleasure in itself. It should be an outpouring of affection, of wanting to be together, of holding and kissing and showing through every touch how much you care for each other.

Inevitably, one experience or one type of touch may feel very good and another less so. Yet a few minutes later (or maybe the next night or the next week), those responses are reversed. Remember, we change from day to day. Just because your partner did not like something one time, do not write it off forever. Be willing to risk trying it again. Maybe this time it will give you both a pleasure you have never had before. Each partner also has the right to say "no" to any proposed sexual activity. Loving partners respect and honor each other's limits and boundaries.

25

Exploring and Negotiating Sexual Meanings

Sara K. Bridges
Robert A. Neimeyer

Type of Contribution: Activity/Homework

Objective

The goal of this activity and the corresponding homework is to help the client understand and communicate more fully about his or her own systems of sexual meanings and those of his or her partner. This expanded awareness should help both partners achieve greater intimacy and sexual satisfaction within their relationship.

Rationale for Use

As complex human beings with diverse backgrounds and ways of making meaning in our lives, we understand and experience sexuality in numerous ways. Taken as a whole, the idea of our sexuality or sexual identity can be a bit overwhelming, making it hard to comprehend fully for ourselves much less communicate clearly to others. The concept of sexual "holons" can be helpful in this way, referring to those parts of our sexuality that are sufficiently complex to be considered whole systems of meanings by themselves, which are in turn nested within a larger system (Zumaya, Bridges, and Rubio, 1999). This exercise helps counselors and clients explore issues related to sexual identity in terms of its component systems—gender, eroticism, interpersonal bonding, and reproduction—thereby providing an organizational structure for mapping sexual meanings and facilitating dialogue about them in the context of individual or couple counseling. As such, this exercise in exploring and negotiating sexual meanings is an expression of constructivist themes in contemporary counseling, helping clients articulate and reconstruct those (inter)personal meanings, feelings, and practices that constrain or enable their relationships with themselves or others (Neimeyer and Mahoney, 1995; Neimeyer and Raskin, 2000).

Instructions

The questions that make up this exercise can be used at two different levels. First, they can provide a framework of assessment for couples counselors or sex therapists, as they begin to piece together a picture of a client's sexual meanings that represent potential strengths or difficulties. Second, the handout, Holonic System of Sexual Meanings, can be used directly by individual clients or couples to guide them in exploring and beginning to negotiate their own sexual meanings and preferences in a relationship. It is often helpful to combine both of these uses in a single case, offering a brief description of the idea of sexuality including four distinct and interacting parts (see description in handout). Once the basic holonic model is clarified, clients can then reflect on each of these four domains, prompted by the questions provided, in the form of a written homework assignment. Because of the delicacy of such personal exploration, however, and the possibility of conflicting meanings and preferences within a couple, ask both partners to keep their responses private until they can be shared with one another in the presence of the counselor.

Finally, it is worth noting that although the various parts or holons can be subject to meaningful exploration by themselves, their greatest utility is in their ability to combine, unify, and connect. As such, illuminating the connections between the areas of gender, eroticism, interpersonal bonding, and reproduction can provide insight into the emergent properties in sexual meaning-making processes in ways not possible if they are solely treated in isolation. For this reason, a sampling of questions to stimulate exploration of the interconnections among these systems of meanings, both within and between members of the couple is also included.

Brief Vignettes

David and Lamar presented for therapy regarding a lack of sexual interest in their relationship. While exploring questions concerning eroticism using the handout, Lamar acknowledged that he had suppressed his private fantasies—which involved light bondage—because he considered them dirty or mean spirited, leading him to shut out feelings of desire in any form. Moreover, David experienced his partner's evident lack of desire in the relationship as a lessening of commitment, constituting a threat to their interpersonal bond. Without this behavioral display of commitment, David tended to withdraw from Lamar, further exacerbating the distance between them. David and Lamar found that by allowing themselves to speak specifically about their respective experiences of sexual desire from within their holonic structures, they could better understand the impasses they had encountered in their sexual relationship. Thus, with only minimal help from a counselor, both men were able to use the holonic map to more fully understand each other's position and also make themselves more clearly understood. This new understanding sparked subsequent problem-solving conversations that allow them both to experiment with new erotic practices without threatening the bond between them.

Jackie was a woman in her late twenties who sought therapy due to complexities in her relationship with Waneen, her female partner of several years. As Jackie sifted through her own evolving sexual identity in response to the holonic questions, she began to recognize that her gender identity had shifted from a presumed heterosexual orientation in her teens, through her exploration of a lesbian identity in her early and mid-twenties, to the emergence of a bisexual identity at present. This shift in gender identity had caused friction with Waneen, as had her expressions of erotic interest in men as well as women. Although Jackie continued to feel a strong bond of love to Waneen, she also felt constrained by the exclusive commitment Waneen required, as well as her partner's unwillingness to discuss the prospect of their having or raising children. Over the course of several sessions of individual and joint therapy, Jackie and Waneen ultimately decided to suspend their romantic relationship and embrace new relationships that corresponded more closely to their divergent needs.

Suggestions for Follow-Up

The initial exploration of holonic meanings can be eye-opening for both counselor and client, leading to sometimes tentative, sometimes spirited exchanges that can "ripple" through several sessions. For this reason, it is often helpful to revisit the holonic mappings periodically over the course of therapy, perhaps asking questions such as, "How has your conception of your gender identity (or erotic preferences, or interpersonal bonds, or feelings about reproduction) changed over time?" "What do you see as your 'growing edge' in this area?" or "What, if anything, still requires attention?" Careful follow-up is especially important when the questions are given as a homework assignment to a client, as deep self-reflection on such intimate questions can sometimes lead to a sense of vulnerability or embarrassment, calling for an empathic and affirming response by the therapist or counselor.

Contraindications

Prior to introducing the holonic model, it is vital that the therapist build rapport with the client to create a safe space for full disclosure of sexual meanings. As always, indications of violence (verbal or physical) or medical concerns (such as vaginismus or difficulties sustaining an erection) should be fully evaluated prior to beginning this exercise. Finally, the negotiation of sexual meanings presumes a certain openness to self-exploration and sufficient levels of empathic communication with the partner to permit moving into a delicate area. For this reason, postpone this exercise until these basic preconditions are met, and suspend it altogether (except in the context of individual counseling) if the client is attempting to disengage from a highly conflicted relationship.

Readings and Resources for the Professional

Fukyama, M. A. and Ferguson, A. D. (2000). Lesbian, gay, and bisexual people of color: Understanding cultural complexity and managing multiple oppressions. In R. M. Perez, K. A. DeBord, and K. J. Bieschke (Eds.), *Handbook of counseling and psychotherapy with lesbian, gay and bisexual clients* (pp. 81-105). Washington, DC: American Psychological Association.

L'Abate, L. and Talmadge, W. C. (1995). Love, intimacy and sex. In G. R. Weeks and L. Hoff (Eds.), *Integrating sex and marital therapy* (pp. 23-34). New York: Brunner/Mazel.

Neimeyer, R. A. and Mahoney, M. J. (Eds.) (1995). *Constructivism in psychotherapy*. Washington, DC: American Psychological Association.

Neimeyer, R. A. and Raskin, J. (Eds.) (2000). *Constructions of disorder: Meaning making frameworks for psychotherapy*. Washington, DC: American Psychological Association.

Regan, P. C. and Berscheid, E. (1999). *Lust: What we know about human sexual desire*. Thousand Oaks, CA: Sage Publications.

Rosen, R. C. and Leiblum, S. R. (Eds.) (1995). *Case studies in sex therapy*. New York: Guilford Publications.

Zumaya, M., Bridges, S. K., and Rubio, E. (1999). A constructivist approach to sex therapy with couples. *Journal of Constructivist Psychology, 12*, 185-201.

Bibliotherapy Sources for the Client

Daniluk, J. C. (1998). *Women's sexuality across the life span: Challenging myths, creating meanings*. New York: Guilford Publications.

Tiefer, L. (1995). *Sex is not a natural act and other essays*. Boulder, CO: Westview Press.

References

Neimeyer, R. A. and Mahoney, M. J. (Eds.) (1995). *Constructivism in psychotherapy*. Washington, DC: American Psychological Association.

Neimeyer, R. A. and Raskin, J. (Eds.) (2000). *Constructions of disorder: Meaning making frameworks for psychotherapy*. Washington, DC: American Psychological Association.

Zumaya, M., Bridges, S. K., and Rubio, E. (1999). A constructivist approach to sex therapy with couples. *Journal of Constructivist Psychology, 12*, 185-201.

Holonic System of Sexual Meanings

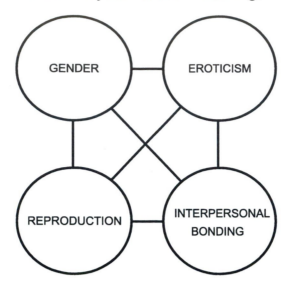

Sexual identity is made up of four interrelated systems of meanings, which differ from one person or relationship to another. Because it can be confusing to sort through these meanings with a partner (or even on one's own), it is often helpful to reflect on each of these areas in turn, as they bear on your thoughts, feelings, and preferences about issues related to gender, erotic pleasure, interpersonal bonding, and reproduction. As a guide, you might find it helpful to try to answer some of the following questions for yourself, before discussing similar questions with your partner. A few suggestions for exploring each of these systems follow, as well as some questions that focus on their interaction. However, other topics related to these areas might occur to you as you reflect on each, so the prompts that follow should be considered only a general guide to how your exploration might evolve.

1. **Gender holon:** the way we see ourselves as female, male, lesbian, gay, bisexual, transgendered, or heterosexual within society and all of the implications this has for our lives. Sample questions:

   How does your personal conception of your gender identity shape your preferred way of relating sexually? What aspects of your gender identity do you value? Are there features of your historical gender identity that you would like to change or leave behind?

   What forms of sexual interaction would fit with your preferred gender role? What forms of interaction would not fit? How have you seen these changing across time?

   Are the gender roles adopted by you and your partner compatible, complementary, or conflictual in their implications for your sexual relationship? How flexible or firm are your respective roles in the relationship? Are there any ways you would like to see this change?

2. **Erotic holon:** our appetite for sexual excitement, pleasure, and orgasm. Sample questions:

   What forms of sexual activity give you pleasure? Are there forms of sexual expression that you avoid? Does this change over time? If so, how?

   What meanings or fantasies enhance or intensify your excitement and erotic potential? What meanings inhibit it?

   How compatible are your erotic preferences with those of your partner? Which aspects of your erotic preferences are most difficult to speak about? Which are most easily misunderstood?

3. **Interpersonal bonding holon:** our capacity to develop intense feelings in regard to the presence or absence, availability or unavailability of another specific human being. Sample questions:

> To what extent do you seek versus retreat from meaningful attachment relationships? How are these forms of drawing close or distancing expressed in words or actions?
>
> Do you experience the emotional bond with your partner as secure or insecure, comfortable or anxious? What forms of interaction between you contribute to each of these outcomes?
>
> Is the form of closeness sought by both of you similar or dissimilar? How might you signal your need for greater connection or space in a way that is constructive for you both?

4. **Reproduction holon:** the human potential to create or foster the development of individuals who are physically similar, but not identical, to those who have nurtured them. Sample questions:

> What role, if any, does having or raising children play in your identity as a person? Has this changed over time, and if so, how?
>
> In what ways do the expressed (or implicit) wishes of others (e.g., biological parents, friends) affect your feelings about having children or not doing so? How can you respond constructively to these wishes without compromising your own preferences?
>
> How compatible are your hopes or wishes concerning the desirability or timing of reproduction with those of your partner? How might such wishes be negotiated?

5. **Holonic interactions:** the subtle interplay among your four systems of sexual meanings, or between your meanings and those of your partner. Sample questions:

> Are some of your holons isolated from the others, so that it is not clear that they connect with other domains of your sexual identity? How would your sense of yourself as a sexual being change if they were more completely integrated?
>
> Are some of your holons bigger or more important than others? What would this look like if you drew them to scale? How would this compare with the holonic structure of your partner?
>
> Is there a distinctive firing order of your holons, that is, does the activation of one (for example, interpersonal bonding) tend to trigger the activation of another (such as eroticism)? Is the sequencing of your activation similar to or different from that of your partner?

26

Enhancing Relationships:
Sex-Role Values of Lesbian and Bisexual Women

Cyndy J. Boyd
Joy S. Whitman
Diane Sobel

Type of Contribution: Activity/Handout

Objectives

This activity is designed to clarify what role sex has in the lives of lesbian and bisexual women, to clarify values these couples have concerning issues of sexuality, and to enhance communication patterns within these couples regarding issues of sexuality.

Rationale for Use

Much of the literature on lesbian couples emphasizes the concept of "fusion," or lack of differentiation, experienced in the relationships (Burch, 1982; Elise, 1986; Krestan and Bepko, 1980; Roth, 1989). It has been suggested that fusion occurs because women have been socialized to be highly attuned and responsive to the needs of others, often to the exclusion of their own needs (Baker Miller and Stiver, 1998). Historically, theorists have noted the problematic aspects of such undifferentiated intimacy, pointing out for instance that individual needs may be neglected and overt conflict completely avoided. A finding by Greene, Bettinger, and Zacks (1996) indicates that healthy lesbian couples do not view this kind of intimacy as detrimental, however; instead, they find it satisfying and facilitative of a robust relationship. Their positive reactions to this level of intimacy may also be understood as a direct result of gender-role socialization, in that women have been encouraged to acquire a high comfort level for emotional closeness, whereas men might find such a dynamic to be less pleasing since they have been socialized to view it as dependent and weak (Goodrich et al., 1988; Mencher, 1990).

Although it must be highlighted that women are able to experience minimal separateness and yet maintain a functional relationship, it is likely that for lesbian couples who are experiencing relationship difficulties, the challenge of managing conflict and asserting individual needs will arise as a theme in therapy. As Bepko and Johnson (2000) state, "dysfunctional lesbian couples seeking therapy may be more vulnerable to patterns of intense conflict and problems negotiating separateness, and these problems may result from one or both partners' overconforming to norms of female conflict avoidance and caretaking" (p. 414). This struggle to accept and resolve differences may be especially pronounced with regard to sexual expression. Since women are socialized to view sexuality primarily as an extension of emotional intimacy, they may be hesitant to express desires that are different from those of their partners, particularly because such an admission may decrease the connectedness that "should" be at the core of their sexual encounters. Furthermore, it may be taboo for some women to admit to sexual preferences that contradict the messages they internalized about appropriate forms of sexual expression for women.

Silence concerning issues of sexuality in a couple can result in significant deficits in functioning and great dissatisfaction for one or both partners. For this reason, therapists must recognize the potential for lesbian couples to find this topic to be exigent. It is also important for therapists to remember that lesbians and bisexual women in same-sex relationships may need both structure and encouragement to delve into this area of discussion.

Instructions

This questionnaire addresses both particular sexual preferences as well as common beliefs underlying the expression of sexuality for many women. It is designed to help therapists introduce this topic and work with their clients' manifest and latent issues regarding styles of sexual expression. It may be used in session as a way to structure a discussion in either individual or couple therapy, or as a homework assignment. If used as homework, the results could be processed in the next session, or if used by a couple before the next session, as a way of facilitating their own dialogue.

Therapists may begin by normalizing the difficulties experienced by many women in discussing and expressing sexuality, given the cultural norms relating to this topic. Following that introduction, therapists can suggest the use of this questionnaire as an aid to clients in finding the language for such an exploration, in normalizing their concerns, and in highlighting some of the central issues. Because the issue of sexuality is more broad and encompassing than the issues covered by this questionnaire, it should be emphasized that this exercise is intended only as a way to begin or further their work rather than as an exhaustive guide on this issue.

Suggestions for Follow-Up

For all clients, this exercise could be used to pinpoint areas to become the focus of ongoing therapy. In addition, once clients have clarified their needs and values through this questionnaire, they may need assistance in communicating them to present or potential partners.

For couples, this questionnaire could be used as a way to begin to talk about differences in this area. The goal would be to work toward the safe expression of individual needs and desires as well as to find a compromise when needs are conflicting.

Contraindications

Clients who have been the victims of sexual abuse or assault would benefit from processing the ways in which those experiences have impacted their current sexuality before focusing on values clarification. If these issues are not addressed, it is likely that residual and intense affect might arise as the result of completing this questionnaire.

Couples who are experiencing physical violence or emotional abuse should address those issues before completing this questionnaire. It is essential that both members of the couple feel safe enough to express themselves fully.

Readings and Resources for the Professional

Baker Miller, J. and Stiver, J. (1998). *The healing connection: How women form relationships in therapy and life*. Wellesley, MA: Wellesley Centers for Women Publications.
Bepko, C. and Johnson, T. (2000). Gay and lesbian couples in therapy: Perspectives for the contemporary family therapist. *Journal of Marital and Family Therapy, 26*(4), 409-419.

Burch, B. (1982). Psychological merger in lesbian couples: A joint ecological and systems approach. *Family Therapy, 9,* 201-208.

Clunis, D. M. and Green, G. D. (2000). *Lesbian couples.* Seattle, WA: Seal Press.

Elise, D. (1986). Lesbian couples: The implication of sex differences in separation individuation. *Psychotherapy, 23,* 305-310.

Goodrich, T. J., Rampage, C., Ellman, B., and Halsted, K. (1988). *Feminist family therapy: A casebook.* New York: W. W. Norton and Company.

Greene, R.-J., Bettinger, M., and Zacks, E. (1996). Are lesbian couples fused and gay male couples disengaged? Questioning gender straightjackets. In J. Laird and R.-J. Green (Eds.), *Lesbians and gays in couples and families: A handbook for therapists* (pp. 185-230). San Francisco, CA: Jossey-Bass.

Krestan, S. J. and Bepko, C. S. (1980). The problem of fusion in the lesbian relationship. *Family Process, 19,* 277-289.

Mencher, J. (1990). Intimacy in lesbian relationships: A critical re-examination of fusion. In J. V. Jordan, S. J. Bergman, C. G. Coll, N. Eldridge, J. Mencher, and J. Baker Miller (Eds.), *Women's growth in diversity: More writings from the Stone Center* (pp. 311-330). New York: Guilford Publications.

Rose, S. M. (2002). *Lesbian love and relationships.* Binghamton, NY: The Haworth Press.

Roth, S. (1989). Psychotherapy with lesbian couples: Individual issues, female socialization, and the social context. In M. McGoldrick, C. Anderson, and F. Walsh (Eds.), *Women in families: A framework for family therapy* (pp. 286-307). New York: W. W. Norton and Company.

Bibliotherapy Sources for the Client

Clunis, D. M. and Green, G. D. (2000). *Lesbian couples.* Seattle, WA: Seal Press.

Rose, S. M. (2002). *Lesbian love and relationships.* Binghamton, NY: The Haworth Press.

References

Baker Miller, J. and Stiver, J. (1998). *The healing connection: How women form relationships in therapy and life.* Wellesley, MA: Wellesley Centers for Women Publications.

Bepko, C. and Johnson, T. (2000). Gay and lesbian couples in therapy: Perspectives for the contemporary family therapist. *Journal of Marital and Family Therapy, 26*(4), 409-419.

Burch, B. (1982). Psychological merger in lesbian couples: A joint ecological and systems approach. *Family Therapy, 9,* 201-208.

Elise, D. (1986). Lesbian couples: The implication of sex differences in separation individuation. *Psychotherapy, 23,* 305-310.

Goodrich, T. J., Rampage, C., Ellman, B., and Halsted, K. (1988). *Feminist family therapy: A casebook.* New York: W. W. Norton and Company.

Greene, R.-J., Bettinger, M., and Zacks, E. (1996). Are lesbian couples fused and gay male couples disengaged? Questioning gender straightjackets. In J. Laird and R.-J. Green (Eds.), *Lesbians and gays in couples and families: A handbook for therapists* (pp. 185-230). San Francisco, CA: Jossey-Bass.

Krestan, S. J. and Bepko, C. S. (1980). The problem of fusion in the lesbian relationship. *Family Process, 19,* 277-289.

Mencher, J. (1990). Intimacy in lesbian relationships: A critical re-examination of fusion. In J. V. Jordan, S. J. Bergman, C. G. Coll, N. Eldridge, J. Mencher, and J. Baker Miller (Eds.),

Women's growth in diversity: More writings from the Stone Center (pp. 311-330). New York: Guilford Publications.

Roth, S. (1989). Psychotherapy with lesbian couples: Individual issues, female socialization, and the social context. In M. McGoldrick, C. Anderson, and F. Walsh (Eds.), *Women in families: A framework for family therapy* (pp. 286-307). New York: W. W. Norton and Company.

Values and Attitudes Regarding the Role of Sex in Relationships

Indicate the extent to which you agree or disagree with each of the following:

1. Sex is necessary for intimacy.

Totally Disagree	Somewhat Disagree	No Opinion	Somewhat Agree	Totally Agree

2. Intimacy is necessary for good sex.

Totally Disagree	Somewhat Disagree	No Opinion	Somewhat Agree	Totally Agree

3. The main purpose of sex in a relationship is to feel closer to the other person.

Totally Disagree	Somewhat Disagree	No Opinion	Somewhat Agree	Totally Agree

4. In their sexual relationships, women have a harder time pursuing other women as opposed to being pursued.

Totally Disagree	Somewhat Disagree	No Opinion	Somewhat Agree	Totally Agree

5. It is OK to have sex with someone just for the fun of it.

Totally Disagree	Somewhat Disagree	No Opinion	Somewhat Agree	Totally Agree

6. Women are not very aware of their sexual needs.

Totally Disagree	Somewhat Disagree	No Opinion	Somewhat Agree	Totally Agree

7. It is OK to have sex with one's "friends."

Totally Disagree	Somewhat Disagree	No Opinion	Somewhat Agree	Totally Agree

8. Even if two people are in a serious relationship, it is OK if one or both of them has sex with somebody outside of the relationship.

Totally Disagree	Somewhat Disagree	No Opinion	Somewhat Agree	Totally Agree

9. It is difficult for women to initiate sex.

Totally Disagree	Somewhat Disagree	No Opinion	Somewhat Agree	Totally Agree

10. It is difficult for a woman to distinguish between her intimate feelings for friends and those she has toward her lover.

Totally Disagree	Somewhat Disagree	No Opinion	Somewhat Agree	Totally Agree

11. A woman's sexual needs are met differently by male partners than by female partners.

Totally Disagree	Somewhat Disagree	No Opinion	Somewhat Agree	Totally Agree

12. Women do not have to be sexual with each other in order to feel intimate.

Totally Disagree	Somewhat Disagree	No Opinion	Somewhat Agree	Totally Agree

13. Women are aware of their partners' sexual needs without asking about them.

Totally Disagree	Somewhat Disagree	No Opinion	Somewhat Agree	Totally Agree

14. Women have trouble asking for their sexual needs to be met by their partner.

Totally Disagree	Somewhat Disagree	No Opinion	Somewhat Agree	Totally Agree

15. Women tend to lose their sense of self when they become intimate with other women.

Totally Disagree	Somewhat Disagree	No Opinion	Somewhat Agree	Totally Agree

SECTION III:
HOMEWORK, HANDOUTS, AND ACTIVITIES FOR GENDER, ETHNIC, AND SEXUAL IDENTITY ISSUES

27

The Sexual Orientation, Gender Identity, and Gender Expression Continuum

Stuart F. Chen-Hayes

Type of Contribution: Activity/Homework

Objective

The goal of this activity is to help clients look at patterns of sexual orientation, gender identity, and gender expression in their past, present, and future for themselves and their partners. It is designed to help broaden gay, lesbian, bisexual, and transgendered (GLBT) clients' conceptualizations of (1) sexual orientation, identity, and behavior self-labeling; (2) personal gender identity and gender expression; and (3) attraction to gender identity and gender expression in a partner.

Rationale for Use

Traditionally, GLBT practitioners and clients have avoided gender identity and gender expression issues in counseling situations due to little or no training in these areas (Chen-Hayes, 2001). Gender identity and gender expression issues, and to a lesser extent sexual orientation issues, continue to be pathologized in medical model contexts (Chen-Hayes, 2001). At the same time, many GLBT clients and counselors feel unsure or uncomfortable about discussing gender identity and gender expression as a part of counseling. This exercise gives a voice for GLBT clients to put gender identity and gender expression in the forefront of counseling along with sexual orientation. As Klein, Sepekoff, and Wolf (1985) expanded upon the Kinsey, Pomeroy, and Martin (1948) scale of sexual orientation to be more inclusive of bisexuality with the Klein Sexual Orientation Grid (KSOG), this exercise broadens the KSOG from a focus on the multiple dynamic variables of sexual orientation to include the multiple dynamic variables related to gender identity and gender expression.

The danger of counselors not including gender identity and gender expression in counseling is that often clients who wish to fully express themselves as gendered beings will ignore or avoid the issues. Counselors who are able to ask and to affirm questions and dialogue related to gender identity and gender expression give permission to clients that it is safe to discuss issues that are otherwise suppressed or pathologized both within and outside GLBT communities. This exercise can be used early in the counseling process as part of an intake or as an evaluative tool for personal growth at any time during the counseling process.

Instructions

Ask clients to rate the sexual orientation, gender identity, and gender expression labels that best fit them in the past, present, and future/ideal on a scale of 1 to 10 (1 = low, 10 = high) using the handouts My Sexual Orientation, Identity, and Behavior, and My Gender Identity/Expression. Next, using the Gender Identities and Gender Expression handout, ask clients to rate their past, present, and future/ideal attractions in terms of gender identity/expression in a partner. Encourage clients to read the Gender Identity and Gender Expression Definitions handout for clarity prior to doing the exercise. Once clients have completed the ratings, counselors are encouraged to discuss a range of questions that may occur for clients:

- How does your gender identity affect your experience as a GLBT person?
- How does gender expression affect your experience as a GLBT person?
- What gender identity/expression attracts you in yourself and others?
- What gender identity/expression is difficult to deal with in yourself and others?
- How does being GLBT affect your masculinity and femininity?
- How do others perceive you in terms of masculinity and femininity?

Brief Vignette

A twenty-two-year-old male of Mexican ethnicity is in counseling because he is unhappy that his family perceives him as feminine. He would like to be more butch, but is attracted only to straight-acting gay, bisexual, and heterosexual men who are *machistas* (feminine gender equivalent of macho). The client states that he likes to do drag and enjoys how he can attract butch men through his feminine attire and attitude but that he yearns to be similar to butch men on the outside, too. He is given the assignment to look at his sexual orientation, gender identity, and gender expression in the past, present, and future in terms of his self-labels, his gender identity, and gender expression, and his partners' gender identity/expression to help clarify his desires and interests. The client discovers that he has always leaned toward a more fem appearance and has always been attracted to butch men. He started doing drag in high school and found that was a way to attract butch men. He would like to start bulking up more and doing drag less to become more butch. The counselor works with him to explore how he does not have to give up his gender identity and interests. Instead, he can expand the roles that he has expressed to include butch as well as fem. The client does not like labels such as "gay" or "transgendered" and chooses not to label either his sexual orientation or gender identity, but he is quite comfortable labeling his gender expression and his partners' gender expression. By assessing his sexual orientation, gender identity, and gender expression, and his potential partners' gender identity/expression through the use of the handouts, the client can discover greater clarity in his own sexual orientation, gender identity, and gender expression as a gay man, as well as clarity about his gender identity/expression attractions in potential partners.

Suggestions for Follow-Up

During and after the counseling process, or in "checkup" sessions, the client or counselor can refer to the handouts to see what, if anything, has shifted over time in terms of client labels, gender identity and gender expression, and partner gender identity/expression in addition to sexual orientation. The client's coming-out process as gay should be taken into consideration as he or she may have additional issues related to coming out in terms of gender identity and expression.

Contraindications

Clients who are just beginning the coming-out process or who fear being vulnerable about their identities related to gender identity and gender expression may find this exercise uncomfortable.

Readings and Resources for the Professional

Chen-Hayes, S. F. (1997). Counseling lesbian, bisexual and gay persons in couple and family relationships: Overcoming the stereotypes. *The Family Journal: Counseling and Therapy for Couples and Families, 5*(3), 236-240.

Chen-Hayes, S. F. (2000). Social justice advocacy with lesbian, bisexual, gay, and trans-gendered persons. In J. Lewis and L. Bradley (Eds.), *Advocacy in Counseling,* (pp. 89-98). Greensboro, NC: Caps Publications (ERIC/CASS).

Chen-Hayes, S. F. (2001). Counseling and advocacy with transgendered and gender-variant persons in schools and families. *The Journal of Humanistic Counseling, Education, and Development, 40*(1), 34-48.

Israel, G. E. and Tarver, D. E. (1997). *Transgender care: Recommended guidelines, practical information and personal accounts.* Philadelphia, PA: Temple University Press.

Klein, F., Sepekoff, B., and Wolf, T. J. (1985). Sexual orientation: A multi-variable dynamic process. In F. Klein and T. J. Wolf (Eds.), *Two lives to lead: Bisexuality in men and women* (pp. 35-50). Binghamton, NY: The Haworth Press.

Namaste, V. K. (2000). *Invisible lives: The erasure of transsexual and transgender people.* Chicago, IL: University of Chicago Press.

Rust, P. (Ed.) (2000). *Bisexuality in the United States.* New York: Columbia University Press.

Bibliotherapy Sources for the Client

Beemyn, B. and Eliason, M. (Eds.) (1996). *Queer studies: A lesbian, gay, bisexual and transgender anthology.* New York: New York University Press.

Bornstein, K. (1994). *Gender outlaw: On men, women, and the rest of us.* New York: Routledge.

Bornstein, K. (1998). *My gender workbook: How to become a real man, a real woman, the real you, or something else entirely.* New York: Routledge.

Queen, C. and Schimel, L. (Eds.) (1997). *Pomosexuals: Challenging assumptions about gender and sexuality.* San Francisco, CA: Cleis.

References

Chen-Hayes, S. F. (2001). Counseling and advocacy with transgendered and gender-variant persons in schools and families. *The Journal of Humanistic Counseling, Education, and Development, 40*(1), 34-48.

Kinsey, A. C., Pomeroy, W. B., and Martin, C. E. (1948). *Sexual behavior in the human male.* Philadelphia, PA: W. B. Saunders.

Klein, F., Sepekoff, B., and Wolf, T. J. (1985). Sexual orientation: A multi-variable dynamic process. In F. Klein and T. J. Wolf (Eds.), *Two lives to lead: Bisexuality in men and women* (pp. 35-50). Binghamton, NY: The Haworth Press.

My Sexual Orientation, Identity, and Behavior

Please rate the sexual orientation, identity, and behavior labels that best fit you in the past, present, and future/ideal on a scale of 1 to 10 (1 = low, 10 = high).

Sexual Orientation, Identity, and Behavior Labels	Past	Present	Future/Ideal
Man who has sex with men			
Man who has sex with men and women			
Man who has sex with women			
Man who has sex with transgendered persons			
Woman who has sex with women			
Woman who has sex with men and women			
Woman who has sex with men			
Woman who has sex with transgendered persons			
Transgendered person who has sex with transgendered persons			
Transgendered person who has sex with men			
Transgendered person who has sex with women			
Transgendered person who has sex with men and women			
Heterosexual identity			
Bisexual identity			
Gay identity			
Lesbian identity			
Two-spirit			
Queer identity			
Questioning			
I don't label my sexual behavior			
I don't label my sexual orientation/identity			
Other: _____			

My Gender Identity/Expression

Please rate the gender identity/expression labels that best fit you in the past, present, and future/ideal on a scale of 1 to 10 (1 = low, 10 = high).

My Gender Identity/Expression	Past	Present	Future/Ideal
Two-Spirit			
Queer			
Questioning			
Transgendered			
Cross-Dresser			
Transsexual			
Drag King			
Drag Queen			
Intersex			
Gender Bender			
Gender Blender			
Traditionally Gendered			
Androgynous			
Stone Butch/Ultramasculine			
Butch/Masculine			
More Butch than Fem			
More Fem than Butch			
Feminine			
Ultrafeminine			
Nontraditionally Gendered			
Gender Role-Playing			
Other: _____			

Gender Identities and Gender Expression

Please rate your past, present, and future/ideal attractions in terms of gender identity/expression in a partner on a scale of 1 to 10 (1 = low, 10 = high).

Gender Identities and Expression That Attract Me	Past	Present	Future/Ideal
Two-spirit			
Queer			
Questioning			
Transgendered			
Cross-Dresser			
Transsexual			
Drag King			
Drag Queen			
Intersex			
Gender Bender			
Gender Blender			
Traditionally Gendered			
Androgynous			
Stone Butch/Ultramasculine			
Butch/Masculine			
More Butch than Fem			
More Fem than Butch			
Feminine			
Ultrafeminine			
Nontraditionally Gendered			
Gender Role-Playing			
Other: _____			

Gender Identity and Gender Expression Definitions

For counselors and clients unfamiliar with the range of gendervariant and transgendered identities, the following definitions are given for clarification (Chen-Hayes, 2001):

Cross-dressers: Heterosexual men who dress in women's clothing and accessories to fulfill gender expression interests and/or for sexual pleasure on a continuum from part time to full time.

Drag kings: Lesbian and bisexual women who wear men's clothing and accessories to celebrate gay pride, question traditional gender expression norms and roles, express nontraditional gender identities, challenge authority, and/or perform or entertain.

Drag queens: Gay and bisexual men who wear women's clothing and accessories to celebrate gay pride, question traditional gender expression norms and roles, express nontraditional gender identities, challenge authority, and/or perform or entertain.

Gender blenders: Persons who challenge traditional dichotomous forms of gender identity/expression by substituting a continuum of external gender role and expression that combines both masculine and feminine clothing and accessories.

Intersex: Persons born with a combination of male and female genitals that may or may not have been surgically altered. Some intersex persons identify as transgendered and others identify as traditionally gendered men or women.

Queer: A term that has had multiple definitions, initially defined in English as different or "odd," and later used by some persons to denigrate GLBT persons. Within the past ten years, the term has been reclaimed by GLBT activists and academics to celebrate GLBT differences as good and deserving to be celebrated. Current usage of the term also includes persons who wish to challenge the essentialist character of terms such as sexual orientation and gender identity/expression and instead define them as socially constructed, fluid, nondiscrete forms of human sexual experience and identity.

Questioning: Persons who are not sure about labeling their identities or behaviors based on sexual orientation, gender identity, or gender expression.

Transgendered: An umbrella term used to describe members of the nondominant gender community (i.e., persons with nontraditional gender identity, gender expression, or role).

Transsexual: Persons whose external and internal gender identity/expression may not match. Persons who go through hormone treatments and sex-reassignment surgery may cross gender and become more congruent in internal and external gender identity/expression (from preoperative to postoperative status). Other transsexuals do not have sex-reassignment surgery and are known as nonoperative. Transsexual persons who have developed congruence in their internal and external gender identity/expression are often referred to as New Men or New Women, or transmen or transwomen.

Two-spirit: An umbrella term that attempts to include the multiple variations of sexual orientation, gender identity, and gender expression found in many traditional indigenous cultures around the world. Two-spirit persons often hold roles of honor and healing in indigenous communities. The expression of two-spirit identity and language is more complex than English-language identities and labels such as lesbian, bisexual, gay, or transgendered.

28

The Sexual Orientation and Gender Identity/Gender Expression Genogram

Stuart F. Chen-Hayes

Type of Contribution: Activity/Homework

Objective

The goal of this activity is to explore family-of-origin and family-of-choice patterns related to sexual orientation and gender identity/expression across multiple generations. For the purpose of this activity, gender identity refers to how persons experience their gender role and behavior internally, and gender expression refers to how persons present themselves in terms of gender roles and behavior externally (they may or may not match) (Chen-Hayes, 2001).

Rationale for Use

Most gay, lesbian, bisexual, and transgendered (GLBT) counseling theorists have looked at either sexual orientation development (D'Augelli, 1994) or gender identity/gender expression development (Bullough and Bullough, 1993). Chen-Hayes and Haley-Banez (2000) enhanced a GLBT identity development model (D'Augelli, 1994) to include gender identity/gender expression issues in addition to sexual orientation in highlighting the main developmental tasks as:

- Exiting heterosexual and traditionally gendered identities
- Developing a personal GLBT identity
- Developing a social GLBT identity
- Becoming a GLBT offspring
- Developing a GLBT intimacy status
- Entering a GLBT community

Combining reflection about family patterns and relationships related to sexual orientation, gender identity, and gender expression allows clients to reduce isolation and connect with potential allies in the family.

This activity can provide greater awareness about sexual orientation, gender identity, and gender expression variations in families of origin and families of choice. By identifying family members who are (or were) perceived as nontraditional in sexual orientation and gender identity/expression, clients and counselors can uncover hidden support, strengths, shared experiences, and family members who would be unsupportive. Learning to map family patterns through the use of genograms has been an effective tool for GLBT clients to reclaim parts of families that sometimes have been cut off from their perceptions. Bringing new or hidden

The author would like to thank Lance T. L. Chen-Hayes for his computer graphic design of the genogram and the GLBT Genogram Symbols handout.

knowledge to the surface in a genogram can provide the impetus for startling changes in clients and their relationships when they reconnect with nontraditional patterns in their own families.

Instructions

Create a genogram over three generations in the client's family of origin and/or family of choice, focusing especially on sexual orientation and gender identity/expression (if known or not). McGoldrick, Gerson, and Shellenberger (1999) provide an excellent resource for learning how to create genograms with multiple examples of famous family genograms and a thorough, easy-to-follow explanation of the symbols used in mapping family relationship patterns. Although McGoldrick, Gerson, and Shellenberger (1999) and Thomlison (2002) do not specifically address sexual orientation or gender identity/expression symbols, clients can be encouraged to use their own creativity on genograms (using rainbow colors, filling in gender symbols as pink or lavender, and so forth). A GLBT sensibility allows a client to easily transgress these traditional genogram gender symbols. Clients may choose to do two separate genograms: one for family of origin and another for family of choice, or a combination of them. The counselor can provide a separate handout, the GLBT Genogram Symbols, to assist clients in understanding how to map relationship patterns in particular using both traditional and GLBT-specific symbols.

Brief Vignette

Bridget, a single lesbian woman of Italian and English ethnicity, identifies as soft butch and comes to counseling after a recent fight with a long-term lover, Elba, a lesbian of Puerto Rican ethnicity who identifies as butch. Although neither woman is out to her family or co-workers, both state that their families of origin accept them at family gatherings. Most family members see them as friends and do not acknowledge anything about their romantic and sexual relationship, even though they are co-parenting a daughter from Elba's former marriage and they have a legal registered domestic partnership in their city. They both feel that they are constrained to the more traditionally feminine roles that their families expect, yet neither of them feels comfortable in traditional gender roles, let alone the clothes, makeup, and ladylike attitudes that go along with expected traditional gendered behaviors and roles. Both women want to reduce their arguing and bickering as a couple as well as their different styles of parenting. They love each other and want to work on their relationship. The counselor suggests that the women do a three-generation genogram to describe the members of their family of origin and how there may be allies for them related to nontraditional sexual practices. The women report that they have numerous lesbian acquaintances, but that they do not see them as a family of choice. Their family genogram highlights sexual orientation and gender identity and gender expression (see Figure 28.1).

In compiling their genogram, the women discuss that there have been several adults on both sides of the family who have been nontraditional in sexual orientation and gender identity/expression. Suspicions of some relatives in terms of nontraditional sexual practices help them see that they are not alone in their families of origin and that they have some allies within their seemingly traditional family structures. Clear patterns emerge over the three generations in terms of who is close to whom and who has conflicted interactions. Clients who examine their relationships to members of their families of origin and reestablish links with other nontraditional family members can powerfully affect current relationships. In this example, the women are encouraged to move toward family members who might be more supportive than how they currently experience or perceive being treated. They are encouraged to look at the relationship patterns and find ways to gain greater support for their relationship from potential ally family

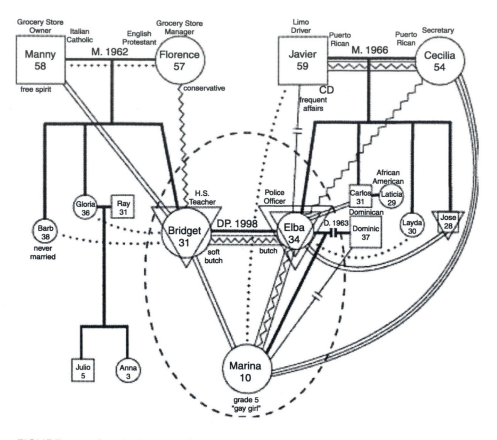

FIGURE 28.1. Gender Identity, Gender Expression, and Sexual Orientation Genogram

members. For example, even though they both believe that Elba's brother is gay, he has never come out officially to Elba and Bridget, nor have they officially come out to him. Although Elba and her father have had a cut-off relationship for over a decade, the counselor encourages her to acknowledge that even with a father who was discovered (by Elba in her early twenties, by accident) to be a cross-dresser (and she chose to cut off her relationship with him entirely at that point rather than disclose the secret to anyone in her family of origin), he and she have a lot in common in terms of their nontraditional sexualities. Although Elba is at first furious with any thought of reconnecting with her father (she was disgusted by his feminine side), the counselor senses Elba has some transphobia and/or internalized sexism that she needs to work through, and that Bridget may be helpful in assisting her to do so. Bridget's work is to help her family of origin see her and her partner in a more overt role over time as she is now coparenting, although her parents have yet to meet their daughter Marina. Bridget, although more comfortable with a range of gender identity and gender expression, in some ways is more hesitant to be open with her family due to fears that they will abandon her because of conservative religious beliefs. Elba can be helpful to Bridget here in supporting her in getting closer to her two sisters as a way to try and open up family dynamics and discussions in a family that has been traditionally quiet about personal matters. By spending time with adult siblings, it is hoped that the women will find allies, and by strengthening these relationships, they will have greater support as coparents, which will take some of the pressure away from their couple dynamics. Marina has also asked questions about why the two women share the same bed, and they have yet to tell Marina they are a lesbian and bisexual couple.

Suggestions for Follow-Up

Clients who discover the nontraditional sexual orientation, gender identity, and gender expression links in families have a powerful resource to draw strength from and to help lessen the isolation of "being the only one" in a family. These messages are strong in most families, yet there is variation in interpretation. Linking the past to the present gives support for how clients can look for strengths in their own families and in challenging heterosexism and transgenderism in their lives. It also gives hope for the future in how clients wish to change relationships in their families and what, if any, messages they want to send to the next generation (be it their own children or other children in their families). Genograms represent one snapshot of a client's perceptions about how relationship patterns evolve in a family, so learning more about the nontraditional members of the family may open up communication or develop new linkages for support and resolution of issues related to family secrets about GLBT issues for members of a couple or family. By using and expanding a genogram over time, one's family tree of relationship patterns becomes a powerful tool to affirm GLBT identity in terms of traditional and nontraditional beliefs about sexual orientation, gender identity, and gender expression.

Questions for follow-up with the client(s) might include:

- Now that you know about new patterns related to sexual orientation, gender identity, and gender expression in your family of origin, how will this affect you and your relationships with your partner and your children?
- What are the similarities and differences in dealing with sexual orientation, gender identity, and gender expression in your family of origin? How have they changed over time?
- How do you see the patterns of relating in your family of origin based on gender roles and expression as similar or different to your current patterns in your couple relationship and in parenting your children?
- Who in your family of origin might you become closer to based on new information?
- As your children become older, what changes might you predict in how you discuss your identities and roles in your family of origin and in your family of choice?
- How do you negotiate your identity as a GLBT person? How do your parents and grandparents negotiate the shift in family dynamics, values, and beliefs based on your GLBT identity?
- How could you build greater social supports in GLBT communities as well as in your family of origin and family of choice?

Contraindications

Genograms are powerful. They can stir up issues that are not related to sexual orientation, gender identity, and gender expression as clients map their perceived patterns of couple and family relationships. Caution is advised to thoroughly prepare clients for the pluses (greater self-knowledge) and minuses (learning family secrets, entering into conversations that might be uncomfortable, the surfacing of unsuspected issues) of similar work.

Readings and Resources for the Professional

Bullough, V. L. and Bullough, B. (1993). *Cross dressing, sex, and gender*. Philadelphia, PA: University of Pennsylvania Press.

Chen-Hayes, S. F. (1997). Counseling lesbian, bisexual and gay persons in couple and family relationships: Overcoming the stereotypes. *The Family Journal: Counseling and Therapy for Couples and Families, 5*(3), 236-240.

Chen-Hayes, S. F. (2000). Social justice advocacy with lesbian, bisexual, gay, and transgendered persons. In J. Lewis and L. Bradley (Eds.), *Advocacy in Counseling* (pp. 89-98). Greensboro, NC: Caps Publications (ERIC/CASS).

Chen-Hayes, S. F. (2001). Counseling and advocacy with transgendered and gender-variant persons in schools and families. *The Journal of Humanistic Counseling, Education, and Development, 40*(1), 34-48.

Chen-Hayes, S. F. and Haley-Banez, L. (2000). *Lesbian, bisexual, gay, and transgendered youth counseling 101: Affirmative practice in schools and families.* Videotape, transcript, and leader guide. Amherst, MA: Microtraining Associates.

D'Augelli, A. R. (1994). Identity development and sexual orientation: Toward a model of lesbian gay, and bisexual development. In E. J. Trickett, R. J. Watts, and D. Birman (Eds.), *Human diversity: perspectives on people in context* (pp. 312-333). San Francisco, CA: Jossey-Bass.

Israel, G. E. and Tarver, D. E. (1997). *Transgender care: Recommended guidelines, practical information and personal accounts.* Philadelphia, PA: Temple University Press.

Laird, J. and Green, R.-J. (Eds.) (1996). *Lesbians and gays in couples and families: A handbook for therapists.* San Francisco, CA: Jossey-Bass.

McGoldrick, M., Gerson, R., and Shellenberger, S. (1999). *Genograms: Assessment and intervention* (Second edition). New York: W. W. Norton and Company.

Namaste, V. K. (2000). *Invisible lives: The erasure of transsexual and transgender people.* Chicago: University of Chicago Press.

Rust, P. (Ed.) (2000). *Bisexuality in the United States.* New York: Columbia University Press.

Thomlison, B. (2002). *Family assessment handbook: An introductory practice guide to family assessment and intervention.* Pacific Grove, CA: Brooks/Cole.

Bibliotherapy Sources for the Client

Bornstein, K. (1994). *Gender outlaw: On men, women, and the rest of us.* New York: Routledge.

Bornstein, K. (1998). *My gender workbook: How to become a real man, a real woman, the real you, or something else entirely.* New York: Routledge.

Feinberg, L. (1993). *Stone butch blues.* Ithaca, NY: Firebrand.

Hutchins, L. and Kaahumanu, L. (Eds.) (1991). *Bi any other name: Bisexual people speak out.* Boston, MA: Alyson Publications.

Lorde, A. (1984). *Sister outsider.* Freedom, CA: Crossing Press.

Queen, C. and Schimel, L. (Eds.) (1997). *Pomosexuals: Challenging assumptions about gender and sexuality.* San Francisco, CA: Cleis.

References

Bullough, V. L. and Bullough, B. (1993). *Cross dressing, sex, and gender.* Philadelphia, PA: University of Pennsylvania Press.

Chen-Hayes, S. F. (2001). Counseling and advocacy with transgendered and gender-variant persons in schools and families. *The Journal of Humanistic Counseling, Education, and Development, 40*(1), 34-48.

Chen-Hayes, S. F. and Haley-Banez, L. (2000). *Lesbian, bisexual, gay, and transgendered youth counseling 101: Affirmative practice in schools and families.* Videotape, transcript, and leader guide. Amherst, MA: Microtraining Associates.

D'Augelli, A. R. (1994). Identity development and sexual orientation: Toward a model of lesbian, gay, and bisexual development. In E. J. Trickett, R. J. Watts, and D. Birman (Eds.), *Hu-*

man diversity: Perspectives on people in context (pp. 312-333). San Francisco, CA: Jossey-Bass.

McGoldrick, M., Gerson, R., and Shellenberger, S. (1999). *Genograms: Assessment and intervention* (Second edition). New York: W. W. Norton and Company.

Thomlison, B. (2002). *Family assessment handbook: An introductory practice guide to family assessment and intervention*. Pacific Grove, CA: Brooks/Cole.

Traditional Genogram Symbols

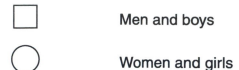

☐   Men and boys

◯   Women and girls

Relationship Lines

....   Distance

^^^^^^^^   Conflict

—| |—   Cut off

════   Close

≡≡≡   Overly close

- The letter M: Marriage

- The letter D: Divorce

- The letter S: Separation

- X through a circle or square: Death

Sexual Orientation Genogram Symbols

         Gay men and boys

         Lesbian women and girls

         Bisexual men and boys

         Bisexual women and girls

         Two-spirit person

- The letters DP: Domestic partnership

- The letters GM: Gay marriage

Gender Identity/Expression Genogram Symbols

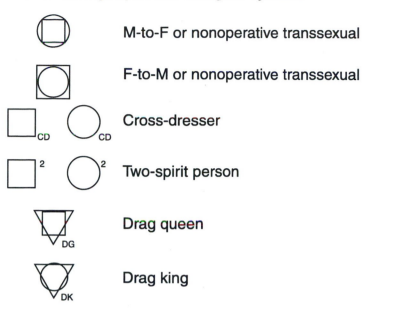

M-to-F or nonoperative transsexual

F-to-M or nonoperative transsexual

Cross-dresser

Two-spirit person

Drag queen

Drag king

- Other gender identity/expression categories can be written underneath the person's name

29

Challenging Multiple Oppressions with GLBT Clients

Stuart F. Chen-Hayes

Type of Contribution: Activity/Homework

Objective

The purpose of this activity is to name, identify, and challenge the past, present, and future effects of multiple oppressions (Lorde, 1984) (i.e., heterosexism, transgenderism, racism, beautyism, linguicism, ableism, classism, sexism, anti-Semitism) that gay, lesbian, bisexual, and transgendered (GLBT) clients often face. Oppression can be defined as prejudice multiplied by power, which is used by members of the dominant group to restrict nondominant group member access to resources on individual, cultural, and systemic levels (Chen-Hayes, 2001c). In naming and labeling these multiple identities, both client and counselor can judge the salience of each cultural identity, whether the client is in the dominant or the target group for oppression, and focus the counseling toward what the client views to be most important. It also allows the counselor to challenge and support areas where the client may not see how internalized or externalized oppression is affecting his or her success and well-being. Internalized oppression occurs when a person believe the myths and lies about his or her nondominant group status and acts accordingly, whereas externalized oppression occurs when members of dominant groups act to restrict resources from members of nondominant groups solely due to membership in that group (Adams, Bell, and Griffin, 1997; Chen-Hayes, 2000; Pharr, 1996). How a person has been, is, or will be targeted (or has targeted others) for oppression, based on the person's nondominant ethnicity, race, class, gender, gender identity/expression, sexual orientation, appearance, language, spirituality/religion, age, and disability, are covered in this exercise.

Rationale for Use

Issues of privilege, power, and access to resources are the keys in counseling and educating persons, particularly GLBT clients, to challenge multiple oppressions (Adams, Bell, and Griffin, 1997; Arredondo et al., 1996; Chen-Hayes, 2000, 2001a,b,c; Lewis and Arnold, 1998; Israel and Tarver, 1997). The areas of oppression that are most salient depend on the client's perceptions as well as the counselor's ability to draw out hidden oppressions that the client may deny or discount. Counselors may assume that if a client is GLBT, heterosexism and/or transgenderism are the central issues to be addressed in counseling. Often, for GLBT persons, other cultural identities and their additive effects with GLBT identities make these other identities as important, if not more so (Israel and Tarver, 1997; Greene, 1997). Instead, using this continuum exercise, clients can make determinations about multiple contexts including heterosexism and transgenderism affecting their lives and their counseling process.

Instructions

The client rates the importance or salience of each of her or his multiple identities on a 1 (low) to 10 (high) scale using the Multiple Identities and Oppressions handout. After making initial rankings, the counselor and client discuss action steps to assist the client with areas where internalized or externalized oppression may have harmed or continue to harm his or her well-being. They mutually set goals to transform the oppressions to give greater power and resources to the client on individual, cultural, and systemic levels. Goals, for example, might include empowering a young gay man who is not "buff and lean" to end his erroneous beliefs of self-hate due to internalized and externalized beautyism and heterosexism. He wants to work on challenging his belief that no one will love a young gay man who is unathletic and fat. A fifty-something transman of color who is nonoperative due to classism (he could never afford the surgery costs), wants to challenge his internalized racism and classism and his erroneous beliefs that white is the "right" look and he should do whatever he can to achieve that look. Instead, he is angry and wants to learn to love himself and other people of color for who they are—not focus on who they are not. A married Jewish bisexual woman with a disability is tired of how the religious men in her life have treated her, her disability, and her sexuality as less-than-normal. She wants to end the internalized anti-Semitism, ableism, and biphobia that have limited her full-life expression.

Brief Vignette

Hyacinth is a forty-five-year-old lesbian mother raising two teenagers, who has recently come out of a heterosexual marriage of twenty years. She identifies as working class, multiracial (Cherokee and English), lives with a disability (chronic fatigue), is a survivor of childhood sexual abuse, and follows earth-centered spirituality. Her ex-husband is also forty-five, of Jewish ethnicity, and was always caring toward her and their children. The ending of the marriage was amiable, as she came out as a lesbian to him and the children. She had lost sexual attraction to him and was seeing women on the side for years prior to their divorce. Although he knew that his wife was lesbian, he stayed in the marriage because he loved her and did not want to harm the kids. She stayed because she was afraid of the economic consequences of being divorced, having married right after high school. She would love to have a long-term relationship with a woman, but it has not worked out in the past. She blames her appearance (she would like to lose forty pounds), and she doubts she will find Ms. Right in the future. She has battled depression at times and has been in counseling with mixed results in the past. Her interests now are to make sure she can support herself and her kids with the loss of income and her disability issues.

Together the counselor and the client work to inventory the multiple oppressions in her life in the past, present, and future. They discuss her strengths and where she has internalized oppression in each of the areas named (i.e., where she believes the myths and lies about her identities— she has internalized beautyism, sexism, heterosexism, ageism, and ableism). She is proud of her multiethnic, racial, and spiritual identities, so she has fought off racism, sexism, sexual perpetration, and other forms of oppression related to her core beliefs and values. The counselor uses the oppression grid to help Hyacinth assess what other areas she can work on to label externalized and internalized oppression in her life. As she has labeled each oppression, Hyacinth and the counselor can work to identify internalized and externalized factors related to the oppression. Next, they can mutually develop specific goals and strategies to challenge both the internal and external oppressions affecting the client. For example, one strategy would be to attend a support group to challenge internalized self-hatred related to being GLBT or to having a disability. Strategies to challenge externalized oppressions could include working with the school board to include curriculum on all ethnic and racial identities and the effects of racism in school curricula or organizing political outreach to create local and state legislation challenging racial profiling or unequal pay for the work of women in employment settings. The counselor and client set goals to work on each of the oppressions in addition to continuing to use cognitive-behavioral methods to relieve her depression (she found this helpful in the past but stopped doing it on a regular basis).

Suggestions for Follow-Up

Ask the client keep a journal of self-defeating thoughts and statements to dispute those thoughts related to oppression and depression. Frame the depression, in part, as the client's internalizing the oppressions and give him or her tools to empower and challenge himself or herself to more realistic, antioppressive thoughts over time. Check to see which oppressions he or she is currently handling, and use those successes to assist the client with other areas of his or her life. Use the survivor skills she developed early on to keep strengthening the other areas of his or her life. The multiple oppressions grid can be used anytime in counseling as a check to see which issues are or are not surfacing in the client's life that need attention.

Contraindications

Clients who begin to realize that they are targets of multiple oppressions may become overwhelmed. They would benefit from developing basic coping skills as well as learning stress-management and anger-management techniques in handling their new awareness and knowledge.

Readings and Resources for the Professional

Adams, M., Bell, L. A., and Griffin, P. (1997). *Teaching for diversity and social justice: A sourcebook.* New York: Routledge.

Arredondo, P., Toporek, R., Brown, S. P., Jones, J., Locke, D. C., Sanchez, J., and Stadler, H. (1996). Operationalization of the multicultural counseling competencies. *Journal of Multicultural Counseling and Development, 24*(1), 42-78.

Chen-Hayes, S. F. (2000). Social justice advocacy with lesbian, bisexual, gay, and transgendered persons. In J. Lewis and L. Bradley (Eds.), *Advocacy in counseling: Counselors, clients, and community* (pp. 89-98). Greensboro, NC: Caps Publications (ERIC/CASS).

Chen-Hayes, S. F. (2001a). Counseling and advocacy with transgendered and gender-variant persons in schools and families. *The Journal of Humanistic Counseling, Education, and Development, 40*(1), 34-48.

Chen-Hayes, S. F. (2001b). The social justice advocacy readiness questionnaire. *The Journal of Lesbian and Gay Social Services, 13*(1/2), 191-203.

Comas-Diaz, L. and Greene, B. (1994). *Women of color: Integrating ethnic and gender identities in psychotherapy.* Thousand Oaks, CA: Sage Publications.

Greene, B. (Ed.) (1997). *Ethnic and cultural diversity among lesbians and gay men.* Thousand Oaks, CA: Sage Publications.

McGoldrick, M. (Ed.) (1998). *Re-visioning family therapy: Race, culture, and gender in clinical practice.* New York: Guilford Publications.

Ponterotto, J. G., Casas, J. M., Suzuki, L. A., and Alexander, C. M. (Eds.) (2001). *Handbook of multicultural counseling* (Second edition). Thousand Oaks, CA: Sage Publications.

Bibliotherapy Sources for the Client

Andrzejewski, J. (Ed.) (1996). *Oppression and social justice: Critical frameworks* (Fifth edition). Needham Heights, MA: Simon and Schuster.

Beemyn, B. and Eliason, M. (Eds.) (1996). *Queer studies: A lesbian, gay, bisexual, and transgender anthology*. New York: New York University Press.

Lorde, A. (1984). *Sister outsider*. Freedom, CA: The Crossing Press.

Pharr, S. (1988). *Homophobia: A weapon of sexism*. Inverness, CA: Chardon Press.

Pharr, S. (1996). *In the time of the right: Reflections on liberation*. Berkeley, CA: Chardon Press.

Rothenberg, P. S. (2001). *Race, class, and gender in the United States* (Fifth edition). New York: Worth.

Rothenberg, P. S. (2002). *White privilege: Essential readings on the other side of racism*. New York: Worth.

Zinn, H. (1999). *A people's history of the United States: 1492-present* (Revised edition). New York: HarperCollins.

References

Adams, M., Bell, L. A., and Griffin, P. (1997). *Teaching for diversity and social justice: A sourcebook*. New York: Routledge.

Arredondo, P., Toporek, R., Brown, S. P., Jones, J., Locke, D. C., Sanchez, J., and Stadler, H. (1996). Operationalization of the multicultural counseling competencies. *Journal of Multicultural Counseling and Development, 24*(1), 42-78.

Chen-Hayes, S. F. (2000). Social justice advocacy with lesbian, bisexual, gay, and transgendered persons. In J. Lewis and L. Bradley (Eds.), *Advocacy in counseling: Counselors, clients, and community* (pp. 89-98). Greensboro, NC: Caps Publications (ERIC/CASS).

Chen-Hayes, S. F. (2001a). Counseling and advocacy with transgendered and gender-variant persons in schools and families. *The Journal of Humanistic Counseling, Education, and Development, 40*(1), 34-48.

Chen-Hayes, S. F. (2001b). The social justice advocacy readiness questionnaire. *The Journal of Lesbian and Gay Social Services, 13*(1/2), 191-203.

Chen-Hayes, S. F. (2001c). Systemic anti-oppression strategies for school counselors as allies affirming queer children, youth, and families of multiracial experience. In K. Kumashiro (Ed.), *Troubling intersections of race and sexuality: Queer students of color and anti-oppressive education* (pp. 163-178). Lanham, MD: Rowman and Littlefield.

Greene, B. (Ed.) (1997). *Ethnic and cultural diversity among lesbians and gay men*. Thousand Oaks, CA: Sage Publications.

Israel, G. E. and Tarver, D. E. (1997). *Transgender care: Recommended guidelines, practical information, and personal accounts*. Philadelphia, PA: Temple University Press.

Lewis, J. A. and Arnold, M. S. (1998). From multiculturalism to social action. In C. C. Lee and G. W. Walz (Eds.), *Social action: A mandate for counselors* (pp. 51-65). Alexandria, VA: American Counseling Association and ERIC/CASS.

Lorde, A. (1984). *Sister outsider*. Freedom, CA: The Crossing Press.

Pharr, S. (1996). *In the time of the right: Reflections on liberation*. Berkeley, CA: Chardon Press.

Multiple Identities and Oppressions

Please rate the importance or salience of each of your multiple identities on a 1 (low) to 10 (high) scale.

Cultural Category and Related Oppression	Past Levels of Internalized/ Externalized Oppression	Present Levels of Internalized/ Externalized Oppression	Future/Ideal
Ethnicity/Ethnic Identity (oppression that may include racism)			
Race/Racial Identity (racism)			
Gender (sexism, heterosexism)			
Gender Identity/Expression (transgenderism, heterosexism)			
Sexual Orientation (heterosexism, transgenderism)			
Social Class (classism)			
Appearance (beautyism)			
Disability Status (ableism)			
Language Status (linguicism)			
Family Type (oppression toward nontraditional families, i.e., single parents, same-gender couples, etc.)			
Spirituality/Religion (anti-Semitism and other oppression toward nondominant religious/spiritual beliefs)			
Trauma/Violence Status (oppression due to emotional, physical, or sexual violence)			
Citizenship Status/Nationality (oppression due to one's citizenship status/nationality)			

30

Who Am I Really? Understanding the Intersection of Sexual and Ethnic Identity

Melody M. Brown
Sheila M. Addison

Type of Contribution: Activity/Handout/Worksheet

Objectives

This activity is intended to promote greater understanding for both client and therapist of how the client's ethnic identity interacts with her or his identity as a sexual minority person. The three goals are to enrich therapeutic conversation, promote self-understanding for the client, and increase therapist sensitivity to the complexity of contextual issues in the client's life.

Rationale for Use

Frequently, clients are unaware of the contextual factors (e.g., race, class, ethnicity, geography, gender) that influence who they are as individuals. Some clients are aware of these factors, but only in isolation from other factors. Exploring the sexual orientation and ethnicity aspects of clients' lives opens the door for them to take an introspective look at themselves not just in the context of relationships with others. It requires them to become more in touch with the different parts of themselves that make the whole and then, in turn, use that knowledge to intentionally interact with others.

Instructions

Request that the client do this worksheet at home, so that you can become more familiar with how the client has navigated the intersection between her or his ethnicity and sexual identity. Give the client the list of questions to be answered by the time of the next visit. Encourage him or her to be as brief or as detailed as necessary to complete the questionnaire. Ask him or her to review the list of questions before ending the session so that you will have the opportunity to make any necessary clarifications. Acknowledge the possibility that this may be the first time the client has ever considered any of the questions listed. Address any concerns, fears, or ambivalence he or she may have about completing the worksheet.

There may be instances where you should offer examples to give the client a clearer picture of how to think about the question. For instance, with the question regarding distinguishing specifics about the client's ethnicity, you can be helpful by providing the following example: "African Americans have a rich history of showing resiliency through hundreds of years of oppression."

When the client returns with the worksheet completed, explore with him or her the experience of completing the worksheet. Ask such questions as, "What was this like for you? How do you see yourself differently than before the worksheet? What positive characteristics about you stand out now that did not before? How has filling out this worksheet changed the way you perceive yourself in relation to both your ethnicity and your sexual identity?" Pay particular attention to any positive regard the client has for her or his ethnicity and link that regard to sexual identity. For example, "You commented on the strength you feel African Americans have through adversity. How does this strength influence you in regard to your sexual identity? How much will your strength and experience with adversity and discrimination as an African American help you when you face the similar adversity as a lesbian?"

Suggestions for Follow-Up

Once the client has begun to internalize the connection between ethnicity and sexual identity, this procedure can be used to explore other contextual factors such as birth order, social class, or geographical area in which he or she was reared.

Contraindications

This exercise may not be effective for clients who have little conscious "connection" to their ethnicity or for those who have been cut off from learning some of the idiosyncrasies of their ethnic identity. Likewise, this activity may not be as useful for those clients at the beginning stages of their sexual awareness or coming-out process.

The therapist should be able to accept and acknowledge the ways in which he or she is privileged regarding aspects of identity; this work should be done prior to attempting this kind of activity with clients (Laszloffy and Hardy, 2000; McIntosh, 1998).

Readings and Resources for the Professional

Boykin, K. (1996). *One more river to cross: Black and gay in America.* New York: Doubleday.

Byrne, J., Clark, J. M., and Michael, L. S. (1995). *Embodying diversity: Identity, (bio) diversity and sexuality.* Boca Raton, FL: Monument Press.

Fukuyama, M. A. and Ferguson, A. D. (2000). Lesbian, gay, and bisexual people of color: Understanding cultural complexity and managing multiple oppressions. In R. M. Perez and K. A. DeBord (Ed.), *Handbook of counseling and psychotherapy with lesbian, gay, and bisexual clients* (pp. 81-105). Washington, DC: American Psychological Association.

Hardy, K. V. (1989). The theoretical myth of sameness: A critical issue in family therapy training and treatment. *Journal of Psychotherapy and the Family, 6*(1-2), 17-33.

Hardy, K. V. and Laszloffy, T. A. (1998). The dynamics of a pro-racist ideology: Implications for family therapists. In M. McGoldrick (Ed.), *Re-visioning family therapy: Race, culture, and gender in clinical practice* (pp. 118-128). New York: Guilford Publications.

Jones, S. R. and McEwen, M. K. (2000). A conceptual model of multiple dimensions of identity. *Journal of College Student Development, 41*(4), 405-414.

Laird, J. (1998). Theorizing culture: Narrative ideas and practice principles. In M. McGoldrick (Ed.), *Re-visioning family therapy: Race, culture, and gender in clinical practice* (pp. 20-36). New York: Guilford Publications.

Laszloffy, T. A. and Hardy, K. V. (2000). Uncommon strategies for a common problem: Addressing racism in family therapy. *Family Process, 39*(1), 35-50.

Leslie, L. A. (1995). Family therapy's evolving treatment of gender, ethnicity, and sexual orientation. *The Family Coordinator, 44*(4), 359.

Longres, J. F. (Ed.) (1996). *Men of color: A context for service to homosexually active men.* Binghamton, NY: The Haworth Press.

McIntosh, P. (1998). White privilege: Unpacking the invisible knapsack. In M. McGoldrick (Ed.), *Re-visioning family therapy: Race, culture and gender in clinical practice* (pp. 147-152). New York: Guilford Publications.

Myrsiades, K. and Myrsiades, L. S. (1997). *Race-ing representation.* Lanham, MD: Rowman and Littlefield Publishers, Inc.

Smith, A. (1997). Cultural diversity and the coming-out process: Implications for clinical practice. In B. Greene (Ed.), *Ethnic and cultural diversity among lesbians and gay men* (pp. 279-300). Thousand Oaks, CA: Sage Publications.

Vasquez, M. J. T. and Eldridge, N. S. (1994). Bringing ethics alive. Training practitioners about gender, ethnicity, and sexual orientation issues. *Women and Therapy, 15*(1), 1-16.

Bibliotherapy Sources for the Client

Boykin, K. (1996). *One more river to cross: Black and gay in America.* New York: Doubleday.

Boykin, K. (1997). Are blacks and gays the same? In M. Lowenthal (Ed.), *Gay men at the millennium: Sex, spirit, community* (pp. 210-221). New York: Jeremy P. Tarcher.

Foulke, M. L. and Hill, R. L. (1997). We are not your hope for the future: Being an interracial lesbian family living in the present. In R. E. Goss and A. A. S. Strongheart (Eds.), *Our families, our values: Snapshots of queer kinship* (pp. 243-249). Binghamton, NY: The Haworth Press.

Hagland, P. E. P. (1998). "Undressing the Oriental boy": The gay Asian in the social imaginary of the gay white male. In D. Atkins (Ed.), *Looking queer: Body image and identity in lesbian, bisexual, gay, and transgender communities* (pp. 277-293). Binghamton, NY: The Haworth Press.

Hardy, J. E. (1997). The river of de-Nile. In M. Lowenthal (Ed.), *Gay men at the millennium: Sex, spirit, community* (pp. 260-262). New York: Jeremy P. Tarcher.

Hardy, K. V. (1989). The theoretical myth of sameness: A critical issue in family therapy training and treatment. *Journal of Psychotherapy and the Family, 6*(1-2), 17-33.

Myrsiades, K. and Myrsiades, L. S. (1997). *Race-ing representation.* Lanham, MD: Rowman and Littlefield Publishers, Inc.

Pegues, C. R. (1998). Piece of man: Redefining the myth around the black male phallus. In D. Atkins (Ed.), *Looking queer: Body image and identity in lesbian, bisexual, gay, and transgender communities* (pp. 259-270). Binghamton, NY: The Haworth Press.

Phillips, L. (1998). "I" is for intersection: At the crux of black and white and gay and straight. In D. Atkins (Ed.), *Looking queer: Body image and identity in lesbian, bisexual, gay, and transgender communities* (pp. 251-258). Binghamton, NY: The Haworth Press.

Roy, S. (1998). Mapping my desire: Hunting down the male erotic in India and America. In D. Atkins (Ed.), *Looking queer: Body image and identity in lesbian, bisexual, gay, and transgender communities* (pp. 271-275). Binghamton, NY: The Haworth Press.

Tanigawa, D. T. (1998). I like my chi-i-sa-i body now. In D. Atkins (Ed.), *Looking queer: Body image and identity in lesbian, bisexual, gay, and transgender communities* (pp. 295-298). Binghamton, NY: The Haworth Press.

Williams, W. L. (1999). *The spirit and the flesh: Sexual diversity in American Indian culture.* Boston, MA: Beacon Press.

References

Laszloffy, T. A. and Hardy, K. V. (2000). Uncommon strategies for a common problem: Addressing racism in family therapy. *Family Process, 39*(1), 35-50.

McIntosh, P. (1998). White privilege: Unpacking the invisible knapsack. In M. McGoldrick (Ed.), *Re-visioning family therapy: Race, culture and gender in clinical practice* (pp. 147-152). New York: Guilford Publications.

Who Am I Really? Sexual and Ethnic Identity Worksheet

What is your ethnicity? (e.g., African American, Irish American, Jewish, American Indian)

What are the specifics about your ethnicity that you feel distinguishes you from those with different ethnic backgrounds?

What do you feel those from other ethnic backgrounds need to know or understand about you and your ethnicity?

What is your ethnic community's attitude regarding your sexual orientation? Is your sexual orientation generally accepted or criticized?

If your community is unaccepting, how have you handled your sexual orientation in relation to being in your community?

What has been your most difficult experience involving your sexual orientation and your ethnicity?

What has been your most validating experience involving your sexual orientation and your ethnicity?

What concerns regarding the worksheet have arisen for you since our last meeting?

31

Facilitating Lesbian Gender Exploration

Heidi M. Levitt
Monica Bigler

Type of Contribution: Activity/Worksheet

Objectives

This activity can be useful to lesbians who are examining issues related to their lesbian gender (e.g., butch, or femme) or their gender expression while in therapy. It identifies both prized and difficult aspects of the butch and femme experience, and can be used to provide a starting point for reflection and discussion about gender identity. A review of this activity can be used to stimulate discussion, either in individual, couple, or family therapy.

Rationale for Use

Within the American lesbian culture, butch/femme lesbianism arose in the 1950s and then faced a period of demise in the 1970s with the second wave of feminism (Faderman, 1991). Feminism brought an androgynous gender aesthetic into lesbian culture; butch women were seen as aping male oppressors and femmes were seen as playing into traditional female roles. In the mid-1980s, however, butch/femme genders began being reexamined by segments of the lesbian communities, and these uniquely lesbian genders began to be reclaimed (Faderman,1993). Due to the strong influence of feminist thought on both heterosexual gender and on lesbian culture, these genders reemerged within different societal and lesbian contexts. They reflected the larger culture's new conceptualization of gender, increasing the fluidity of gender roles in areas such as work, family, and relationship. Instead, these lesbian genders arose with problems and strengths particular to butch and femme women within our era.

In feminist therapy or feminist-oriented therapy, it can be important for therapists to develop an ability to conduct gender-role analyses of lesbian genders to help these women develop a clearer sense of their experiences of oppression as well as the strengths of their gender. Butch lesbians can be seen as facing unique difficulties due to their double discrimination (see Halberstam, 1998). Not only are they lesbian, and challenging expectations around sexual orientation, but they also challenge others' expectations of gender expression. Their nontraditional female gender can act to signal their sexual orientation and can make discrimination on both these counts more likely, particularly within heterosexual society. They may face a series of challenges throughout their development that are distinct from the challenges faced by lesbians of different lesbian genders.

Correspondingly, femme lesbians may experience a number of challenges unique to their gender expression (Harris and Crocker, 1997; Newman, 1995). In a mainstream culture context, they may not be visible as lesbians due to their outer appearance. As a consequence, they may feel forced to verbally assert their lesbian identity at early stages in their social interactions in order to feel true to their identity and to prevent future complications. In a lesbian context, femme women may be faced with discrimination due to their seemingly heterosexual appearance. They may be viewed with suspicion within the lesbian community and may be denied equal status among other lesbian women.

The Lesbian Gender Expression worksheet can be helpful. It can allow lesbians dealing with gender expression issues to normalize their experiences, and it allows therapists or significant others to better understand a client's experiences. Clients may find it difficult to discuss experiences related to lesbian gender, especially with a nonlesbian therapist, so this worksheet can indicate acceptance on the therapist's part as well as permission to discuss issues particular to this gender in therapy. Often, it can be difficult for clients to find words to articulate their experience, and the worksheet can assist by providing initial phrasings and typical experiences. It is designed to address both positive and problematic issues for lesbian women and it may be important to encourage clients to examine both sides of this issue in therapy. This evenhandedness can encourage therapists and clients to avoid pathologizing butch/femme experiences and can help frame gender identity and experience as serving functional purposes in women's lives, as all aspects of identity can be understood to do.

Instructions

Identifying Appropriate Clients

This activity can be used with individual lesbian clients or lesbian couples who are exploring their lesbian gender or gender expression. The women may or may not identify as butch or femme, but they should be in the process of contemplating the role of their gender expression. Therapists do not need to ascertain clients' lesbian gender to present them with the worksheet, as it does not imply an established butch/femme identity. Many of the perspectives presented therein may be shared by lesbians who do not identify as either butch or femme.

Presenting This Activity

This exercise should be presented as a way for clients to begin an examination of their own experience of gender. Therapists may help clients distinguish lesbian issues that are associated with different gender expressions. Lesbians may face unique reactions to their gender expression within both heterosexual and queer cultures. As stereotypical expectations of lesbian gender expression may differ from those of a heterosexual female, lesbians may engender unexpected reactions to their expressed gender. For instance, a lesbian may be accused of "acting straight" by other lesbians when she adopts an otherwise stereotypical femininity, because it conflicts with the expectations of lesbian gender. Similarly, at work, a butch lesbian may be "outed" by her nontraditional appearance and then ostracized by her co-workers or subjected to their prejudicial expectations of lesbians. It is recommended that the therapist avoid categorizing any client as butch or femme if she does not self-identify this way so as not to constrain the woman's own process of conceptualizing her gender or, alternatively, to distance her, as some lesbians may object to butch and femme identities. If clients have not identified themselves as butch or femme, therapists may choose to introduce this exercise with the following description:

> You have been discussing different issues regarding lesbianism and also issues related to the way you feel most comfortable expressing your gender. I have a worksheet that you may want to look at in which lesbians who express their gender in a more butch or femme way discuss the different issues that are important for them. The women represented on this worksheet have discussed various ways in which they have found their gender expression to be both problematic and advantageous. I am not meaning to imply that you are or are not butch or femme, but I thought that there might be some issues that you have in com-

mon with the issues they discuss. The ways they integrate their gender expression may be different than ways you may come to, but they may give you some ideas on how some lesbians are thinking about their gender expression. Perhaps this might be useful for you to look at, and we could discuss whatever comes up for you from this exercise in future sessions.

If a lesbian already identifies as butch or femme, the therapist might modify this introduction by asking the client if she would be interested in looking at a worksheet that identifies issues that other butch/femme women have identified as particular to butch/femme experiences and discussing any ideas that arise in a future session. The therapist might want to make clear that this worksheet does not reflect the experience of all butch and femme women or communities. It is not an assessment of butchness or femmeness, but is provided as a point of departure for the client's own explorations.

Suggestions for Follow-Up

In the session following the distribution of the exercise, the therapist may begin by inquiring about the client's experience in using the worksheet. The therapist can ask the client how she experienced this process, and ask, particularly, if there were any feelings or ideas that arose within her as she was completing this exercise. This reflection can be used to help a client identify aspects of experience that she would like to explore further. Goals can be identified as either short term or long term, to structure her exploration and prizing of her own gender expression. This exercise can be used as the basis for a gender analysis that is reflective of how gender is conceived and/or experienced in some lesbian communities.

Contraindications

This exercise is intended for women who identify as lesbian, although therapists may wish to use it with bisexual women who are exploring their gender identity as well. Women who are struggling with issues around sexual orientation, or coming out, however, probably will need to settle these identity issues before focusing upon their gender expression.

Therapists may need to examine particular aspects of their own homophobia that rarely are confronted when treating femme, androgynous, or undifferentiated lesbians. Butch or femme lesbians may enjoy a gender expression that is problematic for therapists who are not used to women of this lesbian gender. For instance, butch women may sport facial hair, may cross-dress, and may relate in ways that seem more traditionally masculine, and femme women may discuss gender roles that appear to be strangely, or misleadingly, traditional. (Although femme gender may be quite similar to femininity, it also may have unique meanings within lesbian community and entail a strength and power that usually are not subsumed under a feminine gender-expression label.) Therapists may wish to read the worksheet prior to distribution so that they can seek to educate themselves regarding points of butch or femme experience about which they are unaware. This self-examination will be particularly important to preserve the client's safety to explore issues of development, sexuality, and gender expression that might feel taboo or shocking in other contexts. The expression of butch gender will need to be understood not as male, but as uniquely butch lesbian and as a gender expression that can be both functional within their life experiences and prized within certain lesbian communities. Similarly, femme gender expression will need to be seen within a lesbian butch/femme context and not be simplified as sole expression of femininity.

Therapy with lesbians does not necessitate the exploration of gender expression. This exercise may be used in therapy when concerns with gender exploration or gender expression are part of the client's presenting issue.

The problematic issues expressed can be disturbing. It might be difficult for women to begin discussing such painful topics at the beginning of therapy. Rapport should be established prior to introducing this exercise to provide the safety needed for this difficult reflection. The goal of the exercise is to enable these women to better communicate their pain and appreciate their possibilities in order to develop their own understanding of their gender over the course of therapy.

Readings and Resources for the Professional

Faderman, L. (1991). *Odd girls and twilight lovers*. New York: Penguin.
Feinberg, L. (1996). *Transgender warriors: Making history from Joan of Arc to Dennis Rodman*. Boston, MA: Beacon Press.
Halberstam, J. (1998). *Female masculinity*. Durham, NC: Duke University Press.
Harris, L. and Crocker, E. (1997). *Femme: Feminists, lesbians and bad girls*. New York: Routledge.
Lapovsky-Kennedy, E. and Davis, M. D. (1993). *Boots of leather, slippers of gold: The history of a lesbian community*. New York: Penguin.

Bibliotherapy Sources for the Client

Feinberg, L. (1993). *Stone butch blues: A novel*. Ithaca, NY: Firebrand Books.
Munt, S. (1998). *Butch/femme: Inside lesbian gender*. Washington, DC: Cassell.
Nestle, J. (1992). *The persistent desire: A butch-femme reader*. Boston, MA: Alyson Publications.
Newman, L. (1995). *The femme mystique*. Boston, MA: Alyson Publications.

References

Faderman, L. (1991). *Odd girls and twilight lovers*. New York: Penguin.
Faderman, L. (1993). The return of butch and femme: A phenomenon in lesbian sexuality of the 1980's and 1990's. In J. C. Fout and M. Shaw-Tantillo (Eds.), *American sexual politics: Sex, gender and race since the civil war* (pp. 333-351). Chicago, IL: The University of Chicago Press.
Halberstam, J. (1998). *Female masculinity*. Durham, NC: Duke University Press.
Harris, L. and Crocker, E. (1997). *Femme: Feminists, lesbians and bad girls*. New York: Routledge.
Newman, L. (1995). *The femme mystique*. Boston, MA: Alyson Publications.

Lesbian Gender Expression

This worksheet can help you reflect upon and communicate the meaning of your own gender expression/identity. It was based upon interviews with butch and femme-identified women about the difficulties and advantages they experience in relation to their lesbian gender. If you do not identify as butch or femme, you may wish to replace these words with ones that seem to best describe your gender expression. This includes a butch section and a femme section. You may choose to fill out either one or both of these sections, depending upon what feels useful or relevant to you. This can be used as a point of reflection, but is not meant to suggest that these are the only ways that lesbian women can experience their gender expression and is not an assessment of either butchness or femmeness. Some of the issues may be painful or disturbing. You may wish to skip items that do not feel comfortable and put them aside for further thought, or discuss them with your therapist and/or significant other. You are encouraged to develop perspectives and understandings that uniquely work for you in the context of your own life and community. Spaces have been provided for you to write down notes or comments. If you agree with only part of an item, feel free to alter that item to make it work for you. You may choose to reflect upon whether these experiences relate to you or to consider how you might make sense of similar experiences.

BUTCH SECTION

PROBLEMATIC EXPERIENCES	Y/N
The following items were identified by butch-identified lesbians as difficult or painful issues that related to their gender expression.	
Development and Gender Identity	
I have struggled in family with pressures to look more feminine or acceptable.	
In childhood, I often passed as a boy or was expected to be like a boy.	
I felt like I was "the worst thing in the world," or "like I would burn in hell" because I was boyish and lesbian.	
I felt unsure growing up if I was meant to be a girl or a boy.	
Puberty felt like "my body is betraying me."	
Notes/Comments:	
Mainstream Culture	
Others assume that I want to be like a man, or am adopting a male role/attitude.	
Others don't seem to relate to me as female or as maternal.	
People assume I am lesbian—I feel little choice in being "out."	
Men feel hostile toward my being sexual, and they seem to feel more comfortable or even aroused by feminine lesbians—my sexuality feels less safe.	
Male friends sometimes seem to forget that I am a woman and may say sexist things about women in my presence.	
Women seem to be critical of my style of dress or self-presentation at times.	
Some women seem to be afraid of me or just ignore my presence.	
I am mistaken as male (confronted in bathrooms, called "sir," etc.).	
I am treated as a curiosity or novelty at times.	

I worry about being in new situations or meeting new people as they might struggle with recognizing my gender as female. This can be embarrassing, upsetting, or can give me extra work to cope with on top of whatever I am doing.	
I experience harassment due to my gender expression.	
I experience fear of homophobic reactions due to looking lesbian, and I avoid situations or places that I feel might be dangerous.	
Notes/Comments:	
Emotional Experiencing	
I feel like I am processing emotion as both a butch and as a feminine female and then having to choose which approach I want to be dominant. This can be confusing.	
I feel that I have to "take care of myself," and that I shouldn't "get help from anyone."	
I feel that the side of me that reacts as feminine is weaker. I need to be in a safe environment to feel this side.	
I feel that I show my love in more physical ways, by doing chores or the like, while my partners seem to want more intimacy.	
Notes/Comments:	
Lesbian Community	
Some lesbians feel that I am "rocking the boat" by my gender expression.	
People seem to assume I will take on more traditionally male roles.	
I find it hard to be just friends with femme lesbians due to sexual tension and the expectations of a potential for dating.	
I felt like I was born in the wrong place or time—that I was not in a butch/femme community, but I "secretly identified as butch."	
I sometimes feel like I need to be competitive with other butch women.	
I worry about telling others about my femininity as they might question my butchness or I might feel embarrassed.	
Notes/Comments:	
Romantic Relationships	
Others assume that I will want to date femmes and not other types of lesbians.	
I sometimes feel too possessive over my partner, and am now more aware of this.	
Sometimes my partner assumes our romantic relationship will fall into heterosexual roles and I feel misunderstood.	
I feel I am competing with my partner to perform the more butch household chores.	
Notes/Comments:	

Body Image/Sexuality	
I don't feel quite like a woman.	
I feel insecure sometimes about why a woman would prefer to date me instead of a man.	
I feel more comfortable when I dress to downplay my femininity.	
I feel that being sexually penetrated is vulnerable. I like to carefully decide when or if this should occur.	
I feel "in drag" when I look too feminine or feel embarrassed about feminine aspects of my body (e.g., breasts).	
Notes/Comments:	
Children	
I feel embarrassed when children inquire about my gender in public.	
I worry that my children's friends will find my gender expression problematic.	
Notes/Comments:	

POSITIVE EXPERIENCES	Y/N
The following items were identified by butch-identified lesbians as strengths or positive experiences related to their gender expression.	
Developmental and Gender Identity Issues	
My family integrates me as a son and other times as a daughter—it's flexible.	
The identity of butch seems to best help me understand who I am and allows me to present myself as I feel I am.	
My therapist helped my family deal with my being lesbian.	
I feel that my identity of butch helps me accept myself as a woman.	
Notes/Comments:	
Mainstream Culture Issues	
I can increase my safety in at-risk situations by trying to "butch up" or pass as male.	
I am proud of myself for challenging society's gender boundaries.	
I can choose whether I want to react as butch or as more feminine strategically, depending on the situation.	
I can react with humor to people confusing my gender.	
When people struggle with my gender I can use this as an opportunity to talk with them or to educate them.	
Some men feel a camaraderie with me, yet can still be emotional with me at the same time because of my gender expression seeming both male and female.	
Sometimes people automatically place me in a leadership role or treat me with respect.	
I am glad that I don't need to worry about men asking me out or flirting with me.	

Heterosexual women can flirt with my "masculine attitude," yet still confide in me as another woman.	
Being out lets me openly address lesbian issues and rights and be more political.	
Notes/Comments:	
Emotional Experiencing	
I can choose whether I want to feel emotions as butch or femme, depending on the situation and on how safe I feel in the moment.	
Dressing butch allows me to guard my energy when I feel vulnerable.	
I have let go of shame for looking like a guy, and now enjoy being butch.	
Notes/Comments:	
Lesbian Community	
It's easier to be friends with other butch women since it is assumed that we will probably not date each other.	
I feel a mutual respect with other butch women for our "similar pain" and our strength. This provides safety and makes it easier to get support from them.	
I am happiest in lesbian communities that embrace butch/femme as valid and important parts of lesbian culture.	
I like it when these genders are understood as flexibility in the lesbian community.	
I like being visibly "out" as other lesbians will more easily approach me.	
In the lesbian community, I have found butch mentors who help me feel more comfortable with accepting myself and dealing with my feelings.	
Notes/Comments:	
Romantic Relationships	
I can pass as male and can be public with my affections toward my girlfriend.	
I find in talking to other butch women that we have similar difficulties in being vulnerable in our relationships. This mutual support is helpful.	
I experience some femmes as allies, as they understand my concerns based on experiences with prior butch partners.	
I feel flexibility in determining myself; taking more traditionally female roles at times does not diminish my identity as butch.	
Notes/Comments:	
Body Image/Sexuality	
I feel more powerful and sexier when I am being or dressing butch.	
I can enjoy sharing common ideas of desire and sexuality with other butch women.	
Now that I understand butchness, I can see how I am attractive to women and how butch women aspire to a different aesthetic than feminine women.	

I understand my sexuality better through my identification as butch.	
I have learned to enjoy my sexuality as butch, especially as I see it as distinct from sexual dominance.	
I can feel more comfortable or take more pleasure in flirting as butch.	
Notes/Comments:	

Children	
I can be a role model, as a lesbian who accepts herself and feels comfortable with her gender expression.	
I feel I am "paving the road" for future generations by being visibly out.	
I can educate children who ask me about my gender by asking them why gender should matter.	
Notes/Comments:	

FEMME SECTION

PROBLEMATIC EXPERIENCES	Y/N
The following items were identified by femme-identified lesbians as difficult or painful issues that related to their gender expression.	
Developmental and Gender Identity Issues	
I wasn't sure if I should identify as femme because I thought it meant I was weak and thought it placed me in the role of being an object.	
I felt that being lesbian meant that you had to be butch or androgynous.	
I feel I have to fight to shake others' idea that femmes are subservient.	
My family is confused about my sexuality; they are having a hard time understanding the combination of me being femme and being lesbian at the same time.	
My family has a hard time understanding my role in my relationship.	
When I came out, femmes were not visible in my lesbian community, nor was there a particular language/vocabulary involved with being femme, and thus I had a difficult time finding lesbians with whom I could identify.	
Due to my feeling tough or dominant, at first I assumed I could not identify as femme.	
It was harder for me to identify as lesbian as I wasn't attracted to women who are considered traditionally beautiful. I could only call myself lesbian after I began meeting butch or androgynous-looking women.	
Notes/Comments:	
Mainstream Culture	
There is controversy when I try to explain my femmeness to straight girlfriends as they only can see my relationship through the eyes of heterosexual sexism and not through the eyes of lesbian culture.	

It upsets me when men act as though my sexuality is for their amusement.	
Sometimes men who know I am lesbian seem more homophobic or strange with me after they see me with my girlfriend.	
People seem to think that a woman who dresses feminine cannot be assertive. They may expect me to be weak, and are surprised by my assertiveness and physicality.	
I find it hard to be out as people will assume I am heterosexual. I need to always verbalize my sexual orientation.	
Others assume that my relationship is governed by heterosexual gender roles.	
I don't like men hitting on me and not believing that I am lesbian.	
I often feel a pressure in social situations (workplace, friendships) to "come out" as soon as possible, since people might otherwise assume that I am heterosexual.	
Notes/Comments:	
Lesbian Community	
I find I don't get taken as seriously as a lesbian.	
Sometimes I am treated by other lesbians as though I am not bright.	
I experience harassment from other lesbians because of my gender expression.	
I feel like I have to "come out" to my lesbian community as a femme and assert myself as a lesbian.	
Sometimes other lesbians seem to accuse me of wanting to pass as straight.	
I feel angry when other lesbians are disrespectful of my relationship.	
Some members of my community accuse my partner and me of trying to imitate a hetero-sexual lifestyle.	
Notes/Comments:	
Romantic Relationships	
Sometimes I feel guilty for being attracted to other femme women.	
I feel a need to protect my partner from feeling too vulnerable or too feminine in public.	
I feel guilty as, in public, I am treated better than my girlfriend sometimes.	
Sometimes I worry what others think if my girlfriend acts too butch in public.	
I sometimes feel I have to perform roles in my relationship that don't necessarily fit with who I am.	
I am surprised that some straight and lesbian friends attribute traditional gender roles in my relationship due to our femme/butch appearance, while, in actuality, our roles may be blurry or even be reversed at times.	
Notes/Comments:	
Body Image/Sexuality	
Sometimes I find it hard to know how to relate sexually with my partner as she can feel vul-nerable with certain sexual acts or with my sexual assertion.	
I feel that I had to learn that being femme doesn't restrict one to being sexually passive.	

Sometimes I wonder how to communicate about expectations about sex with my partner.	
I am not always sure whether intimacy means the same for me as it does for my partner.	
Notes/Comments:	

POSITIVE EXPERIENCES	Y/N
The following items were identified by femme-identified lesbians as strengths or positive experiences related to their gender expression.	
Developmental and Gender Identity Issues	
I feel that being femme identified allows me to feel more positive about myself.	
Instead of having to prove myself as lesbian by being more butch, I feel I can relax and be myself.	
Feeling powerful and bright goes hand in hand with how I experience my gender and my sexuality.	
My identity as femme has led me to experience pride over my ability to express who I am fully as a person.	
I feel that my femme identity helps me understand myself as a lesbian.	
I am interested in the diversity in femme experience (e.g., butchy femmes).	
Notes/Comments:	
Mainstream Culture	
I feel as though part of my political work as a femme woman is to create recognition of the diversity among lesbians.	
I am accepted more easily into mainstream culture than nonfemme lesbians, and can therefore use my admission to educate others about lesbian issues.	
I perceive lesbian gender to be on a continuum, rather than being categorized into a male-female dichotomy. This can be hard to relate to heterosexual friends.	
My femmeness allows me to be political about lesbian issues as I can seem less threatening.	
Coming out as a lesbian and femme has raised my awareness of social injustice in connection with sexual orientation, gender, race, and class issues.	
Notes/Comments:	
Lesbian Community	
I feel a sisterly closeness with other femme women due to the expectation that we won't date each other.	
I can flirt with whomever I want and be respected.	
Models of femmeness in the lesbian community have been important for my feeling positive about myself as lesbian.	
I enjoy being in a lesbian community in which I can be true to myself without fear of compromising my femmeness.	

My nonbutch/femme friends in the lesbian community communicate acceptance of and interest in my gender expression.	
Notes/Comments:	
Romantic Relationships	
I like feeling complimented or catered to by my partner. It makes me feel cared for and appreciated.	
I like having a clear lesbian gender. It is disturbing for me to imagine switching genders with my partner (e.g., her wearing a dress or me wearing a dildo).	
There is much more fluidity in my lesbian relationship gender roles than there was in my heterosexual relationships.	
I feel that flirting with women is different than with men because both of us are women and there is no heterosexual power differential.	
Often I enjoy the sexual play with my partner, in which I may invite her to initiate sexual interaction.	
Notes/Comments:	
Body Image/Sexuality	
Being femme means looking good for myself and not caring about others' opinions.	
I have learned to feel positive about my feminine qualities by becoming comfortable about myself.	
I experience myself not as passive, but as sexy and powerful.	
I enjoy feeling sexy for my lesbian partner and knowing that this is subverting the traditional expectation that women only look sexy for men.	
I feel that my femmeness often increases in interaction with positive sexuality.	
Notes/Comments:	
Children	
I can show younger lesbians that being feminine does not mean you are any less lesbian.	
Notes/Comments:	

SECTION IV:
HOMEWORK, HANDOUTS, AND ACTIVITIES
FOR SPECIFIC ISSUES

32

A Coming-Out Ritual:
Using Spirituality to Enhance Resilience

Eve M. Adams

Type of Contribution: Activity/Homework

Objective

The goal of this activity is to help gay, lesbian, and bisexual (GLB) individuals who are in the beginning of the coming-out process improve their self-esteem while integrating their newly developed GLB identity. Individuals are asked to enter a meditative state and bring to mind positive aspects of themselves and their community. By creating a ritual that GLB people can practice regularly, they can honor the process of coming to know their more authentic selves in an intentional, positive, and sacred way.

Rationale for Use

Although issues of spirituality and religion have been examined within the therapeutic context to varying degrees, there has been a recent resurgence of interest to bring the spiritual more fully into the counseling process (Faiver et al., 2001). Spirituality is a transcultural phenomenon that helps people address their problems (Faiver et al., 2001). More specifically, all cultures have spiritual rituals to help people negotiate life transitions (Arrien, 1993). Rituals are conscious acts or ceremonies that help us recognize a change is occurring and can provide support through it. Usually these acts have a sacred intention (Arrien, 1993).

The use of spirituality in counseling is particularly complex when working with GLB clients. As Sweasey (1997) opines, "the message seems clear: homosexuality plus religion can only equal bad news" (p. ix). Although many GLB individuals have felt unwelcomed and rejected by the practice of all major religions, the desire to integrate their spiritual and sexual/affectional selves is still strong. The interplay between these two aspects of self is a dynamic process.

According to D'Augelli and Garnets (1994), "Coming out is a complex sequence of events through which individuals acknowledge, recognize, and label their sexual orientation and then disclose it to others throughout their lives" (p. 302). The coming-out process is a rite of passage for all GLB people that could be enhanced by a ritual that helps GLB individuals feel more positive about their newly acquired gay identity. For many gays and lesbians the most common rites of passage are their first visit to a gay bar or their first same-sex sexual encounter; but these events have no ceremonies attached to them that have sacred intention and the conscious acknowledgement of the new part of oneself and the new path one is on. Providing an intentional, sacred ritual can be an important therapeutic contribution to the coming-out process.

In addition to recognizing one's sexual orientation, there is often the task of acknowledging the impact of heterosexism, or oppression due to heterosexual bias. There is a great deal of fear for many gays and lesbians when they think about coming out. Often the fear is that, "I won't be able to handle the conflict/tension/rejection that might arise if the truth were known," or "I can't bear to lose this person, family, or community that is so much a part of my life." As Jeffers (1987) points out in her book *Feel the Fear and Do It Anyway,* all fears can be distilled to one basic fear, "I can't handle _____." In order to help GLB individuals face their fears and trust that they have the resilience to handle such potential rejections, they need help in recognizing their internal and external resources.

In addition, these fears are not necessarily reality, but rather perceptions of potential future negative feedback (Adams and Mitton, 1998). In fact, Adams and Mitton found that perceptions of how participants thought others might react to them coming out was significantly related to their level of self-hatred (internalized heterosexism) and self-esteem. That is, the lower one's self-esteem, the greater the internalized heterosexism (or negative feelings about being gay), the more negative one assumes will be the reaction from those to whom one might disclose one's sexual orientation. Thus, it is essential that therapists help GLB clients maintain or increase their self-esteem and their belief that they can negotiate this difficult passage.

Spiritual rituals that increase self-esteem and resilience can help make the coming-out process more empowering and help GLB people feel more positive about who they are as they incorporate their sexual orientation and integrate it with their spiritual selves. These rituals reinforce the importance of understanding ourselves better, getting to know our most authentic selves, and accepting who we are. In addition, such rituals can also enhance an optimistic spirituality in general (Borysenko, 1994), particularly for those GLB individuals who have been raised with the belief that God is a vengeful and punishing parent, and they deserve to be punished for their wickedness.

The following ritual is a combination and adaption from several meditative rituals including the cradling exercise, the warrior posture (Arrien, 1993), and the loving-kindness meditation (Kabat-Zinn, 1994; Kornfield, 1993). This activity can be given to clients in group or individual modalities. It is best for clients to practice it outside the therapeutic context, so that it can become a regular practice in their lives.

Instructions

Prior to suggesting this activity, make sure your clients are willing to address the coming-out process in a spiritual way. As a prelude to this activity, suggest to clients that they try to spend some of each day in solitude reflecting on how they want to feel and act as people in the early stages of coming out, as well as how they can support themselves and what their strengths are if they do experience an interpersonal loss. For example, you could ask your clients to reflect on the question, "What are your internal and external resources if your parents were to reject you and cut you off financially?" Explain to clients the importance of rituals as part of the coming-out process in order to acknowledge their strengths in the face of the potential interpersonal losses that GLB people may face. Such acknowledgments also help to decrease your clients' levels of internalized heterosexism, as well as help them to cope with heterosexism at the institutional and individual levels.

Tell your clients that to do this activity they need to be in a quiet place, free of interruptions. They should lie down on the floor or bed on their back with their arms stretched out. After several slow deep breaths, they should place their right hand over their heart and their left hand on their right hand. The purpose of the hand position is to cradle the heart, as the laying of hands is a healing tradition (Arrien, 1993). As they lie there, they are to slowly acknowledge their strengths (e.g., that they are honest about who they are); talents (e.g., they are able to make friends easily); the traits they like about themselves (e.g., that they are intelligent); the ways they have contributed (and are contributing) to others (e.g., being a good listener); and finally the love they have given and received (e.g., naming specific relations with family, friends, and lovers). As they think about these things, it is important to directly confront any internalized heterosexism by recognizing that they are this unique combination of talents, qualities, contributions, and love because they are gay, lesbian, or bisexual. In fact, by accepting their GLB identity and helping others overcome their heterosexism, they are making a tremendous contribution to society.

One variation on the ritual is to shift the ritual from a reclining/healing mediation to a standing/empowerment mediation (Arrien, 1993), in which the clients stand with one hand over their heart and the other hand between the navel and ribcage. As they go through the ritual, they can visualize themselves as a tree. Although they will still be engaging in the process of focusing on inner and outer resources, the meditation has two distinct parts. As clients create their list of traits and abilities and the love and support they have received, they can visualize each of these elements as the tree roots that will provide grounding and nourishment. This visualization can enhance their sense of resilience. When clients create their list of contributions and the love and support they have given to others, they can visualize each of these elements as the branches of their tree that they offer to others, and which also provides them with a sense of present or future external accomplishments. This part of the visualization can enhance feelings of self-esteem.

To end the ritual, a prayer may be said. Clients may choose to create one themselves; however, you might want to suggest a loving-kindness prayer to them as well. Loving-kindness meditations have been practiced for over 2,500 years (Kornfield, 1993) and they are particularly effective at reducing self-loathing and feelings of inadequacy (Kabat-Zinn, 1994). It is important to convey that being healed is meant in the context of being healed from any internalized oppression, specifically internalized heterosexism, and any other self-criticism.

The other aspect to the loving-kindness meditation is to expand these feelings of acceptance and love to others in their lives. First these feelings may be extended to those closest to them and later to those with whom conflict may exist. The latter might include those with whom your clients are considering disclosing their sexual orientation. The entire ritual should be practiced several times a day.

Suggestions for Follow-Up

Some clients will need help identifying their strengths and contributions. You might suggest that they read de la Huerta's (1999) book for a variety of examples of the contributions GLB individuals have made, particularly in the sacred realm. In addition, because the ritual is solitary in nature, it is important to balance out this inner work with external validation. As Bandura's (1986) theory of reciprocal determinism would suggest, creating a more supportive environment will help GLB individuals feel better about themselves. However, creating a supportive environment requires that they already feel positive about themselves and act accordingly with others. Thus it is essential that therapists affirm their clients' positive perceptions of self, assess their clients' ability to view themselves positively before and after attempting the ritual, and help their clients explore which people in their environment would be most likely to provide external validation, support, and a sense of community.

Contraindications

Although this exercise is capable of producing deep feelings of peace and serenity, it may not be appropriate for everyone. Clients who are experiencing significant depression that makes it difficult for them to think of anything positive about themselves or who engage in extensive ruminations would probably find such an activity demoralizing or distressing. Also, because this activity is a form of relaxation, clients who experience dissociative episodes might be better served by engaging in such an activity under their therapist's supervision. Of course this activity would not be appropriate to use with those clients whose adherence to certain organized religions would make such an activity taboo. It is not necessary for someone to be spiritually focused to engage in this activity, as meditation is not inherently spiritual (Kabat-Zinn, 1994). For such people, the activity could be presented as a self-esteem–building exercise.

Readings and Resources for the Professional

Adams, E. M. and Mitton, F. (1998). Internalized heterosexism and the gay/lesbian identity development process. Poster session at the American Psychological Association, San Francisco, CA.

Arrien, A. (1993). *The four-fold way: Walking the paths of the warrior, teacher, healer, and visionary*. San Francisco: HarperSanFrancisco.

Bandura, A. (1986). *Social foundations of thought and action: A social cognitive theory*. Englewood Cliffs, NJ: Prentice-Hall.

Borysenko, J. (1994). *Fire in the soul: The new psychology of spiritual optimism*. New York: Warner Books.

D'Augelli, A.R. and Garnets, L.D. (1994). Lesbian, gay, and bisexual communities. In A. R. D'Augelli and C. J. Patterson (Eds.), *Lesbian, gay, and bisexual identities over the lifespan: Psychological perspectives* (pp. 293-320). New York: Oxford University Press.

Faiver, C., Ingersoll, R. E., O'Brien, E., and McNally, C. (2001). *Explorations in counseling and spirituality: Philosophical, practical, and personal reflections*. Belmont, CA: Brooks/Cole.

Jeffers, Susan (1987). *Feel the fear and do it anyway*. New York: Fawcett Columbine.

Kabat-Zinn, J. (1994). *Wherever you go there you are: Mindfulness meditation in everyday life*. New York: Hyperion.

Kornfield, J. (1993). *A path with heart: A guide through the perils and promises of spiritual life*. New York: Bantam.

Sweasey, P. (1997). *From queer to eternity: Spirituality in the lives of lesbian, gay and bisexual people*. London: Cassell.

Bibliotherapy Sources for the Client

Arrien, A. (1993). *The four-fold way: Walking the paths of the warrior, teacher, healer, and visionary*. San Francisco, CA: HarperSanFrancisco.

Borysenko, J. (1994). *Fire in the soul: The new psychology of spiritual optimism*. New York: Warner Books.

de la Huerta, C. (1999). *Coming out spiritually: The next step*. New York: Jeremy P. Tarcher/ Putnam.

Jeffers, Susan (1987). *Feel the fear and do it anyway*. New York: Fawcett Columbine.

Kabat-Zinn, J. (1994). *Wherever you go there you are: Mindfulness meditation in everyday life*. New York: Hyperion.

Kornfield, J. (1993). *A path with heart: A guide through the perils and promises of spiritual life*. New York: Bantam.

References

Adams, E. M. and Mitton, F. (1998). Internalized heterosexism and the gay/lesbian identity development process. Poster session at the American Psychological Association, San Francisco, CA.

Arrien, A. (1993). *The four-fold way: Walking the paths of the warrior, teacher, healer, and visionary*. San Francisco, CA: HarperSanFrancisco.

Bandura, A. (1986). *Social foundations of thought and action: A social cognitive theory.* Englewood Cliffs, NJ: Prentice-Hall.

Borysenko, J. (1994). *Fire in the soul: The new psychology of spiritual optimism.* New York: Warner Books.

D'Augelli, A.R. and Garnets, L.D. (1994). Lesbian, gay, and bisexual communities. In A. R. D'Augelli and C. J. Patterson (Eds.), *Lesbian, gay, and bisexual identities over the lifespan: Psychological perspectives* (pp. 293-320). New York: Oxford University Press.

de la Huerta, C. (1999). *Coming out spiritually: The next step.* New York: Jeremy P. Tarcher/Putnam.

Faiver, C., Ingersoll, R. E., O'Brien, E., and McNally, C. (2001). *Explorations in counseling and spirituality: Philosophical, practical, and personal reflections.* Belmont, CA: Brooks/Cole.

Jeffers, Susan (1987). *Feel the fear and do it anyway.* New York: Fawcett Columbine.

Kabat-Zinn, J. (1994). *Wherever you go there you are: Mindfulness meditation in everyday life.* New York: Hyperion.

Kornfield, J. (1993). *A path with heart: A guide through the perils and promises of spiritual life.* New York: Bantam.

Sweasey, P. (1997). *From queer to eternity: Spirituality in the lives of lesbian, gay and bisexual people.* London: Cassell.

33

Reconciling with Religion/Exploring Spirituality

Sharon Horne
Nicole Noffsinger Frazier

Type of Contribution: Activity/Homework

Objective

This activity is designed for clients who are struggling with the integration of their faith and their sexual identity. It is intended to be a structured exploration of religious practices and spiritual beliefs. Clients will be asked to identify their specific spiritual and/or religious beliefs and then encouraged to explore how these spiritual beliefs can be met. Finally, homework assignments that guide clients on an exploration of community religious resources and opportunities for spiritual growth in practice and belief are provided.

Rationale for Use

Many gay, lesbian, bisexual, and transgendered (GLBT) clients struggle to integrate their sexual orientation with their religious and/or spiritual beliefs (Gage Davidson, 2000). Affirmation of a person's basic goodness, the development of community, and connection with a higher being or creator are three basic purposes of spirituality for GLBT people (O'Neill and Ritter, 1992). Scholars propose that GLBT persons' needs for religious and/or spiritual communities may be more urgent than heterosexuals' (Fortunato, 1982; O'Neill and Ritter, 1992). Due to the stigma placed on them by a heterosexist society, GLBT individuals may encounter more difficulties in finding a supportive spiritual community (Gage Davidson, 2000). Unfortunately, all too often, "traditional organized religion, rather than assisting with integration and wholeness, often fragments individuals by seeming to demand that individuals change or be forgiven for their very nature" (Ritter and O'Neill, 1989, p. 10). In some instances, this conflict causes GLBT individuals to leave their religious communities or to remain silenced about their sexual orientation within their faith community. Still others leave their spiritual communities and seek out GLBT-welcoming faith communities or become members of a GLBT-affirming community associated with their traditional faith. However, integrating sexual orientation and religious beliefs can be difficult and challenging, and many individuals who struggle with this issue will seek guidance in a therapeutic setting (Fortunato, 1982; Haldeman, 1996).

Instructions

This exercise can be utilized in individual, couple, or group therapy, and can be assigned as homework for client(s) to engage in independently, or it can be utilized in session as a shared exploration for the therapist(s) and client(s). Client(s) will be instructed to complete the following questionnaire and then therapist or client can score the questionnaire. The main purpose of the questionnaire, however, is to elicit an initial analysis of spiritual values and needs in the life of the client(s). Instructions are listed that will guide the therapist through the intervention.

Suggestions for Follow-Up

Because this activity is intended to initiate exploration of spiritual beliefs/practices and needs, therapists should follow up on a weekly basis. Therapists should plan sufficiently for time in session to discuss clients' experiences between sessions, particularly when homework assignments require client exploration of community resources and events. If the integration of spirituality and sexual identity remains a salient issue with clients, the exercise can be repeated in six months or a year for further clarification of the clients' needs.

Contraindications

This exercise is intended for clients of all faith traditions and communities. It should not be used with clients who are content with their faith community, and may not be appropriate for clients who have chosen not to be affiliated with any spiritual community and are now struggling with the integration of spirituality and sexual identity. In addition, the activity makes an assumption that clients have a traditional faith community; although the exercise may still be relevant for these clients, the therapist may want to amend the questionnaire to reflect the clients' current spiritual beliefs.

Readings and Resources for the Professional

Clark, J. M., Brown, J. C., and Hochstein, L. M. (1990). Institutional religion and gay/lesbian oppression. In F. W. Bozett and M. B. Sussman (Eds.), *Homosexuality and family relations* (pp. 265-284). Binghamton, NY: The Haworth Press.

Comstock, G. D. and Henking, S. E. (1997). *Que(e)rying religion: A critical anthology*. New York: Continuum.

Fortunato, J. E. (1982). *Embracing the exile: Healing journeys of gay Christians*. New York: Seabury Press.

Gage Davidson, M. (2000). Religion and spirituality. In M. Perez, K. Debord, and K. Bieschke (Eds.), *Handbook of counseling and psychotherapy with lesbian, gay, and bisexual clients* (pp. 409-433). Washington, DC: American Psychological Association.

Haldeman, D. (1996). Spirituality and religion in the lives of lesbians and gay men. In R. P. Cabaj and T. S. Stein (Eds.), *Textbook of homosexuality and mental health* (pp. 881-896). Washington, DC: American Psychiatric Press.

Jones, S. L. (1994). A constructive relationship for religion with the science and profession of psychology: Perhaps the boldest model yet. *American Psychologist, 49,* 184-199.

O'Neill, C. and Ritter, K. (1992). *Coming out within: Stages of spiritual awakening for lesbians and gay men*. San Francisco: Harper and Row.

Ritter, K. and O'Neill, C. (1989). Moving through loss: The spiritual journey of gay men and lesbian women. *Journal of Counseling and Development, 68,* 9-15.

Bibliotherapy Sources for the Client

Empereur, J. L. (1998). *Spiritual direction and the gay person*. New York: Continuum.

Glaser, C. (1998a). *Come home: Reclaiming spirituality and community as gay men and lesbians*. Gaithersburg, MD: Chi Rho Press.

Glaser, C. (1998b). *Coming out as sacrament*. Louisville, KY: Geneva Press.

Glaser, C. (1999). *The word is out: Daily reflections on the Bible for lesbians and gay men*. London: Westminster John Knox Press.

Kolodny, D. R. (2000). *Blessed bi spirit: Bisexual people of faith*. New York: Continuum Publishing Group.

McCall Tigert, L. (1996). *Coming out while staying in: Struggles and celebrations of lesbians, gays, and bisexuals in the church*. Cleveland, OH: United Church Press.

McNeill, J. J. (1996). *Taking a chance on God: Liberating theology for gays, lesbians, and their lovers, families, and friends*. Boston, MA: Beacon Press.

Stuart, E., Braunston, A., and Edwards, M. (1998). *Religion is a queer thing: A guide to the Christian faith for lesbian, gay, bisexual and transgendered persons*. Cleveland, OH: Pilgrim Press.

Sweasey, P. (1997). *From queer to eternity: Spirituality in the lives of lesbian, gay, and bisexual people*. United Kingdom: Cassell Academic.

White, M. (1995). *Stranger at the gate: To be gay and Christian in America*. New York: Plume Press.

Internet Resources

GLBT Muslims

Al-Fatiha (2001). Retrieved online August 2, 2002, from <http://www.al-fatiha.net>.

TransMuslims (2001). Retrieved online August 2, 2002, from <http://groups.yahoo.com/group/transmuslims>.

LGBTQ Muslim Youth (2001). Retrieved online August 2, 2002, from <http://groups.yahoo.com/group/lgbtqMuslimYouth>.

Roman Catholic

Dignity (2001). Retrieved online August 2, 2002, from <www.dignityUSA.org>.

Episcopal

Integrity (2001). Retrieved online August 2, 2002, from <www.integrityusa.org>.

Jewish

World Congress of Gay, Lesbian, Bisexual, and Transgendered Jews (2001). Retrieved online August 2, 2002, from <www.glbtjews.org>.

Church of Latter Day Saints/Mormon

Affirmation (2001). Retrieved online August 2, 2002, from <www.affirmation.org>.

Lutheran

Lutherans Concerned North American (2001). Retrieved online August 2, 2002, from <http://www.lcna.org>.

United Methodist

Affirmation (2001). Retrieved online August 2, 2002, from <www.umaffirm.org>.

Seventh-Day Adventist

Kinship International, Inc. (2001). Retrieved online August 2, 2002, from <www.sdakinship. org>.

Christian

Universal Fellowship of Metropolitan Community Churches (2001). Retrieved online August 2, 2002, from <www.ufmcc.com>.

References

Fortunato, J. E. (1982). *Embracing the exile: Healing journeys of gay Christians*. New York: Seabury Press.

Gage Davidson, M. (2000). Religion and spirituality. In M. Perez, K. Debord, and K. Bieschke (Eds.), *Handbook of counseling and psychotherapy with lesbian, gay, and bisexual clients* (pp. 409-433). Washington, DC: American Psychological Association.

Haldeman, D. (1996). Spirituality and religion in the lives of lesbians and gay men. In R. P. Cabaj and T. S. Stein (Eds.), *Textbook of homosexuality and mental health* (pp. 881-896). Washington, DC: American Psychiatric Press.

O'Neill, C. and Ritter, K. (1992). *Coming out within: Stages of spiritual awakening for lesbians and gay men*. San Francisco, CA: Harper and Row.

Ritter, K. and O'Neill, C. (1989). Moving through loss: The spiritual journey of gay men and lesbian women. *Journal of Counseling and Development, 68*, 9-15.

Exploration of Religious/Spiritual Needs

This questionnaire is designed to assist you in identifying what your religious/spiritual needs and community values may be. Please answer the following questions about religious faith using the scale below. Indicate the level of agreement (or disagreement) for each statement, then add up the total number of points for each scale. Upon completion, you may want to discuss your answers with your therapist.

Spirituality Inventory (S)	Disagree 0	Uncertain 1	Agree 2	Strongly Agree 3
1. My spiritual/religious faith community is a very important aspect of my identity.	☐	☐	☐	☐
2. I am an active participant in a religious/spiritual community.	☐	☐	☐	☐
3. My religious/spiritual faith provides me with a sense of purpose in my life.	☐	☐	☐	☐
4. My religious/spiritual community provides me with a vital support network.	☐	☐	☐	☐
5. I look to my faith community for direction in my life.	☐	☐	☐	☐
6. My faith community is an important part of my family of origin and extended family.	☐	☐	☐	☐
7. My faith community provides me with a sense of peace and solace when I am in need.	☐	☐	☐	☐
8. The majority of my friends and family belong to my religious/spiritual faith community.	☐	☐	☐	☐

Total Score _____

Score of 0-11: *Low S.* You may be questioning whether your spiritual needs are currently being met. You may be very certain that your spiritual faith is not meeting the needs you may have for sense of purpose, connection, peace, and support.

Score of 12-17: *Moderate S.* Your spiritual community is important to you and you find value in your faith community for a number of reasons. However, your current faith may not be meeting all of your spiritual needs.

Score of 18-24: *High S.* Your spiritual community is an extremely important part of your life. It provides you with a support network, feelings of connection, purpose, and peace, and allows you to be actively involved.

GLBT Assessment (G)	Disagree 0	Uncertain 1	Agree 2	Strongly Agree 3
1. My faith community considers being homosexual a sin or against the faith.	☐	☐	☐	☐
2. My faith community is not gay, lesbian, and bisexual affirming.	☐	☐	☐	☐

	Disagree	Uncertain	Agree	Strongly Agree
3. I am not comfortable being out in my faith community.	☐	☐	☐	☐
4. My faith community accepts GLBT members only if they do not openly disclose their sexual orientation.	☐	☐	☐	☐
5. My faith community accepts "sinners" but condemns the "sin" of homosexuality.	☐	☐	☐	☐
6. My faith community will not perform commitment ceremonies for same-sex couples.	☐	☐	☐	☐
7. My faith community does not hold coming-out ceremonies for GLBT people.	☐	☐	☐	☐
8. My faith community does not recognize anniversaries of same-sex couples.	☐	☐	☐	☐
9. My faith community recognizes marriage as an institution only between a man and a woman.	☐	☐	☐	☐
10. My faith community has no "out" GLBT members (the majority of the community knows they are GLBT).	☐	☐	☐	☐
11. I would feel uncomfortable disclosing my sexual identity to the leaders of my faith community.	☐	☐	☐	☐
12. My faith community addresses homosexuality negatively.	☐	☐	☐	☐

Total Score _____

Score of 0-11: *Low Negativity.* Your score indicates that for the most part you feel comfortable within your spiritual community with regard to your sexual identity. This may include being out in your community, celebrating same-sex relationships, or feeling affirmed by your community for being GLBT. However, there may be one or two areas in which you are uncertain or where your faith community fails to be affirming.

Score of 12-23: *Moderate Negativity.* Your score indicates that although your current faith community probably has some negative practices toward GLBT individuals, you may be uncertain about your faith community's stance toward GLBT people, seeking affirmation for same-sex relationships, or whether you would be comfortable being out in your faith community.

Score of 24-36: *High Negativity.* Your score indicates that your current faith community is highly negative toward GLBT individuals. It is likely that your faith community does not support GLBT people in disclosing their sexual identities, does not recognize same-sex relationships, and considers homosexuality incompatible with your faith community.

Action Assessment (A)	Disagree 0	Uncertain 1	Agree 2	Strongly Agree 3
1. I feel a need to resolve the conflict between my sexual identity and the teachings of my faith community regarding homosexuality by exploring my spirituality.	☐	☐	☐	☐
2. I feel safe to suggest changes in my faith community so that they can better accommodate my needs as a GLBT person.	☐	☐	☐	☐
3. I feel safe talking with my family regarding changing my faith community.	☐	☐	☐	☐

4.	Leaving my faith/religious community is a viable option if my spiritual needs are not being met in my current community.	❑	❑	❑	❑
5.	I would like to explore faith communities affiliated with my current belief that are GLBT affirming.	❑	❑	❑	❑
6.	I am interested in finding or creating spiritual communities that are GLBT affirming, even if they are outside my faith.	❑	❑	❑	❑

Total Score

Score of 0-5: *Low Active.* Your score indicates that making changes may be uncomfortable for you at this time. You may be interested in further exploring your spiritual needs but currently are unable to initiate changes within your community or change faith communities.

Score of 6-11: *Moderately Active.* Your score indicates that although you are interested in making some changes with regard to your faith community, you are also uncertain about how or whether to make other changes. For example, this may mean that you desire to make changes within your faith community (e.g., inquiring as to the faith community's stance toward GLBT, talking with your family about your faith and sexual identity) but are not wanting to completely change faith communities.

Score of 12-18: *Highly Active.* Your score indicates a strong interest in making changes so that your faith community is congruent with your sexual identity. This may include making changes within your current faith community (e.g., advocating for recognition of commitment ceremonies or anniversaries) or altering your current spiritual community.

Exploration of Spiritual/Religious Options

Therapists should engage clients in a full exploration of possible conflict among scores on spirituality (S), GLBT assessment (G), and action assessment (A). For example, individuals scoring high (S), high (G), and high (A) would most likely be in urgent need of assistance in exploring alternatives to their current faith community. These individuals indicate strong spiritual faith values while finding themselves in a highly non–GLBT-affirming community, but endorsing strong interest in changing their current faith community. Clients scoring low in two or more areas most likely are not seeking therapy for spirituality issues. Clients scoring high (S) and (G), but not (A), may need more intensive exploration of the meaning of their spirituality and what support systems they may have at their disposal to cope with negative messages from their spiritual community.

This questionnaire is intended to be used as a resource to inform therapists of clients' current spiritual needs and is not meant to be utilized as an assessment of clients' spirituality. Clients are encouraged to be open and disclosing of their needs. It is necessary for therapists to explore the potential losses and life disruptions that could occur with a change of faith or community before assigning homework or other interventions.

Homework

1. Ask the client to explore possible alternatives for a GLBT-affirming community within his or her own faith/church affiliation/community. For example, if the client is affiliated with a non–gay-affirming Southern Baptist church, he or she could be encouraged to visit a GLBT-affirming American Baptist branch of the church to see if this approach to Baptist faith is compatible with his or her needs. This exercise is valuable for moderate-high (S), moderate-high (G), and moderate-high (A).
2. Ask the client to explore a GLBT-affirming faith/church community outside his or her original faith/church. This may include locating the local Universal Fellowship of Metropolitan Community Church, United Church of Christ, the Quaker Society of Friends, or the Unitarian Church. This exercise is valuable for low-moderate (S), moderate-high (G), and high (A).
3. Ask the client to engage in a Web-based exploration of GLBT-affirming support networks within faiths. Each majority faith in the United States and North America has its own organization that has embraced GLBT-identified members without abandoning the majority church/faith (e.g., the Episcopalian Church [Integrity]; Roman Catholic [Dignity]; Judaism [World Congress of Gay, Lesbian, Bisexual and Transgender Jews]; Mormon [Affirmation]; Muslim [Al-Fatiha Foundation]; Seventh-Day Adventist [Kinship]). If there is not a local chapter, therapists can explore how clients can become affiliated with these groups either by Internet, locating the nearest chapter, or creating a local chapter themselves. This exercise is appropriate for moderate-high (S), moderate-high (G), and high (A).

34

Facilitating Spiritual Wellness with Gays, Lesbians, and Bisexuals: Composing a Spiritual Autobiography

Randall L. Astramovich

Type of Contribution: Activity/Homework

Objective

This homework activity was designed to help foster healthy spiritual development in gays, lesbians, and bisexuals (GLB), by emphasizing spiritual wellness. Composing a spiritual autobiography can help GLB clients identify and value their unique spiritual-growth process, and clarify specific areas of past spiritual experience that may hamper healthy spiritual development.

Rationale for Use

Throughout history, spirituality has been considered a naturally occurring part of human development and a significant component of healthy psychological adjustment (Grant and Epp, 1998). In order to facilitate spiritual growth, individuals have customarily affiliated with an organized religious faith within their individual culture. GLB people, however, have experienced discrimination and rejection from traditional organized religions in their quest for spiritual growth (Barret and Barzan, 1996). Although some GLB people have found solace and welcoming from more liberal religious groups, or from GLB-affirming churches (e.g., Universal Fellowship of Metropolitan Community Churches), other gays, lesbians, and bisexuals have sought spiritual development outside traditional Judeo-Christian religions (Ritter and O'Neill, 1989). Perlstein (1996) identifies six approaches GLB individuals have typically chosen in order to integrate spirituality into their lives. These include remaining closeted in mainstream religion, coming out and joining a religious subgroup, joining mainstream religion as an openly GLB person, joining a GLB church, forming an individual relationship with a higher power, and creating a unique spirituality built upon extended families and friends in the GLB community.

Regardless of the specific spiritual path taken, in order for spiritual development to progress in a healthy manner GLB people must assess whether their approach fosters spiritual wellness. According to Chandler, Holden, and Kolander (1992), spiritual wellness involves a balanced approach to spirituality that serves as a prerequisite to healthy spiritual development. An individual's present level of spiritual wellness may be influenced by past religious and spiritual experiences. For many GLB individuals, a major element in achieving spiritual wellness involves the exploration of their unique spiritual path in light of past intolerance and discrimination from many religious faiths. Ultimately, GLB people must find a spiritual path that is affirming and contributive to wholeness and balance in their lives.

Spirituality can comprise a significant part of an individual's identity and it may have positive or negative consequences upon an individual's self-esteem (Grant and Epp, 1998). Therefore, attaining a healthy spiritual perspective can contribute to psychological wellness. Assessing their past spiritual experiences and their current spiritual life may help GLB clients acquire insight into their spiritual paths and make necessary adjustments in order to achieve spiritual wellness. Traditional Judeo-Christian religious affiliation may foster spiritual wellness for some GLB people. However, those not coming from Judeo-Christian backgrounds, or those unsatisfied with the Judeo-Christian faiths, may seek spiritual wellness through other spiritual paths including Islam, Buddhism, Hinduism, paganism, Greek mythology, Wicca, and Native American spiritual traditions (Davidson, 2000). Thus, for GLB people the achievement of spiritual wellness may occur through myriad forms, depending upon their unique personal and spiritual needs.

Although traditional psychotherapy has often minimized, or even excluded, spiritual and religious concerns of clients, therapists today must acknowledge and affirm the role of religion and spirituality in the lives of their clients. A main role of the therapist in helping GLB clients achieve spiritual wellness includes encouraging them to explore the role spirituality plays in their identity (Haldeman, 1996). Because spiritual exploration and cultivating spiritual insight can play a significant role in a GLB client's search for self-identity (Lynch, 1996), therapists should be able to propose activities designed to foster spiritual wellness to GLB clients.

Instructions

Composing a spiritual autobiography encourages GLB clients to assess their own level of spiritual wellness, and it may help them identify areas for future growth and balance on their individual path of spiritual development. As Grant and Epp (1998) point out, an individual's views of spirituality often reflect projections of themselves. Therefore, composing a spiritual autobiography is both a deeply personal and a spiritual endeavor. Ultimately, as clients' self-perceptions change, their individual spirituality changes as well. This exercise was designed to foster spiritual reflection and is not specifically religious. However, its use does not preclude incorporation of a specific religious perspective and it may be successfully adapted to the clients' religious preferences and current religious practice. The goal is to help GLB clients foster wellness in their spiritual lives and ultimately guide them in healthy spiritual development.

In order to prepare clients for the process of composing their spiritual autobiography, it is important to emphasize the individual and unique nature of spiritual development. It may be helpful to speak with clients about past spiritual experiences and current spiritual beliefs, and to discuss the impact of these upon their current level of psychospiritual well-being. In addition, clients should be instructed that their spiritual autobiography might incorporate numerous media of expression. For example, some artistically inclined clients may choose to paint or draw pictures of significant experiences, and others may write a series of poems or compose music or songs symbolic of their experiences. Therapists should welcome and encourage a variety of creative endeavors in the clients' spiritual autobiography. Presenting the spiritual autobiography to clients as a portfolio of significant artifacts related to their individual spirituality may help them utilize their creativity in this activity. Composing a spiritual autobiography should be viewed as an ongoing homework activity for clients, as its completion may take many weeks.

The creation of a spiritual autobiography by GLB people may be conceptualized as a triptych comprised of three significant themes: spiritual heritage, sexual orientation and spirituality, and cultivating spiritual wellness. Clients should be encouraged to explore each theme in a variety of contexts. The Spiritual Autobiography handout gives some suggested questions for clients to consider when exploring each of the three themes, and also lists some possible mediums of expression. Clients should be encouraged to share their experiences during weekly counseling sessions, as they make progress on their autobiography.

During the exploration of spiritual heritage, clients should be encouraged to examine how their views of spirituality have been influenced, both positively and negatively, by past experiences. Clients may even create a spiritual time line, highlighting significant spiritual or religious events in their lives from childhood through adulthood. Exploring sexual orientation and spirituality helps GLB clients identify conflicts surrounding their spiritual heritage and their sexual orientation. Clients are asked to explore their comfort level with being GLB and how this impacts their spirituality. Furthermore, clients are encouraged to explore how being GLB impacts their participation in organized religious or spiritual activities. During the last stage of the spiritual autobiography, clients explore their current level of spiritual wellness and determine the role spirituality plays in their lives today. Finally, clients are encouraged to identify the qualities of a balanced spiritual life and determine ways they may foster these qualities in their own lives.

Suggestions for Follow-Up

The composition of a spiritual autobiography frequently leads to significant interaction during counseling sessions. Often GLB clients struggle with deep-rooted religious beliefs that are incongruent with a positive GLB identity. Therapists should therefore be prepared to help clients explore these significant concerns as they arise. In addition, clients may decide to share their insights with significant others in their lives, including clergy or spiritual leaders when appropriate. Often therapists will want to help clients process the impact of this activity upon their relationships with family, friends, and significant others. Although further counseling may not specifically focus on the clients' spiritual and religious experiences, the composition of a spiritual autobiography may play a significant role in helping them achieve balance in their lives.

Contraindications

This exercise requires a great deal of energy and introspection from clients. Therefore, it is not recommended for individuals experiencing extreme life crises, psychosis, or other severe mental illness. Writing a spiritual autobiography may be fruitful for these clients, however, once they have achieved some degree of physical and psychological stability. Furthermore, some clients may not be compelled to explore spiritual development as part of their counseling. Therapists must therefore refrain from pressuring them to explore spiritual concerns in counseling sessions. Composing a spiritual autobiography is thus best suited for clients specifically expressing a desire to explore and enhance their spirituality.

Readings and Resources for the Professional

Barret, R. and Barzan, R. (1996). Spiritual experiences of gay men and lesbians. *Counseling and Values, 41,* 4-15.

Chandler, C. K., Holden, J. M., and Kolander, C. A. (1992). Counseling for spiritual wellness: Theory and practice. *Journal of Counseling and Development, 71,* 168-175.

Davidson, M. G. (2000). Religion and spirituality. In R. M. Perez, K. A. DeBord, and K. J. Bieschke (Eds.), *Handbook of counseling and psychotherapy with lesbian, gay, and bisexual clients* (pp. 409-433). Washington, DC: American Psychological Association.

Grant, D. and Epp, L. (1998). The gay orientation: Does God mind? *Counseling and Values, 43,* 28-33.

Haldeman, D. C. (1996). Spirituality and religion in the lives of lesbians and gay men. In R. P. Cabaj and T. S. Stein (Eds.), *Textbook of homosexuality and mental health* (pp. 881-896). Washington, DC: American Psychiatric Press.

Lynch, B. (1996). Religious and spirituality conflicts. In D. Davies and C. Neal (Eds.), *Pink therapy: A guide for counselors and therapists working with lesbian, gay, and bisexual clients* (pp. 199-207). Philadelphia, PA: Open University Press.

Perlstein, M. (1996). Integrating a gay, lesbian, or bisexual person's religious and spiritual needs and choices into psychotherapy. In C. J. Alexander (Ed.), *Gay and lesbian mental health: A sourcebook for practitioners* (pp. 173-188). Binghamton, NY: The Haworth Press.

Ritter, K. Y. and O'Neill, C. W. (1989). Moving through loss: The spiritual journey of gay men and lesbians. *Journal of Counseling and Development, 68,* 9-15.

Bibliotherapy Sources for the Client

de la Huerta, C. and Fox, M. (1999). *Coming out spiritually: The next step.* Los Angeles, CA: J. P. Tarcher.

Empereur, J. L. (1998). *Spiritual direction and the gay person.* New York: Continuum.

Johnson, E. C. and Johnson, T. (2000). *Gay spirituality: The role of gay identity in the transformation of human consciousness.* Los Angeles, CA: Alyson Publications.

O'Neill, C. and Ritter, K. (1992). *Coming out within: Stages of spiritual awakening for lesbians and gay men.* San Francisco, CA: Harper and Row.

References

Barret, R. and Barzan, R. (1996). Spiritual experiences of gay men and lesbians. *Counseling and Values, 41,* 4-15.

Chandler, C. K., Holden, J. M., and Kolander, C. A. (1992). Counseling for spiritual wellness: Theory and practice. *Journal of Counseling and Development, 71,* 168-175.

Davidson, M. G. (2000). Religion and spirituality. In R. M. Perez, K. A. DeBord, and K. J. Bieschke (Eds.), *Handbook of counseling and psychotherapy with lesbian, gay, and bisexual clients* (pp. 409-433). Washington, DC: American Psychological Association.

Grant, D. and Epp, L. (1998). The gay orientation: Does God mind? *Counseling and Values, 43,* 28-33.

Haldeman, D. C. (1996). Spirituality and religion in the lives of lesbians and gay men. In R. P. Cabaj and T. S. Stein (Eds.), *Textbook of homosexuality and mental health* (pp. 881-896). Washington, DC: American Psychiatric Press.

Lynch, B. (1996). Religious and spirituality conflicts. In D. Davies and C. Neal (Eds.), *Pink therapy: A guide for counselors and therapists working with lesbian, gay, and bisexual clients* (pp. 199-207). Philadelphia, PA: Open University Press.

Perlstein, M. (1996). Integrating a gay, lesbian, or bisexual person's religious and spiritual needs and choices into psychotherapy. In C. J. Alexander (Ed.), *Gay and lesbian mental health: A sourcebook for practitioners* (pp. 173-188). Binghamton, NY: The Haworth Press.

Ritter, K. Y. and O'Neill, C. W. (1989). Moving through loss: The spiritual journey of gay men and lesbians. *Journal of Counseling and Development, 68,* 9-15.

Spiritual Autobiography:
Possible Questions for Exploration and Media of Expression

I. Spiritual Heritage

- What role did religion or spirituality play in my family of origin?
- How did members of my family and peer group view religion or spirituality during my childhood, adolescence, and early adulthood?
- Who were the significant spiritual or religious leaders that played a part in my spiritual development?
- How are my religious or spiritual perspectives today influenced by my spiritual heritage?
- In my life today, how have I incorporated, changed, or discarded the religious and spiritual traditions of my past?

II. Sexual Orientation and Spirituality

- What are the historical representations of homosexuality in the spiritual or religious affiliations of my past?
- How did my childhood religious or spiritual affiliations view homosexuality?
- How do I view my own sexual orientation?
- How comfortable am I with being open about my sexual orientation?
- What have I done to resolve my own discomfort over religious intolerance of homosexual orientations?
- How did my sexual orientation shape the way I view myself as a spiritual person?
- How has coming out influenced my religious or spiritual beliefs?
- What significance does being homosexual or bisexual have in my participation in organized religion and spirituality today?

III. Cultivating Spiritual Wellness

- What role does spirituality play in my general well-being?
- How does organized religion or spiritual affiliation fit into my life as a GLB individual?
- How do I define "spiritual wellness"?
- What are some of the significant qualities of a spiritually well person?
- How does one live a balanced religious or spiritual life?
- What are some areas that I want to enhance on my spiritual path?

Suggested Media of Expression

- Journal writing
- Audio- or videotaping
- Composing music
- Collecting and listening to recordings of significant music
- Painting, drawing, illustrating, sculpting
- Photography
- Needlework, sewing, quilting
- Meditation
- Cinematherapy
- Bibliotherapy

35

Body As Self: Resolving Body Image Disturbances in Gay Men

Scott D. Pytluk

Type of Contribution: Activity

Objective

This activity can be implemented in individual, couple, or group psychotherapy/counseling. For self-identified gay men or for men early in their gay identity development, preoccupation with body appearance, distorted body image, and a general preference for the concrete versus abstract-emotional can be sources of great psychic distress and can forestall general positive emotional development. The following clinical suggestions are meant to assist such men in moving beyond the tangible realm of their physical bodies in an effort to deepen emotional awareness and to set the therapeutic stage for greater structural change.

Rationale for Use

It is widely acknowledged that gays, lesbians, and bisexuals develop their sexual identities and their overall personalities in a sociocultural, familial, and, ultimately, intrapsychic environment that is rife with negative attitudes, beliefs, and feelings about their burgeoning sexual identity (Reynolds and Hanjorgiris, 2000; Troiden, 1993). Psychotherapists familiar with sexual minorities know from experience that it is not an unreasonable leap for their clients to generalize these inevitably internalized attitudes to a damaged sense of self-worth in general. When the "mirroring function" performed by parents, peers, and society (i.e., reflections and affirmations of an individual's value and very existence) so critical in the early psychic development of a cohesive and sturdy self is inconsistent at best, and virtually absent at worst, the self emerges as fragmented, uncertain, and often self-defeating (Wolf, 1988).

Sociocultural messages that their desires and most deep-seated sense of self are defective, frightening, sick, and/or repulsive bombard gay men and are transmitted in the family environment as well. For example, it is easy to see how catastrophic for psychic development chronic experiences of even subtle rejections and interpersonal withdrawals are on the part of a male caregiver (heterosexual or not) who responds to a young gay boy's erotic and loving approaches with actions as seemingly insignificant as a slight phobic stiffening of the body (Isay, 1989).

Some of these boys develop into men who continue to seek the positive mirroring experiences they so lacked early on in the form of great efforts at creating a beautiful body that can be "seen" and recognized as such. For a subset of these men, such a focus on the body can become virtually all-consuming. Even if solely a significant preoccupation, however, displacement of the internal onto the external, the body, comes with a cost: a lack of recognition of underlying internal emotional experience. Not acknowledging his own internal world, the gay man himself in effect repeats the trauma of the poor mirroring experience he underwent at the hands of his most often unwitting caregivers. This process is actually one way to understand the kind of internal process that results from internalized homophobia. The psychological consequences are myriad: low self-esteem, unsatisfying intimate relationships, substance abuse, self-sabotage, anxiety, and depression, among other psychological troubles (Shidlo, 1994). Therapeutic work aimed at fostering an awareness of the gay male client's internal experience, thereby providing some of the needed affirmative mirroring, is critical in treating symptoms and promoting emotional development in general.

Instructions

The therapist should attempt the following activity only after good rapport and a strong working alliance are established with the client, as well as after some exploratory therapeutic work has already been accomplished.

Step 1

Gay men with body image preoccupations or disturbances will likely focus much attention on their bodies in session. Once this is sufficiently the case, so that the client will not experience the therapist's focus on the body as alien, the therapist might ask the client to take a moment to focus on particular statements the client might have just made. More specifically, for example, a client might have just been commenting on how "lumpy," "weak," or "small" he found himself feeling yesterday morning. He might go on to say that he added a half-hour to his already strenuous regular workout at the gym to manage those negative feelings. The therapist might then suggest that the dyad spend some time exploring those descriptors (i.e., lumpy, weak, and small)—requesting that the client elaborate on them, comment on their frequency, describe their intensity, verbalize any visual images that might accompany them, or wonder about how he feels in the moment discussing them.

Step 2

This next step entails the therapist pointing out to the client that those same "descriptors" he had been attributing to his *body* might also be useful markers of his feelings about his *self*. With a client for whom such an abstraction is difficult to understand in the moment, the therapist might accomplish the same goal in a more concrete manner. For instance, the therapist might isolate and even write down one of the client's statements (e.g., "I just felt that my stomach was so lumpy yesterday," or "I was horrified to see how small my torso was when I looked in the mirror"). Then, the therapist might ask the client to say aloud or write the same sentence substituting "me," "I," "myself," etc. for the body words in the sentence. For example, the therapist might suggest: "You know, I wonder if we might try something together? You often speak of parts of your body in unforgiving and negative terms. I sometimes find myself wondering whether you might also be referring to how you feel about yourself in general. What if you were to substitute the word 'I' for the words 'my torso' in the statement you just made? Would you be willing to do that and say it out loud?" If the client agrees he would say: "I was horrified to see how small I was. . . ." If the client does not agree, the therapist can model making the substitution. Next, the therapist should spend a significant amount of time exploring the client's responses to the connection the dyad just made, focusing on affects, further cognitive or emotional associations the client makes, etc. For example, the therapist might simply ask, "What did it feel like to hear yourself make that statement? I noticed that you grimaced while you made the substitution. What does the grimace mean for you? What did it feel like to have me encourage you to recognize how negatively you view yourself at times?" or "I wonder what other thoughts or memories entered your mind while you uttered that statement aloud."

Step 3

This step is quite important at this stage in the intervention sequence, but might be more clinically appropriate after the dyad has had more experience working through repeated iterations of this activity. Simply, the purpose of this step is to assist the client in identifying the triggers for the negative feelings about his body in the first place. For example, the client who believes his stomach looks "lumpy" and is dissatisfied with a torso he perceives as "small," might have felt slighted the night before when his new boyfriend ended the evening earlier than expected. This kind of interpersonal event has internal consequences in the form of stimulating the emergence of negative feelings about the self that have a long history in the client's psychology. Teaching the client that his feelings about his body/self are not random, thereby fostering the client's curiosity about cause and effect sequences in his emotional life, will begin to enable the client to undo some of the effects of deficient mirroring and promote further development. For example, the therapist might observe: "Now that we have both realized that your frequent negative self-perceptions of your body are likely also to reflect negative perceptions of your self in general, let's see if we can determine what events, either inside or outside yourself, might trigger such negative thoughts. I believe that these thoughts, however frequent and ingrained, are triggered by something in the present. Do you have any ideas about this?" If the client does not seem to be able or willing to proceed, the therapist should check in about the client's response to the question. Then, if the client chooses to proceed, the therapist might scan his or her memory for examples from the current or prior sessions. The therapist might follow with: "Well, I think I might be able to think of something. It occurs to me that earlier in today's session, before you launched into your complaints about your body, you told me that your new boyfriend had ended your evening earlier than you had hoped for. You also suggested that you were very hurt by this. How might your hurt feelings lead to thoughts or feelings about yourself?"

Reiterations of this step of the intervention sequence over time might seek to reach increasingly deeper layers of the client's internal experience. For instance, once the client understands the ways in which his experience the night before with his new boyfriend elicited negative feelings about his body and self, it might be even more therapeutic to establish connections with the client between this kind of current event with experiences from the client's past. To move into this stage of the intervention, the therapist might simply ask: "What other similar experiences have you had that we could talk about now? When have you experienced a hurtful, disappointing, angering, or painful interaction that led you to feel badly about yourself? These might even go as far back as your childhood years." Later, if appropriate, it might be helpful for the therapist to summarize by pointing out directly that early hurt, pain, and anger might have been so formative as to be carried with the client to all his relationships and to color his overall sense of self.

Step 4

At this stage of the exercise, especially after the first occasions of its use in session, the therapist would do well to "check in" with the client about his feelings about the intervention, his feelings toward the therapist for attempting it, his questions, and his general feelings in the moment. Sample therapist questions/statements might include: "How do you feel right now, in this moment? What has this process been like for you today? What do you feel toward me now, as I have asked you to look deeply inside and maybe feel some painful feelings?" or "I wonder if any questions come to mind that you might want to ask me right now?"

Suggestions for Follow-Up

The most important follow-up is to repeat the exercise in future sessions in an effort to work through in a satisfactory manner the complexities of the issues it attempts to remediate. Frequent "checking in" with the client about his experience of this kind of therapeutic work is critical. It is not uncommon for some clients to react to the activity with resistances to tapping into these kinds of emotional depths in the form of reconsidering and rejecting their significance in sessions following the activity, avoiding further exposure and experiences of vulnerability by missing subsequent sessions, and, in extreme cases, prematurely discontinuing treatment. The therapist should be prepared to address these resistances in an open and therapeutic manner.

The therapist accustomed to employing more directive interventions and assigning extra-session homework in his or her clinical work might find it useful to suggest that the client attempt the intervention sequence at home. The therapist might instruct the client to pay attention to additional negative feelings about his body that might emerge outside the session and to jot these down. The client might then be asked to consider what triggers might have promoted the negative feelings and to write those down as well. Finally, any connections to past experience might also be recorded. This assignment could act as a stimulus for further therapeutic work in future sessions.

Contraindications

This activity is not appropriate as a primary intervention for gay men with severe eating-disorder symptoms such as significant restriction of diet, purging behaviors, dangerously compulsive exercise, use of body-enhancing drugs or supplements, serious body dysmorphic disorder, and/or suicidality. With such men, symptom-focused interventions should be the primary focus, perhaps supplemented with the proposed activity after symptoms have sufficiently remitted.

Further, as insight-oriented clinical work can be highly stimulating and can even foster regressions, use your best clinical judgment in employing this activity with clients with more fragile personality organizations such as clients with diagnosed personality disorders.

Readings and Resources for the Professional

Cornett, C. (1995). *Reclaiming the authentic self: Dynamic psychotherapy with gay men.* Northvale, NJ: Jason Aronson, Inc.

Drescher, J. (1998). *Psychoanalytic therapy and gay men.* Hillsdale, NJ: The Analytic Press.

Garner, D. M. and Garfinkel, P. E. (1997). *Handbook of treatment of eating disorders* (Second edition). New York: Guilford Publications.

Isay, R. A. (1989). *Being homosexual: Gay men and their development.* New York: Farrar, Strauss, and Giroux.

Reynolds, A. L. and Hanjorgiris, W. F. (2000). Coming out: Lesbian, gay, and bisexual identity development. In R. M. Perez, K. A. DeBord, and K. J. Bieschke (Eds.), *Handbook of counseling and psychotherapy with lesbian, gay, and bisexual clients* (pp. 35-55). Washington, DC: American Psychological Association.

Shidlo, A. (1994). Internalized homophobia: Conceptual and empirical issues in measurement. In B. Greene and G. M. Herek (Eds.), *Lesbian and gay psychology: Theory, research, and clinical applications* (pp. 176-205). Thousand Oaks, CA: Sage Publications.

Troiden, R. R. (1993). The formation of homosexual identities. In L. D. Garnets and D. C. Kimmel (Eds.), *Psychological perspectives on lesbian and gay male experiences* (pp. 191-217). New York: Columbia University Press.

Wolf, E. (1988). *Treating the self.* New York: Guilford Publications.

Bibliotherapy Sources for the Client

Isay, R. A. (1996). *Becoming gay: The journey to self-acceptance*. New York: Pantheon.

Pope Jr., H. G., Phillips, K. A., and Olivardia, R. (2000). *The Adonis complex: The secret crisis of male body obsession*. New York: Simon and Schuster, Inc.

References

Isay, R. A. (1989). *Being homosexual: Gay men and their development*. New York: Farrar, Strauss, and Giroux.

Reynolds, A. L. and Hanjorgiris, W. F. (2000). Coming out: Lesbian, gay, and bisexual identity development. In R. M. Perez, K. A. DeBord, and K. J. Bieschke (Eds.), *Handbook of counseling and psychotherapy with lesbian, gay, and bisexual clients* (pp. 35-55). Washington, DC: American Psychological Association.

Shidlo, A. (1994). Internalized homophobia: Conceptual and empirical issues in measurement. In B. Greene and G. M. Herek (Eds.), *Lesbian and gay psychology: Theory, research, and clinical applications* (pp. 176-205). Thousand Oaks, CA: Sage Publications.

Troiden, R. R. (1993). The formation of homosexual identities. In L. D. Garnets and D. C. Kimmel (Eds.), *Psychological perspectives on lesbian and gay male experiences* (pp. 191-217). New York: Columbia University Press.

Wolf, E. (1988). *Treating the self*. New York: Guilford Publications.

36

Feelings and Meaning Associated
with Unwanted Sexual Behavior

Andrew B. Suth

Type of Contribution: Activity/Handout/Homework

Objective

The goal of this activity is to identify feelings and fantasies regarding the need for psychological restitution of unwanted sexual behavior. The Sexual Behavior Questionnaire (SBQ) is designed to help elicit some of the latent meanings through association of behavior and feelings or events leading to that behavior. It may be especially helpful in eliciting these connections by normalizing the subject matter in an arena that is often shrouded in secrecy, shame, and guilt.

Rationale for Use

Shame and guilt around sexuality is particularly present in the gay, lesbian, bisexual, and transgendered (GLBT) community (Cohler and Galatzer-Levy, 2000). Often, healthy sexual behavior has been relegated to "the closet" due to a culture where sexual minorities are deemed pathological (Sedgwick, 1990; Levine and Troiden, 1988). Many individuals who grew up with the notion that their sexual fantasies and thoughts were nonnormal were psychologically condemned to repressing and hiding their feelings (Cohler and Galatzer-Levy, 2000), as well as to continual experiences of self-hate (Domenici and Lesser, 1995). The pain of these experiences contributes to a cycle of shame, guilt, and secrecy that impacts their sexual behaviors. Further, sexuality in general in this culture has elements of forbiddenness while simultaneously having properties of tension release and restitution of painful internal feelings. Unfortunately, the relief from pain is often fleeting, and the behaviors cause either interpersonal problems (such as tension within a romantic relationship) or intrapsychic tension (such as self-rage). The SBQ is designed to help the therapist and patient move beyond the cycle of shame, guilt, secrecy, and self-rage toward connecting to the root of these behaviors. This can have the effect of helping a client move toward painful feeling states such as depression, depletion, emptiness, and rage that, once uncovered, can be addressed more directly. These experiences often help clients to understand meaning in their behavior, to develop more self-understanding and acceptance, and finally, by addressing the painful root of the behavior, to develop an alternative restitution based on a therapeutic relationship to replace or reduce unwanted behavior.

Please note that these types of behavior are often highly shame producing and difficult for clients even to discuss. Terms such as *sexual addiction* and *sexual compulsion* are often means of ascribing moral or cultural judgment rather than addressing the nature and meaning of the behavior (Levine and Troiden, 1988). By adopting a stance that de-emphasizes the moral castigation often present in both therapist and client with one that encourages alleviation of self-rage through meaning-making, the therapist allows the exploration of some of the most painful and least revealed topics in treatment. This is especially useful in a brief therapy where this may not unfold in the course of a set time frame without a structured tool. Finally, this topic often evokes much within the therapist as well. The SBQ is designed to help both focus on meaning and in doing so may help clarify issues of countertransference for the therapist.

Instructions

The SBQ could be used in a variety of ways. Mainly, it is designed as a homework tool to employ in brief therapy. When therapy time is limited, the therapist can use the SBQ to address issues of importance when they may otherwise not be addressed spontaneously. If a client identifies unwanted sexual behavior as problematic, the therapist can ask him or her to use the SBQ at the time of the next sexual experience. In this way, the therapist sets a tone for thoughtful discussion of meanings behind the client's behavior versus a tone of abstinence, which can reinforce feelings of shame as well as serve to shut down a discussion. Therefore, the client is instructed to take a copy (or several copies) of the SBQ after the session to fill out if he or she experiences a sexual act that evokes negative feelings during the week. The client is then asked to bring the completed questionnaire to the next session. The therapist can use the SBQ to help connect feelings and behaviors as well as to more openly address the role these behaviors have in restituting his or her self. In this way, the therapist can help not only through understanding but also through creating a relationship that can begin to address the early needs of the client and replace the pain from earlier self-object experiences (Siegel, 1996; Kohut, 1984). This can be done in a shorter time frame than conceived originally by self-psychologists (Gardner, 1999), and the SBQ can aid in that process.

A second way the instrument can be used is as a tool for the therapist to guide discussion. In other words, the therapist need not administer the SBQ as homework, but instead can use the instrument to frame a discussion when a client addresses unwanted sexual behavior.

Suggestions for Follow-Up

The SBQ can be used as a weekly part of therapy. It can be filled out with any subsequent event and the therapist can discuss changes or key points that continue to be addressed each time. In addition, by using it regularly, the SBQ can serve a self-monitoring effect so that behavior becomes increasingly connected with the affective motivation that may engender it.

Contraindications

The discussion of these issues must flow first from an established empathic relationship. Thus, the SBQ does not replace the important relational characteristics of therapy. In this regard, it may be wise to wait until an adequate rapport is established before use to avoid premature termination of therapy due to intolerable feelings that are as yet unsafe to address. In addition, the SBQ as homework is designed for brief therapy. In long-term therapy, its secondary use as a frame of discussion for the therapist may be more appropriate.

Readings and Resources for the Professional

Bollas, C. (1992). Cruising in the homosexual arena. In C. Bollas, *Being a character: Psychoanalysis and self-experience* (pp. 144-164). New York: Hill and Wang.

Cohler, B. J. and Galatzer-Levy, R. M. (2000). *The course of gay and lesbian lives: Social and psychoanalytic perspectives*. Chicago, IL: The University of Chicago Press.

Colgan, P. (1988). Treatment of identity and intimacy issues in gay males. In E. Coleman (Ed.), *Integrated identify for gay men and lesbians: Psychotherapeutic approaches to well-being* (pp. 101-123). Binghamton, NY: The Haworth Press.

Domenici, T. and Lesser, R. C. (Eds.) (1995). *Disorienting sexuality: Psychoanalytic reappraisals of sexual identities*. New York: Routledge.

Eisenman, R. (1987). Sexual acting out: Diagnostic category or moral judgment. *Bulletin of the Psychonomic Society, 25*, 387-388.

Gardner, J. (1999). Using self psychology in brief psychotherapy. *Psychoanalytic Social Work, 36*, 43-85.

Isay, R. (1989). *Being homosexual: Gay men and their development*. New York: Farrar, Straus and Giroux.

Kohut, H. (1984). *How does analysis cure?* Chicago, IL: University of Chicago Press.

Levine, M. P. and Troiden, R. R. (1988). The myth of sexual compulsivity. *The Journal of Sex Research, 25*, 347-363.

Sedgwick, E. (1990). *Epistemology of the closet*. Berkeley, CA: University of California Press.

Siegel, A. (1996). *Heinz Kohut and the psychology of the self*. New York: Routledge.

Silverstein, C. (1991). When the therapist is more anxious than the patient. In C. Silverstein (Ed.), *Gays, Lesbians and their therapists* (pp. 240-252). New York: W. W. Norton and Company.

Bibliotherapy Sources for the Client

Handel, L. (2000). *Now that you're out of the closet, what about the rest of the house?* Naperville, IL: Sourcebooks.

Isay, R. (1996). *Becoming gay: The journey to self-acceptance*. New York: Henry Holt and Company.

Monette, P. (1992). *Becoming a man: Half a life story*. San Francisco, CA: Harper.

Penn, R. (1997). *The gay men's wellness guide*. New York: Henry Holt and Company.

References

Cohler, B. J. and Galatzer-Levy, R. M. (2000). *The course of gay and lesbian lives: Social and psychoanalytic perspectives*. Chicago, IL: The University of Chicago Press.

Domenici, T. and Lesser, R. C. (Eds.) (1995). *Disorienting sexuality: Psychoanalytic reappraisals of sexual identities*. New York: Routledge.

Gardner, J. (1999). Using self psychology in brief psychotherapy. *Psychoanalytic Social Work, 36*, 43-85.

Kohut, H. (1984). *How does analysis cure?* Chicago, IL: University of Chicago Press.

Levine, M. P. and Troiden, R. R. (1988). The myth of sexual compulsivity. *The Journal of Sex Research, 25*, 347-363.

Sedgwick, E. (1990). *Epistemology of the closet*. Berkeley, CA: University of California Press.

Siegel, A. (1996). *Heinz Kohut and the psychology of the self*. New York: Routledge.

Sexual Behavior Questionnaire (SBQ)

This questionnaire is designed to help you identify feelings and thoughts associated with sexual behavior. The answers you provide are helpful to understand the meaning of feelings you have in relation to the sexual behavior that you are exploring. Discussing the answers to these questions with your therapist will help you connect what you are feeling with what you may be doing. Please fill out this questionnaire as close as you can to the sexual behavior that you want to examine.

1. I am concerned by the following sexual behavior:

2. The last time this occurred was:

3. Immediately before the behavior, I felt:

4. Immediately before the behavior, I thought:

5. My day before the behavior was like:

6. I dreamed the following the night before this behavior:

7. Immediately after the behavior, I felt:

8. Immediately after the behavior, I thought:

9. When engaged in the behavior, I imagined I would have felt:

10. The feelings I felt before this behavior reminded me of these other feelings in my life/in my past:

11. The thoughts I felt before this behavior reminded me of these other thoughts in my life/from my past:

12. The feelings I felt after this behavior reminded me of these other feelings in my life/in my past:

13. The thoughts I felt after this behavior reminded me of these other feelings in my life/in my past:

37

An Alphabet of GLBT and Disability Issues

Katherine Schneider

Type of Contribution: Activity/Homework

Objective

The goal of this activity is to provide a springboard for exploring various issues related to being gay, lesbian, bisexual, or transgendered (GLBT) and having a disability/illness.

Rationale for Use

Therapists who are familiar with multicultural issues, including those faced by GLBT clients, typically have little or no training regarding disability issues (Olkin, 2000). Therapists with the most training on disability issues, rehabilitation counselors, have had very little exposure to GLBT issues (McAllan, 1994).

The double oppression experienced by the one out of seventy Americans who has a disability and is GLBT may lead to increased isolation and stress. The looksism, or favoring of young physically attractive bodies, particularly present in the gay male community, and the asexual stereotype of people with disabilities may lead to distortions in physical self-concepts. Healthy identity development may also be hindered by the double stigma of disability/illness and GLBT status (Corbett, 1994).

Counselors may suffer not only from lack of knowledge and resources for clients, but also from a lack of comfort in even asking the questions. For these reasons, the counselor may wish to answer the questions for himself or herself before giving them to the client. For example, a nondisabled counselor might wish to answer the D-disability coming-out story questions for the first person with a disability he or she knew or for the person with a disability he or she feels closest to.

Instructions

The twenty-six topics raised by the questions in this Alphabet Exercise are similar to questions often asked during intake interviews. However, the emphasis is on how the disability/illness component of the GLBT person's identity influences all areas of his or her life. By asking these questions, the therapist can help the client tell his or her story in such a way that both the therapist and the client can better understand the impact of the disability/illness in shaping the GLBT client's identity.

At the end of the initial intake session, the therapist could hand the client a worksheet with these twenty-six topics on it and ask the client to fill out any of them that he or she believes were not covered thoroughly enough during the intake. Alternatively, during the therapy process, the therapist could ask the client to pick a set of questions and journal about them outside of therapy.

As the client's experiences are heard, both by the therapist and by the client, connections will occur to the client that help him or her in integrating the disability/illness into a positive identity.

Suggestions for Follow-Up

During therapy, there may be changes in views of some of the areas covered by the alphabet. It might prove useful for the client and therapist to look through the alphabet areas occasionally and discuss what has and has not changed. This discussion could be used to focus further therapy.

Both counselor and client may wish to read the books and visit the Web sites listed under Bibliotherapy Sources for the Client. Bibliotherapy (particularly the narratives listed) and finding community on the Web can help to lessen the alienation the GLBT client with a disability/illness may feel.

Contraindications

Counselors who feel very uncomfortable interacting with GLBT or people with a disability should not use this exercise and may wish to find other therapists in their community to whom they can refer clients with these characteristics. Therapists who feel the kind of discomfort that comes from limited experience may decide to do their own bibliotherapy and work with a client while getting some collegial supervision from a therapist who is more familiar with GLBT and disability issues. Clients who have not considered their disability/illness as part of their identity may have difficulty with these questions and may wish to consider them throughout therapy rather than only at the beginning. This exercise may help the client integrate his or her disability into his or her identity.

Special Instructions

For the visually impaired or learning-disabled client, the therapist may wish to give him or her the alphabet in an alternate format such as on disk or in braille.

Readings and Resources for the Professional

Corbett, J. (1994). A proud label: Exploring the relationship between disability politics and gay pride. *Journal of Applied Rehabilitation Counseling, 9*(3), 343-357.

McAllan, L. C. (1994). Addressing the needs of lesbian and gay clients with disabilities. *Journal of Applied Rehabilitation Counseling, 25*(1), 26-35.

Olkin, R. (2000). *What psychotherapists should know about disability.* New York: Guilford Publications.

Bibliotherapy Sources for the Client

Brownworth, V. and Raffo, S. (Eds.) (1999). *Restricted access: Lesbians on disability.* Seattle, WA: Seal Press.

Clare, E. and Pharr, S. (1999). *Exile and pride: Disability, queerness and liberation.* Cambridge, MA: South End Press.

Fries, K. (1997). *Body remember: A memoir.* New York: Dutton.

Griffin, S. (1999). *What her body thought.* Scranton, PA: HarperCollins.

Luczak, R. (Ed.) (1997). *Eyes of desire: A deaf gay and lesbian reader.* Los Angeles, CA: Alyson Publications.

Panzarino, C. (1994). *The me in the mirror*. Seattle, WA: Seal Press.
Tremain, S. (Ed.) (1996). *Pushing the limits: Disabled dykes produce culture*. London: Women's Press.

Internet Resources

Ability. (2001). Retrieved online August 2, 2002, from <http://www.ability.org.uk/>.
American Council of the Blind (2001). Retrieved online August 2, 2002, from <www.acb.org>.
Bent (2001). Retrieved online August 2, 2002, from <www.bentvoices.org/home.html>.
Disability and Gender Resources (2001). Retrieved online August 2, 2002, from <www.disabilitystudies.com/gender.htm>.
Disability Resources on the Internet (2001). Retrieved online August 2, 2002, from <http://disabilityresources.org>.
Gay Disabled Webring (2001). Retrieved online August 2, 2002, from <http://quest.apana.org.au/~tlang/gaydisabled>.
Gayscape Disabilities (2001). Retrieved online August 2, 2002, from <www.gayscape.com/gayscape/dis.html>.
Levine, A. (2001). Sexuality Information and Education Council of the United States. Retrieved online August 2, 2002, from <www.siecus.org/pubs/biblio/bibs0009.html>.
Passing Twice (2001). Retrieved online August 2, 2002, from <www.geocities.com/westhollywood/3323>.
Queergirlies (2001). Retrieved online August 2, 2002, from <www.gimpgirl.com/lists/queergirlies>.
The Deaf Queer Resource Center (2001). Retrieved online August 2, 2002, from <www.deafqueer.org>.

References

Corbett, J. (1994). A proud label: Exploring the relationship between disability politics and gay pride. *Journal of Applied Rehabilitation Counseling, 9*(3), 343-357.
McAllan, L. C. (1994). Addressing the needs of lesbian and gay clients with disabilities. *Journal of Applied Rehabilitation Counseling, 25*(1), 26-35.
Olkin, R. (2000). *What psychotherapists should know about disability*. New York: Guilford Publications.

Alphabet Exercise

A-access: What access issues do you face because of your disability/illness? Physical access? Information access? Are there ways this counseling or the counselor could be more accessible?

B-body beautiful: How do you think and feel about your body? Are there parts of your body or functions of your body that you have a hard time accepting? Is your body beautiful? Why or why not?

C-coming-out story: What is your coming-out story? Are you out to yourself? Others? In what areas of your life are you not out and why?

D-disability coming-out story: What is your disability/illness story? If your disability/illness is not a visible one, do you tell others about it? Why or why not?

E-empowerment: In what areas of your life do you feel empowered to do your best and aim high? Who and what helps empower you? Who and what disempowers you?

F-friendships: Who are your friends? Are your family members friends? Why or why not? Who are your allies and support people?

G-gifts: What are the gifts you have to share with the world? Are you sharing them? If not, what stands in the way?

H-health care: Are you getting GLBT- and disability/illness-friendly health care? Does this include sexual health care? If not, what needs to happen for you to access the health care you need?

I-identity: Who are you? Answer this question twenty times in terms of roles, adjectives that describe you, etc.

J-joy: What gives you joy in life? How much of your life is joyful? Is this the same as happy to you? Why or why not?

K-knowledge: Do you know enough about your disability/illness? Your legal rights? Your personal rights, such as the right to be safe?

L-love: Whom do you love? Do you love yourself? Who loves you?

M-model: What is your model of disability/illness? Is it a defect for which you feel embarrassed? A medical condition to be treated, rehabilitated, and compensated for? A difference to be proud of?

N-no: What are you saying "no" to? Are some options closed to you because of your disability/illness or your GLBT status? Are your "no's" decisions or defeats?

O-object: Do you ever feel treated as an object of pity? An object of fetishistic or voyeuristic curiosity? What do you do when you feel this way?

P-pride: Do you feel GLBT pride? Disability/illness pride? Why or why not?

Q-queer: What is your model of GLBT status? What words do you use to describe your identity in this area? Why don't you use other common words?

R-role models: Who are your GLBT role models? Your disability role models? If you could have lunch with three people living or dead, who would they be?

S-spirituality/religion: Where is God, your Higher Power, or your spiritual/religious beliefs in dealing with your GLBT status? Your disability/illness? Are you a member of a faith community? If so, how do they deal with you as a disabled person? A GLBT person?

T-thriver: At this point in your life, do you feel like a victim? A survivor? A thriver? Why?

U-unite: What groups are you a member of? Are you in any GLBT groups? Disability groups? Why or why not?

V-value: How do you value and nurture yourself? Do you take better care of others or yourself? What would you have to do to take better care of yourself?

W-work: Are you working? A student? A volunteer? A parent/caregiver? What is your life work?

X-express yourself: Which feelings do you express? To whom? Which ones do you hide? Why?

Y-yes: What do you say "yes" to? Are they decisions or defeats? Does your disability/illness make you more or less likely to say "yes?" In what situations?

Z-zest: Where are you zany, and full of zest and zip? Who do you laugh around? Where do you feel fully alive?

38

Same-Sex Domestic Violence:
Establishing a Safety Plan with Victims

Ned Farley

Type of Contribution: Activity

Objective

The goal of this activity is to help victims of same-sex domestic violence create a safety plan and take responsibility for their safety.

Rationale for Use

A pattern of intimidation and emotional abuse often accompanies domestic violence, which can result in the victim experiencing confusion regarding his or her relationship and responsibility for the violent behavior. In addition, within the gay, lesbian, bisexual, and transgendered (GLBT) communities, both knowledge of and access to resources is often limited, and sometimes nonexistent (Hamburger, 1996; Renzetti, 1992). Services that are available to victims of heterosexual abuse may not be sensitive to or even aware of same-sex domestic violence. Sexual minorities often do not trust the police or the legal system to understand or protect them, thus they may be afraid of or resistant to accessing these systems even when they are available. For this reason, the therapist may be the client's only resource; therefore, he or she must be able to provide guidance in these situations. In addition, it is important that attention to and understanding of cultural factors be taken into consideration (Mendez, 1996).

It is imperative to help victims of same-sex domestic violence understand the cycle of violence and, more important, to understand and develop a means for protecting themselves. By helping clients develop a safety plan, the clinician is helping them learn to take responsibility for themselves and their safety, especially when they choose to remain in the abusive relationship.

Historically, work with victims of same-sex domestic violence has been conducted in support groups. There are arguments, however, for the need and availability of individual therapy (Farley, 1992; Lobel, 1986). With this in mind, although working with victims of same-sex domestic violence is preferably done in group therapy, at times working individually is either clinically appropriate or the only modality available.

This exercise can be used effectively in either a group or individual setting. It is geared toward working with victims and focuses on helping them devise a workable safety plan, an especially important skill when they have chosen to remain in the violent relationship. This exercise can be utilized across time, and is not limited to a single session. In addition, it should be established as an important skill that can be utilized after therapy has ended.

Instructions

Establishing a safety plan is best done within the therapeutic hour, with continued work for the client between sessions. Considering that it is not uncommon for victims to first need crisis work, and depending on circumstances the remaining work might be short term, it is imperative to develop the safety plan early on in treatment. By utilizing the following questions as the context for development of the plan, the therapist can help the client think through the important components for establishing his or her safety. List the questions on a handout, with room for written responses. Use a session (or part of a session) to review the handout and to brainstorm potential scenarios that can help the client think through his or her answers. Then, in the same session, or at the latest the following session, create in writing the plan itself. Finally, using the plan as a guideline, have the client put in place the necessary items and protocol for following through with the safety plan when needed. It is not recommended that the client be asked to take the form home or discuss it with his or her partner. For the sake of safety, he or she needs to keep this confidential, and share the plan only with the therapist, as well as the person or persons who they will utilize as their safe house. The ultimate focus of this exercise is to establish a plan of action that will allow the client to leave a dangerous situation and go to a predesignated safe house that is outside of the knowledge of the abuser.

- *Who* do you know that might be able to provide you with a safe environment if your partner becomes violent or is moving toward violence? This should be someone that your partner does not know and would have a difficult time tracing, for example a work acquaintance, a friend of a friend, a shelter, or some other person/place not inside the circle of friends and acquaintances already known to the perpetrator. *Note:* In some cases, and if the client has the financial resources, a motel or hotel may be an option. For victims of same-sex domestic violence, the "who" is especially important. In general cases of domestic violence, the victims are often socially isolated. This may be even more pronounced within same-sex relationships. As such, the person who might provide safety and support needs to be someone that the victim can be open with, not only about the violence that is occurring but about his or her sexual orientation. If the client is limited in terms of who he or she is "out" to, a preliminary step of identifying some potential support persons who the client feels comfortable enough to come out to might be in order.
- *What* do you need to have in order to leave a potentially violent situation? This includes access to a means of transportation, keys, money, clothes, phone numbers which might include your therapist, a domestic violence hot line, your safe house number, your physician, your lawyer, etc. If you are leaving such a situation, you need to be prepared to stay away until the danger is past, or perhaps permanently. Do not leave behind anything that you cannot live without. *Note:* It is important that all of these resources are identified as sensitive to the needs of GLBT people. It is part of a good counselor/therapist's role to ensure that resources used for referral are sexual minority sensitive.
- *Where* can you hide a bag with the above necessary items that you can easily access in times of crisis? Can you have a packed bag already at the designated safe house, or do you need to have it somewhere else that is easily accessed? (This might be with a friend or perhaps at your workplace.)
- *When* do you leave? Clearly if you are in imminent danger, you need to get out fast. Make sure you have a plan to be able to do this, with access to everything you need at a moment's notice. If things are escalating but not yet at a danger point, how will you decide when it is safe to leave without raising suspicion? (For example, if you work outside the home, perhaps leave from work to the safe house, rather than going home first. This, of course, means having your bag packed and ready at the workplace.)

- *How* will you get to your safe location? Is there someone you can call or do you need to ensure that you have a set of car keys hidden for such a circumstance? If you are taking public transportation, make sure you have money, phone numbers, and a schedule handy.

Vignette

Sam is a twenty-eight-year-old Iranian-American gay male. He has been involved in a long-term relationship with Joseph, a thirty-year-old Caucasian American of Irish and German descent. They have been together for almost four years, although living together for only two years. Sam works part time and is in graduate school studying social work. He hopes to work with immigrant families in an agency setting that focuses on transitional services for immigrant populations. Joseph works as a junior vice president for a nationally known bank. Sam reports no history of medical or psychological concerns, no history of drug or alcohol use, and no history of violence in either his family of origin or previous adult relationships. He reports that Joseph has utilized psychotherapy previous to this relationship, but has not talked about the reason, other than in vague terms. Sam was aware early in their relationship that Joseph seemed to have a difficult time dealing with stress and tended to have angry outbursts, often triggered by apparently mundane events. Historically, these outbursts involved yelling, breaking things, and verbal name-calling, but never to the point that Sam felt concern for his personal safety. However, over the past year, these outbursts have become more violent and frequent, with Joseph verbalizing threats to Sam's safety, and on at least two occasions pushing and shoving him. Sam states that they have few close friends, and Joseph seems to get a bit jealous if Sam plans on meeting with friends or school acquaintances on his own. He has come to therapy because he is reporting that his own stress level has increased, resulting in decreased sleep, increased levels of anxiety, and the declining quality of his school and work performance.

Sam has not entered therapy in crisis. However, his therapist, having appropriately conducted a screening for domestic violence, feels it is important to develop a safety plan with Sam in the event that things escalate at home. Sam reports loving Joseph, but realizes that the behavior is out of control. He has done some studying about different forms of family violence through his social work program, and he has come to realize that this is what is going on for him. Fortunately, Sam lives in an urban area with a fairly strong gay community, including clinicians familiar with same-sex domestic violence. At the second session, Sam and the therapist go over a checklist of the questions that will help Sam create a workable safety plan. The following is what they agreed to:

- *Who:* Sam has identified a friend from his social work program who he believes will agree to be his safe house. This is someone who he studies with at school, but is not someone that Joseph knows in any way. Sam has not even shared this person's name with Joseph, in large part due to Joseph's jealous streak. If this person is unable to play this role for Sam, he has someone at his workplace that might fit the bill. It is a woman, again unknown by his partner, whom Sam has talked to about the abusive behavior. She herself was a victim of domestic violence in a previous marriage.
- *What:* Sam has a car, thus has transportation. He also works part time, so he has some independent financial support. Although Joseph has pushed the idea of combining their finances, up to this point no action has been taken in that regard. Sam plans on packing a bag with extra clothing, toiletries, some cash, a credit card beyond what he has in his wallet, and important phone numbers, including his therapist and the local crisis hot line.
- *Where:* Sam's plan is to keep the bag at his friend's house. He will keep an extra car key hidden in his car. The therapist told him that there are spare key boxes that magnetically at-

tach to the underbelly of cars. He can pick one up at a local auto store. The therapist suggests that Sam might want to consider buying a cell phone, too, and keeping it in his car.

- *When:* Sam and his therapist have briefly discussed the cycle of violence, with the intention of having a deeper discussion during later sessions. At this point, Sam has some awareness of the things that seem to trigger Joseph, and hopes that he can make a decision to leave at the first sign of abuse, rather than waiting until it escalates. Either way, by having his safety plan and items in place, Sam believes he can walk out the door and get away with relative success, mostly due to advance planning and the fact that he is not dependent on someone else to transport him. If the violence escalates, or at some point Sam comes to the realization that he does not feel safe going home, he knows that he can put his plan into action from either work or school.
- *How:* As previously stated, fortunately Sam has access to his own transportation. He realizes that his job is to keep his car in good repair and full of gas, and he has the spare key readily accessible.

Suggestions for Follow-Up

There are two areas that the therapist should consider for follow-up with the client. The first is ensuring that the client has found someone who agrees to operate as his or her safe house, and to cement that as much as possible. It is important that the client share the necessary information with this person about what is going on, especially since he or she has agreed to open up his or her home to the client. Although slight, there is some risk involved if the abuser found out where the client was staying (thus the reason behind identifying a person and/or place that is not connected to either partner's social circle or easily identified). Second, it might be useful to discuss back-up plans, especially regarding transportation and access to legal services. Beyond this, the continued discussion and education of the client about the cycle of violence, and how to identify where the relationship is in this cycle, is critical.

Contraindications

There are few, if any, contraindications for the use of this exercise. Rather, there are ways in which the exercise would be expanded or adapted. If there were children involved, there would be a need to identify how to make sure the children are included in any safety plan. This sometimes means separate plans, as the children may not all be in the same place at the same time. In addition, in cases involving children, there is a necessity to attend to legal issues, especially concerning no-contact orders and/or potential custody issues. In every case, a cultural assessment component to the therapeutic work is necessary. It is imperative that the therapist understands and takes into consideration any cultural history and factors that would contribute to the decisions made about both the relationship and the safety plan.

Readings and Resources for the Professional

Farley, N. (1992). Same-sex domestic violence. In S. Dworkin and F. Gutierrez (Eds.), *Counseling gay men and lesbians: Journey to the end of the rainbow* (pp. 231-242). Alexandria, VA: American Counseling Association.

Hamburger, L. K. (1996). Intervention in gay male intimate violence requires coordinated efforts on multiple levels. In C. Renzetti and C. Miley (Eds.), *Violence in gay and lesbian domestic partnerships* (pp. 83-92). Binghamton, NY: The Haworth Press.

Hammond, N. (1989). Lesbian victims of relationship violence. *Women and Therapy, 8,* 89-105.

Kanuha, V. (1990). Compounding the triple jeopardy: Battering in lesbian of color relationships. In L. S. Brown and M. P. Root (Eds.), *Diversity and complexity in feminist therapy* (pp. 169-184). Binghamton, NY: The Haworth Press.

Lobel, K. (Ed.) (1986). *Naming the violence: Speaking out about lesbian battering*. Seattle, WA: Seal Press.

Mendez, J. (1996). Serving gays and lesbians of color who are survivors of domestic violence. In C. Renzetti and C. Miley (Eds.), *Violence in gay and lesbian domestic partnerships* (pp. 53-60). Binghamton, NY: The Haworth Press.

Renzetti, C. (1992). *Violent betrayal: Partner abuse in lesbian relationships*. Thousand Oaks, CA: Sage Publications

Renzetti, C. and Miley, C. H. (Eds.) (1996). *Violence in gay and lesbian domestic partnerships*. Binghamton, NY: The Haworth Press.

Bibliotherapy Resources for the Client

Lobel, K. (Ed.) (1986). *Naming the violence: Speaking out about lesbian battering*. Seattle, WA: Seal Press.

NiCarthy, G. (1986). *Getting free: A handbook for women in abusive relationships*. Seattle, WA: Seal Press.

References

Farley, N. (1992). Same-sex domestic violence. In S. Dworkin and F. Gutierrez (Eds.), *Counseling gay men and lesbians: Journey to the end of the rainbow* (pp. 231-242). Alexandria, VA: American Counseling Association.

Lobel, K. (Ed.) (1986). *Naming the violence: Speaking out about lesbian battering*. Seattle, WA: Seal Press.

39

Same-Sex Domestic Violence: A Tool for Batterers

Ned Farley

Type of Contribution: Activity

Objective

The goal of this activity is to help perpetrators of domestic violence understand and track how their anger and/or rage escalates into violence, and ultimately learn how to control their violent behavior.

Rationale for Use

Batterers in same-sex relationships have limited access to resources and often have little trust in the legal system. In addition, especially for female perpetrators, there is both an internalized sense of shame as well as an overt stigma attached to expressing anger and violence (Hammond, 1986). For both men and women who are perpetrators in same-sex relationships, internalized homophobia may also contribute to the abuse dynamics (Benowitz, 1986). Although anger itself is not the cause of domestic violence, feelings of anger (sometimes repressed and/or denied) often are the catalyst for rage and violence. In intimate relationships, this anger and subsequent rage has little to do with the partner himself or herself, and everything to do with the perpetrator's own history of abuse and violence in his or her family of origin. One of the many useful tools to help perpetrators of domestic violence understand what happens during the cycle of violence is an anger journal. This particular tool helps the perpetrator slow down time and look carefully at the triggers and subsequent thoughts and feelings that lead to violent outbursts. Consideration and understanding of cultural factors are crucial to providing clinically appropriate services (Kanuha, 1990).

Therapeutic work with batterers has historically been conducted in groups. With perpetrators of same-sex domestic violence, group work is still seen as the optimal intervention (Farley, 1992). However, there are times that group work might not be available, thus individual therapy is utilized (Byrne, 1996). In either case, the following exercise can be used in either group or individual therapy. This assignment is to help perpetrators understand the role anger and violence play in their lives and in their relationships. This exercise can be utilized across time, and is not limited to a single session. In addition, it should be established as an important skill that can be utilized even after therapy has ended.

Instructions

This exercise is useful if first done in session, with the client using it outside of sessions at any time that he or she begins to experience angry feelings. The only instruments necessary are paper and pen or pencil. A bound journal might help to keep a record of experiences and can serve as an educational tool for the future. For the sake of practice in session, the therapist/counselor should ask the client to recall an experience of feeling angry, or a recent violent outburst. If it is the latter, it is important to help the client slowly backtrack from the outburst to the feelings that led up to it. In this way, there will be an opportunity to see the connections between feelings and behaviors, and learn how to ask the questions necessary to understand the etiology of the feelings. Many counselors/therapists who work with perpetrators utilize some form of anger journal in their treatment. The following, adapted from Farley and Wilder (1992), are useful questions to consider when keeping an anger journal:

- How intense is your anger (rate on a scale of 1 to 10)?
- What sensations do you experience in your body when you first feel anger; as your anger grows; when you feel out of control?
- Describe your behavior as the tension builds; when you first feel angry; as you become enraged.
- Describe the situation.
- What did you do with your feelings? Did you express them? If yes, how? Did you escalate them? Did you suppress them? Did you take a time-out? Did you act them out?
- What are you feeling now? What might be under the anger?
- What are you thinking? What kind of self-talk goes on before, during, and after your violence?
- What can you do to calm yourself down? How can you take care of yourself?

Vignette

Katrina is a thirty-nine-year-old biracial female of Chinese and Danish descent. She has been involved in a ten-month relationship with Vonda, who is forty and of African-American descent. They met through mutual friends, and have not yet moved in together. Katrina is employed full time as a social worker, working in a hospital setting with cancer patients. Vonda is employed full time as a middle school teacher. Katrina reports a history of violence in her family of origin, predominantly, but not exclusively, with her father abusing her mother and her oldest brother. She reports some history of alcohol abuse for herself, but this stopped after college. She smokes cigarettes, but uses alcohol only occasionally. There is no report or evidence of any other substance use. Katrina has been in counseling before, after the end of her previous relationship of ten years. She reports that she was violent in that relationship, and the reason she self-referred into therapy at this point is to avoid that behavior in her current relationship. Both she and Vonda have noted an increase in verbal abuse over the past two months. This is of concern to Katrina. In her previous relationship, the violence escalated to the point that her ex-partner wound up in the hospital with a broken arm and multiple bruises and contusions.

Katrina's counselor asks her to remember the last time she was out of control with Vonda. This was easy, it had happened just days before this session. She and Vonda were in the car on the way to a friend's birthday party. It was taking place outside in a park that neither of them had been to before. Katrina was driving, and they were lost. Vonda offered to read the map sent to them with the instructions, but Katrina refused, stating she could get there on her own. As the tension mounted with Katrina's frustration, Vonda suggested stopping somewhere to ask for help. Katrina began yelling and threatening to "just turn around and go home." Fortunately at this point, they saw a sign directing them to the park entrance; however, Katrina had difficulty calming down and continued to be verbally abusive toward Vonda. Needless to say, it ruined their experience of the party, and Vonda threatened to leave the relationship unless Katrina received some help.

As Katrina began to tell the story, her counselor asked her to consider the eight questions previously stated. Katrina reported that she experienced her anger as about a 7 on a scale of 1 to 10, with 10 being very intense. As she remembered the incident, she reported feeling her body tense up as she realized that she was lost and angry with herself for getting lost. As the anger intensified, she was aware that her body tingled, almost as though electricity was running through it. She states that when she explodes, she usually is totally unaware of her body, almost as if she has left it completely behind. Luckily, this particular incident did not escalate to that point. She continues to explore her responses, and reports that although she raised her voice and began yelling at Vonda, she never shared that she felt out of control of the situation, and was angry with herself for getting them lost. As she thinks about the event, she remembers that getting mad at Vonda was a way to avoid her own feelings of fear about being in a situation that she felt was beyond her control. She blamed Vonda for reading the instructions incorrectly, when in fact she now realizes she was so intent on finding the park that she did not really listen to what Vonda was saying. Vonda's suggestion to stop and ask for directions was experienced as total failure by Katrina. Her self-talk during this time was a mixture of blaming Vonda and finding ways to make Vonda responsible, while berating herself for being stupid. As she thinks back on the situation, Katrina realizes she has a hard time coming up with ways to calm herself down. After some discussion with her counselor, Katrina begins to identify the use of deep breathing as one technique that might help her calm down. It will take some more work and discussion to come up with others.

Suggestions for Follow-Up

Continued work and practice with the anger journal, especially at the moment that anger emerges, will be the most important part of learning to stop the anger from escalating into rage and violence. Including the anger journal work as part of the ongoing therapy process is critical. It is suggested that clients report on their use of the journal at each session, and include in this a discussion of what they are learning about themselves and their feelings. Crucial to this process is to support clients in having their feelings, including those that are uncomfortable, such as anger and fear, while helping them see that expression needs to happen in healthy ways, not in ways that are destructive to themselves or others. It is not the feeling that is abusive, but rather the behaviors that are chosen to express them.

In addition, it will be important to understand clients' cultural backgrounds, and the cultural beliefs and understandings about anger and violence. Does this contribute to the clients' understanding of not only their feelings, but also their beliefs about themselves and their relationships? About domestic violence?

Contraindications

The use of the anger journal seems quite appropriate and helpful for most clients. In some part, this is due to the fact that the anger journal as a tool can be adapted to include attention to cultural factors. Usually, such a tool is not going to be helpful in situations where the anger and violence appear to be (or have been diagnosed to be) attached to a mental disorder such as schizophrenia (as an example) where the anger and/or violence might in fact be due to psychosis rather than due to domestic violence as we understand it. This is true in the treatment of perpetrators in general. If there is a clearly diagnosed mental disorder in which the symptomology often includes anger and violence, then the therapist needs to sort through whether the client is really appropriate for domestic violence treatment versus more intensive psychological or psychiatric therapy.

Readings and Resources for the Professional

Farley, N. (1992). Same-sex domestic violence. In S. Dworkin and F. Gutierrez (Eds.), *Counseling gay men and lesbians: Journey to the end of the rainbow* (pp. 231-242). Alexandria, VA: American Counseling Association.

Gondolf, E. (1993). Treating the batterer. In M. Hansen and M. Harway (Eds.), *Battering and family therapy* (pp. 105-118). Thousand Oaks, CA: Sage Publications.

Klinger, R. (1991). Treatment of a lesbian batterer. In C. Silverstein (Ed.), *Gays, lesbians and their therapists: Studies in psychotherapy* (pp. 126-142). New York: W. W. Norton and Company.

Renzetti, C. and Miley, C. H. (Eds.) (1996). *Violence in gay and lesbian domestic partnerships.* Binghamton, NY: The Haworth Press.

Bibliotherapy Sources for the Client

Sonkin, D. and Durphy, M. (1985). *Learning to live without violence: A handbook for men.* San Francisco, CA: Volcano Press.

Stamps, W. (1992). Betrayal of passion. *On Our Backs, 7* (July/August), 31-35.

References

Benowitz, M. (1986). How homophobia affects lesbians' response to violence in lesbian relationships. In K. Lobel (Ed.), *Naming the violence: Speaking out about lesbian battering* (pp. 198-201). Seattle, WA: Seal Press.

Byrne, D. (1996). Clinical models for treatment of gay male perpetrators of domestic violence. In C. Renzetti and C. H. Miley (Eds.), *Violence in gay and lesbian domestic partnerships* (pp. 107-117). Binghamton, NY: The Haworth Press.

Farley, N. (1992). Same-sex domestic violence. In S. Dworkin and F. Gutierrez (Eds.), *Counseling gay men and lesbians: Journey to the end of the rainbow* (pp. 231-242). Alexandria, VA: American Counseling Association.

Farley, N. and Wilder, M. (1992). Gay/lesbian perpetrator treatment, Part I—Theory; Part II—Practice. Workshops presented at Gay/Lesbian Domestic Violence National Conference, Minneapolis, MN.

Hammond, N. (1986). Lesbian victims and the reluctance to identify abuse. In K. Lobel (Ed.), *Naming the violence: Speaking out about lesbian battering* (pp. 190-197). Seattle, WA: Seal Press.

Kanuha, V. (1990). Compounding the triple jeopardy: Battering in lesbian of color relationships. In P. Elliott (Ed.), *Confronting lesbian battering: A manual for the battered women's movement* (pp. 142-157). St. Paul, MN: Lesbian Battering Intervention Project.

40

Helping HIV-Positive Gay Men on Antiretroviral Therapy Maintain Their Medication Adherence

Perry N. Halkitis
Leo Wilton

Type of Contribution: Activity

Objective

The goal of this activity is to help therapists work with clients who (1) need to develop routines for medication adherence, or (2) may face situational challenges to their adherence. It helps clients to develop routines for medication adherence and to develop strategies to overcome those obstacles or situations that may be out of the norm of their daily existence and thus interfere with medication regimens. This activity is intended for use with clients who express concern about their medication-taking behaviors or who are initiating the use of highly active antiretroviral therapy (HAART) and are concerned about their abilities to follow the required dosing patterns. Although the activity was initially designed for use with gay men, it is equally effective for all clients regardless of sexual orientation, gender, or age who are on combination therapy and who are struggling with adherence. This may also be applied to adherence behaviors regarding non-HIV medications.

Rationale for Use

The recent implementation of combination antiretroviral therapies, also known as HAART, has been heralded as a medical breakthrough in the treatment of HIV/AIDS. Due to the persistence of reservoirs of HIV in human cells, it has become apparent that eradication of HIV, first suggested in 1995 (Ho et al., 1995), is becoming a less likely scenario. This suggests that for those with HIV infection, lifelong therapy with HAART may be necessary. Ultimately, the effectiveness of HAART regimens in their ability to delay progression of the disease is dependent on adherence.

Medication adherence, also referred to as medication compliance, is defined as the extent to which a person's behavior in terms of taking medications coincides with recommended schedule given by a health professional (Sacket, Haynes, and Taylor, 1979). Adherence to antiretroviral regimens is affected by a complex array of factors (Crespo-Fiero, 1997; Kalichman, Catz, and Ramachandran, 1999) and occurs in the context of lives already burdened by socioeconomic, psychological, cultural, and health challenges (Halkitis, 1998, 2000; Halkitis and Kirton, 1999). Unfortunately, the effectiveness of HAART is based on extremely high levels of adherence. Recent work has shown adherence rates of 90 to 95 percent or greater are necessary for HAART to be effective (Chaisson, 1999; Paterson et al., 1999), and that a 10 percent decline in adherence results in a 16 percent increase in AIDS-related mortality (Hogg et al., 2000) and a doubling of HIV-1 RNA blood levels. The failure to maintain strict adherence to HAART can result in the proliferation of virus that may become drug resistant (Flexner, 1998; Hecht et al., 1998; Vanhove et al., 1996). Genetic variants of HIV that are resistant to antiretrovirals, as well as a reversal of viral suppression, have been identified among HIV-positive persons reporting even slight disruptions in their medication regimen (Shafer et al., 1998). As a consequence, HIV-positive persons who are unable to adhere to their regimens may experience greater progression of HIV-related medical complications (Andrade et al., 2000; Hogg et al., 2000), as well as the potential transmission of drug-resistant strains to others through unprotected sexual behavior, posing similar treatment restrictions and initiating a more relentless epidemic without effective treatments (Halkitis and Wilton, 1999; Hecht et al., 1998; Routy et al., 2000; Wainberg and Friedland, 1998).

Complicating the situation, resistance to one medication in a class of antiviral drugs has the potential to become cross-resistant, or resistant to other medications within that same class of drugs, rendering no available or limited treatment options for HIV-infected persons (Palmer, Shafer, and Merigan, 1999; Schapiro et al., 1999). Antiviral treatment failure due to viral resistance may lead to an accelerated progression of HIV and the development of a plethora of viruses causing opportunistic infections (Moorman et al., 1998).

Numerous psychological, emotional, interpersonal, and cognitive factors have been related to HAART adherence (Halkitis, 1998). Yet the identification of an adherent personality remains elusive, a fact that is quite apparent when studying the adherence behaviors of gay men (Halkitis et al., in press). Instead, for many gay men, situational factors appear to most adversely affect adherence behaviors. Those who successfully adhere to their medications have seamlessly interwoven the medication-taking behavior into the fabric of their lives, and have developed routines or systems for taking their medications on time. This may include the development of social support systems, the use of gadgets such as beepers, or the association of medication taking with other life events such as brushing one's teeth, or watching the same television show each day (Halkitis and Kirton, 1999). Those who have developed such systems are more successful in their adherence behaviors.

However, when life circumstances interfere with the daily medication-taking routines of the individual, then he or she is likely to miss doses of HAART (Halkitis, 2000). For example, vacations or time from home are likely examples of poorer adherence because the individual's daily medication-taking routine is somewhat different. Similarly, social situations in which the serostatus of the HIV-positive person is not known to others may interfere with adherence to HAART. In both these types of situations, the underlying obstacle is the fact that the individual is removed from his or her normal life contexts and daily routine.

Instructions

1. Prior to the session, the therapist should ask the client to write out the names of the HIV medications that he or she is currently taking, frequency of taking the medications, number of pills per dose, and times of the day at which the medications are taken.
2. At the beginning of the activity, the therapist and the client should review the medication regimen so that the therapist is familiar with the required demands of timing and dosing.
3. The therapist may then say, "Many people struggle with taking their HIV medications as prescribed by their HIV health care provider. Have you experienced this difficulty?" This should be an open-ended discussion allowing the client to freely express any frustrations he or she may be experiencing with adherence.
4. Ask the client to describe the routines that he or she has developed to make sure the client takes his or her medications on time. It should be noted that some clients will have elaborately developed systems that allow them to adhere properly, and others may not have those routines developed, especially if they have recently initiated HAART. In the latter

case, the remainder of the activity may then focus on the development of routines, as outlined in step five.

5. Provide the client with a sheet of paper that lists the twenty-four hours of the day, and ask him or her to fill in the activities that he or she undertakes on a typical day. After this is completed, the therapist and client should review the day's activities and mark the times of the day that the client is required to take HIV medications. The activity should focus on linking the medication times to a specific activity of the day such that the activity becomes linked with the medication-taking behavior. The activity should focus on helping the client use the day's activities as cues to the times that he or she is required to dose his or her medications.

6. The therapist then says, "Sometimes people who are on HIV medications find that other life events and activities interfere with their usual medication-taking routines. Some people experience these life events as obstacles to taking their medications. For example, if a person is on vacation, at a party, or in an emergency situation with a loved one, this represents an obstacle to one's usual routines. Have you ever experienced such situations?" The client should be given the opportunity to share stories that indicate this type of situation.

7. The therapist and client should then develop a list of these situations experienced in the client's past, present, and anticipated future that interfere with his or her medication adherence. After exploring this list with the client, the therapist should work with the client to develop strategies that could be implemented to avoid missing a dose of his or her medications. The therapist should say, "Let's look at the first situation that you listed as an obstacle to your adherence. Imagine you are in this situation in the future. What could you do to avoid missing your medication?" The therapist and client should work to help the client visualize the situations and develop strategies for negotiating obstacles in all the situations listed by the client.

8. If the client does not face such obstacles, then the client may focus on situations that he or she imagines would be problematic for adherence or situations that he or she has avoided in fear that it might interfere with his or her adherence. Again, the goal of the activity should be to visualize those situations and brainstorm how one would maintain adherence despite being in those situations.

Suggestions for Follow-Up

It is suggested that this activity be used on a quarterly basis or during significant events in the client's life (e.g., birthdays, holidays, vacations), using the same format, and the goal should always be to help empower the client with strategies so that adherence issues are overcome. Similarly, it is suggested that the activity be revisited every time the client is prescribed a new regimen by his or her health care provider. Thus, the therapist will be responsible for either communicating with the health care provider about these matters or by asking the client about his or her medications on an ongoing basis. If the client experiences difficulty in adhering to his or her medication regimens, the therapist may decide to explore which obstacles impede the client from taking his or her medications, particularly by using steps three and six.

Contraindications

The issue of medication adherence is dependent on several factors, including the clients' understanding and acceptance that HAART will improve the quality of their lives. Some clients will seek alternative therapies such as acupuncture, meditation, or the use of Chinese herbs to treat their HIV. These treatments may actually undermine adherence to the clients' HIV medications (Halkitis, Remien, and Wolitski, 1999). In those types of situations, it will be imperative that the therapist balance the activity with an understanding of the clients' alternative approaches and sensitivity to why those appropriates are sought out by them. In other cases, patients may experience emotional distress and thus miss doses of medication as a means of compromising their health. Finally, for those clients who were extremely ill prior to the onset of HAART, it is important for the therapist to consider the implications of "Lazarus Syndrome," which has been described as the survival of many HIV-positive individuals after a period of prolonged sickness due to the implementation of new treatments. For these individuals, living in and of itself may represent an enormous challenge, especially if they were prepared to die and then had their health somewhat restored because of these treatment advances. In such situations, the therapist will need to address both the process of living and the will to live in conjunction with the issues of medication adherence such that there is an acceptance of the treatments that work to prolong life.

Readings and Resources for the Professional

Deeks, S. G., Smith, M., Holodniy, M., and Kahn, J.O. (1997). HIV-1 protease inhibitors: A review for clinicians. *Journal of the American Medical Association, 227,* 145-153.
Halkitis, P. N. (1999). American Psychological Association Directorate on AIDS, adherence fact sheet. Retrieved from <http://www.apa.org/pi/aids/adherence.html>.
Halkitis, P. N. and Kirton, C. (1999). Self-strategies as means of enhancing adherence to HIV antiretroviral therapies: A Rogerian approach. *New York State Journal of Nursing, 30*(2), 22-27.
Halkitis, P. N. and Wilton, L. (1999). Beyond complacency: The effects of treatment advances on HIV transmission. *Focus: A Guide to AIDS Research and Counseling, 14*(5), 1-5.
Holzemer, W. L., Corless, I. B., Nokes, K. M., Turner, J. G., Brown, M. A., Powell-Copre, G. M., Inouye, J., Henry, S. B., Nicholas, P. K., and Portillo, C. J. (1999). Predictors of self-reported adherence in persons living with HIV disease. *AIDS Patient Care and STDs, 13*(3), 185-197.
Meichenbaum, D. and Turk, C. (1987). *Facilitating treatment adherence: A practitioner's guidebook.* New York: Plenum.

Bibliotherapy Sources for the Client

Chesney, M. A. (1997). Compliance: How you can help? *HIV Newsline,* June, pp. 67-72.
Halkitis, P. N. (1997). Sticking to it!: Protease inhibitors and the challenge of adherence. *The Volunteer: Gay Men's Health Crisis, 14*(5), 4-5, 18.
New York State Department of Health (1999a). *New treatments for HIV: A guide for people with HIV.* New York: Author.
New York State Department of Health (1999b). *Staying on schedule: How to take the new treatments for HIV.* New York: Author.

Internet Resources

AIDSmed (2001). Retrieved online August 2, 2002, from <www.aidsmeds.com>.
The Body (2001). Retrieved online August 2, 2002, from <www.thebody.com>.

References

Andrade, A., Wu, A., Selnes, O., Hill, C., Letzt, A., Seifert, R., Kaseman, D., Myers, W., Lefkowitz, J., and McArthur, J. C. (2000). Feasibility study of the disease management assistance system: A potential adherence device. Paper presented at the Seventh Conference on Retroviruses and Opportunistic Infections, San Francisco, CA. February.

Chaisson, R. E. (1999). Take as directed? Adherence and outcomes of therapy. Paper presented at the Sixth Conference on Retroviruses and Opportunistic Infections, Chicago, IL. February.

Crespo-Fiero, M. (1997). Compliance/adherence and care management in HIV disease. *Journal of the Association of Nurses in AIDS Care, 8*(4), 43-54.

Flexner, C. (1998). HIV-protease inhibitors. *New England Journal of Medicine, 338,* 1281-1292.

Halkitis, P. N. (1998). Advances in treatment of HIV disease: Complexities of adherence and complications for prevention. *The Health Psychologist, 20*(1), 6-7, 14.

Halkitis, P. N. (2000). HIV in the new millennium: Treatment advances and the complexities of adherence. Paper presented at the HOPE Training Conference, American Psychological Association, New Orleans, LA. January.

Halkitis, P. N. and Kirton, C. (1999). Self-strategies as means of enhancing adherence to HIV antiretroviral therapies: A Rogerian approach. *New York State Journal of Nursing, 30*(2), 22-27.

Halkitis, P. N., Parsons, J. T., and Wolitski, R., and Remien, R. H. (in press). Adherence to HIV antiviral treatments in a community based sample of men who have sex with men. *AIDS Care.*

Halkitis, P. N., Remien, R., and Wolitski, R. (1999). Adherence to protease inhibitors and other antiretrovirals among HIV+ MSM. Paper presented at the International AIDS Biopsychosocial Conference: AIDS Impact, Ottawa, Canada. July.

Halkitis, P. N. and Wilton, L. (1999). Beyond complacency: The effects of treatment on HIV transmission. *FOCUS: A Guide to AIDS Research and Counseling, 14,* 1-4.

Hecht, F. M., Grant, R., Petropoulos, C., Dillon, B., Chesney, M. A., Tian, H., Hellmann, N. S., Bandrapalli, N. I., Digilio, L., Branson, B., and Kahn, J. O. (1998). Sexual transmission of HIV-1 variant resistant to multiple reverse-transcriptase and protease inhibitors. *New England Journal of Medicine, 339,* 307-343.

Ho, D. D., Neuman, A. U., Perelson, A. S., Chen, W., Leonard, J. M., and Markowitz, M. (1995). Rapid turnover of plasma virions and CD4 lymphocytes in HIV-1 infection. *Nature, 373*(6510), 123-126.

Hogg, R. S., Yip, B., Chan, K., O'Shaughnessy, M. V., and Montaner, J. S. G. (2000). Non-adherence to triple combination therapy is predictive of AIDS progression and death in HIV-positive men and women. Poster presented at the Seventh Conference on Retroviruses and Opportunistic Infections, San Francisco, CA. February.

Kalichman, S. C., Catz, S., and Ramachandran, B. (1999). Barriers to HIV/AIDS treatment and treatment adherence among African-American adults with disadvantaged education. *Journal of the National Medical Association, 91,* 439-446.

Moorman, A. C., VonBargen, J. C., Pallella, F. J., and Holmberg, S. D. (1998). Pneumocystis varinii pneumonia incidence and chemoporphylaxis failure in abulatory HIV-infected patients. *Journal of Acquired Immune Deficiency Syndromes and Human Retrovirology, 19*(2), 182-188.

Palmer, S., Shafer, R. W., and Merigan, T. C. (1999). Highly drug resistant HIV-1 clinical isolates are cross-resistant to many antiretroviral compounds and current clinical development. *AIDS, 13*(6), 661-667.

Paterson, D., Swindells, S., Mohr, J., Brester, E., Vergis, C., Squier, M., Wagener, M., and Singh, N. (1999). How much adherence is enough? Perspective study of adherence to protease inhibitors therapy using MEMs caps. Paper presented at the Sixth Conference on Viruses and Opportunistic Infection, Chicago, IL. February.

Routy, J. P., Brenner, B., Salomon, H., Quan, Y., Campos, A.-F., Rouleau, D., Lefebvre, E., Coté, P., Leblanc, R., Tsoukas, C., Conway, B., Sekaly, R., Wainberg, M. A., and Investigators of the Quebec Primary Infection Study (2000). Transmission of dual and triple-class drug-resistant viral variants in primary/early HIV-1 infection (PHI) in Montreal. Paper presented at the Seventh Conference on Retroviruses and Opportunistic Infections, San Francisco, CA. February.

Sackett, D., Haynes, R. B., and Taylor, D. W. (1979). *Compliance in health care*. Baltimore, MD: Johns Hopkins University Press.

Schapiro, J., Winters, M. A., Lawrence, J. and Merigan, T. C. (1999). Clinical cross resistance between HIV protease inhibitors saquinavir and indinavir and correlations with genotypic mutations. *AIDS, 13*(3), 359-365.

Shafer, R. W., Winters, M. A., Palmer, S., and Merigan, T. (1998). Multiple concurrent reverse transcriptase and protease and multidrug resistance of HIV-1 isolates from heavily treated patients. *Annals of Internal Medicine, 128,* 906-911.

Vanhove, G. F., Schapiro, J. M., Winters, M. A., Merigan, T. C., and Blaschke, T. F. (1996). Patient compliance and drug failure in protease inhibitor monotherapy. *Journal of the American Medical Association, 276,* 1955-1956.

Wainberg, M. A. and Friedland, G. (1998). Public health implications of antiretroviral therapy and HIV drug resistance. *Journal of the American Medical Association, 279,* 1977-1983.

41

The Balancing Act: Two Lesbian Moms

Lisa A. Hollingsworth
Mary J. Didelot

Type of Contribution: Activity/Handout

Objective

This activity helps couples bring definition and balance into their relationships. The activity can be used with lesbians entering into a new relationship, as well as with couples who have been in a relationship for some time and are currently recognizing the degenerative effect created by the lack of role definition and imbalance.

Rationale for Use

When a lesbian enters into a relationship with a lesbian who has a child or children, the parenting role of this new family member is undefined. This lack of definition generates an imbalance that transcends all aspects of the relationship, and in the worst case scenario, can eventually lead to the collapse of the relationship itself. Society readily recognizes the biological parent with a heterosexual family paradigm as the "real" parent (Dalton, Bielby, and Bielby, 2000). Within a lesbian family unit, this attitude is exacerbated. The societal rejection of the nonbiological parent, as well as the lesbian family unit as a whole, results in invalidation. The most forceful examples of this invalidation can be seen within the lack of legal rights of lesbian-headed families (Slater, 1995). This perception, coupled with the inherent societal challenges to lesbian relationships in general, inhibits both the formation of definition of the parental roles and the performance of the parental roles (Slater, 1995). Without that definition of the roles, then, "these lesbian parents are especially exposed to the social vulnerability imposed on parenting lesbian families" (Slater, 1995, p. 96).

Furthermore, in any family with a stepparent, there will be disagreements concerning child rearing. Within the lesbian family unit, such disagreements have potential to escalate so intensely that the relationship itself will collapse (Lewin, 1993). The potential is fueled by the societal attitude that an individual lesbian mother is acting in a gender-appropriate manner, but concomitantly sees a two-parent lesbian family as acting in a gender-inappropriate manner (Dalton, Bielby, and Bielby, 2000). It is important, however, to issue the caveat that not all lesbians who enter into a relationship with a woman who has children wish to take a parenting role (Berzon, 1988; Lewin, 1993). Thus an assumption of willingness to participate in parenting can be devastating to the biological parent and the relationship itself. Interestingly enough, the biological parent often perceives entering into a relationship as an act that will give her more support in child rearing (Lewin, 1993).

All of these external stressors, grounded in the dominant society's perceptions of the lesbian family unit, support an unhealthy power imbalance in child rearing. "Even individuals (e.g., lesbian friends, parents, and the child's teacher) who are fully aware of each woman's relationship to the child sometimes refuse to acknowledge their dual-mothering arrangement" (Dalton, Bielby, and Bielby, 2000, p. 6). Therefore, there is a foundational need within lesbian families for a conscious, proactive approach to parenting roles in order to forge healthy partnerships and family units.

Instructions

After the couple's initial intake session, the therapist should schedule an immediate individual session for each client. Professional ethics standards should be consulted before suggesting this to clients during the initial session (e.g., release of confidential information forms which will allow the therapist to share information from either client with her partner). The focus for these one-time individual sessions will be the exploration of the foundational question for the biological parent and the foundational question for her new partner or current partner. Individual sessions are important for exploration without any inhibitors to truth and genuine feelings.

The therapist should first, within an individual session, discuss with the partner who is the nonbiological family member the following foundational issue. It is of no significance whether the relationship is new or ongoing. The dialogue may proceed as follows:

> Parenting within a lesbian relationship is riddled with both societal pressure and internal family pressures that will stress your partnership. I realize you may know this, but I need you to consciously give this consideration. However, we both also know that parenting can be an extremely wonderful experience. You must give this conscious consideration also because it is really necessary for the health and longevity of your relationship and your mental health that you and I discuss your willingness or lack of willingness to actively participate as a parent. It is quite all right if you have no interest whatsoever in taking on parenting responsibilities. However, it will not be OK if you say you want to take on the responsibilities but really don't want to. You need to be totally honest about this and explore your feelings thoroughly because this will affect your relationship and other areas as well. I purposefully asked your partner not to attend this session so that we can explore this together without you worrying about your feelings hurting your partner. Just a reminder, though, the information you share with me may be shared in the joint session. So the question is, do you want to participate in the relationship as a parent? If so, how do you envision your roles and responsibilities as a coparent?

If the client does not wish to participate in the partnership as a parent, or wishes to stop parenting, this needs to be presented and explored in the next counseling session with both partners present. The approach presented in this chapter should not be pursued if this is the case. It is important, however, to applaud the honesty of either of these decisions and to ameliorate the guilt that may result from either of these decisions. If the decision is to parent or continue parenting, the following steps should be taken according to the paradigm presented here.

Concomitantly, there needs to be an individual session with the biological parent. Her willingness to allow another to parent with her should be addressed. This session may include an exploration of her needs as they relate to the role of parent, and her expectations of her partner's role as parent. The dialogue may proceed as follows:

> You know intimately the societal stressors that are placed upon lesbian parents. I would like you to consider for a moment the pressure that will be (is) placed upon you by society when it comes to two lesbians parenting a child or children. Because of this, we need to make certain you know with some degree of certainty that you want your partner in a parenting role. If you do, we need to explore the limits, if any, of that participation. You need to explore these issues honestly and thoroughly because this will affect your relation-

ship and other areas as well. I purposefully asked your partner to not attend this session so you can voice your feelings freely without worrying about hurting her. However, remember that the information you share with me will be shared in the couple's session. If you do not want your partner to participate in parenting your children, please do not feel guilty. It is quite all right to feel this way. But if you do, we need to explore to what extent you wish to see her role as parent extended. If you do wish her to coparent, how do you envision your partner's roles and responsibilities?

If the biological parent does not wish for her partner to participate in parenting, this needs to be presented and discussed in the next session with both partners present and the approach suggested in this activity should not be pursued. If the biological parent wants active participation by the partner, then this should be explored with the couple at the next session, according to the paradigm presented in the following.

At the next couple's session, the therapist should begin by validating the decisions by the biological parent to have the partner participate in the parenting process, and the partner's decision to participate in the parenting. The therapist should then introduce the following participation levels to assist the couple in delineating parenting responsibilities.

A. *No decision power*. The nonbiological parent is to make no decisions in this area whatsoever. This parent is expected to defer all decisions in this area to the biological parent. Also, this parent is not to either (a) anticipate the biological parent's decision or (b) discuss the anticipated decision with the child.

B. *Limited decision power*. Clients will decide upon the conditions. For instance, if the biological parent is unavailable, the partner may make the decision to explain to the child(ren) that since the biological parent is not available, she will make the decision this time. An example involves finances. The decision to give the child(ren) money for a haircut may be made when the biological parent is not available. However, the decision to give the child money for a different haircut or hair coloring may be made only by the biological parent.

C. *Decision power is equal*. Under any and all circumstances, either partner may make any decision surrounding the child(ren). Whenever possible, however, consultation should take place between the partners before making decisions that have significant consequences for the child(ren) and/or family. This team approach serves two purposes: (1) it minimizes disagreements, and (2) it presents a united stand in the parental partnership.

Once the participation levels and ramifications of these levels are explored, understood, and applied to the clients' relationship, the Participation Chart should be completed. It should be noted by the therapist that the list of activities is not exhaustive as presented and needs to be honed to each particular family. It is highly recommended that the couple take into consideration the child's feelings in this activity, and then enlist his or her input in an age-appropriate manner. For example, the couple may decide to have equal decision making in school-related decisions. However, a child or adolescent may be uncomfortable having "two moms" show up for parent-teacher conferences.

This Participation Chart not only will initiate dialogue on parenting responsibilities, but will help focus the couple on a thorough discussion of parenting responsibilities and roles. The strength of this paradigm is its conscious and proactive approach to the challenges of lesbian parenting. It will result in a clear definition of each parent's role and lead to a balance of power within the parenting component of the relationship. The resulting definition and balance, then, will strengthen the couple as parents and partners.

Suggestions for Follow-Up

It is strongly suggested that, once the roles are defined, each parent keep an informal record of the effectiveness, progress, and satisfaction of these definitions within the reality of the family's daily living. A few follow-up sessions should be scheduled for this purpose, to explore possible necessary adjustments, including input from the child(ren).

Once these definitions have been honed, it is also highly suggested that the responsibilities be shared with the child(ren) in a family session. During this session, it is extremely important for the therapist to speak to the validity of the family unit and how adherence to the decisions surrounding responsibility will help support and strengthen the family unit.

Whatever level of participation is agreed upon, it might be suggested that an initial period of no parenting by the stepparent be instituted. This will help the new stepparent build a relationship with the child(ren) without the constraints of parenting. This too needs to be discussed in a family session.

Contraindications

There may be some children who refuse to recognize the validity of the relationship and therefore the validity of the family unit. If this is so, then there must be some foundational, individual work with the children before they are asked to accept the family unit and their places within the unit.

Readings and Resources for the Professional

Clunis, D. M. and Green, G. D. (1995). *The lesbian parenting book: A guide to creating families and raising children.* Seattle, WA: Seal Press.

Slater, S. (1999). *The lesbian family life cycle.* Chicago, IL: University of Illinois Press.

Tasker, F. L. and Golombok, S. (1998). *Growing up in a lesbian family: Effects on child development.* New York: Guilford Publications.

Wright, J. M. (1998). *Lesbian step-families: An ethnography of love.* Binghamton, NY: The Haworth Press.

Bibliotherapy Sources for the Client

Clunis, D. M. and Green, G. D. (1995). *The lesbian parenting book: A guide to creating families and raising children.* Seattle, WA: Seal Press.

Drucker, J. (1998). *Families of value: Gay and lesbian parents and their children speak out.* Cambridge, MA: Perseus Publishing.

Howey, N. and Samuels, E. (2000). *Out of the ordinary: Essays on growing up with gay, lesbian, and transgendered parents.* New York: St. Martin's Press.

References

Berzon, B. (1988). *Permanent partners: Building gay and lesbian relationships that last.* New York: Plume.

Dalton, S. E., Bielby, C., and Bielby, D. D. (2000). That's our kind of constellation. *Gender and Society, 14*(1), 36-62.

Lewin, E. (1993). *Lesbian mothers: Accounts of gender in American culture.* Ithaca, NY: Cornell University Press.

Slater, S. (1995). *The lesbian family life cycle.* New York: The Free Press.

Participation Chart

Activity/Area of Concern	Level of Decision Making (e.g., No Input, Limited Input, or Equal Input)	Limits
Discipline and behavior		
School-related issues (e.g., parent-teacher conferences)		
Allowance		
Curfew		
Dress		
Nutrition		
Household chores		
Homework		
Peer relationships		

Additional spaces are available to modify the chart to fit the couples' needs.

42

Family Care Planning for Gay, Lesbian, Bisexual, and Transgendered Parents: Creating Healthy Living Environments for Adults and Children

Ron McLean

Type of Contribution: Activity

Objective

Gay, lesbian, bisexual, and transgendered (GLBT) parents face many challenges from society in general. Similar to most heterosexual parents, GLBT parents desire to raise their children in ways that promote health and growth. The goal of this activity is to help GLBT parents improve their awareness and intention of how they will parent their children.

Rationale for Use

We live in a society in which most parents expend substantial energy in raising their children, and many feel shame and guilt if they are not successful. For GLBT individuals and parents, however, additional energy must be expended to address societal prejudice and discrimination toward those who do not identify as heterosexual. Plenty of evidence suggests that a large number of people still believe that being a member of a sexual minority and a parent are incompatible (Colberg, 1997; Falk, 1993; Herek, 1998). Many of the basic institutions, such as legal and religious systems, that help to construct our society have long histories of oppressing sexual minorities through their policies and practices. For example, although small changes have been made, many states in the United States have laws that prevent or limit sexual minorities from becoming foster and/or adoptive parents due to deeply held negative beliefs (Abel, 2000; Yang, 1999). It can be asserted that GLBT parenthood occurs within a context of oppression.

How does cultural oppression affect GLBT individuals, parents, and their families? Similar to other oppressed groups in this country, the practice of oppression fosters at least three debilitating characteristics for sexual minorities. First, it propagates misinformation about GLBT individuals and parents which promotes self-hate (e.g., internalized homophobia, heterosexism), and encourages others to hold prejudicial beliefs about GLBT individuals and families (e.g., "everyone should be heterosexual") (Herek, 1993; Isensee, 1997). Second, oppression contributes to the powerlessness and second-class citizenry of GLBT individuals and families because it denies access to goods and services or rights and privileges that are taken for granted by heterosexuals (e.g., being denied a family membership at a local fitness center because your gay family constellation is not recognized by the facility). Third, oppression offers little or no support for GLBT individuals and families to develop and be valued for who they are (e.g., few role models portray GLBT families positively in the media). The significant lack of cultural support and sanction increases the potential for feelings of alienation, isolation, and depression, which has a negative impact on GLBT families (Loiacano, 1993). Oppressive cultural forces against sexual minorities are embedded in our society which promote homophobia, heterosexism, and denial of rights, and provide meager or no support for GLBT families (Isensee, 1997; Laird and Green, 1996).

When considering the cultural context in which GLBT parenthood develops, it is imperative for mental health counselors and other helping professionals to develop tools that will assist GLBT individuals and couples in confronting cultural oppression, lessening its impact on their family life, and improving skills in raising their children. One method is called the Family Care Plan (FCP). The FCP is designed to have a twofold purpose. First, utilizing a family-systems perspective, the model provides an educational component to help GLBT individuals and/or parents understand the interconnectedness between their family dynamics and cultural oppression (Carter and McGoldrick, 1988; Gladding, 1998). An additional educational component, although not unique to GLBT parents, has been included because it is important for healthy individual and family development. This educational component is intended to impart knowledge that will allow GLBT individuals to acquire specific skills in such areas as writing a parent mission statement, understanding the basic needs of children, teaching cooperation and respect, managing problematic behaviors, and explaining stress management. The FCP educational component gives GLBT individuals and parents an opportunity to increase their awareness about how cultural toxins affect family functioning, and it helps these families conceptualize how they would like to parent their children. This type of cognitive clarity builds the sexual minority parents' self-esteem and confidence, and it enhances GLBT parents' ability to withstand the culturally oppressive forces against them.

The second component of the FCP is an action-oriented phase in which the GLBT parent is coached to develop the FCP and "take action" that is consistent with his or her parental mission statement. Although the following categories are not an exhaustive list, they are useful in constructing an action plan. The categories are: chosen and biological familial support, developmental needs of children, social and economic support, individual and couple development, and social justice. GLBT individuals, couples, and parents may use these categories as guides to determine how they will negotiate relationships or create activities that positively support family maintenance.

The following are examples of how each category might be used to help GLBT parents construct a family plan:

1. *Chosen and biological familial support.* The GLBT parent makes a decision about the level of support he or she feels from his or her important family members. For example, if the parent has a hostile and homophobic birth family, he or she may consciously decide to align more closely with family-of-choice members.

2. *Developmental needs of children.* In addition to basic needs, the GLBT parent must acquire the skills to help children deal with the stigma associated with GLBT families. For example, sexual minority parents must teach children about appropriate sexual orientation disclosure and problem solving regarding being teased.

3. *Social and economic support.* In an effort to reduce stress, the GLBT parent determines ways of providing support for his or her own family beyond the resources of the extended family and close associates, especially financial support. Making decisions about support groups, volunteering, and stable employment are examples of providing support beyond immediate family.

4. *Individual and couple development.* In addition to mastery of developmental tasks essential to self or couple optimal functioning, the GLBT parent must determine how he or she will identify as a member of a sexual minority and its implications for his or her immediate family. For example, sexual minority persons who have a strong self-identity seem to have

a better sense of well-being and coping capacity than individuals who experience significant ambivalence regarding their sexual identity. However, GLBT parents who decide to be more visible increase the potential of stigmatization.

5. *Social justice.* The GLBT parent's welfare, similar to members of other oppressed groups, is affected by social injustice. The GLBT parent would be encouraged to explore his or her feelings and determine whether he or she wishes to promote a social justice initiative and at what level. Social activism ranges from supporting an initiative anonymously to being a highly visible advocate (Barret, 1998).

In sum, GLBT parents who possess a basic understanding of the interconnectedness of family dynamics and external forces, develop a parenting plan, and take corrective action to address the needs of the family will become more confident in their ability to create a healthy environment for their children's development. The FCP is particularly important for GLBT parents because it provides a method for these parents to construct positive images of their parenting experiences, challenges myths about sexual minorities as parents (e.g., child molesters), and develops concrete strategies for their own self-care and the care of their children.

Instructions

1. Introduce a family-systems view of the family unit by exploring: (a) how other system levels (e.g., individual, nuclear family, community, workplace, and other sociopolitical-cultural issues) affect the family unit, and (b) how negative belief patterns (e.g., gay shame), developmental transitions (e.g., coming-out process of a GLBT family), and unpredictable crises (e.g., untimely death of a GLBT parent with AIDS) can generate severe stress if left unaddressed. Parents may be provided with the following reflection statements:

    A. When thinking about system levels, what issues, at each level, influence you and your family the most? (For example, the counselor may help the GLBT parent explore his or her own homophobia and highlight how input from other systems levels such as biological family's ridicule of your sexual orientation, religious institution advocacy against sexual minority parents, and workplace failure to provide health care to diverse families, all contribute to his or her internalized homophobia, which, left unaddressed, will most likely have a negative outcome on the parenting process.)

    B. Describe the belief patterns, myths, secrets, etc., that are problematic for your family. (For example, in GLBT families, children will: contract AIDS, confuse sex roles, be molested, have a diminished sense of well-being, or GLBT parent must be a super mom or super dad.)

    C. Describe the major stressors that are problematic for your family.

2. Help GLBT parents understand the developmental and relational needs of children. *Developmental needs* include: (a) the basic needs—safety, food, shelter, and clothing; (b) the need for a regular schedule; and (c) the need for clear lines of authority. *Relational needs* include: (a) the need to care and be cared for; (b) the need for honesty and objectivity in relationships; (c) the need to communicate one's feelings; (d) the need to hold ambiguous and negative feelings; and (e) the need to accept one's own body (Garanzini, 1995). *Specific needs of children whose parents are GLBT* include: (a) learning appropriate disclosure of parents' sexual orientation; (b) having a safe environment to ask questions and express feelings about the parents' sexual orientation; (c) being supported in their own coming-out process; and (d) learning coping strategies to deal with the stigma directed toward GLBT families. GLBT parents may be provided with the following reflection questions:

    A. In what areas am I doing well in meeting my child's developmental and relational needs? Why?

    B. In what areas do I need to improve?

    C. What skills do I need to acquire to help my child address such GLBT issues as: the family's coming-out process, appropriate disclosure, external prejudice, family member homoprejudice, and expressing his or her own feelings about sexuality?

3. Assist GLBT parents in developing a parent mission statement. This is a useful tool to help them clarify their parenting philosophy and short- or long-term goals in succinct form. A mission statement can be a powerful reminder to GLBT parents regarding their purpose during rough times. These parents may be asked to reflect on the following questions:

    A. What is my purpose as a parent?

    B. Given the cultural context of oppression in which GLBT parenthood is embedded, in what way will my mission statement reflect my intentions about how I will respond to cultural oppression?

4. Evaluate GLBT parents' current style of parenting and, if lacking, look for ways to integrate strategies that promote cooperation and respect in parent-child relations. At this point, a caveat is offered: when it comes to parent-child interactions, sexual orientation per se is not unique and becomes less important compared to caring adults who provide consistent and long-term care for a child. Further, the current discussion is offered as an adjunct to the previous discussion not because it is unique to GLBT parents but because improving parent-child relations is a central goal to most parents in general. Therefore, the following section briefly discusses strategies that promote cooperation and respect in children based on the work of Faber and Mazlish (1980).

    Respect within the current context refers to how one model values the other when discipline is necessary. Respectful discipline includes: (a) avoiding corporal punishment, (b) expressing feelings strongly without attacking the child's self-esteem, (c) stating your expectations, (d) showing the child how to make amends, (e) giving the child a choice, (f) taking action if the child continues to not meet the stated expectation, and (g) problem solving. Strategies that promote cooperation refer to creating a helping climate and consist of (a) describing the problem, (b) giving information, (c) avoiding lecturing—saying it with a word, (d) talking about your feelings, and (e) writing a note. GLBT parents may be asked to respond to the following reflection questions:

    A. In what ways do I convey respect for my child(ren)?

    B. In what ways do I solicit cooperation in my family?

    C. How would I describe weaknesses in my parenting style?

    D. As a GLBT identified parent, what unique attributes do I bring to being a parent? How can I use these attributes to improve parent-child relations?

Brief Vignette

Tara is a lesbian mother who lives in a midwestern town with her two children (Tim, age eight; Natalie, age six). Her familial support consists of a homophobic father and brother. Although she is not close to either of them, they do help her out with child care. Her mother is deceased. Tara describes herself as shy and having few friends. She is employed in an entry-level position, but takes pride in maintaining her own apartment and raising her children.

Recently, Tara began dating a lesbian woman named Christi. Christi has a strong lesbian identity and considers herself an activist. As the relationship progressed, Christi began to take on the role of parent with the children. She also became more verbal about problematic family dynamics. For example, Christi complained about Tara's internalized homophobia, unassertive parenting style, and her father's disrespectful treatment of them as a couple (e.g., he repeatedly tells Tara that her relationship is wrong). Eventually tension escalated into a verbal confrontation between Christi and Tara's father, which strained the already tenuous relationship between Tara and her dad.

Tara initially came for help because she felt depressed and emotionally unavailable to her children due to tension in her family. She admitted she felt torn between the demands of her partner and her father. After some exploration, it became clear that there were dynamics within the immediate family and extended family that needed to be addressed if she was going to relieve her depressive symptoms and have more energy to spend with her children.

For at least three reasons, the FCP can be a useful tool to assist Tara and her family in gaining a sense of stability during a family transition. First, the educational component can be used to help Tara increase awareness and understand the interconnections between levels of cultural oppression and her dysfunctional family dynamics (e.g., depressive symptoms or emotional unavailability toward her children). One example is to underscore homophobia as a cultural current that is flowing throughout this family and how it has intensified since the addition of a new family member, Tara's partner Christi. The observable manifestations of this negative current are indicative of her marked inattention to her children and increased symptoms of depression.

Second, following the exploration of negative cultural forces that influence interactional patterns in her family, the counselor can work with Tara to decide how she would like for things to be different. Constructing a parental mission statement is a strategy that can begin to facilitate the cognitive clarity that will be necessary for Tara to think about what kind of parent she would like to be to her children and what parental barriers (e.g., internalized homophobia or co-parenting conflict) will need to be eradicated. For example, a portion of Tara's parental mission statement might concentrate on boosting her sense of self and setting boundaries that lessen homophobic interactions with her birth family. Lessening homophobic interactions in her immediate family will likely allow Tara to free up emotional energy that could be better used to care for her children.

Third, the counselor coaches Tara to develop an FCP and "take action" that is consistent with her parental mission statement. Certain categories can be used as guides to construct Tara's FCP. When considering her current situation, at least three of the previously mentioned categories need immediate attention:

1. Familial support (e.g., establishing boundaries to decrease homophobic interactions)
2. Individual and couple concerns (e.g., lesbian identity acceptance; couple's intimacy and parenting role development)
3. Social support (e.g., support network expansion beyond biological family)

For each category, the counselor would help Tara develop specific action steps and offer support as she attempts to execute her plan. As Tara gains cognitive clarity about the impact of the negative cultural currents impacting her family, constructs new ways to care for her family, feels supported, and takes action to execute her FCP, she begins to feel more competent in her role as a parent and as a partner.

Suggestions for Follow-Up

The counselor's primary task is to provide education, coaching, and support for the GLBT individual, couple, or parent motivated to construct a healthy family environment. By utilizing the FCP model, the counselor assists the GLBT client in addressing cultural oppression, clarifying an action plan that addresses major family issues, and, most important, taking action.

After an action plan has been established, it is important to provide a period of time for the execution of the plan and evaluation. Generally, a period of thirty to sixty days is utilized. It is also recommended that bibliotherapy be used as an adjunct to the FCP to increase the client's knowledge base. For example, returning momentarily to our case, additional reading for Tara in such areas as assertive communication and GLBT intimate relationships would be recommended because these are areas in which she has skill deficits. Finally, if and when it became appropriate, Tara's partner and father could be invited to be a part of "constructing a healthy family environment."

Contraindications

The FCP can be a powerful tool to help GLBT persons construct family realities that are healthy for children. However, two issues stand out as possible limitations to using this method:

1. There is a need for moderate intellectual capacity and high motivation for change. The psychoeducational component of the FCP model attempts to enhance cognitive clarity in the hopes that one becomes motivated to change. However, some GLBT individuals will gain insight but lack the motivation to make changes in their family environments due to their fears of oppression. In the case of Tara, we could assume that one reason she may have tolerated the homophobia in her birth family was due to the fear of losing her only biological relatives. Tara's fear, then, diminishes her motivation to change.
2. Changing family structure requires a long-term commitment, as reconstructing individual or family structures is difficult and confusing. This type of family work requires substantial time, information acquisition, and execution. For some GLBT clients, their needs may be more urgent and severe (e.g., GLBT clients who feel suicidal after disclosing their sexual orientation).

In each of these cases, the FCP is not likely to be useful, and the counselor may better serve the client by assisting him or her in seeking other treatment modalities.

Readings and Resources for the Professional

Barret, R. L. and Robinson, B. E. (2000). *Gay fathers: Encouraging the hearts of gay dads and their families.* San Francisco, CA: Jossey-Bass.

Gottman, J. S. (1990). Children of gay and lesbian parents. In F. W. Bozett and M. B. Sussman (Eds.), *Homosexuality and family relations* (pp. 177-196). Binghamton, NY: The Haworth Press.

Laird, J. and Green, R. J. (Eds.) (1996). *Lesbians and gays in couples and families: A handbook for therapists.* San Francisco, CA: Jossey-Bass.

Tasker, F. L. (1997). *Growing up in a lesbian family: Effects on child development.* New York: Guilford Publications.

Bibliotherapy Sources for the Client

Borhek, M. (1983). *Coming out to parents: A survival guide for lesbians and gay men and their parents.* New York: Pilgrim Press.

Charlesworth, E. A. and Nathan, R. G. (1985). *Stress management: A comprehensive guide to wellness.* New York: Atheneum.

Drucker, J. (1998). *Families of value: Gay and lesbian parents and their children speak out.* New York: Insight Books.

Faber, A. and Mazlish, E. (1980). *How to talk so kids will listen and listen so kids will talk.* New York: Avon Books.

Martin, A. (1993). *The lesbian and gay parenting handbook.* New York: HarperCollins.

References

Abel, S. (2000). Becoming fathers. *Parent, 14*(8), 132-137.

Barret, B. (1998). Gay and lesbian activism: A frontier for social action. In C. Lee and G. Walz (Eds.), *Social action: A mandate for counselors* (pp. 83-98). Washington, DC: American Counseling Association.

Carter, B. and McGoldrick, M. (1988). *The changing family life cycle* (Second edition). New York: Gardner.

Colberg, M. (1997). Clinical issues with gay and lesbian adoptive parenting. In S. K. Roszia, A. Baran, and L. Coleman (Eds.), *Creating kinship* (pp. 115-123). Portland, OR: Dougy.

Faber, A. and Mazlish, E. (1980). *How to talk so kids will listen and listen so kids will talk*. New York: Avon Books.

Falk, P. J. (1993). Lesbian mothers: Psychosocial assumptions in family law. In L. D. Garnets and D. C. Kimmel (Eds.), *Psychological perspectives on lesbian and gay male experiences* (pp. 420-436). New York: Columbia University.

Garanzini, M. J. (1995). *Child-centered, family-sensitive schools: An educator's guide to family dynamics*. Washington, DC: National Catholic Education Association.

Gladding, S. T. (1998). *Family Therapy: History, theory, and practice* (Second edition). Englewood Cliffs, NJ: Prentice-Hall.

Herek, G. M. (1993). The context of antigay violence: Notes on cultural and psychological heterosexism. In L. D. Garnets and D. C. Kimmel (Eds.), *Psychological perspectives on lesbian and gay male experiences* (pp. 89-108). New York: Columbia University.

Herek, G. M. (Ed.) (1998). *Stigma and sexual orientation: Understanding prejudice against lesbians, gay men, and bisexuals*. Thousand Oaks, CA: Sage Publications.

Isensee, R. (1997). *Reclaiming your life: The gay man's guide to love, self-acceptance, and trust*. Los Angeles, CA: Alyson Publications.

Laird, J. and Green, R. J. (Eds.) (1996). *Lesbians and gays in couples and families: A handbook for therapists*. San Francisco, CA: Jossey-Bass.

Loiacano, D. K. (1993). Gay identity issues among black Americans: Racism, homophobia, and the need for validation. In L. D. Garnets and D. C. Kimmel (Eds.), *Psychological perspectives on lesbian and gay male experiences* (pp. 364-375). New York: Columbia University.

Yang, A. (1999). *From wrongs to rights: Public opinion on gay and lesbian Americans moves toward equality*. New York: Policy Institute of the National Gay and Lesbian Task Force.

43

Making Connections:
Parallel Process in Lesbian and Bisexual Women's Recovery from Addiction and Healing from Homophobia

Elizabeth P. Cramer

Type of Contribution: Activity/Handout/Homework

Objective

The goal of this handout/homework is to assist lesbian and bisexual substance abusers in drawing parallels between the negative consequences of active addiction and their experience as a population of women who are oppressed because of their sexual orientation. In addition, the handout delineates positive results of both recovery from addiction and healing from the wounds of homophobia. Engaging in parallel process is useful for clients who are faced with similar internal and external experiences in more than one area of their lives. For example, by making connections among similar experiences, clients are able to apply the lessons learned in one area to another.

Rationale for Use

There is disagreement in the literature about the relative incidence and severity of substance abuse in heterosexual women versus lesbian and bisexual women (Williams, Qualls, and Wilson, 1994). There is a common understanding, however, that addiction among lesbian and bisexual women needs to be addressed by incorporating a framework that recognizes the unique internal and environmental stressors that affect this population (Williams, Qualls, and Wilson, 1994). Among these stressors are societal attitudes and expectations regarding restrictive gender roles, which contribute to issues that female substance abusers present in treatment, such as dependency, stigmatization, powerlessness, guilt, and shame (Hughes and Wilsnack, 1997). These stressors are not only customary for females who are addicted, but they also describe the experience of living as a lesbian or bisexual woman in a homophobic environment.

Lesbian and bisexual women who are addicted can benefit from drawing parallels in their lives: their lived experience as addicted persons in a society that stigmatizes addicts parallels with their existence as lesbian or bisexual women in an environment that discriminates against people with sexual orientations that are different from the norm. A conceptualization of recovery—from addiction and from homophobic societal responses—can further the connection between their lives as addicted persons and their lives as sexual minorities. Internalized homophobia can provide the bases for the shame, despair, and alienation that contribute to active addiction. As McNally and Finnegan (1992) note in their study about lesbian recovering alcoholics:

Accepting and internalizing their alcoholic identities enabled them to explore, accept, and internalize their lesbian identities which, in turn, enabled them to continue to transform and strengthen their alcoholic identities. . . . Even in sobriety, external and internal homophobia was still the most difficult and painful barrier to accepting and internalizing a positive lesbian identity. Nevertheless, the women's work in sobriety enabled them to experience their lesbian identity as an integral part of their overall identity. (p. 96)

Instructions

Although this handout was originally developed for use with a group for female substance abusers, it may be used with individual clients or couples. The handout comprises two graphics. The first comprises interlocking boxes and the second is quotes that illustrate the concepts in the boxes.

The therapist distributes the handout and then explains each of the concepts in the boxes and uses the quotes to provide examples of those concepts. The therapist solicits examples from the client's life to begin to make connections between the experience of being addicted and of being lesbian or bisexual.

The therapist would begin with the handout, Common Issues in Being Addicted and in Being Gay. The following is an example of how to work with a client on one of the concepts: shame.

THERAPIST: Women who are addicted often talk about the shame they feel because of their problem with alcohol or other drugs. They share how badly it makes them feel when people give them a look of disgust or tell them how sick they are. Gay (or lesbian) or bisexual women often feel shame because other people tell them, or they believe themselves, that they are not normal or that they are committing a sin. Let's look at the quote under shame. [Have the client read the quote.]

SHAME: At seventeen I had no conception of what it meant to plan a career or to take care of myself. It seemed so easy to pick up a drink at a party. I was afraid my female friends would reject me if I told them I was a lesbian. I did not know any other lesbians then.

THERAPIST: Can you think of a time when you felt shame because of being an addict? Because of being gay, lesbian, or bisexual?

CLIENT: [Describes incident(s) of shame.]

THERAPIST: There are similar experiences in life when someone is addicted or someone is gay. People can be judgmental, cruel, and not very accepting of substance abusers and gay people. Let's move on to the next one, despair and loneliness.

After each of the common issues is presented and discussed, the therapist can move on to the Recovery: Positive Self-Identity, Sense of Community, Freedom, Lack of Dependency handout. One quote is featured that illustrates all of these concepts. Just as the therapist was assisting the client in making connections between the negative consequences of addiction and of a stigmatized sexual orientation, the therapist now draws parallels between recovery from addiction and healing from homophobia.

The therapist presents and discusses the four concepts of recovery and offers the quotes to illustrate recovery and healing. The therapist asks the client where she would put herself along the journey of recovery, noting that the four boxes represent the ideal in recovery and that most people are somewhere along the path toward these.

For homework, the client is asked to write down the specific steps she could take to move herself closer to the concepts in the recovery graphic. For example, if she puts herself at the beginning of a path toward positive self-identity, ask her to write down three steps she could take to move toward a more positive self-identity. If she has trouble thinking of anything, offer a suggestion or two, such as "read books by lesbian alcoholics/addicts who have been in recovery for a long time and who have a strong self-esteem."

Suggestions for Follow-Up

In future sessions, when a client mentions feelings and/or experiences with which she is struggling and that are related to the Common Issues in Being Addicted and in Being Gay handout, the therapist can assist the client in making the connection between the issues. For example, a client who recently began a new job comes into a session with a concern about her co-workers discovering that she is recovering from addiction. The therapist can remind the client about the fear box on the quotes handout, and inquire as to whether the client has felt that same fear about others finding out that she is lesbian or bisexual.

Similarly, when a client demonstrates that she is moving along the path of recovery from addiction and/or the wounds of homophobia, the therapist can pull out the recovery quote and assist her in noting the areas of growth. As an example, a client is proud to share with her therapist that she went to her first Gay Narcotics Anonymous meeting. The therapist responds with praise and encouragement and observes that the client is moving along in her journey toward recovery by developing a sense of community (a box on the handout).

Contraindications

Lesbian and bisexual female clients who are in active addiction may be unable or unwilling to examine the Common Issues in Being Addicted and in Being Gay handout. If these clients do not consider themselves to have an addiction, they may be unable to draw any parallels between their lives as addicts and as lesbian or bisexual women. Conversely, clients who are uncertain about their sexual orientation, or who are so deeply closeted that they do not want to discuss any issues related to sexual orientation, would most likely not benefit from this handout. Furthermore, a client who holds negative feelings about both identities (as addict and as lesbian or bisexual woman) may find the exercise to be more disheartening than enlightening.

This handout can be appropriate for clients of various socioeconomic, racial, ethnic, and educational backgrounds. The therapist should be sensitive to the client's unique background. Thus, he or she should take care to explain the handout in a way that is comprehensible to each client.

Readings and Resources for the Professional

Bepko, C. (Ed.) (1991). *Feminism and addiction*. Binghamton, NY: The Haworth Press.

Hall, J. M. (1990). Alcoholism recovery in lesbian women: A theory in development. *Scholarly Inquiry for Nursing Practice: An International Journal, 4*(2), 109-122.

Hughes, T. L. and Wilsnack, S. C. (1997). Use of alcohol among lesbians: Research and clinical implications. *American Journal of Orthopsychiatry, 67*(1), 20-36.

Kelly, J. (1994). *Preventing alcohol and other drug problems in the lesbian and gay community*. Sacramento, CA: California Department of Alcohol and Drug Programs.

McNally, E. B. and Finnegan, D. B. (1992). Lesbian recovering alcoholics: A qualitative study of identity transformation. A report on research and applications to treatment. *Journal of Chemical Dependency, 5*(1), 93-103.

Roth, P. (Ed.) (1991). *Alcohol and drugs are women's issues: Volume one. A review of the issues*. Metuchen, NJ: Scarecrow Press.

Skinner, W. F. (1994). The prevalence and demographic predictors of illicit/licit drug use among lesbians and gay men: The Trilogy Project. *American Journal of Public Health, 84*(8), 1307-1310.

Van Den Bergh, N. (Ed.) (1991). *Feminist perspectives on addictions.* New York: Springer Publications.

Williams, P., Qualls, R., and Wilson, D. (Eds.) (1994). *Lesbians, gay men, and bisexuals: Alcohol, tobacco, and other drugs resource guide.* Rockville, MD: National Clearinghouse for Alcohol and Drug Information.

Bibliotherapy Sources for the Client

A.A. Grapevine, Inc. (1976). *AA for the woman.* New York: Alcoholics Anonymous World Service, Inc.

A.A. Grapevine, Inc. (1989). *AA and the gay/lesbian alcoholic.* New York: Alcoholics Anonymous World Service, Inc.

Kominars, S. B. (1989). *Accepting ourselves: Twelve-step journey of recovery from addiction for gay men and lesbians.* New York: Harper and Row.

Runbeck, M. L. (1954). *A letter to a woman alcoholic.* New York: Alcoholics Anonymous World Service, Inc.

Whitfield, C. L. (1987). *Healing the child within.* Pompano Beach, FL: Health Communications, Inc.

References

Hughes, T. L. and Wilsnack, S. C. (1997). Use of alcohol among lesbians: Research and clinical implications. *American Journal of Orthopsychiatry, 67*(1), 20-36.

McNally, E. B. and Finnegan, D. B. (1992). Lesbian recovering alcoholics: A qualitative study of identity transformation. A report on research and applications to treatment. *Journal of Chemical Dependency, 5*(1), 93-103.

Williams, P., Qualls, R., and Wilson, D. (Eds.) (1994). *Lesbians, gay men, and bisexuals: Alcohol, tobacco, and other drugs resource guide.* Rockville, MD: National Clearinghouse for Alcohol and Drug Information.

Common Issues in Being Addicted and in Being Gay

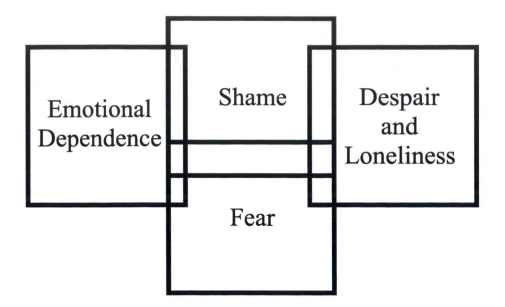

Emotional Dependence   Shame   Despair and Loneliness

Fear

Recovery: Positive Self-Identity, Sense of Community, Freedom, Lack of Dependency

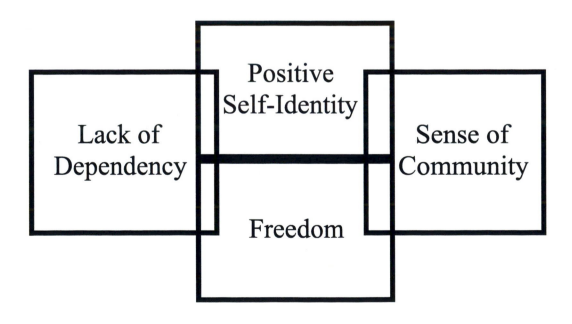

Lack of Dependency   Positive Self-Identity   Sense of Community

Freedom

Quotes for Common Issues in Being Addicted and in Being Gay

Shame, Despair and Loneliness, Fear, Emotional Dependence

Shame

At seventeen I had no conception of what it meant to plan a career or take care of myself. It seemed so easy to pick up a drink at a party. I was afraid my female friends would reject me if I told them I was a lesbian. I did not know any other lesbians then. (A.A. Grapevine, 1989, p. 5)

Despair and Loneliness

Then I was arrested twice within three months for driving while intoxicated. My house of cards was tumbling down. Not even alcohol was my friend anymore. I had abandoned self, friends, and God. All that remained were intensive blackouts, the alcohol that my body demanded, and the despair that accompanied each drink. (A.A. Grapevine, 1989, p. 6)

Fear

No longer were we center stage. Instead we were passing out and waking up full of fear, not knowing where we were or who we were with. We started wondering what was real in our lives. (A.A. Grapevine, 1989, p. 6)

Emotional Dependence

I truly believed I could not emotionally survive alone, and so I attached myself to lovers with an extraordinary level of dependence. I was terrified of being abandoned, and the bottom line of each of these relationships was that I would do anything to prevent these lovers from leaving me. Self-esteem and self-respect were unknown to me. I felt worthless and so I acted accordingly. (A.A. Grapevine, 1989, p. 7)

Recovery: Positive Self-Identity, Sense of Community, Freedom, Lack of Dependency

Life is developing along lines that bring satisfaction, joy, love, and a sense of accomplishment and a sense of peace to me. I feel capable of dealing with the disappointments and frustrations that once overwhelmed me. I now see such things as a normal part of living, not just the punishment meted out to me. This knowledge frees me to genuinely enjoy the good things when they come along. Today I am free of my dependency upon alcohol and my need for other people to supply my identity. Thanks to A.A. I am free to be who and what I am, and free to actively participate in my own life. There is no greater gift, and I will be forever grateful. (A.A. Grapevine, 1989, pp. 10-11)

Source: A. A. Grapevine, Inc. (1989). *AA and the Gay/Lesbian Alcoholic.* New York: Alcoholics Anonymous World Service, Inc.

44

Examining Links Between Drug or Alcohol Use and Experiences of Homophobia/Biphobia and Coming Out

Farzana Doctor

Type of Contribution: Activity/Handout

Objective

This activity helps gay, lesbian, and bisexual (GLB) clients understand potential links between changes in their drug or alcohol use and the experiences of coming out and coping with homophobia/biphobia. It highlights the coming-out process as an ongoing and potentially difficult one for most GLB people, and identifies the use of drugs or alcohol as an attempt to cope with homophobia. It can be used as a group exercise or in individual therapy.

Rationale for Use

The coming-out process can be both difficult and joyful for a GLB person. Societal homophobia/biphobia can create an impediment to his or her development of a positive identity as well as cause day-to-day stressors (Cabaj, 2000; Hicks, 2000). Many GLB people adapt healthfully to these stressors, and others develop coping strategies that have negative consequences to their health and well-being. One such way that many clients cope with tasks of developing identity is with drug or alcohol use.

Substance abuse may help with some of the initial tasks of coming out, and may function as a coping strategy for difficult feelings associated with it. Many writers have discussed the importance of the bar and rave cultures in GLB communities as being both a safe place for GLB people who are coming out and a potential risk for developing substance abuse problems (Collins and Howard, 1997; Kauth, Hartwig, and Kalichman, 2000).

Although the role of heterosexism and homophobia in substance abuse is unclear, it is clear that oppression can instill negative self-perception and shame in GLB people (Substance Abuse and Mental Health Services Administration, 2001). Clinical experience has shown that homophobic experiences and coming-out stressors can exacerbate an already developing drug or alcohol use problem, or create one. Some clients have noticed that their abuse of drugs or alcohol helped them repress their same-sex or bisexual feelings, which only became conscious after they moderated or stopped their drug or alcohol use. Others noticed that although their drug or alcohol use increased somewhat during their coming-out process, they were able to return to more limited or moderate use after a period of stabilization.

This activity has been used with GLB clients who have identified a concern about their drug or alcohol use in individual and group therapy. It explores potential links between their coming-out process and substance abuse. When used with this population, some clients have recognized weak links, and others identify that homophobia and coming out have been major factors in their drug or alcohol abuse. Such identification allows clients and therapists to develop related recovery or treatment goals to address triggers or high-risk situations.

Instructions

If completing this activity individually, follow Steps A and C. If this activity is being used in a group, follow all three steps.

Step A

Prior to introducing the activity, it is useful to have some discussion or provide some psychoeducation about coming-out processes and homophobia/biphobia. For example, in a therapy group the facilitator may want to give a brief presentation about theories on coming-out stages to stimulate group discussion. Individually, a therapist may want to provide this information more informally, perhaps by providing a handout or suggesting reading materials on coming-out theories. Clinical experience has shown that clients are often very interested in discussing how their own experiences connect with these theories. Many clients comment that they have few opportunities or role models from which to learn about developmental stage theories relevant to their lives.

Step B

Next, ask clients to share a piece or a summary of their own coming-out stories. The facilitator should emphasize that each person's coming-out experience will be unique and that there is no "correct" way to come out. It is suggested that the facilitator share part of his or her own coming-out experience as a way to model the exercise, taking care to maximize the benefits of his or her self-disclosure. For example, the facilitator may want to share coping strategies used and highlight how each coming-out story will be unique and mediated by experiences of race, class, ability, and age, among other areas of privilege and oppression. (I have chosen to share that it was useful for me to meet other South Asian lesbians to normalize and validate my own lesbian identity and also how I used this community support to help me when I was coming out.) When all the group members have finished sharing, ask the group for any reactions/impressions about hearing the stories.

Step C

Next, distribute the handout. If in a larger group, group members should be asked to pair up to complete it. Encourage clients to jot down the approximate age(s) that correspond with the items in the two columns. Note that there may be more than one age that corresponds with each item. (For example, the coming-out process, or the drug or alcohol use may have been interrupted and reinitiated again at a later point. Once clients have completed their sheets, they should begin to look at whether any of the ages duplicate across the two columns. For example, someone may have listed age twenty-one as a time when he or she began to come out to family. Age twenty-one may also have been a time when his or her drug or alcohol use began to change in some way.) Clients should then discuss any potential correlations and write down any comments they have in the "comments" column. Some will note that the convergence represents a direct correlation, and others may need to write down other influences or events that had an effect on them. (For example, age twenty-one could also have been an age when other difficulties were experienced.) In a group, clients are then asked to share their impressions with the entire group. In individual therapy, the clinician can then ask the client to discuss any reactions about the exercise and its implications.

Clinical experience has shown that clients have a variety of responses to this activity, including feelings of sadness that homophobia or biphobia has hurt them and/or feelings of pride that they have come a long way in their process. Some clients have been quick to point out that they are fine with their sexual orientation, or that they feel societal oppression has not affected them. I question whether some clients feel that it would be a personal shortcoming to acknowledge that they could be vulnerable to oppression. GLB people often are forced to "toughen up" in the face of oppression, and this activity may be painful for some.

In terms of specific links between homophobic experiences and substance abuse, clients' responses may be, but are not limited to, the following:

- use increased to cope with feeling "different" prior to coming out
- use increased to cope with staying closeted at work or with loved ones
- use increased to cope with social discomfort or to "fit in" at GLB events and bars
- use increased to cope with social discomfort or internalized homophobia at a meeting, in dating, or when having sex
- use increased to cope with bashing or other overt homophobic/biphobic experiences
- used to cope with fears of, or actual rejection by, loved ones
- same-sex or bisexual attractions became conscious when stopping or reducing drug or alcohol use
- use reduced as comfort with identity increased
- unsure of any links as use began prior to any awareness of GLB identity
- unsure of any links as other factors, such as childhood trauma, appear to correlate more directly with substance abuse

Suggestions for Follow-Up

For clients who recognize links between their drug or alcohol use and coming-out and homophobic/biphobic experiences, it may be appropriate to consider whether these issues continue to be triggers or high-risk situations for substance abuse. Many clients have stated that the identification of triggers is helpful for relapse prevention. The following are some examples.

Client A recognizes that she has used marijuana to cope with experiences of rejection by friends and family who belittled and denied her bisexual identity. She may want to consider whether this is still a trigger for her. Does the memory of, or isolation caused by those rejections, trigger problematic marijuana use? Has she used marijuana to cope with subsequent rejection or potential rejection? How has she internalized this rejection and homophobia? What supports or resources could be helpful to Client A if she faced this experience today?

Client B realizes that once she quit using alcohol and cocaine she was attracted to women. She remembers having some same-sex attractions when she was younger, but she refused to acknowledge them at the time. She feels that her alcohol and drug use may have helped her repress these feelings. Now that she has a goal to remain abstinent, she recognizes that internalized homophobia may be a trigger for substance abuse, and that she will need support to develop a positive lesbian identity as she moves through her coming-out process.

Client C is aware that his alcohol abuse started when he began to come out to himself and frequent gay bars. Many years have passed and heavy drinking at the bars has continued to be a habit. Client C wishes to become only a moderate drinker, and will need to examine the triggers that exist for him at gay bars, and whether he can learn to socialize at a bar without drinking heavily. Client C may also need to consider alternative ways to have fun and connect with the gay community.

Contraindications

The links between drug or alcohol use and experiences of coming out and homophobia are as diverse as the coming-out experience itself. It is important to note that many GLB people move through homophobia and coming out without using substances to cope. Others may not identify the link between the drugs or alcohol and coming out, but rather link it with other stressors in their lives. As with any other discussion about GLB people, it is important to avoid reductive or stereotypical claims about their experiences.

Readings and Resources for the Professional

Collins, B. and Howard, B. (1997). Lesbians and gay men. In S. Harrison and V. Carver (Eds.), *Alcohol and drug problems: A practical guide for counselors* (pp. 249-274). Toronto: Addiction Research Foundation.

Green, R. and Laird, J. (1996). *Lesbians and gays in couples and families: A handbook for therapists*. San Francisco, CA: Jossey-Bass Publishers.

Guss, J. (Ed.) (2000). Sex like you can't even imagine: "Crystal," crack, and gay men. *Journal of Gay and Lesbian Psychotherapy, 3*, 105-122.

Perez, R., Debord, K., and Bieschke, K. (2000). *Handbook of counseling and psychotherapy with lesbian, gay and bisexual clients*. Washington, DC: American Psychological Association.

Bibliotherapy Sources for the Client

Hutchins, L. and Kaahumanu, L. (1991). *Bi any other name: Bisexual people speak out*. Boston: Alyson Publications.

Kettelhack, G. (1999). *Vastly more than that: Stories of lesbians and gay men in recovery*. Center City, MN: Hazelden Press.

Kominars, K. and Kominars, S. (1996). *Accepting ourselves and others: A journey into recovery from addictive and compulsive behaviours for gays, lesbians and bisexuals*. Center City, MN: Hazelden Press.

Loulan, J. (1987). *Lesbian passion: Loving ourselves and each other*. Minneapolis: Spinsters Ink.

Penelope, J. and Wolfe, S. (1989). *The original coming out stories*. Freedom, CA: The Crossing Press.

Ratti, R. (1993). *A lotus of another colour*. Boston, MA: Alyson Publications.

Silvera, M. (1991). *Piece of my heart: A lesbian of colour anthology*. Toronto: Sister Vision Press.

References

Cabaj, R. (2000). Substance abuse, internalized homophobia, and gay men and lesbians: Psychodynamic issues and clinical implications. *Journal of Gay and Lesbian Psychotherapy, 3*, 5-24.

Collins, B. and Howard, B. (1997). Lesbians and gay men. In S. Harrison and V. Carver (Eds.), *Alcohol and drug problems: A practical guide for counselors* (pp. 249-274). Toronto: Addiction Research Foundation.

Hicks, D. (2000). The importance of specialized treatment programs for lesbian and gay patients. *Journal of Gay and Lesbian Psychotherapy, 3*, 81-94.

Kauth, M., Hartwig, M., and Kalichman, S. (2000). Health behavior relevant to psychotherapy with lesbian, gay and bisexual clients. In R. Perez, K. Debord, and K. Bieschke (Eds.), *Hand-*

book of counseling and psychotherapy with lesbian, gay and bisexual clients (pp. 435-456). Washington, DC: American Psychological Association.

Substance Abuse and Mental Health Services Administration (2001). A provider's introduction to substance abuse treatment for lesbian, gay, bisexual, and transgender individuals (DHHS Publication No. [SMA] 01-3498). Rockville, MD: U.S. Government Printing Office.

Examining the Links Between Drug and Alcohol Use and Experiences of Homophobia/Biphobia and Coming Out

My age(s) when I was . . .	Comments and Correlations	My age(s) when I was . . .
Just beginning to understand that I was "different":		Experimenting with alcohol or drugs:
Feeling confused about my sexual orientation:		Beginning to use on a regular basis (developing a pattern of use or routine, higher tolerance, etc.):
Suppressing my sexual orientation (times I have been mostly closeted):		Beginning to develop some dependence on alcohol or drugs (to have fun, to relax, to cope, etc.):
Beginning to tolerate my sexual orientation:		Increased dependence and negative consequences of use:
First same-sex crush: First same-sex kiss: First same-sex relationship: First time coming out to friend or family member: First time going to a GLB bar: First time going to GLB event: First time joining a GLB group/ organization:		Times in my life that I tried to quit or cut down: Times when I began to recognize problem use: Times when I sought help for the use:
Times in my life that I've dealt with homophobic/biphobic rejection or violence:		Times in my life when my use was in control:

45

Out in the Workplace: A Cost-Benefit View

Lisa A. Hollingsworth
Mary J. Didelot

Type of Contribution: Activity/Handout

Objective

This activity will help gay, lesbian, and bisexual (GLB) clients balance career needs with the expression of their sexual orientation.

Rationale for Use

As GLB-advocacy efforts for equity move forward, the workplace is now the targeted focus (Gore, 2000). In order to benefit from workplace equity policies, GLB job candidates and current employees must be out in the workplace. This puts GLB employees in the very difficult position of deciding between coming out in the workplace or staying in the closet. To be considered in this decision is the reality of heterosexism in the workplace. Heterosexism is "social disadvantage designed to enforce 'traditional' cultural values that include negative stereotypes of homosexuality . . ." (Gore, 2000, p. 284). Exacerbating this issue is the fact that GLB people constitute a hidden minority group that does not necessarily receive public compassion for its struggles.

According to deCharms (1975), if a GLB person is intentionally passing at work, he or she becomes a pawn because the work environment now controls his or her behavior. The behavior therefore is not reflective of the authentic self. The authentic self, though, needs outlets for expression. Since "people search for environments that will let them exercise their skills and abilities, express their attitudes and values, and take on agreeable problems and roles" (Holland, 1973, p. 4), the work environment must allow for the level of "outness" that is needed by the GLB person in order for the environment and the person to be healthy. How can a therapist, then, help a client achieve this balance between career needs and the expression of sexual orientation? According to Orzek (1996), a therapist needs to first look to the client's:

1. own emphasis on sexual orientation;
2. frame of reference for sexual orientation; and
3. stage of identity formation.

It is important to recognize and respect the client's own perceptions of sexual orientation needs and values regarding the disclosure of sexual orientation in order to keep the therapist from overemphasizing the needs and values *for* the client (Orzek, 1996).

Within the arena of career counseling, the person-environment matching process is extremely important (Chojnacki and Gelberg, 1994). Orzek's (1996) three aforementioned keys (emphasis, frame of reference, and identity formation) must also be an integral part of this process for

GLB clients. It is this addition that differentiates career counseling for heterosexuals from career counseling for GLB clients. These concepts are also at the foundation of the most critical career question for GLBs: Should I come out at work?

Instructions

In order to aid a GLB client in his or her decision about coming out or not at work, carefully examine (1) the indicators that coming out would prove to be successful, (2) the benefits of staying in the closet, (3) the personal costs of staying in the closet, and (4) the reasons other GLB persons come out at work.

The therapist should first recognize that there are two indicators of a successful coming-out process as identified by Hancock (2000): (1) psychological disposition and (2) the availability of interpersonal support. These issues are important because those who have been successful feel a sense of satisfaction with their identity and have strong support systems, especially if this is true within their work environment. Knowing how the client perceives these two areas of indication will help the therapist identify a starting point and goals for therapy. Taking all of this into consideration, the therapist may then use the following narrative with the client:

> When we talk about coming out at work, I always ask my clients some important questions to begin the decision-making process:
>
> 1. How do you feel about being lesbian/gay?
> 2. Are you comfortable with that part of yourself?
> 3. Do you feel a sense of satisfaction with whom you are?
> 4. Are the people who know you are lesbian/gay supportive of you?
> 5. Do they speak of your sexual orientation in positive terms?
> 6. Are they accepting of you?
> 7. Are people at work who know you are lesbian/gay supportive of you?
> 8. Do people at work speak of lesbian/gay employees in positive terms?
> 9. If I asked you to list your supporters, who would be on that list?

An important part of the intake process should be the Sexual Identity Formation (SIF) Stages handout, which is based on Cass's (1979) model of sexual identity formation. The counselor should know where the client perceives himself or herself on this scale. In order to accurately assess the client in this process, critical questions are listed under each category to help the therapist. Once the SIF is completed, the therapist will be able to judge the degree of perceived "outness" and level of expression of sexual orientation the client requires in order to be comfortable within the work environment. Clients in Stages 1 through 4 would more than likely not be ready to come out in the workplace. In Stages 1 through 3, the GLB identity is not fully accepted or understood by the client. During Stage 4, the client has only begun to test the waters of outness and therefore not only is the identity extremely fragile but the risk of rejection is very high. A client in Stage 5 would more than likely have to be cautioned about making a rash decision to come out. A client in Stage 6 would more than likely be successful and comfortable with coming out at work. The therapist may use the following narrative to introduce and conclude this activity:

> I am going to go over the SIF with you in order for me to see how out you wish to be and need to be in the workplace. Because we do not all have the same need or desire to express sexual orientation in different environments, I want to know how *you* see yourself in the work environment. From there, we can look to some costs and benefits of coming out.

Before we move on, let me make certain that I have a good grasp of how you feel about coming out at work. From your responses on the SIF, I get the impression that you need a work environment that is _____ (e.g., not open to GLB persons, somewhat open to GLB persons, completely open to GLB persons, or completely open to and legally protects GLB persons). Do I understand you correctly? Is what I said an accurate representation of how you feel? Do you have anything to add to or modify what I have concluded?

Once the therapist has a clear picture of the client's need for "outness," the therapist should then move to the Benefits and Costs Summary (BCS) of the Workplace Closet handout. This is a tool to help the client organize his or her thoughts, and begin the balancing process between career needs and expression of sexual orientation. The therapist may approach the BCS in the following manner:

This BCS lists some of the benefits of staying in the closet. These benefits have been identified by GLB individuals over the years. They are very common and also may be quite fitting for you at *this* time in your life. If you have thought of any of these or believe that these statements are true for you, let's check them off and talk about them. Together, we'll look to see what these statements mean to you personally in your life, where you are in the SIF model, and your career choice(s).

It is important that the responses on the BCS be discussed thoroughly so that the therapist knows the client's comfort level with himself or herself in the workplace. When the BCS and discussion are concluded, the therapist may wish to summate:

I have listened carefully to your responses. Here is the picture I have received about your views of the personal benefits you will receive by staying in the closet: [restates client's responses]. Am I correct? Would you like to add anything or modify my picture?

The next step would be to look at the negative aspects of staying in the closet. A similar dialogue of introduction, process, and conclusion that was used for the benefits will work well for this topic. Again, however, be sure to emphasize the normalcy and the dynamic nature of these feelings and thoughts. The client may or may not feel the same way a month from this session.

The therapist should then move to the worksheet titled Why Come Out at Work? (WCOW). The therapist may initiate this discussion:

I want to go over some reasons many GLB individuals do come out at work, despite all the risks. Let's check off the reasons that reflect your needs and comfort level. As we do or do not check off a particular statement, let's discuss why the statement does or does not reflect you at this time in your life. Then, when we have completed the worksheet, I'll summarize what I have heard you say about your needs and comfort level. As always, if you need to add anything or modify my summary in any way, please feel free to do so.

After all three worksheets have been completed and thoroughly discussed, the therapist should think through the responses and create a narrative that integrates the client's stage of identity, the importance of the need and comfort level to express his or her sexual orientation in the workplace, and the type of overall working environment the client desires. These findings should then be presented and thoroughly discussed with the client. After the discussion, the client should be on firm ground to make a decision to stay in the workplace closet or come out to everyone or just a few trusted colleagues within the work environment.

Suggestions for Follow-Up

Coming out is a dynamic process. Therefore, follow-up sessions should be scheduled to reflect upon this process and the resultants of it. Approaches may include:

1. Revisiting the SIF;
2. Revisiting the WCOW;
3. Discussing with the client his or her current perceptions of overall comfort level at work since the decision to come out or not to come out was made; and
4. Discussing his or her "outness" comfort level.

Contraindications

If the therapist perceives any notions of strong internalized homophobia and/or sexual identity confusion, these issues must be addressed before proceeding further in the process.

Readings and Resources for the Professional

Frisko, A. and Silverstein, S. (1996). *Straight jobs, gay lives: Gay and lesbian professionals, the Harvard Business School, and the American workplace*. New York: Touchstone.

Rosi, R. and Rodriguez-Nogues, L. (Eds.) (1995). *Out in the workplace: The pleasure and perils of coming out on the job*. Los Angeles, CA: Alyson Publications.

Bibliotherapy Sources for the Client

The Gay Financial Network (2001). Retrieved online August 2, 2002, from <http://www.gfn.com>.

Gay, Lesbian, and Straight Education Network (2001). Retrieved online August 2, 2002, from <http://www.glsen.org/>.

Mickens, E. and Isaacson, D. (1994). *The 100 best companies for gay men and lesbians*. New York: Pocket Books.

Waldron, J. (1996). Statutory protection for gays and lesbians in private employment. *Harvard Law Review, 109*(7), 16-26.

References

Cass, V. C. (1979). Homosexual identity formation: A theoretical model. *Journal of Homosexuality, 4*, 219-235.

Chojnacki, J. and Gelberg, S. (1994). Toward a conceptualization of career counseling with gay/lesbian/bisexual persons. *Journal of Career Development, 21*(1), 3-10.

deCharms, R. (1975). *Personal causation*. New York: Academic Press.

Gore, S. (2000). The lesbian and gay workplace. In B. Greene and G. L. Croom (Eds.), *Education, research, and practice in lesbian, gay, bisexual, and transgendered psychology* (pp. 282-302). Thousand Oaks, CA: Sage Publications.

Hancock, K. A. (2000). Lesbian, gay, and bisexual lives: Basic issues in psychotherapy training and practice. In B. Greene and G. L. Croom (Eds.), *Education, research, and practice in lesbian, gay, bisexual, and transgendered psychology* (pp. 91-130). Thousand Oaks, CA: Sage Publications.

Holland, J. L. (1973). *Making vocational choices*. Englewood Cliffs, NJ: Prentice-Hall.

Orzek, A. M. (1996). Career counseling for the gay and lesbian community. In S. Gelberg and J. Chojnacki (Eds.), *Career and life planning with gay, lesbian, and bisexual persons* (pp. 23-33). Alexandria, VA: American Counseling Association.

Sexual Identity Formation (SIF) Stages

The following questions were generated to explore your level of "outness." Your counselor will want to discuss your answers with you so that he or she may know how you see yourself as an individual who is gay, lesbian, or bisexual.

Stage 1: Identity Confusion

1. Have you realized that you may be gay, lesbian, or bisexual?
2. Have you begun to consider the possibility of a gay, lesbian, or bisexual identity?
3. Do you find yourself denying or making excuses for gay, lesbian, or bisexual behavior or previous gay, lesbian, or bisexual sexual activity?

Stage 2: Identity Comparison

4. Have you accepted your gay, lesbian, or bisexual behavior or gay, lesbian, or bisexual sexual behavior, but still identify as heterosexual?
5. Do you fear the reactions of others when you tell them you are gay, lesbian, or bisexual?
6. Have you attempted to contact gay, lesbian, or bisexual individuals for information?

Stage 3: Identity Tolerance

7. Have you begun to initiate gay, lesbian, or bisexual relationships?
8. Have you entered the gay, lesbian, bisexual community?
9. Do you still identify as heterosexual in most social and professional situations?

Stage 4: Identity Acceptance

10. Do you now accept your gay, lesbian, or bisexual identity?
11. Have you disengaged somewhat from heterosexual friendships?
12. Have you begun to disclose your identity to carefully selected people only?

Stage 5: Identity Pride

13. Have you immersed yourself into the gay, lesbian, and bisexual culture?
14. Have you found yourself valuing gay, lesbian, and bisexual culture over heterosexual culture?
15. Have you disengaged yourself from the heterosexual culture and heterosexual friends?
16. Have you been extremely conscious that your gay, lesbian, or bisexual identity is predominate?

Stage 6: Identity Synthesis

17. Have you found that your sexuality is only a part of whom you are?
18. Have you integrated your gay, lesbian, or bisexual culture into the dominant, heterosexual culture?
19. Have you engaged in gay, lesbian, or bisexual friendships as well as heterosexual friendships?

Benefits and Costs Summary (BCS) of the Workplace Closet

This will help you and your counselor begin to balance your career needs with your need to express your sexual orientation. Circle the numbers for the statements that reflect your individual needs.

Benefits

1. Relationships are easier for me to make and maintain at work if my co-workers only suspect me of being gay, and I never confirm it.
2. I am safer, physically and emotionally, at work if I'm not out.
3. I can feel free to speak out for gay, lesbian, and bisexual rights if no one knows I'm gay. I'm more effective that way.
4. I can feel free to ask for favors (e.g., being a late for work to go to a physician's appointment, leaving early for a family matter, etc.) from time to time without co-workers thinking I want special "rights."
5. Co-workers will view my political statements as more fair if I am not out.
6. My job will less likely be in jeopardy if I am not out.
7. I am more likely to be promoted if I am not out.
8. I can wait until I'm really comfortable with my sexuality before I come out at work.
9. I should come out to family and/or friends first before I come out at work.
10. Other: _____.

Costs

1. I am constantly afraid of being outed by someone with whom I work.
2. I feel really isolated at work. I can't discuss social experiences with my co-workers.
3. There are co-workers who continually "bait" me to see if they can get me to "admit" I'm gay, lesbian, or bisexual.
4. I am afraid of a co-worker blackmailing me.
5. I feel I can't socialize with co-workers.
6. I feel I can't have co-workers to my home for dinner.
7. I feel I can't have any heterosexual friends at work.
8. I don't have the support of out gay, lesbian, and bisexuals at work.
9. I am lying about myself and my life to my co-workers.
10. I realize if I am not out at work, I will not be able to file a report if someone does discriminate against me.

Further Costs in a Relationship

11. My ex-lover or any future ex-lover can always use my sexual orientation as a threat against me.
12. I will be seen as "single" by co-workers when, in actuality, I have a good relationship.
13. I cannot bring my partner to office parties or other social events.
14. I feel I'm not being respectful of my relationship or my partner by not being out to co-workers.
15. Other: _____.

Why Come Out at Work? (WCOW)

Check off statements that reflect your own thoughts about why it might be important for you to come out at work.

Personal Reasons

_____ 1. If my relationship ends, I can get emotional support from friends at work.
_____ 2. No one can threaten to out me.
_____ 3. I do not have to pretend to be heterosexual.
_____ 4. I do not have to lie to my employer or co-workers about my life.
_____ 5. I do not have to be afraid to have co-workers see me in a social situation with my gay, lesbian, or bisexual friends.
_____ 6. I can be authentic all the time.
_____ 7. I can have a single, integrated identity, not a dual identity.
_____ 8. I can allow others to be friends with the real me.
_____ 9. I can tell my co-workers about my partner.
_____ 10. If my partner becomes ill, or dies, I can tell my employer and take advantage of employee benefits if available.

Professional Reasons

_____ 11. I can have professional support from other gay, lesbian, or bisexual persons.
_____ 12. I can have valuable business networking with other gay, lesbian, or bisexual professionals.
_____ 13. I can entertain business associates in my home.
_____ 14. I can take my partner to appropriate business functions and office parties.

Political Reasons

_____ 15. I can educate co-workers about gay, lesbian, or bisexual lifestyles and cultures.
_____ 16. If my co-workers know I'm gay, they will find it harder to believe the myths and stereotypes.
_____ 17. In the workplace, I can speak out and challenge ignorance about the gay, lesbian, or bisexual lifestyles and cultures.
_____ 18. I can help gain respect for gay, lesbian, or bisexual people.
_____ 19. I can help change corporate policy and create benefits for domestic partnerships.
_____ 20. I can help create or refine corporate policies on discrimination.
_____ 21. I can incorporate my beliefs and my culture into my everyday life.
_____ 22. I can be a role model within the gay, lesbian, and bisexual community.
_____ 23. Other: _____.

46

Managing Stress:
Helping Gays, Lesbians, and Bisexuals Cope with Coming Out in the Workplace

Reginald Tucker

Type of Contribution: Activities/Homework

Objective

The goal of this activity is to help gay, lesbian, or bisexual (GLB) clients manage the disclosure of their sexual identity and learn new coping skills as they address the decision to come out in the workplace.

Rationale for Use

The client seeking therapy for support in the process of coming out to co-workers and/or supervisors introduces many new challenges for the therapist. Specifically, the client must learn healthy methods for managing disclosure of his or her GLB identity and also learn new coping skills for managing the potential stigma that may accompany disclosure of this identity. Cain (1991) asserts that many researchers view self-disclosure as the indicator of a positive gay identity and also the means to achieve self-acceptance for gay men. However, the decision to disclose one's homosexuality can create a stressful and anxiety-producing experience for the GLB client.

In assessing the level at which the client is considering coming out in the workplace, the therapist must also determine the client's present consciousness or awareness of his or her sexual identity and the degree to which he or she is currently out in other areas of his or her life. This determination by the therapist will assist in the assessment of how, when, and if the GLB client should disclose his or her sexual orientation in the workplace. Prince (1995) postulates that gay men at the beginning stages of coming out may not be cognizant of the impact that their progressing gay identity will have on their career behavior. Particularly, they may not have considered how to come out to co-workers or how they will integrate their current or future partners into work-related social functions.

Instructions

In order to help the client anticipate and cope with the impact of his or her sexual identity on his or her career behavior, the technique articulated by Meichenbaum and Deffenbacher (1988) of stress inoculation training (SIT) may be used. This skill-based approach will provide a sense of protection from stress similar to the protection that an individual receives from an inoculation from disease (Shannon, 1994). The premise behind this approach is to prepare the client for the stressful interaction prior to its actual occurrence. The exercises presented here will assist the therapist in providing tools to the GLB client for identity disclosure management and coping as he or she decides to come out to his or her co-workers and/or supervisors.

The SIT model includes three stages of therapy: education, skills acquisition, and application. The first stage centers on the therapeutic relationship between the therapist and the client. The role of the therapist in this stage is to create a collaborative and warm environment. The therapist should be prepared for the client to be anxious regarding his or her decision to come out in the workplace. Therefore, the therapist will assist the client in developing a plan of action for disclosure in such a way as to limit the amount of anxiety experienced. The goals of the education stage are to help the client become more conscious of the situations and thoughts that produce anxiety about coming out in the workplace, and to focus on the effectiveness of the coping skills that the client currently uses to manage his or her anxiety.

To ensure the effectiveness of the skill-based approach prescribed by the exercises in this activity, the therapist should begin by becoming acquainted with the techniques used by the client to manage his or her identity outside of the workplace. Exercise #1 may help the client identify the techniques that he or she uses to manage his or her GLB identity in personal domains. The therapist should encourage the client to provide as much detail as can be remembered in Exercise #1. The information received from the client's responses will reveal how the client has previously managed the disclosure of his or her GLB identity. In addition, the responses will inform the therapist of the client's preferred methods of coping with such interactions.

In addition to assessing the client's coping skills and identity-management techniques, the therapist and client should assess the client's work environment. That is, would the client's work environment provide the social support necessary to handle the disclosure? Subtle and overt displays of homophobic attitudes or fundamental religious attitudes in the workplace may well present a challenge for the GLB client deciding to disclose his or her sexual orientation. Exercise #2 will help the client and therapist assess the client's work environment to determine if it has previously provided support for such disclosure.

If the therapist and the client determine that the client's workplace will not provide the desired social support, they should evaluate two courses of action. First, the client should determine if coming out in the workplace is in his or her best interest. That is, will the process of coming out in the workplace benefit the client psychologically and assist him or her in developing a positive GLB identity? Second, the client must determine from where in his or her current social support network will he or she receive the support necessary to manage the stress and anxiety that accompanies such an interaction. Exercise #3 is a tool to help the client and the therapist assess the client's current social support network.

Subsequent to determining the level of support present in the client's life, the therapist and the client can begin working on the coping skills necessary to reduce the anxiety related to coming out in the workplace. The therapist can use Exercises #4 and #5 to help the client improve his or her coping strategy selection process. The use of Exercise #4 will assist the client in assessing his or her current coping strategies and also aid in developing the coping skills necessary to reduce the anxiety related to coming out in the workplace. Exercise #5 will document the automatic thoughts and negative self-talk of the client to help him or her identify the situations that may trigger the anxiety related to coming out in the workplace.

The therapist can use Exercise #6 as a self-instruction technique for the client. Self-instruction training can be defined as a set of statements used by the client to manage a stressful situation. It is important that the statements are significant to the client and not mere "catch phrases to be repeated mindlessly" (Shannon, 1994, p. 348). The statements used in self-instruction are used as cognitive counteractions to the stressful and anxiety-producing event of coming out in the workplace.

Suggestions for Follow-Up

In order for the GLB client to maintain low levels of anxiety and stress related to being out in the workplace, he or she must develop and sustain appropriate coping and identity management skills. The therapist should ask the client to practice saying the statements in Exercise #6. In addition, the therapist may suggest that Exercise #5 be completed on a periodic basis. The therapist can follow up on the statements added to Exercise #6 to ensure that the statements are affirming, and he or she can follow up on the responses on Exercise #5 to ensure that the same situations are not continuously creating setbacks for the client. As the client continues to utilize the tools learned, the therapist should encourage him or her to discuss the improvements made and to recognize the source of the improvements. That is, the therapist and the client should attribute the improvements to the change in the client as a person (Meichenbaum and Deffenbacher, 1988). Also, it is important when using SIT that the therapist be aware that the client may experience setbacks (e.g., choosing to delay coming out at work). However, such setbacks should be viewed as learning experiences and opportunities for the client to practice his or her coping skills. In addition, the client should be reminded that SIT will not eliminate the anxiety and stress of coming out in the workplace, but it will provide tools that he or she can use to positively adapt to the situation.

Contraindications

This activity is contraindicated for GLB individuals who have yet to explore the possibility of coming out in the workplace. Also, this activity may be inappropriate for individuals at the beginning stages of sexual identity development. These individuals may need to concentrate on coming out to themselves prior to focusing on coming out to others.

Readings and Resources for the Professional

Cain, R. (1991). Relational contexts and information management among gay men. *Families in Society: The Journal of Contemporary Human Services, 72*(6), 344-352.

Kanuha, V. K. (1999). The social process of "passing" to manage stigma: Acts of internalized oppression or acts of resistance? *Journal of Sociology and Social Welfare, 26*(4), 27-46.

McCarn, S. R. and Fassinger, R. E. (1996). Revisioning sexual minority identity formation: A new model of lesbian identity and its implications for counseling and research. *The Counseling Psychologist, 24*(3), 508-534.

Meichenbaum, D. H. and Deffenbacher, J. L. (1988). Stress inoculation training. *The Counseling Psychologist, 16*(1), 69-90.

Prince, J. P. (1995). Influences on the career development of gay men. *The Career Development Quarterly, 44*, 168-177.

Shannon, C. (1994). Stress Management. In D. K. Granvold (Ed.), *Cognitive and behavioral treatment: Methods and treatment* (pp. 339-352). Pacific Grove, CA: Brooks/Cole Publishing Company.

Bibliotherapy Sources for the Client

Diamant, L. (1993). *Homosexual issues in the workplace.* Washington, DC: Taylor and Francis.

Hardin, K. N. (1999). *The gay and lesbian self-esteem book.* Oakland, CA: New Harbinger Publications.

References

Cain, R. (1991). Relational contexts and information management among gay men. *Families in Society: The Journal of Contemporary Human Services, 72*(6), 344-352.

Meichenbaum, D. H. and Deffenbacher, J. L. (1988). Stress inoculation training. *The Counseling Psychologist, 16*(1), 69-90.

Prince, J. P. (1995). Influences on the career development of gay men. *The Career Development Quarterly, 44*, 168-177.

Shannon, C. (1994). Stress Management. In D. K. Granvold (Ed.), *Cognitive and behavioral treatment: Methods and treatment* (pp. 339-352). Pacific Grove, CA: Brooks/Cole Publishing Company.

Exercise #1

1. Think about a time when you disclosed your sexual orientation to an individual or group and you received a positive response. Describe the situation.

   a. Discuss your feelings *prior* to disclosure.

   b. What were some of your thoughts and feelings regarding this person or group of persons to whom you disclosed *prior* to disclosure?

   c. What were some of your thoughts and feelings regarding this person or group of persons to whom you disclosed *following* disclosure?

   d. Do you currently correspond with this person or group of persons? Why or why not?

   e. Describe your feelings and thoughts regarding your sexuality *following* the disclosure?

2. Think about a time when you disclosed your sexual orientation to an individual or group and you received a negative response. Describe the situation.

   a. Discuss your feelings *prior* to disclosure.

   b. What were some of your thoughts and feelings regarding this person or group of persons to whom you disclosed *prior* to disclosure?

   c. What were some of your thoughts and feelings regarding this person or group of persons to whom you disclosed *following* disclosure?

   d. Do you currently correspond with this person or group of persons? Why or why not?

   e. Describe your feelings and thoughts regarding your sexuality *following* the disclosure?

Exercise #2

Section A

1. Are you aware of any other gay, lesbian, or bisexual individuals within your organization? If yes, go on to question #2. If no, go to Section B.

2. Are the gay, lesbian, or bisexual individuals within your organization "out" regarding their sexuality?

3. What is your perception of the staff's response to gay, lesbian, or bisexual workers who are open regarding their sexuality?

4. What is your perception of management's response to gay, lesbian, or bisexual workers who are open regarding their sexuality?

5. How does your organization show that it values its employees? Is this shown to all employees equally?

Section B

6. Does anyone within your organization know your sexual orientation? If so, name the individual and discuss how he or she discovered your sexual orientation.

7. Why do you want to disclose your sexual orientation in your workplace?

8. What are the benefits of disclosure?

9. To whom would you disclose first, second, and third? Discuss why you would choose these individuals.

10. Discuss your thoughts and feelings regarding how you think these individuals will respond to your disclosure.

11. Does your organization have policies protecting employees against discrimination based on sexual orientation?

12. If so, what are the penalties for individuals who violate this policy? Are you aware of any violations to this policy?

Exercise #3

Assessing Social Support Network

Write your name in the center circle. In the boxes extending from the circle, write the names of people who provide emotional, mental, financial, physical, and spiritual support to you. If necessary, you may add more boxes. After you have completed the exercise, rate each box according to how much you depend on the individual(s) written in the box for support. See below for the rating scale.

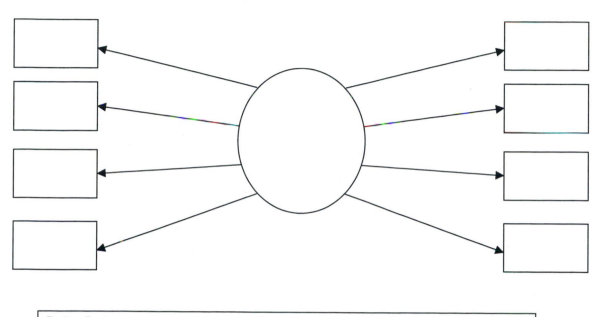

Rating Scale

1 = I rely on the person(s) rarely
2 = I rely on the person(s) sometimes
3 = I rely on the person(s) often
4 = I rely on the person(s) almost always
5 = I rely on the person(s) on a daily basis

Exercise #4

How would you respond to each of the three following scenarios? Carefully consider each, and respond honestly.

1. When coming out to a close friend, you suddenly realize that he or she has an extreme dislike for individuals who engage in sexual activities with persons of the same sex. Your friend says that he or she believes that such behavior is unnatural and that the people who engage in such practices are unnatural too.
   a. Describe the thoughts you would have as you listen to this friend.
   b. What would you say to him or her?
   c. Would such a statement affect your friendship?
   d. How would this affect your next coming-out experience?

2. A friend reveals during a group outing that he or she is attracted to members of his or her same gender. This disclosure is made to the entire group. This group does not know of your sexual orientation. A few of the individuals in the group react negatively to the disclosure.
   a. Describe the thoughts you would have as you listen to this friend.
   b. Do you disclose your sexual orientation?
   c. Do you support your friend's disclosure?
   d. How does the reaction of the group affect how you feel about your sexuality?

3. You disclose your sexual orientation to a family member that you thought would be unsympathetic; however, the family member is surprisingly sympathetic and informs you that he or she has always known about your sexuality and will continuously love and care for you.
   a. Describe the thoughts you would have as you listen to this family member.
   b. How does this unsuspecting reaction affect your thoughts and feelings about this family member?
   c. Does this response affect your notions about your sexuality?
   d. How would this affect your next coming-out experience?

Exercise #5

Complete the four sentences below as they relate to your work experiences. Please attempt to complete the worksheet on the day the anxiety-provoking event actually takes place.

1. Today at work the situation that caused the greatest anxiety regarding my sexuality was

_____

_____

_____

2. I responded to the anxiety by _____

_____

_____

3. When I think about the situation now I feel _____

_____

_____

4. If this situation were to happen again, I would respond _____

_____

_____

Exercise #6

The following are five statements that can be used to help you overcome your anxious feelings regarding coming out in the workplace. Notice that there are blank spaces for numbers 6 to 10. For these numbers, please fill in five statements that are personally relevant (i.e., use co-workers' names and exact situations).

1. The responses of my co-workers and/or supervisors are not a reflection of me as a person.

2. It is OK to put my feelings and attitudes before the feelings and attitudes of my co-workers and/or supervisors. I am responsible to me first.

3. It is OK if I choose not to come out now. I can decide when and if I am ready to come out at work.

4. A little anxiety is not a bad thing. It reminds me to use the coping skills I have learned.

5. I am not a bad person because I am gay, lesbian, or bisexual.

6. _____

7. _____

8. _____

9. _____

10. _____

47

A Rainbow of Allies

Todd M. Sigler

Type of Contribution: Activity/Homework/Handout

Objective

The goal of this activity is to help gay, lesbian, bisexual, and transgendered (GLBT) clients assess their current support structure and evaluate its assets and liabilities.

Rationale for Use

For GLBT individuals, connecting with and developing a sense of belonging in the larger GLBT community is a critical developmental task after they come out to themselves (Cass, 1979; Coleman, 1981-1982; Dank, 1971). The development of an inner sense of community and belonging leads to an increased sense of support, a reduction in isolation, and a reduction (or perhaps elimination) of self-hate, and facilitates the developmental stages of the coming-out process (Cass, 1979; Coleman, 1981-1982; Troiden, 1979).

Because GLBT individuals are an invisible minority to the larger community, and in fact to each other (Coleman, 1987; Herek, 1990; Ross, 1978; Weinberg, 1972), deliberate attempts must be made to connect with the GLBT community. Although the connection with and the process of accessing support within the GLBT community may be easy for some GLBT individuals, it poses significant obstacles to others. Geography, level of "outness," ability, and internal and external homonegativity may play significant factors in individuals' abilities to reach out to and develop a sense of community (Grossman and Kerner, 1998; Nesmith, Burton, and Cosgrove, 1999). These challenges may place GLBT individuals at greater risk for difficulties in identity development and healthy social adjustment.

The following handouts use the rainbow flag to help GLBT clients assess their support systems and bolster their GLBT identities. The rainbow flag has become the recognized colors of pride for the GLBT community. It is incorporated into these exercises because rainbows that occur in nature are not discrete from one color to the next. Each color blends into its neighbor. The rainbow flag is discrete between the colors. GLBT individuals may benefit most from thinking of their support systems and allies as both discrete and nondiscrete. For example, a parent may initially be unsupportive. However, as the parent and the GLBT individual continue to work on their relationship, the parent may come to be seen as a supportive ally. This may also be true of friends, co-workers, spiritual leaders, etc. Therefore, the use of the rainbow flag with and without discrete boundaries is deliberate.

Instructions

The therapist can use this activity with clients in individual or couple therapy. The therapist first must educate clients about the developmental tasks of coming out. Both Cass (1979) and

Coleman (1981-1982), as well as all other models of coming out, indicate that an early step in the process is the connection with and the development of a support system.

Tell clients that you have a guided exercise that will assist them in identifying members of their current support systems and assessing the amount of support they feel from each member. In addition, clients will have a sense of which areas of their support systems they need to develop further. Distribute the Rainbow of Allies worksheet and the Rainbow of Allies Key. Instruct clients to generate a list of significant and important people in their lives. The list should include partners, family, friends, co-workers, acquaintances, neighbors, and people from other areas of life (church, synagogue, sports teams, leisure activity groups, etc). Clients should write the list of people that are important or significant in their lives on the Important People in My Life worksheet. Then clients can use the Rainbow of Allies Key to indicate for each person on the list the people to whom they (a) are out, (b) would like to come out, and (c) will not come out at this point.

When this is completed, give clients the Rainbow of Allies worksheet. Inform them that the flag on the worksheet should be colored to match the rainbow flag. Ask clients to take the list of important people in their lives (with the code written next to each name) and write each name on their list in the corresponding color in the rainbow. Then either discuss with them or ask them to journal about the Consider the Following Questions worksheet.

Suggestions for Follow-Up

This exercise may generate questions for clients about how to develop social support systems. Specifically, they may question where and how to meet other GLBT individuals. Therapists should be prepared with local and Internet-based resources to help clients meet other GLBT individuals. This may also bring to light clients' skill deficits in the areas of relationship building, dating, and social interaction. Therapists should be prepared to assist clients with these skills (or refer them to someone who can) if the need should arise as a result of clients' assessment of their support system. Therapists should also be aware that this may cause clients to focus on the things they are not getting in their current relationships. The feelings related to this may need to be included in therapy as well.

Contraindications

This activity may not be appropriate for individuals who are still working on coming out to themselves. Clients should have a reasonable internal comfort with their gay, lesbian, or bisexual orientation.

In addition, in its current format the exercise is not particularly accessible to individuals with congenital blindness. Possible adaptations would be to use a chromatic musical scale or different short musical phrases. Each half step on the chromatic scale could stand for one of the colors of the rainbow. A short musical phrase such as a few bars from Beethoven's Fifth or First movement could stand as a color, then four other short recognizable musical phrases could be used to stand for the remaining colors. For braille users, in the portion of the exercise that asks clients to place a circle, square, or triangle, it may be more accessible to have them place a 1, 2, or 3 in front of the number rather than the circle, square, or triangle.

Readings and Resources for the Professional

Cass, V. (1979). Homosexual identity formation: A theoretical model. *Journal of Homosexuality, 4*(3), 219-235.

Coleman, E. (1981-1982). Developmental stages of the coming out process. *Journal of Homosexuality, 2*(2-3), 31-43.

Coleman, E. (1987). Assessment of sexual orientation. *Journal of Homosexuality, 14*(1-2), 9-24.

Dank, B. (1971). Coming out in the gay world. *Psychiatry, 34,* 180-197.

Gillian, M. (2000). *Checklist: A bisexual, gay, lesbian, transgender bibliography.* Anaheim, CA: Odd Girls Press.

Grossman, A. and Kerner, M. (1998). Support networks of gay male and lesbian youth. *Journal of Gay, Lesbian and Bisexual Identity, 3*(1), 27-46.

Hampton, M. and Norman, C. (1997). Community-building in a peer support center. *Journal of College Student Development, 38*(4), 357-364.

Herek, G. (1990). The context of antigay violence: Notes on cultural and psychological heterosexism. *Journal of Interpersonal Violence, 5*(3), 316-333.

Neal, C. and Davies, D. (2000). *Issues in therapy with lesbian, gay, bisexual and transgendered clients.* Philadelphia, PA: Open University Press.

Nesmith, A., Burton, D., and Cosgrove, T. (1999). Gay, lesbian and bisexual youth and young adults: Social support in their own words. *Journal of Homosexuality, 37*(1), 95-108.

Remafedi, G. (1987). Adolescent homosexuality: Psychosocial and medical implications. *Pediatrics, 79,* 331-337.

Reynolds, A. and Koski, M. (1993/1994). Lesbian, gay and bisexual teens and the school counselor: Building alliances. *The High School Journal, 77*(1-2), 88-94.

Rosenfeld, L. and Richman, J. (1997). Developing effective social support: Team building and the social support process. *Association of Applied Sport Psychology, 9,* 133-153.

Ross, M. W. (1978). The relationship of perceived societal hostility, conformity, and psychological adjustment in homosexual males. *Journal of Homosexuality, 4*(2), 157-168.

Stein, T. (1996). Homosexuality and homophobia in men. *Psychiatry Annals, 26*(1), 37-40.

Troiden, R. R. (1979). Becoming a homosexual: A model of gay identity acquisition. *Psychiatry, 42,* 362-373.

Weinberg, G. (1972). *Society and the healthy homosexual.* New York: St. Martin's Press.

Welch, P. (1996). In search of a caring community: Group therapy for gay, lesbian and bisexual college students. *Journal of College Student Psychotherapy, 11*(1), 27-40.

Bibliotherapy Sources for the Client

Berzon, B. (1990). *Permanent partners: Building gay and lesbian relationships that last.* New York: E. P. Hutton.

Brown, M. and Rounsley, C. (1996). *True selves: Understanding transsexualism.* San Francisco, CA: Jossey-Bass.

Eichberg, R. (1990) *Coming out: An act of love.* New York: Penguin Books.

Esterberg, K. (1997). *Lesbian and bisexual identities: Constructing communities, constructing selves.* Philadelphia, PA: Temple University Press.

Hutchinson, L. (1990). *Bi any other name: Bisexual people speak out.* Boston, MA: Alyson Publications.

Outland, O. (2000). *Coming out: A handbook for gay men.* Boston, MA: Alyson Publications.

Penn, R. (1998). *The men's wellness guide: The National Lesbian and Gay Health Association's complete book of physical, emotional and mental health and well-being.* New York: Henry Holt and Company.

Rhodes, R. (1994). *Coming out in college.* Westport, CT: Bergin and Garvey.

Schwartz, C. and Pollack, R. (1995). *The journey out: A guide for and about lesbian, gay and bisexual teens.* New York: Viking.

Signorile, M. (1995). *Outing yourself: How to come out as lesbian or gay to your family, friends, and coworkers*. New York: Fireside.

Stringer, J. (1990). *The transsexual's survival guide to transition and beyond*. King of Prussia, PA: Creative Design Services.

Vargo, M. (1998). *Acts of disclosure: The coming out process of contemporary gay men*. Binghamton, NY: The Haworth Press.

Internet Resources

The Gay.Com Network (2001). Retrieved online August 2, 2002, from <http://www.gay.com>.

Planet Out (2001). Retrieved online August 2, 2002, from <http://www.planetout.com>.

Human Rights Campaign (2001). Retrieved online August 2, 2002, from <http://www.hrc.org>.

References

Cass, V. (1979). Homosexual identity formation: A theoretical model. *Journal of Homosexuality, 4*(3), 219-235.

Coleman, E. (1981-1982). Developmental stages of the coming out process. *Journal of Homosexuality, 2*(2-3), 31-43.

Coleman, E. (1987). Assessment of sexual orientation. *Journal of Homosexuality, 14*(1-2), 9-24.

Dank, B. (1971). Coming out in the gay world. *Psychiatry, 34,* 180-197.

Grossman, A. and Kerner, M. (1998). Support networks of gay male and lesbian youth. *Journal of Gay, Lesbian and Bisexual Identity, 3*(1), 27-46.

Herek, G. (1990). The context of antigay violence: Notes on cultural and psychological heterosexism. *Journal of Interpersonal Violence, 5*(3), 316-333.

Nesmith, A., Burton, D., and Cosgrove, T. (1999). Gay, lesbian and bisexual youth and young adults: Social support in their own words. *Journal of Homosexuality, 37*(1), 95-108.

Ross, M. W. (1978). The relationship of perceived societal hostility, conformity, and psychological adjustment in homosexual males. *Journal of Homosexuality, 4*(2), 157-168.

Troiden, R. R. (1979). Becoming a homosexual: A model of gay identity acquisition. *Psychiatry, 42,* 362-373.

Weinberg, G. (1972). *Society and the healthy homosexual*. New York: St. Martin's Press.

Rainbow of Allies

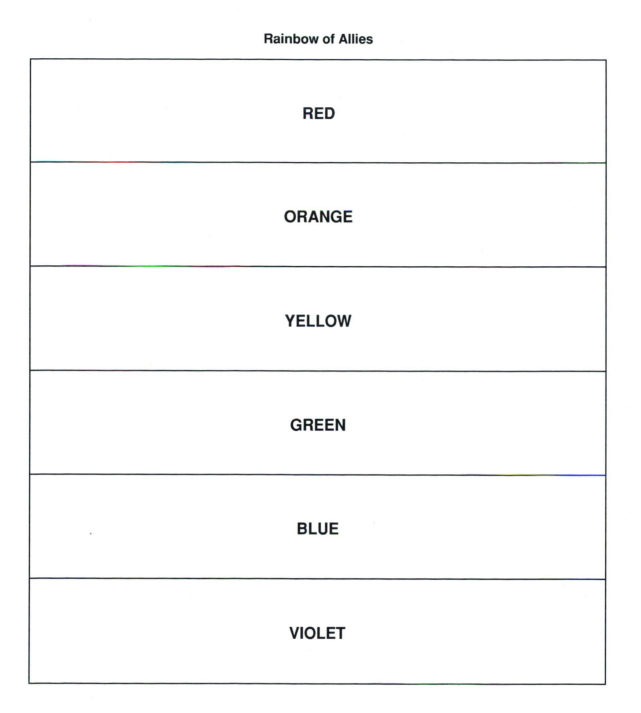

RED

ORANGE

YELLOW

GREEN

BLUE

VIOLET

Rainbow of Allies Key

Red (Life): These are the people to whom you are out, by whom you are accepted, and who provide you with support and nurturance. These people contribute in positive and healthy ways to your life as a GLBT person.

Orange (Healing): These people are friendly and positive. They say and do things that are supportive and show tolerance, but they are not nurturing. They contribute to your healing from oppression. They appear to support you intellectually, but their personal values and beliefs are not supportive.

Yellow (Sun): These are the people to whom you have begun to drop clues and hints about your sexual orientation. You have not discussed it directly, but you have been ambiguous enough in casual conversation to leave the door open for the discussion. Perhaps you have sent up some "test balloons" and they have generally responded positively and in a supportive manner to GLBT conversations and issues. These people provide "lip service" to the idea of tolerance. These people may be supportive on many issues, but then say or do something that highlights a certain level of negativity (e.g., they don't believe that GLBT individuals should be schoolteachers or parents). Their actions, behaviors, and words leave you with an en-LIGHT-ened view of their potential as positive, accepting, supportive, and nurturing.

Green (Nature): These are the people to whom you would like to come out. You hope they will be supportive and nurturing.

Blue (Harmony): These are the people whose words and actions have made them appear to be nonsupportive and nonnurturing. They may not say or do things deliberately that are destructive, but their particular lens on sexual orientation prevents them from saying or doing supportive and/or nurturing things. These individuals may say things such as, "I just don't agree with it." They do not contribute to harmony in your life.

Violet (Spirit): These are people to whom you are not out, whom you have felt would not be supportive, and who would not accept and nurture your sexual orientation. These individuals behave in ways and say things that are hostile, destructive, and leave you feeling rejected and bad. These people siphon energy off your healthy spirit.

Important People in My Life

Place an appropriate symbol next to each name you list.

Circle {O} the names of the people to whom you are out right now.

Square {□} the names of people to whom you would like to come out soon.

Triangle {∇} the names of people to whom you will not come out at this point.

_____   _____

_____   _____

_____   _____

_____   _____

_____   _____

_____   _____

_____   _____

_____   _____

_____   _____

_____   _____

_____   _____

_____   _____

Consider the Following Questions

1. When I look at my Rainbow of Allies (or the lack of them),

   I feel . . .

   I can see that . . .

   I wish . . .

2. Are the people in my Rainbow of Allies flag aware of their impact on my life?

3. Have individuals in my life moved between colors?

   If so, in what direction did they move?

   Why?

   What "caused" their movement to a more supportive or a less supportive color?

4. Is there anyone that I can say something to that will allow them to move to a more supportive and nurturing color?

5. Is there anyone that I need to move back a color?

6. How much of my time do I spend with people in each color?

7. Is there a better balance for me right now?

8. In order to find potential people for my Rainbow of Allies, I need to . . .

   (e.g., join a support group/find a counselor/talk honestly to my partner, family, friends, co-workers, spiritual leader/break off my relationship with . . .)

9. This month, in order to build my Rainbow of Allies, I will . . .

10. This week, in order to build my Rainbow of Allies, I will . . .

11. Today I am going to begin by . . .

48

Assisting Gay, Lesbian, and Bisexual Youth in Finding a Community

Molly L. Grimes
Scott D. Pytluk

Type of Contribution: Activity/Homework

Objective

The goal of this activity is to help the therapist assist gay, lesbian, and bisexual (GLB) youth in finding their own community of gay or gay-friendly peers. The therapist is advised to follow a three-step process in this endeavor, such that the first step entails an *exploration* of the client's feelings; the second step includes an *action,* bringing the client closer to his or her community; and the third step requires a *follow-up* procedure, during which emotions are processed.

Rationale for Use

Research has shown that, more and more, youth in this country are coming out as gay, lesbian, or bisexual during their teen years, rather than deferring this process until adulthood (Hershberger and D'Augelli, 2000). Certainly, adolescence itself can be quite a disruptive and difficult period for even the most well-adjusted teens, and adding the element of sexual orientation to this mix may be more troubling to GLB youth. It is widely understood that the coming-out process is a difficult one, particularly if the individual coming out is left without support (Savin-Williams, 1990). GLB youth often find themselves feeling isolated from, and even harassed by, their school-age peers (Gibson, 1989). Therefore, it may be helpful for a client to engage herself or himself in the GLB youth community in a safe and strategic manner. This client may be able to cultivate a supportive and accepting network that can substitute for the peer group lost due to her or his sexual orientation, and also learn from these new peers that she or he is not alone or abnormal in her or his experience.

Instructions

Prior to having a client actually take any specific action toward discovering her or his own community, it is essential that the therapist and client explore the emotions associated with this action. This exploration period, Step 1, should be viewed as equally important as the action itself, and the therapist should be willing to devote a substantial amount of time to this endeavor.

During this exploration phase, the therapist is encouraged to assist the client in examining the feelings she or he has associated with finding a community of GLB peers. The therapist should be sure to help the client discuss both the fears and hopes associated with this process, and care should be taken to address these hopes and fears adequately before moving the client along to the next step. (For a list of suggested questions, see the Fears and Hopes handout.) In addition, the therapist and client should discuss important logistical concerns, such as issues of safety (i.e., does the client fear that her or his safety may be compromised if chosen action inadvertently "outs" her or him to family or peers?).

It is also important that the therapist discuss whatever associations the client may have with this process pertaining to the therapist. For example, the therapist should encourage the client to discuss what it is like for the therapist to be suggesting a homework activity, and great pains should be taken to ensure that this exploration stage is a *collaborative* process. In addition, the therapist may want to consider her or his own sexual orientation when discussing this topic with the client. If the therapist is gay, does the client feel as though she or he is being pressured into coming out or joining the community? If the therapist is heterosexual, does the client feel that the therapist may be suggesting activities that only appear safe to someone outside of her or his own group? Because this issue of therapist sexual orientation adds a more complicated element to this process, it is strongly encouraged that the therapist always inquire about the client's questions regarding the therapist's intentions, and that those questions are then answered.

Once this period of exploration has been adequately accomplished, the client and therapist should move on to Step 2. Again, this process begins with a period of collaborative brainstorming, during which the client and therapist attempt to decide on an activity to bring the client closer to finding a GLB community. This activity should feel safe to the client, but should also be a very small step outside of her or his current comfort zone. (For a list of suggested brainstorming questions, see the Brainstorming handout.)

The client may wish to engage in several different activities. For example, she or he may choose to spend some time chatting in a GLB youth Internet chat room, or she or he may choose to attend a gay/straight alliance meeting at her or his school or one nearby. In addition, many coffee shops around the country now offer GLB youth nights, and this is a viable option. If the client feels uncomfortable taking an action step as those mentioned, she or he might wish to choose one of those steps as a goal, rather than as a starting point. For example, if the client wishes to attend a GLB youth night at a local coffeehouse, but is currently uncomfortable taking that step, a possible step for this client may be simply making a phone call to a local GLB youth foundation to find out where and when those GLB nights take place. In addition, the therapist and client are encouraged to use therapy time for engaging in a role-play of the given action if the client feels this will assist her or him.

After the specific action has been chosen, the therapist and client should agree on a time by which this action should be completed. If the client feels that the step is small enough that she or he can complete the step in the period between therapy sessions, it is suggested that she or he do so. It is also recommended that the client spend time recording some of the feelings she or he experiences during the action itself, either in the form of a journal or a simple laundry list format, so that she or he and the therapist are able to process these feelings together, after the fact. If the client appears to be struggling with how to journal her or his feelings, the therapist might consider adapting the questions supplied in Fears and Hopes to form a handout as a resource to guide the client through the journaling process. (For a list of suggested questions to include in a client handout, see asterisked items in the Fears and Hopes handout.)

Suggestions for Follow-Up

After the client has completed her or his action, the therapist and client should move into the follow-up period, Step 3, during which the client's feelings and experience are discussed. If for some reason the client returns to therapy having been unable to go through with her or his chosen action, the therapist should return to Step 1 to determine what is preventing the client from acting. If the client has been able to complete the action, the therapist should encourage the client to discuss what this experience was like for her or him and how she or he perceives the outcome to have been. If the client expresses dissatisfaction with her or his experience, the therapist should be sure to explore these feelings and should work to determine the underlying meaning of her or his unhappiness with the action. For example, did the action simply not suit the client's taste in activity, or is the client experiencing shame at having made a movement toward joining the GLB community? If the client expresses satisfaction with her or his chosen experience, this too should be processed, and the therapist and client should discuss the implications associated with the client's enjoyment of the activity.

Finally, the client and therapist should discuss the entire process of choosing an action and going through with it, and should determine whether the client wishes to continue in this manner. If the client wishes to select another action, the three-step process should begin again, and care should be taken not to eliminate the exploration stage of the process. If the client wishes to alter the process in some way, the therapist and client should work collaboratively to do so.

Contraindications

In order to ensure that this process is helpful to a client, it is essential that the therapist establish a strong relationship with him or her, such that the therapist is aware of the client's current emotional and developmental stance. The therapist is advised not to suggest this action for a client who is currently unprepared to enter the GLB community. If the client feels great shame or fear about her or his sexual orientation and subsequently wishes to distance herself or himself from the community, this should be respected. In such a situation, therapy should focus elsewhere until such a time when movement toward a community seems more appropriate.

In addition, even if the client does wish to engage herself or himself in the GLB community, it is essential that the therapist not recommend that she or he do so if it appears that it is likely that the client's safety may be compromised in the process. For example, if parents of the client have threatened to remove her or him from the family home if she or he were to become a part of the gay community, this concern should absolutely be addressed prior to engaging in an action.

In a more logistical sense, the therapist is encouraged to be aware of potential limitations the client may have in her or his ability to take an action. For example, a client of low socioeconomic status may not have access to the Internet or may not have transportation to coffeehouses; subsequently, the therapist should work with the client to choose a cost-free action. Similarly, the therapist should be sensitive to other factors that may affect the client's involvement in the GLB community. For example, the therapist should be mindful of the additional stress an African-American client may be experiencing when engaging herself or himself in the GLB community, as she or he must deal with issues of race as well as issues of heterosexism.

Readings and Resources for the Professional

D'Augelli, A. R. (Ed.) (1998). *Lesbian, gay, and bisexual identities over the lifespan: Psychological perspectives*. New York: Oxford University Press.

Gibson, P. (1989). Gay male and lesbian youth suicide. *Report of the secretary's taskforce on youth suicide*. Washington, DC: U.S. Department of Health and Human Services.

Hershberger, S. L. and D'Augelli, A. R. (2000). Issues in counseling lesbian, gay, and bisexual adolescents. In G. M. Perez, K. A. De'Bord, and K. J. Baschke (Eds.), *Handbook of counseling and psychotherapy with lesbian, gay, and bisexual clients* (pp. 225-247). Washington, DC: American Psychological Association.

Patterson, C. J. and D'Augelli, A. R. (Eds.) (2001). *Lesbian, gay, and bisexual identities and youth: Psychological perspectives*. New York: Oxford University Press.

Savin-Williams, R. C. (1990). *Gay and lesbian youth: Expressions of identity*. New York: Hemisphere Publishing Corporation.

Savin-Williams, R. C. and Cohen, K. M. (Eds.) (1997). *The lives of lesbian, gay, and bisexuals: Children to adults*. Fort Worth, TX: Harcourt Brace College Publishing.

Bibliotherapy Sources for the Client

Internet Resources

Youth Resource (2001). Retrieved online October 3, 2001, from <http://www.youthresource. com.>

Gay Teen Resource (2001). Retrieved online October 3, 2001, from <http://www. gayteenresource. com>.

Kurfew (2001). Retrieved online October 3, 2001, from <http://www.kurfew.com>.

OutProud (2001). Retrieved online October 3, 2001, from <http://www.outproud.org>.

Planet Out (2001). Retrieved online October 3, 2001, from <http://www.planetout.com>.

Parents, Families, and Friends of Lesbians and Gays (2001). Retrieved online October 3, 2001, from <http://www.pflag.org>.

Books

Heron, A. (Ed.) (1994). *One teenager in ten: Testimony by gay and lesbian youth*. Boston, MA: Alyson Publications.

Hutchins, L. and Kaahumanu, L. (1991). *Bi any other name: Bisexual people speak out*. Boston, MA: Alyson Publications.

Kaufman, G. and Raphael, L. (1996). *Coming out of shame*. New York: Doubleday Books.

Hotline

1-888-THE-GLNH (the Gay and Lesbian National Hotline)

References

Gibson, P. (1989). Gay male and lesbian youth suicide. *Report of the secretary's taskforce on youth suicide*. Washington, DC: U.S. Department of Health and Human Services.

Hershberger, S. L. and D'Augelli, A. R. (2000). Issues in counseling lesbian, gay, and bisexual adolescents. In G. M. Perez, K. A. De'Bord, and K. J. Baschke (Eds.), *Handbook of counseling and psychotherapy with lesbian, gay, and bisexual clients* (pp. 225-247). Washington, DC: American Psychological Association.

Savin-Williams, R. C. (1990). *Gay and lesbian youth: Expressions of identity*. New York: Hemisphere Publishing Corporation.

Fears and Hopes

How does it feel to be thinking about becoming a part of the GLB community?*

Do you feel safe taking action at this point?

Do you feel that becoming a part of the GLB community would have some risks for you?

What types of risks would you be taking by becoming a part of the GLB community?*

It is understandable that you might be afraid about this process. Can you talk a little about what types of fears you might be experiencing?*

What is the scariest part of this whole process?*

What do you think it *means* to be a member of the GLB community?*

What do you picture when you envision the GLB community?

How do you think things will change for you once you have become a member of the GLB community?*

When you picture the worst possible outcome of this experience, what do you envision?*

Is there a specific outcome of this process that is particularly scary for you?

Is there something you want us to really work hard to prevent from happening in this process?

When you picture the best possible outcome of this experience, what do you envision?*

If you could design this experience to be just perfect, how would things look?

Is there a certain aspect of this experience that you really want us to focus on to try to make this a good experience?

What would it be like for you if this experience were a negative one?

What do you think it would mean for you if this experience were a negative one?

Do you think you would feel like a different person if this experience were a negative one?*

Do you think you would feel different about being GLB if this experience were a negative one?*

What would it be like for you if this experience were a positive one?

What do you think it would mean for you if this experience were a positive one?

Do you think you would feel like a different person if this experience were a positive one?*

Do you think you would feel different about being GLB if this experience were a positive one?*

---

*Items to include as a resource for clients seeking help with journaling.

Brainstorming

Do you currently take part in any activities?

What types of activities do you really enjoy?

What activities do you participate in that allow you to feel safe?

Are there certain activities that you really do not enjoy?

What activities are available for GLB youth in your community?

Can you look into some of those activities so that you can pick one?

Have you learned about certain activities in the GLB community that sound particularly interesting to you?

Have you heard about certain activities in the GLB community that sound particularly bad or scary to you?

Are any of the activities that you enjoy available in the GLB community?

Can you think of any ways that we might be able to decide on an activity for you that allows you to participate in an activity we know you enjoy, and also allows you to immerse yourself in the GLB community?

Is there any activity about which we have spoken that really jumps out at you as being perfect for merging your interests with the GLB community?

What safety precautions do you think you need to take for this experience?

If you are using your computer for this, can your parents or siblings access your e-mail?

Will you need others to drive you to your activity, and will this be safe?

Will you have to rely on others to help you complete this process, and how will you explain this to them?

Are you going to have to lie to people in order to follow through with this experience, and how will that feel?

Does this plan lead to you being "outed"?

Are there people who may find out about your sexuality that you wish would not?

49

Negotiating Relationships with Ex-Partners

Joy S. Whitman
Cyndy J. Boyd

Type of Activity: Activity/Handout

Objective

The goal of this activity is to help gay, lesbian, and bisexual (GLB) clients make decisions about how to have friendships with ex-partners.

Rationale for Use

As a result of being marginalized by their families of origin due to their sexual orientation, having a need for a role model and social support within the GLB communities, and needing help in maintaining positive GLB identities, GLB individuals typically create a family of choice (Bepko and Johnson, 2000; Nardi, 1982; Nardi and Sherrod, 1994; Weston, 1997). These chosen families serve similar functions as would families of origin in terms of providing support, rituals, caregiving, and spaces for holiday gatherings. Without these families, GLB people can feel isolated and alone.

A family of choice can be created from a variety of sources, such as selected members of the family of origin, heterosexual and GLB friends, and GLB ex-partners (Bepko and Johnson, 2000; Nardi, 1982; Nardi and Sherrod, 1994; Weston, 1997). This inclusion of ex-partners is not uncommon and can be attributed to the relatively small size of GLB communities as compared to heterosexual communities, the reliance on ex-partners as caregivers in case of illness or disease, and the social norms found within those GLB communities (Becker, 1988; Bepko and Johnson, 2000; Kirkpatrik, 1989; Rothblum et al., 1995; Slater, 1994; Stanley, 1996; Weston, 1997).

Since the inclusion of ex-partners into a family of choice is seen as customary, it is deserving of support and exploration from the therapist. Moreover, since the inclusion of ex-partners into a family of choice is so common, those clients who do not want to include their ex-partners, yet feel compelled to do so, can benefit from this kind of examination as well. This activity and handout will help clients decide whether and how to include these important people into their families of choice and the positions ex-partners can have, especially when clients are in a new romantic relationship.

Instructions

Clients may not ask the question of how to include their ex-partners in their lives since they may not realize that careful exploration of such relationships warrants attention. It may be up to the therapist to raise this issue after a recent breakup so that clients may review their decision-making process. Initiating such discussion can convey to the client your understanding of family of choice and the inclusion of ex-partners into that family, as well as the importance this ex-partner may still have in the client's life.

Once this topic has been broached, use the Draw Your Family of Choice handout to help the client illustrate graphically who is in his or her family of choice. Ask your client to omit her or his ex-partner for now. Be sure to spend time exploring the placement, roles, functions, and longevity of her or his family of choice so that when the client is asked to include the ex-partner, she or he has thoroughly explored all other relationships. Then guide the client to include her or his ex-partner into the diagrams, again spending ample time exploring that relationship.

After the client has diagrammed her or his family of choice, use the Negotiating Relationships with Ex-Partners handout to facilitate a deeper understanding of the client's desires, fantasies, and ideas about how he or she would like to include her or his ex-partner in his or her life.

Suggestions for Follow-Up

If the client has made a decision to include an ex-partner in her or his family of choice, discussing how to present this to the current partner will be a next step. Inviting the client's partner to a session in order to draw upon the support and structure of therapy is an option. Role-playing with the client about how to discuss this with her or his partner is an alternative method.

As a result of engaging in this activity, the client may realize that he or she would like to redefine the relationship with the ex-partner. She or he may need help in discussing and defining these new parameters with his or her ex-partner. Again, role-playing this discussion or inviting the ex-partner into a session may be helpful.

Exploring a client's desire to include an ex-partner into her or his family of choice can bring to the surface issues beyond the presenting one of ex-partners. A client may realize that he or she has few people in this family of choice, or that his or her family of choice consists of people who are not emotionally and/or physically close. This could cause some distress for the client, which would require a shift in focus away from ex-partner inclusion toward the client's available support network. Attention to shoring up the client's family of choice may then take precedence.

Contraindications

None. Whether the relationship with an ex-partner has been abusive or caring, engaging in this activity with the client will help illuminate the nature of that relationship and will facilitate an exploration of inclusion or exclusion into the client's family of choice.

Readings and Resources for the Professional

Becker, C. S. (1988). *Unbroken ties: Lesbian ex-lovers*. Boston, MA: Alyson Publications.

Bepko, C. and Johnson, T. (2000). Gay and lesbian couples in therapy: Perspectives for the contemporary family therapist. *Journal of Marital and Family Therapy, 26*(4), 409-419.

Hite, S. (1987). *Women in love: A cultural revolution in progress*. New York: Alfred A. Knopf.

Kirkpatrik, M. (1989). Lesbians: A different middle-age? In J. Oldham and R. Liebert (Eds.), *New psychoanalytic perspectives: The middle years* (pp. 135-148). New Haven, CT: Yale University Press.

Nardi, P. M. (1982). Alcohol treatment and the non-traditional "family" structures of gays and lesbians. *Journal of Alcohol and Drug Education, 27*(2), 83-89.

Nardi, P. M. and Sherrod, D. (1994). Friendships in the lives of gay men and lesbians. *Journal of Social and Personal Relationships, 11*, 185-199.

Rothblum, E. D., Mintz, B., Cowan, D. B., and Haller, C. (1995). Lesbian baby boomers at midlife. In K. Jay (Ed.), *Dyke life: From growing up to growing old, a celebration of the lesbian experience* (pp. 61-76). New York: Basic Books.

Slater, S. (1994). *The lesbian family life cycle*. New York: The Free Press.

Stanley, J. L. (1996). The lesbian's experience of friendship. In J. S. Weinstock and E. D. Rothblum (Eds.), *Lesbian friendships: For ourselves and each other* (pp. 39-59). New York: New York University Press.

Weston, K. (1997). *Families we choose*. New York: Columbia University Press.

Bibliotherapy Sources for the Client

Becker, C. S. (1988). *Unbroken ties: Lesbian ex-lovers*. Boston, MA: Alyson Publications.

Weston, K. (1997). *Families we choose*. New York: Columbia University Press.

References

Becker, C. S. (1988). *Unbroken ties: Lesbian ex-lovers*. Boston, MA: Alyson Publications.

Bepko, C. and Johnson, T. (2000). Gay and lesbian couples in therapy: Perspectives for the contemporary family therapist. *Journal of Marital and Family Therapy, 26*(4), 409-419.

Kirkpatrik, M. (1989). Lesbians: A different middle-age? In J. Oldham and R. Liebert (Eds.), *New psychoanalytic perspectives: The middle years* (pp. 135-148). New Haven, CT: Yale University Press.

Nardi, P. M. (1982). Alcohol treatment and the non-traditional "family" structures of gays and lesbians. *Journal of Alcohol and Drug Education, 27*(2), 83-89.

Nardi, P. M. and Sherrod, D. (1994). Friendships in the lives of gay men and lesbians. *Journal of Social and Personal Relationships, 11*, 185-199.

Rothblum, E. D., Mintz, B., Cowan, D. B., and Haller, C. (1995). Lesbian baby boomers at midlife. In K. Jay (Ed.), *Dyke life: From growing up to growing old, a celebration of the lesbian experience* (pp. 61-76). New York: Basic Books.

Slater, S. (1994). *The lesbian family life cycle*. New York: The Free Press.

Stanley, J. L. (1996). The lesbian's experience of friendship. In J. S. Weinstock and E. D. Rothblum (Eds.), *Lesbian friendships: For ourselves and each other* (pp. 39-59). New York: New York University Press.

Weston, K. (1997). *Families we choose*. New York: Columbia University Press.

Draw Your Family of Choice

1. Draw a time line with the date of coming out to self as the beginning point and the present or near future as the end point. Along that time line, include the names of your family of choice as it is now so that you have a chronological picture of the development of this family. Include the roles or functions of these people in your life. These roles or functions are to include both past and present functions since these roles may have changed over time. You might want to create symbols to signify different roles or functions, such as a heart to indicate someone who helps you to feel loved, a bicycle or golf club for someone with whom you recreate, or an angry face for someone with whom you often argue. Make sure to include family of origin if those people are included in your family of choice.

2. Below that, draw another picture with you in the middle and your family of choice around you indicating emotional and physical distance or closeness. Be aware that someone with whom you may be emotionally close may be physically distant.

3. Add to this drawing pieces of the time line, such as time when individuals entered your life and the roles and functions they have played in the past and in the present.

4. Now, as you look at the drawings, include your ex-partner in them, making sure that you include the roles or functions and distance or closeness that he or she presently maintains with you and that you maintain with him or her.

5. Finally, use the questions in the Negotiating Relationships with Ex-Partners handout to help you explore this ex-partner's place in your life relative to other people in your family of choice.

Negotiating Relationships with Ex-Partners

1. How long has it been since we ended our relationship?

2. How sexually attracted am I to my ex-partner?

3. How emotionally attracted am I to my ex-partner?

4. What feelings do I still have toward my ex-partner?

5. Why do I want to maintain a relationship with my ex-partner?

6. What are the pros and cons of maintaining a relationship with my ex-partner?

7. What kinds of boundaries, emotional and sexual, do I want to create with my ex-partner?

8. What roles or functions do I want to play in my ex-partner's life and what roles or functions do I want my ex-partner to play in mine?

9. How do I want to maintain this relationship while in a new romantic or sexual relationship? Where do I want my ex-partner to fit into my present relationship?

10. If my ex-partner were not in my life, who else in my family of choice could take on the roles or functions and emotional or physical closeness or distance that my ex-partner has fulfilled? How would I feel if that were to happen?

Index

❏ **YES!** Please rush me the following book(s)

❶ ❏ The Therapist's Notebook
Homework, Handouts, and Activities for Use in Psychotherapy

❏ $49.95 soft. ISBN: 0-7890-0400-3 _____ Quantity

Order this book online at: www.HaworthPressInc.com/store/product.asp?sku=1567

❸ ❏ The Therapist's Notebook for Families
Solution-Oriented Exercises for Working with Parents, Children, and Adolescents

❏ $39.95 soft. ISBN: 0-7890-1244-8 _____ Quantity

Order this book online at: www.HaworthPressInc.com/store/product.asp?sku=4645

❷ ❏ The Therapist's Notebook for Children and Adolescents
Homework, Handouts, and Activities for Use in Psychotherapy

❏ $39.95 soft. ISBN: 0-7890-1096-8 _____ Quantity

Order this book online at: www.HaworthPressInc.com/store/product.asp?sku=4742

❹ ❏ The Therapist's Notebook for Lesbian, Gay, and Bisexual Clients
Homework, Handouts, and Activities for Use in Psychotherapy

❏ $39.95 soft. ISBN: 0-7890-1252-9 _____ Quantity

Order this book online at: www.HaworthPressInc.com/store/product.asp?sku=4743

Order Today!

PAYMENT OPTIONS

❏ **BILL ME LATER.** ($5.00 service charge will be added.) (Not available on individual orders outside US/Canada/Mexico. Minimum order: $15. Service charge is waived for jobbers/wholesalers/booksellers.)

P.O.# _____

Signature _____

❏ **PAYMENT ENCLOSED.** $ _____
Payment by check or money order must be in U.S. or Canadian dollars drawn on a U.S. or Canadian bank.

❏ **PLEASE CHARGE TO MY CREDIT CARD:**

❏ Visa ❏ MasterCard ❏ AmEx ❏ Discover ❏ Diners Club ❏ Eurocard ❏ JCB

Account _____

Exp. Date _____

Signature _____

May we open a confidential credit card account for you for possible future purchases? ❏ Yes ❏ No

FINAL TALLIES

COST OF BOOK(S)	
POSTAGE & HANDLING See chart at right.	
IN CANADA Please add 7% for GST. NFLD, NS, NB: Add 8% for province tax.	
State Tax NY, OH & MN add local sales tax.	
FINAL TOTAL	

POSTAGE AND HANDLING:

If your book total is:	Add this amount:
up to $29.95	$5.00
$30.00 – $49.99	$6.00
$50.00 – $69.99	$7.00
$70.00 – $89.99	$8.00
$90.00 – $109.99	$9.00
$110.00 – $129.99	$10.00
$130.00 – $149.99	$11.00
$150.00 – and up	$12.00

US orders will be shipped via UPS; Outside US orders will be shipped via Book Printed Matter. For shipments via other delivery services, contact Haworth for details. Allow 3–4 weeks for delivery after publication. Based on US dollars. Booksellers: Call for freight charges.

• If paying in Canadian funds, please use the current exchange rate. Payment in UNESCO coupons welcome.
• Individual orders outside the US/Canada/Mexico must be prepaid by check or credit card.
• Prices in US dollars and subject to change without notice.

ADDITIONAL INFORMATION

Please fill in the information below or **TAPE YOUR BUSINESS CARD IN THIS AREA.**

NAME _____

INSTITUTION _____

ADDRESS _____

_____

CITY _____

STATE/PROVINCE _____

ZIP/POSTAL CODE _____

COUNTY (NY Residents only) _____

COUNTRY _____

PHONE _____

FAX _____

E-MAIL _____

PLEASE PRINT OR TYPE CLEARLY.

May we use your e-mail address for confirmations and other types of information? ❏ Yes ❏ No

We appreciate receiving your e-mail address and fax number. Haworth would like to e-mail or fax special discount offers to you, as a preferred customer. We will **never share, rent, or exchange** your e-mail address or fax number. We regard such actions as an invasion of your privacy.

THIS FORM MAY BE PHOTOCOPIED FOR DISTRIBUTION.

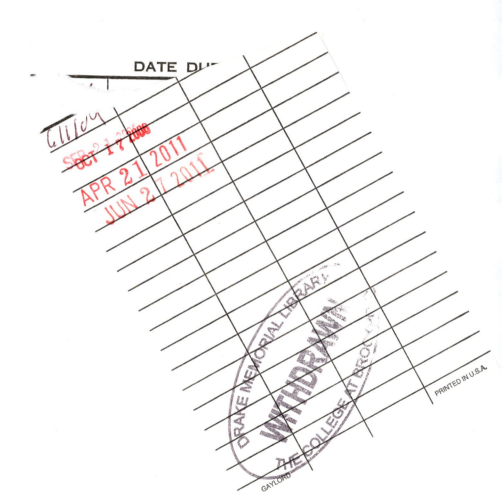